THE SPECIAL GUEST COOKBOOK

ALSO BY ARLENE EISENBERG

Alive and Well: Decisions in Health
(with Howard Eisenberg)

THE SPECIAL GUEST COOKBOOK

Elegant Menus and Recipes for Those Who Are:

ALLERGIC TO CERTAIN FOODS
BLAND DIETERS / CALORIE COUNTERS
CHOLESTEROL CONSCIOUS
DIABETIC / HYPOGLYCEMIC
KOSHER / MILK SENSITIVE
OVOLACTO VEGETARIAN
PRITIKIN PROSELYTES
SALT-AVOIDING
STRICTLY VEGETARIAN

Arlene Eisenberg, Heidi Eisenberg,
Sandee Eisenberg, RN

BEAUFORT BOOKS, INC.
New York/Toronto

Library of Congress Cataloging in Publication Data
Eisenberg, Arlene.
The special guest cookbook.

Includes index.
1. Cookery. I. Eisenberg, Heidi.
II. Eisenberg, Sandee. III. Title.
TX652.E36 641.5'63 81-17106
ISBN 0-8253-0090-8 AACR2

Published in the United States by Beaufort Books, Inc.,
New York. Published simultaneously in Canada by
General Publishing Co. Limited

Designer: Ellen LoGiudice
Printed in the U.S.A. First Edition

10 9 8 7 6 5 4 3 2 1

For
Mimi and Gramps who taught us all guests are special,
the men in our lives who patiently tasted and tested,
and, of course, the special guests who inspired
this book.

A special thank you to Rabbi David Teutsch, for advice
and suggestions.

Note: All recipes and menus in *The Special Guest Cookbook* adhere to dietary laws and are suitable for use in the kosher kitchen.

THE SPECIAL GUEST COOKBOOK

Contents

Introduction

The rose-hued candlelight danced gracefully across the richly embroidered Madeira cloth, reflecting a thousand times in the cut-crystal goblets before bouncing brilliantly off the gleaming silver. A full-bodied Burgundy, newly come of age, breathed quietly on the mahogany buffet; the air, perfumed with an intoxicating blend of food aromas was enriched, too, with unobtrusively melodious chamber music.

The gracious hostess, elegant in her at-home silks and pearls, had thought of everything. At least she thought she had, until the meal she'd spent weeks planning and days shopping for and preparing began.

One guest, a distinguished playwright, had been warned just weeks earlier about the dangerously high levels of cholesterol in his blood. Glumly following his doctor's strict directives, he could do no more than pick at the perfectly rare roast beef, the rich Yorkshire pudding, the Caesar salad—lavished with egg yolks, cheese, and butter-tossed croutons. Another guest, a young vegetarian editor accustomed to skipping main courses and making her meal out of salad, vegetables, and side dishes, found she could make a meal out of nothing at all. The Caesar salad had been tossed with anchovies, and the

Yorkshire pudding had derived its richness largely from roast-beef drippings. A third guest, halfway to her weight-loss goal, sat with grim determination through the calorie-laden main courses only to succumb—with immediate remorse and self-hatred—to the chocolate mousse that followed. The ovolacto vegetarian was fortunately able to quell her by-then ferocious hunger pangs with a large helping of the creamy dessert; the playwright, alas, was not.

Watching the dinner party of dreams dissolve into an entertaining nightmare, the martyred hostess, needless to say, lost her own appetite. And try as the remaining three "normal" guests did to do justice to her culinary efforts, the bulk of the once-elaborate dinner ended up in aluminum foil that evening to be fed reheated to family, or worse still, to Fido.

The plight of that hostess and her guests is not, in this era of dietary obsession, the least bit uncommon. Similar scenes are reenacted in homes across the country as well-intentioned hosts and hostesses unwittingly serve what their guests can't—or won't—eat. When, for instance, the boss, who has been following a strict low-salt diet since his hypertension was diagnosed, comes to dinner, when best friends who have suddenly gone vegetarian are invited for cocktails, when in-laws (Dad's got to watch his cholesterol and saturated fats) are visiting for the weekend, or when one of the millions of Americans currently attempting to lose weight is a brunch guest.

The trend is clear. Today's hosts and hostesses must confront appetites and attitudes that are no longer as homogenized as a quart of milk. More and more people are doing their own thing dietarily, and entertaining these people has become complicated and confusing.

Some once-hospitable folks are now, understandably, taking the cowardly way out: they've stopped inviting their difficult-to-feed friends. A doctor we know, a vegetarian and, more recently, a follower of the Pritikin program, has had increasing difficulty in finding friends courageous enough to entertain him. Dinner invitations for him and his wife are becoming more and more rare.

My husband and I, kosher for nearly thirty years and cholesterol conscious for the past dozen, do occasionally find friends game enough to feed us. But while their intentions may be the best, the results aren't always. Like the time Debbie Reynolds, then Mrs. Eddie Fisher, tried to surprise us with kosher steaks at a dinner party. The meat turned out to be not kosher, but "kosher style," a common and confusing category in the state of California. While Debbie, Eddie, and their other guests dined (a bit guiltily, I suspect) on steak, we ate scrambled eggs.

At least the Fishers tried. Many other potential hosts and hostesses, intimidated by the fear of possible pitfalls, never try at all. *The Special Guest Cookbook* is dedicated to helping people like us, our doctor friend, and millions of other Americans with dietary peculiarities, garner more dinner invitations. And to helping those cordial and courageous folks who would rather invite than switch friends, avoid the kind of embarrassment that can result when they extend an invitation without the proper preparation.

For those rare souls who never get to entertain a special guest, this book provides a new approach to entertaining that spotlights delicious and interesting food low in the ingredients that just about everyone is—or feels he or she should be—cutting down on: fat, sugar, and salt. At the same time, it supplies a wide variety of easy to prepare and highly nutritious recipes for family use. With very few exceptions, ingredients called for are "natural," containing no additives of any kind. But the dishes they go into are not so blatantly healthy or radically exotic as to frighten off either cook or diner. On the surface, they differ little from the kinds of foods you ordinarily like to serve your guests.

Before we go on to the special diets, we'd like to share some tips with you, collected during the years we've spent as special guests, and the equal number of years we've been entertaining other special guests.

The problem guest doesn't usually expect to be catered to, and because some guests won't volunteer the fact that they are vegeterian, or watching their cholesterol or salt-intake, or are sensitive to milk, routinely root out guests' dietary problems or quirks when you invite them. If you keep a guest file, note such requirements on the guest's card so that you won't have to ask again. If the problem is not as black-and-white as being allergic to a particular food—mangoes, for instance—refer to the Questions to Ask Your Special Guest section in the appropriate chapter, and elicit the necessary additional information.

Once you've determined your special guest's needs, you can proceed to plan your menu. If you're not entertaining other dieters at the same meal, you can simply pick a menu suitable to that guest's diet, and serve it to everyone. Alternately, you can offer two main courses, one that's suitable for your problem guest, and one that's not. In that case, only the special diet guest need know the difference thus eliminating for him or her the possible embarrassment of being singled out.

Only as a last resort should you prepare just enough of a special main course and side dishes for your problem guest. Say, for instance, you are having a theme dinner party and only spicy Indian food is on the menu. A good friend, who is automatically included on all your guest lists, has recently been diagnosed as having an ulcer, and has been advised to avoid all strong spices. In that case, call her and tell her of your dilemma. Offer her the option of joining the party and eating a specially-prepared bland meal, or just skipping the invitation altogether.

After you've ascertained who you'll be cooking for, you can head for the market. In general, the best way to shop for problem guests is to go as far back to nature as possible. Stick to foods that have nothing added to them: fresh fruits and vegetables, natural grains such as rice, bulgur, kasha, and pastas, meats, fish, or poultry (depending upon your guest's dietary needs).

Only in the dairy department will "natural" usually be less suitable than processed. For most diets, you will want to buy dairy products from which most or all of the fat has been removed. Then you'll want to check for other unsuitable additions.

The easiest way to be sure that all the ingredients in a dish are acceptable on your special guest's diet is to prepare it from scratch. Whenever possible, eschew prepared salad dressings, sauces, breads, frozen entrees, and desserts and opt for homemade.

But, your job as a considerate host or hostess doesn't end when you've finished cooking. Even the best of planning and the purest of intentions can be upset if you don't serve the meal properly. Always remember the following.

• **Allow for self-service.** It's very elegant to serve your company French style. But the guest who's been served double of what he can eat of rice pilaf, or has been given something he can't eat at all, will either eat what he shouldn't, or leave it. In either case he will be unhappy.

• **Prepare food so that guests can easily take small portions.** Eight-ounce steaks, capon halves, and extra large baked potatoes will either lead to diet devastation or unnecessary food waste. Try to limit meat, fish, and poultry portions to 3 or 4 ounces each, keeping plenty of extra on hand for those who wish seconds. Cut large potatoes in quarters, or use small ones; serve small baked apples instead of enormous ones.

• **Serve the trimmings on the side.** Unless the sauces, salad dressings, and other condiments and garnishes are suitable for everyone at the table, pass or serve them separately. Offer options whenever possible, two vegetables, for instance, or two kinds of sauce.

• **Keep the seconds, breads, and other temptations off the table.** Staying on any kind of diet, whether self- or doctor-prescribed, is difficult. You can make it less difficult for your dieting guest by not letting temptation stare him or her in the face. Out-of-sight, out-of-mind. Do, however, keep serving dishes nearby on a buffet or warming cart for guests who want more.

• **Always serve something simple.** If you make it a practice to serve some kind of fresh salad (dressing on the side), at least one ungarnished steamed vegetable, and to provide a bowl of fresh fruit along with any other desserts, you'll almost always be sure of having something for everyone. Only those who must avoid dietary fiber would be unable to make a meal out of such basic fare.

• **Don't be a food or drink pusher.** Saying no once is difficult. A second time is very difficult. A third offer may be completely impossible to refuse. Rarely will a guest be too shy to say yes to something he or she really wants. Haven't we all been talked into taking seconds of something we really didn't want by an over-exuberant hostess? Think about that the next time you catch yourself pushing food or drink.

• **Provide choices in beverages, too.** Your special guest may be allowed just one alcoholic drink, or none at all. Either way, you should always have available a wide variety of non-alcoholic alternatives: water, seltzer (no calories, salt, or sugar), club soda (added salt, but no added sugar or calories), diet soda, (try the new ones sweetened with aspartame; it's safer than saccharine, according to some authorities), tomato and vegetable juices, and fruit juices. Though wine with meals has become a ritual in many homes, guests who can't wine while they dine will appreciate your serving a choice of iced water, juice, or other non-alcoholic beverages. For toasts, the pleasant muscatel or regular grape juices are especially appropriate.

After dinner, do provide decaffeinated teas and coffee for guests who can't tolerate (or want to cut back on) caffeine, especially in the evening. If it's available in your market, use the freshly ground, water-processed decaffeinated coffee. Decaffeinated teas, too, come in many varieties; offer a choice if you can. Or, offer some of the non-caffeine hot beverages listed in Recipes, pages 545 to 548. Also, offer appropriate choices of sweeteners (saccharine or aspartame [APM], the new low-calorie sweetener described in the Recipe Glossary, turbinado sugar and/or honey, as well as ordinary sugar) and coffee lighteners (whole milk, cream, skim milk, half-and-half, and/or non-dairy creamer).

• **Don't be your guest's conscience.** Your job is to provide a meal that is suitable to your guest's special dietary needs. From there, it's up to him or her. Unless it's a close friend who whispers plaintively,

"Please stop me if I dig into that pasta," allow your guests freedom of choice. It's their diet, not yours.

• **Don't feel sorry for your special guest.** He's probably working hard at not feeling sorry for himself. If you must serve something that your guest can't try, don't moan sympathetically, "Oh, you poor thing, you don't know what you're missing." Chances are good your guests knows all too well what he's missing and won't appreciate your reminding him of it. Except to privately inform him that the dish isn't suitable to his diet, no comment is preferable.

• **Don't make an announcement that the food is for a special diet.** Be discreet. Unless your problem guest's special diet is common knowledge, keep the fact that all or part of the meal is specially prepared between you and your dieting guest. When we tested some special diet recipes on family, we brought out a lovely apricot mousse. As soon as Aunt Irene heard that it was a low calorie and low cholesterol dessert, the dear lady stubbornly refused a single bite. Proud of her "naturally" slim figure even well into her sixties, she announced, "I don't eat diet food." And while the other guests devoured the mousse appreciatively, she went without dessert. Chances are that if you keep the information to yourself and your dieting guest, no one else will notice the dietetic differences. A good friend of ours, for instance, once dug into one of our creamy, fluffy, rich-tasting desserts and declared ecstatically, "This is *my* kind of food—rich and fattening." We laughed—and finally told her that the "fattening" dessert was virtually calorieless.

Entertaining special guests will never be completely problem free. But if you follow the recipes, menus, and advice in this book as closely as possible, you'll never suffer the sometimes embarrassing consequences of entertaining special guests without special preparation. And, even if you make a mistake or two, your guest will know that you've tried. One particularly gracious host, the charming Barone Ricasoli, took us to lunch many years ago after a fascinating tour of his Chianti vineyards and his old family castle. As kosher travelers, we'd never had trouble eating in Italy. There was always, at the very least, pasta with marinara or butter sauce on the menu. The small local *ristorante* the Barone ushered us into, though, was an exception to that rule. There was nothing on the menu at all besides meat and seafood dishes, but we eventually discovered that there was something in the kitchen we *could* eat: boiled potatoes. They'd be tasty with butter and filling enough.

The Barone could have eaten anything on the menu. But, *noblesse oblige,* he elected to eat potatoes with his guests. Not once did he make us feel that our "different" customs were causing him to be deprived of a good meal.

As you will discover through *The Special Guest Cookbook,* you can be every bit as gracious a host as the Barone Ricasoli when entertaining your problem guests. And, better still, you can do it without letting them eat potatoes.

ARLENE EISENBERG

The Weight-Conscious Guest

Future historians, sifting through the artifacts of our civilization, examining diet pill bottles, diet food packages, diet books and magazines, and doubtless, the ruins of several thousand reducing salons and spas, may conclude that we were a people as obsessed with weight loss as with sex. They would probably be right, too.

That preoccupation with weight loss can present a serious obstacle to today's host or hostess. Diane, thin as a rail, says she can't touch the glorious chocolate rum soufflé you spent all afternoon preparing. "Just looking at it makes me gain weight," she moans. Plump, ever-dieting Janine turns it down for more obvious reasons. But, eyeing the other guests who have already proclaimed, "The diet starts first thing tomorrow morning," and are unabashedly asking for seconds, Diane and Janine may eventually succumb to temptation. And hate themselves—and maybe you—in the morning.

We don't believe that dinner parties, weekends at the beach, or brunches in town should be spartan affairs. Social gatherings are for eating, drinking, and enjoying. But there's more enjoyment for all when guests know that what they're eating today won't show up on the scale tomorrow.

Our low-calorie menus and recipes don't follow any particular diet plan, fad or otherwise. In fact, they aren't strict day-to-day diet fare at all. They're the kinds of dishes that you might ordinarily serve guests, only decalorized.

Weight Control Basics

If you haven't dieted lately (or even if you have) you may not be aware that the road to weight loss is no longer paved meagerly with cottage cheese and celery sticks.

It's true that in order to lose weight, food intake must be limited to fewer calories than are required to meet energy needs, forcing the body to burn fat for energy, and consequently, melting pounds away. And it is also true that if more calories are taken in than are needed, they are, alas, stored as fat.

But a limited caloric intake needn't leave the dieter walking around with an empty, growling stomach and an unsatiated appetite, deprived of its just desserts. Such dietary deprivation may well lead to self pity—and binge eating. Satisfying, filling meals are the mainstay of a successful weight-reducing program.

One good way to keep your weight-conscious guests satisfied and filled is by letting them eat fiber. Fiber-rich foods, in combination with plenty of non- or low-calorie liquids, are naturally satisfying for several reasons. For instance, they require more chewing time, giving the dieter a chance to recognize the sensation of "fullness" before he or she overeats. The extended chewing time, too, gives the dieter a psychological boost.

But fiber food is more than filling. The heavy mass formed by fiber and water speeds up food transit through the gastrointestinal tract, allowing less time for absorption of calories, and reducing absorption by as much as 5 percent. The high-fiber miracle-workers now recommended for dieters include raw vegetables and fruits with peels intact, whole grains, bran, beans, seeds, and nuts. Plenty of exercise, too, can work miracles for dieters. Disco dancing at a party or a set of tennis before brunch will help the dieting guest burn the calories you serve.

Another way dieters can beat the scales is to eat early in the day, when, according to recent chronobiological studies, the body burns calories more efficiently. Keep this in mind when inviting weight-watchers; a hearty brunch or a four o'clock dinner is kinder to their diets than a midnight supper.

Though, happily, dieters can modify the way their bodies handle calories, they can't afford to become overconfident. In the final analysis, calories—no matter when they're consumed, or what form they're consumed in—*do* count. And if you undertake to entertain weight-conscious guests, you become a partner in keeping those calories under control.

How to meet the challenge? First of all, use those veteran diet-devastaters, fat and sugar, sparingly in cooking and serving. Foods high in fat should be restricted because of their unforgivably high calorie contents. They contain more than twice as many calories per gram as carbohydrates or proteins. Four ounces of full-fat Cheddar cheese, for example, contain about 450 calories, whereas low-fat cottage cheese boasts only 80 to 90 calories per 4-ounce portion. Four ounces of tuna fish in oil, drained, add 230 calories to your guest's count, while 4 ounces in water add only half that amount.

Sugar's sin isn't only in its calorie content; it's in its emptiness. Because sugar is void of nutrition, the dieter who consumes a lot of it is either going to fall short on nutritive needs, or do a lot of extra eating to compensate. The first option can lead to weakness, fatigue, and eventual abandonment of the diet, the second to weight gain.

This doesn't mean that you can't serve any fat or sugar to dieters, just that you should keep the use of these foods to a minimum. Build your meals around low-calorie, high-nutrient main courses: fish, chicken, turkey, lean veal, and beef. Accompany the entrée with generous portions of salads, vegetables, and fruits, and round out the menu with smaller servings of foods that have moderate calorie counts, and are important both nutritionally and psychologically: breads, rice, pastas, cereals, and potatoes. To garnish or otherwise enhance the taste, texture, and color of low-calorie dishes use higher calorie foods, such as cheese, nuts, and mayonnaise, in very small quantities.

Since the psychological aspects of dieting are crucial to its success, don't ignore the aesthetics of the food you're serving. No matter how dietetic a meal is, it ought to be attractively and elegantly presented. To remove the element of self-pity ("Everyone else gets to eat chocolate mousse, and I'm stuck with this lousy apple") try to serve the same foods to all your guests, without singling your dieting guest out. A mountain of curried popcorn, for instance, can easily replace a bowl of mixed nuts for non-dieting and dieting guests alike. Ditto a pâté made from mushrooms, rather than pork fat and liver, or a broth laced with sherry from which the alcohol has been boiled out, leaving its heady taste and fragrance, but not its calories. Also consider chicken breasts stuffed with vegetables and herbs, pasta tossed with mushrooms and cauliflower or zucchini and stock (instead of oil), a cheesecake or pumpkin chiffon pie that you've cleverly eliminated a chunk of calories from—without eliminating a bit of the appeal. No one need be the wiser for your machinations, or the fatter.

What you serve your weight-conscious guests may be less important than how you serve it. To make eating at your house less of a potential diet threat, allow guests to serve themselves, so that dieters can take as little as they wish of foods that are limited on their diets, and as much as they wish of "free" foods. Make it easy to take small portions. Serve small chicken cutlets, small baked potatoes, thin slices of cake. Bake tiny 1½-inch muffins, or biscuits cut into 1½-inch rounds, that dieters can take one of, and non-dieters can take more of. Pass gravies, sauces, dressings, and toppings separately.

Have food available for seconds, but don't leave the serving platters on the dining table itself; such temptation may defeat even the strongest willed of dieters. Dieters are much less likely to pile their platter high a second time if they have to stroll over to the sideboard, buffet, or warming cart.

Whatever you do, don't be a food or drink pusher. When a guest says "no thank you" to seconds, don't press or plead. It's hard enough to say no the first time. And, if your dieting guest gives in on your second try, he or she will surely share some of the blame for the diet setback with you.

Questions to Ask Your Weight-Conscious Guest

1. *Are you on a low-calorie or balanced nutrient type of diet similar to Weight Watchers?* If so, all of our menus and recipes for the Weight Conscious guest (*LC*) will work. If not, ask:

2. *What kind of diet are you on?* Guests can't expect you to prepare a meal in accordance with a particular fad diet. If you can manage to cater to their needs without too much trouble, go ahead. If, however, the diet is totally impossible to incorporate into your menu, we suggest that you extend your invitation again once their diet is ended. Most fad diets are, fortunately, short lived.

Weight-Conscious Shopping

Label reading can either make or break shopping for the weight-conscious guest. And whether or not your mission is successful will depend on what part of the label you read. For example, if you see the word "dietetic" slashed across a bar of chocolate or a box or crackers, beware. Though the manufacturer might want you to believe that his product is low in calories, it might very well not be. "Dietetic" may only signify that the chocolate bar is sugar-free, or that the crackers are low in salt, and not that they are any lower in calories than their high-sugar or high-salt counterparts. Also misleading to those shopping for a weight-conscious guest are the terms "health food," "wholesome," or "natural"; none are indicators of calorie reduction. Even a product labeled "no sugar added" doesn't proclaim a product suitable for a weight-watcher. Honey and sorbitol, the two sweeteners which most often replace sugar, are both high in calories.

But while you can't rely on everything you read on a label, two sections will prove invaluable. One is the nutrition listing, which is appearing on more and more products these days. Because the listing will give you a calorie count per serving, you can use it to compare a given product with a similar one. Generally, foods that contain more than 150 calories per serving (except for main courses, which can run up to 400 calories) should be avoided.

Required reading, too, for anyone shopping for a weight-conscious guest is the list of ingredients. By law, ingredients must be listed in order of quantity used in a product, with the most abundant item listed first, the least, last. Consequently, a high-fat, high-calorie product is easy to spot, and easy to avoid when shopping for a dieting guest. Shortening, oil, cream, or other fat will be near the top of the list. Products, on the other hand, which contain no shortening, or list shortening at the bottom of a long list of ingredients, will be comparatively low in calories. Sugar at the top of an ingredient list may indicate that the product in question is devoid of food value, and thus a poor choice for weight-conscious guests, who ought to spend their daily calorie allotments on high nutrient foods.

As in most special diet shopping, the very best approach when stocking up for a dieting guest is to look for foods in their most natural state. Generally, additions add calories. Fresh fruits and vegetables are lower in calories than fruits packed in sugar, or vegetables frozen in butter or cheese sauce. Plain yogurt is lower in calories than flavored, sweetened yogurt. Unsweetened applesauce is lower in calories than the sugar-added variety. Raw chicken, which you can prepare in a low-calorie manner, is a far better bet than ready-made chicken in barbecue sauce, or fried chicken. Plain oats are lower in calories than hot cereals which have been flavored with sugar or maple syrup.

Some foods, of course, are loaded with calories even in their most natural state. Nuts of all kinds (except chestnuts), avocados, dried fruits, smoked fish, sausage, bacon, and beef should either be avoided or purchased and used in very small quantities.

"Calorie-controlled" or "light" prepared foods, which can now be found in every section of the supermarket, can be used in a pinch. We don't, however, recommend them for elegant entertaining.

When shopping for your main course, always consider fish first. Non-fatty fishes, including scrod, cod, flounder, halibut, haddock, tilefish, perch, pike, sea bass, sole, lobster, oysters, scallops, and shrimp, are the lowest calorie selections. Next are the slightly fatter fishes, such as striped bass, trout, bluefish, mackerel, swordfish, and, then, the most fatty fishes, including pompano, butterfish, sardines, salmon, and tuna. When poultry—the next best calorie buy—is going to headline at your dinner party, always opt for breasts over dark meat, and remove all skin *before* cooking. Lean veal follows chicken and turkey in calorie count, and is followed in turn by lean beef. Remember, whenever purchasing meat in a butcher shop, ask the butcher to remove all visible fat for you. If you've bought your meat in a supermarket, you'll have to do the trimming yourself.

Cooking for the Weight-Conscious Guest

What you do with your basic "low-calorie" purchases once you get them into your kitchen will have a major effect on how caloric they'll be when they get to your dinner table. As in low-calorie shopping, the first commandment of low-calorie cooking is: thou shalt minimize fat. Unless you wish to sabotage your guests' diet, you can't prepare their meal with any fat-based method of cooking. Frying, sautéing in oil, stir-frying in oil, broiling in butter, and basting with butter or other fats, are, without exception, unacceptable. Instead, steam, boil, broil "dry," roast, bake, or sauté with minimal or no fat. (See Recipe Glossary, p. 154, for directions on fat-free sautéing.)

A lot of creativity can take the place of a lot of calories. Make your dips, for instance, with low-fat cottage cheese, yogurt, pureed vegetables, or tofu rather than with sour cream or cream cheese. Serve unbuttered, air-popped corn in the place of high-fat nuts and potato chips alongside your cocktails. Dress salads with a stock-based dressing, rather than a mayonnaise- or oil-based one. Top baked potatoes with BUTTERMILK-CHIVE DRESSING (252), instead of sour cream or butter. Top pancakes with FRUITED YOGURT (428) or BERRY SAUCE (430), instead of melted butter and maple syrup. Prepare sauces and creamed soups with skim milk, instead of whole, evaporated skimmed milk instead of cream. Broil fish fillets in lemon and wine, instead of butter. Use ice milk in a bombe dessert instead of ice cream. Whip desserts light, fluffy, and nearly calorie-less with egg whites or whipped evaporated skimmed milk. Cut the calories in butter (or margarine) by whipping with water, as described in the Recipe Glossary, p. 148. Lend flavor to sauces and gravies with dry wine, cooked for several minutes to evaporate the alcohol and its calories; add plenty of fresh herbs and spices.

Weight-Conscious Menus

Because weight control programs vary widely, present your dieting guests with plenty of choices. A selection of crudités at a cocktail party, or before dinner, gives weight-conscious guests something virtually calorie-free to nibble on and assuage his hunger. Adding a low-calorie dip will make it easier for your guest to stay away from caloric offerings, by satisfying taste cravings. Keep plenty of diet sodas, seltzer, club soda, and mineral water on hand for guests who don't want to waste their calories on alcohol.

At mealtime, let your guests help themselves. Small portions—a taste of this and a taste of that—allow for optimum pleasure during the meal, and minimum pain the following morning. The only exception to the less-is-more rule is in vegetables and undressed salads. Pass bountiful bowls of each, along with low-calorie dressings for your dieting guests, regular dressing for those who are not dieting. Appetites occupied by low-calorie salads and steamed, fat-free vegetables, your weight-conscious guests won't be tempted to ruin their diets with seconds of higher-calorie foods. Don't feel like you have to limit your menu to rabbit foods, though. Go ahead and serve modest amounts of pasta, rice, or beans, if you wish, but without high-fat, high-calorie sauces. If dessert isn't a low-calorie creation, at least favor your weight conscious guest with a bowl of fresh fruit, so that resisting the Mocha Bavarian won't be completely out of the realm of possibility. Finally, because most diets require a substantial fluid intake, always keep plenty of iced water, diet or club soda within your dieter's reach.

The dishes in our weight-conscious menus are not, as we have said, diet fare in the most stringent sense. They are, however, substantially calorie-reduced, so that they should bring about no unpleasant repercussions on the morrow.

Menus for Guests on Weight-Control Diets

Breakfasts

I

Orange Slices, Lime Wedge
Hot Bulgur Cereal with Cinnamon and Raisins, Scoop of Hoop Cheese (30)

II

Whole Wheat Buttermilk Pancakes (55), *Berry Sauce* (430)
Cheesecake (441)

Brunches

I

Cold Spiced Tomato Juice (557)
Mixed Seasonal Fruit, Fruited Yogurt (428)
Granola Muffins (26)

II

Macédoine of Winter Fruit (476)
Herbed Mushroom Angel Crepes (43)
Watercress-Apple Salad (225)
Fluffy Pineapple Mousse (455)
Cookie Treats (532)

Lunches

I

Mushrooms a la Grecque (173)
Halibut and Melon Salad on Bibb Lettuce (240)
Whole Wheat French Bread (9)
Strawberry Sorbet (468)

II

Cream of Tomato Soup (93)
Spinach-Mushroom Sformato (340)
Whole Wheat Italian Bread (15)
Airy Apple Parfait (434)

Barbecues

I

Vegetables a la Grecque (178)
Grilled Fish Steaks (406)

Rice, Snow Pea, and Water Chestnut Salad (236)
Sliced Tomatoes
Tossed Greens, Light Vinaigrette (258)
Fresh Fruit Kabobs (474)

II
Baba Ghanoush (101), *Vegetable Chips* (383)
Hawaiian Chicken Kabobs (405)
Bok Choy Salad (192)
Mango Ice (460)
Almond Cookie Thins (525)

Cocktail Parties
I
Mushroom "Nuts" (129)
Vegetables a la Grecque (178)
Curried Mushroom Dip (104), Crudités (383)
Lo-Cheese Spread (113), *Melba Squares* (16), *and Zucchini Rounds* (383)
Lomi Lomi Salmon (176)
Cheese-Stuffed Snow Peas (152)
Crumb and Nut-Stuffed Mushrooms (148)
Eggplant Caviar-Stuffed Cherry Tomatoes (107)
Melon or Pineapple Cubes with Lime Dip (489)

II
Air-Popped Seasoned Popcorn (131)
Gazpacho Dip (108), *Crudités* (383)
Eggplant Caviar (106), *Melba Squares* (16), *and Zucchini Rounds* (383)
Mushrooms a la Grecque (173)
Tofu Tidbits (159)
Mushroom-Stuffed Zucchini (154)
Fresh Fruit Kabobs (474)

Dinners
I
Eggplant Caviar (106), *Pita Bread Triangles, and Black Olives*
Tunisian Chicken Breasts (313)
Minted Green Beans (386)
Tossed Greens, Coriander Dressing (254)
Light Baklava (541)
Turkish Coffee

II
Asparagus Pepperonata (164)
Chicken Cacciatore (303)
Angel Hair Pasta with Matchstick Zucchini (358)
Arugula Salad (188)
Fluffy Pineapple Mousse (455)
Shreddies (522)

III
Mushrooms a la Grecque (173)
Yucatecan Fish (295)
Rice and Celery Pilaf (364)
Watercress, Orange, and Fennel Salad (227)
Orange Sorbet Supreme (464)
Lemon Cookie Thins (530)

IV
Seviche (177)
Chicken Mayan Style (309)
Zucchini Rice (372)
Mexican Salad (202)
Pineapple Chiffon Pie (538)

Buffets
I
Stuffed Peppers (150)
Chilean Fish Stew (278)
Whole Wheat Italian Bread (15)
Spinach-Apple Salad (215)
Orange Sorbet Supreme (464)

II
Chilled Gazpacho (77), *Celery Swizzle-Stick*
Poached Whole Fish (284), *Dill Sauce* (421)
Sweet and Sour Cucumber Salad (195)
Sunchoke-Zucchini Salad (221)
Tossed Greens, Light Vinaigrette (258)
Strawberries Romanoff (499)
Angel Cream (543) *or Fruited Yogurt* (428)

Suppers
I
Onion Bouillabaisse (95)
Whole Wheat Italian Bread (15)

Watercress, Orange, and Fennel Salad (227)
Baked Apples (479)

II
Salmon Mousse I (287), *Melba Squares* (16)
Dilled Yogurt-Cucumber Salad (197)
Peach Sorbet (465)

The Cholesterol-Cautious Guest

It was over fifteen years ago that we first entertained a guest who was on a low-cholesterol diet. In those blissfully ignorant days before health and nutrition consciousness, our guest was something of an oddity, and we prepared for his arrival with little knowledge and a great deal of trepidation.

Today the guest who limits his cholesterol is no longer an oddity; he is nearly in the majority. Almost everyone we know seems to have altered his or her diet in that direction, either on the advice of a doctor, as a precautionary or preventative measure, or just because everyone else is doing it. Friends report that beef is making only rare guest appearances on their tables, while fish, poultry, and veal star regularly; that margarine has taken over their butter dishes; that vegetable oils are their shortening of choice; and that skim milk is the only milk in their fridge.

In response to this dietary revolution, restaurants have begun featuring fish and poultry on their menus, and chefs have learned how to broil fish without the lavish globs of butter once deemed necessary, for those who request their entrée "dry." The food industry has begun turning out long lines of cholesterol-free and cholesterol-reduced products: polyunsaturated vegetable oils, skim milks and skim-milk cheeses, low-cholesterol cheeses, ice milks, eggless mayonnaises, and so on.

All this makes the cholesterol-cautious dieter one of the easiest to cater to. Your other guests will notice hardly anything unusual about your low-cholesterol meals, except, of course, that they are unusually delicious.

Low-Cholesterol Basics

In spite of the occasional conflicting reports (often sponsored by egg, meat, and dairy industry interests) most medical authorities agree with the American Heart Association that dietary changes can reduce the risk of heart attack. They believe the evidence is strong enough to support *all* Americans reducing consumption of fats—especially saturated fats—and cholesterol to what is believed to be safe, or prudent, levels, while increasing intakes of complex carbohydrates, especially those high in dietary fiber.

The guest who is following a low-cholesterol diet has probably been instructed to limit the following foods because they are high in cholesterol or in saturated (hardened) fats:

- Eggs, including those used in cooking (1 egg yolk contains 250 to 300 milligrams of cholesterol, a whole day's allowance for many)
- Organ meats, such as liver, heart, tongue, kidneys, brains (1700 milligrams of cholesterol per 3-ounce serving), giblets, and sweetbreads
- Shellfish, such as shrimp, lobster, and scallops
- Beef, lamb, pork, ham, bacon, goose, duck, or fatty cuts of any meat
- Luncheon meats, cold cuts (salami, bologna, head cheese, pastrami, corned beef, etc.), sausages, and frankfurters
- Butter, lard, fat back, salt pork, suet, bacon or meat drippings, chicken, or other poultry fat
- Vegetable shortenings that are hydrogenated, high in saturated fats, such as palm oil, coconut oil, Crisco, and cocoa butter
- Vegetable oils low in polyunsaturates, such as olive and peanut oil (recent studies suggest these can be used in moderation)
- Coconut and chocolate (but not cocoa)
- Whole milk and cream, and dairy products made from them including: hard, soft, and processed cheeses, sour cream, yogurt, ice cream

- Poultry skins
- Baked goods, processed, and convenience foods that contain any of the above ingredients

Questions to Ask Your Cholesterol-Cautious Guest:

1. *Do you use egg substitutes?* If your guest does, you have the choice of using these low-cholesterol blends of egg whites, oils, and flavorings, or using egg whites (two whites for each whole egg) whenever whole eggs are called for in a recipe. Egg substitutes *cannot* be used to replace egg whites in a recipe.

2. *Must you restrict your salt intake?* If so (the combination of restricting salt and dietary cholesterol is quite common, as both have been linked with heart disease), read and follow the advice in Chapter Four, The Low-Salt Dieter. Use recipes that are suitable for both diets.

3. *Must you limit all fats?* There is growing evidence that excessive intake of fats of any kind is linked to disease, including heart disease and cancer. If your guest is limiting his or her fat consumption, you can still use just about any of the recipes which are suitable for a low-cholesterol diet (*LCh*), as the majority of them are low in all dietary fats. Pritikin recipes (*P*), which are virtually fat-free, are particularly appropriate choices.

4. *Must you limit your sugar intake?* Because high sugar intake is related to high levels of triglycerides—another blood fat linked to heart disease risk—many of those watching their cholesterol are also watching their sugar intake. If your guest is, read Chapter Three, The Guest on a Low-Sugar Diet, and select recipes that are both low in cholesterol (*LCh*), and in sugar (*D*). In most cases, the low-cholesterol dieter won't be following a no-sugar diet, just a low-sugar one. If so, you can use almost any of the recipes in this book which are suitable for a low-cholesterol diet; they are, with few exceptions, either sugar-free or significantly sugar-reduced.

Cholesterol-Cautious Shopping

Thanks to a very strong and persistant consumer demand for cholesterol-reduced products, shopping for a cholesterol-cautious guest is fast becoming an easy proposition. Supermarket shelves are today lined with all of the staples of a low-cholesterol diet, notably, polyunsaturated vegetable oils (the best: safflower, sunflower, corn, sesame, and soybean oils), margarines with high ratios of polyunsaturated to saturated fats (4 to 2 or better), and yolkless "imitation" mayonnaise.

As usual, it's the convenience foods that make your supermarket work complicated. A quick perusal of labels on ready-to-eat dinners, baked goods, frozen foods, cake and cookie mixes, ready-to-spread frostings, and nearly everything else that has been processed, will reveal a larder full of forbidden fats, including hydrogenated shortening, partially hydrogenated shortening, vegetable fat, coconut oil, cocoa butter, palm oil, lard, beef fat, chicken fat, and butter. And making matters worse still, most convenience products will also contain one or more of the following cholesterol-laden ingredients: eggs or egg yolks, cheese, whole milk, creams, coconut, and/or chocolate.

Ready-to-eat fried foods including fried chicken and fish, french fries, hash browns, hush puppies, potato and other snack chips, donuts, potato pancakes, onion rings, and egg rolls are more often than not fried to their delightful, crisp, golden brown hue in a forbidden shortening. Peanut butter, popcorn, and roasted nuts may also contain forbidden fats. Even chocolate—thanks to its cocoa butter—is a no-no. But cocoa, from which the saturated fat has been removed, can go into your shopping cart.

The dairy case is also an obstacle course of potential pitfalls for the cholesterol-cautious shopper. Bypass all whole milk and whole milk products, including evaporated milk, full-fat cheeses, ice cream, creams, and butter; all are unacceptably high in cholesterol. Settle only for skim milk (lower in cholesterol than 1 or 2 percent milks), low- or non-fat yogurt, low-fat cottage cheese (1 percent or less), low-fat pot cheese, low-fat buttermilk (80 or 90 calories per 8-ounce glass), low-cholesterol cheese (made with liquid vegetable oils instead of cream), low-fat/low-cholesterol cheeses (some imports contain 5 percent butterfat or less, and taste as good as fattier cheeses), hoop cheese (made from whey, and as rich tasting as ricotta, despite its lack of fat, salt, and cholesterol), farmer cheese (not very low in fat, but considerably lower than cream cheese), and sapsago, or "green" cheese (made from skim milk and fresh mown clover). Part-skim milk cheeses are available, but be aware that they are not always low in fat or cholesterol. Imitation sour cream and cream cheese products, too, can be loaded with saturated fats.

In spite of their notoriously high cholesterol count, you don't have to cross eggs off your shopping list. Buy them, but use only the whites. Or, if you prefer, use egg substitutes.

At the fish counter, choose from fresh, frozen, dried, smoked, or canned fish (except when it is canned in a prohibited oil), but not shellfish. Not only is fish cholesterol-free, it may actually help lower blood cholesterol levels.

Poultry, including chicken and turkey, but not goose and duck, is low in cholesterol, particularly the white meat. Skinless and boneless breasts of chicken are an especially good purchase for the low-cholesterol dieter, and save you the troublesome, but necessary, task of skinning.

If you can't bear to bypass beef altogether, at least keep away from the marbled and fatty cuts. Veal makes an elegant, though expensive "meaty" alternative to beef, and is relatively low in cholesterol. Again, though, opt for the leaner cuts.

Once in the produce department you can truly let yourself go, filling your shopping cart as high as you please with fresh fruits and vegetables which, in addition to being filling, nutritious, and cholesterol-free, have been credited, thanks to fiber content, by some medical researchers with reducing blood cholesterol levels. If you choose to buy frozen vegetables, steer clear of those frozen in butter or cheese, or any other sauce which might contain hidden fats.

You can feel equally free when selecting rice, pasta, grains (barley, buckwheat groats, triticale, millet), legumes (beans, peas, soybeans), nuts, seeds (sunflower, sesame, pumpkin, poppy), and, of course, herbs and spices. If any of these products, though, have seasonings added, check the label to see that no prohibited fats have been added as well. And avoid egg noodles, unless you can locate a "yolkless" egg noodle.

Cholesterol-Cautious Cooking

With the exception of frying, you can use just about all of your favorite cooking techniques when preparing for the low-cholesterol dieter. When you do use shortening, use polyunsaturated oils or margarines, rather than butter, lard, hydrogenated vegetable shortenings, or other prohibited fats. But keep in mind that foods cooked in stocks or wines, with as little added fat as possible, are preferable. Butter is out, too, on bread, easily replaced by margarines which are high in polyunsaturates, nut or fruit butters, or tofu spreads.

Though you have already obtained a lean cut of meat, you'll want to trim it of any remaining visible fat. Trim fat off poultry, too, and remove the skin before cooking. Discard the fat that cooks out of meats and poultry; skim meat juices and stocks used for gravies, or sauces and soups. The easiest and most effective method for skimming is to chill the liquid, and remove the fat that hardens at the top.

Two egg whites can be substituted for one whole egg in most recipes. Alternately, use egg substitutes according to the proportions recommended on the package. They'll work well in cooking and some baking, in omelets, French toast, pancakes, waffles, and breadings. They can't, however, be used as a substitute for whipped egg whites in baking or desserts.

When a recipe calls for egg yolks to thicken sauces or soups, use corn or potato starch, or a bit of instant mashed potato instead. The small amount of egg yolk in a spoonful of mayonnaise won't destroy a cholesterol-cautious dieter's regime, but a cupful could. Therefore, serve oil and vinegar, not mayonnaise-based salads, and favor dressings made with polyunsaturated oil.

Since creams—both sweet and sour—and whole milk are high in cholesterol and saturated fats, you'll have to substitute low-fat equivalents in your cooking. You'll find these will do a fine job in everything from creamed soups to bechamel (white) sauces, and even in frozen desserts. Substitute as follows: skim milk for whole milk, evaporated skimmed milk for cream (if chilled until ice crystals begin forming, you can whip evaporated skimmed milk for use in desserts), low-fat yogurt for whole milk yogurt, low-fat buttermilk for whole milk buttermilk.

Low-fat cheese can also take the place of higher-fat products in cooking. Low-fat (1 percent milkfat) cottage cheese substitutes flawlessly for the standard 4 percent milkfat cottage cheese, and contains about 75 percent less fat per ounce. Hoop or low-fat pot cheese makes an excellent substitute for ricotta or cream cheese in all baking and cooking, and, blended with skim or buttermilk, makes a fine dip.

Cholesterol-Cautious Menus

It's true that your guest is probably allowed three eggs a week, and beef every now and then. But since you don't know what he was served at a dinner party last night, or will be eating tomorrow, you'd be considerate to plan the most cholesterol-free meal possible. Our menus *are* cautious. So don't feel that you can't add a dab of mayonnaise to a sauce, or a sliced egg to a salad. Just be careful not to overdo it when altering the basic menu plan, unless, of course, you are substituting one of our low cholesterol recipes for another.

Menus for Guests on Low-Cholesterol Diets

Breakfasts

I

Macédoine of Winter Fruit (476)
Hot Bulgur Cereal with Cinnamon and Raisins (30)
Apple Coffee Cake I (500)

II

Marinated Mango (486)
Muesli (34) *or Homemade Granola* (32), *Seasonal Fruits and Skim Milk*
Whole Wheat Raisin Bread (21), *Apple Butter*

Brunches

I

Blended Fruit Juice (562), *Lime Wedge*
French Toast with Brandied Apples (62)
Vegetarian Sausage
Bran Muffins (22)

II

Seedless Grapes with Rum and Yogurt (485)
Spinach-Cheese Quiche (61)
Green Salad, Vinaigrette
Peach Cobbler (452)

Lunches

I

Cream of Tomato Soup (93)
Mushroom-Rice Angel Crepes (44)
Watercress, Orange, and Fennel Salad (227)
Wine-Poached Fruit (478)

II

Chilled Apple-Wine Soup (66)
Viva La Salad (249)
Granola Muffins (26), *Apple Butter-Tofu Spread* (548)
Strawberry-Yogurt Pie (540)

Barbecues

I

Chicken Sate (404)
Chutney Rice (365)

Grilled Curried Eggplant (412)
India Salad (199)
Chapatis (7)
Gingered Fruit (473)
Date-Nut Crescents (515)

II
Gazpacho (77)
Herbed Fish Flambé (407), *Soyo-Remoulade* (270)
Coal-Roasted Potatoes (415), *Buttermilk-Chive Dressing* (252)
Vegetable Slaw (224)
Fruit-Nut Sundae (472)

Cocktail Parties
I
Mushroom-Almond Pâté (117)
Indonesian Chicken Nuggets (158)
Baba Ghanoush (101), *Crudités* (383), *and Pita Bread Triangles*
Falafel Pie (347)
Melon Cubes with Lime Dip (489)

II
Cheese-Stuffed Snow Peas (152)
Mushroom-Stuffed Zucchini (154)
Lomi Lomi Salmon (176)
Vegetable Pâté (126), *Whole Rye Crackers*
Spinach-Cheese Strudel (144)
Almond-Stuffed Dates
Walnut-Stuffed Prunes

Dinners
I
Apple-Wine Soup (66)
Poached Salmon (284), *Sauce Verte* (426)
Okra and Tomatoes (389)
Rice, Snow Pea, and Water Chestnut Salad (236)
Onion-Walnut Loaves (18)
Peaches Caramel Flambé (494), *Brandied Angel Cream* (544)

II
Creamless Zucchini Soup (83)
Veal Roast, Minted Cranberry Glaze (330)
Glazed Carrots, Turnips, and Peas (380)
Kensington Salad (201), *Creamy Citrus Dressing* (253)

Pears Flambé (495)
Lace Cookies (520)

III
Zucchini, Tomato, and Basil Appetizer (179)
Stuffed Fish in Phyllo (290)
Five-Grain Pilaf (369)
Peas a la Française (391)
Boston Lettuce and Hearts of Palm Salad (193), *Garlic-Sesame Dressing* (256)
Praline-Baked Bananas (482)

IV
Cream of Hazelnut Soup (87)
Stuffed Chicken Breasts in Phyllo (302)
Brown Rice and Triticale Pilaf (363)
Fresh Stir-Fried Kale and Julienne Carrots (399)
Herbed Vegetable Salad (198)
Marzipan-Stuffed Pears (447)
Pecan Balls (521)

Buffets
I
Vegetables a la Grecque (178)
Gazpacho Verde (78)
Salmon Mousse I (287), *Cucumber Garnish*
Spinach and Red Pepper Salad (219), *Sweet and Sour Dressing* (272)
Gourmet Rice Salad (234)
Whole Wheat Italian Bread (15)
Sesame Bread Sticks
Cassis Sorbet (457)
Lace Cookies (520)

II
Eggplant Caviar (106), *Olives, Black Bread, and Margarine*
Lemon Chicken with Mushrooms and Hazelnuts (308)
Stir-Fried Broccoli (398)
Saffron Rice (371)
Whole Wheat Italian Bread (15)
Wine-Poached Fruit (478) *on Angel Cake*

Suppers
I
Caponata (102), *Melba Squares* (16)
Cold Pasta Primavera (337)

Arugula Salad (188)
Light Tortonis (470)
Almond Cookie Thins (525)

II
Cold Sesame Noodles and Bean Sprouts (169)
Tangerine Chicken (312)
Fluffy White Rice (370)
Bok Choy Salad (192)
Marinated Pineapple (487), *Lichee Nuts*
Almond-Nut Cookie Thins (526)

The Guest on A Low-Sugar Diet

When you think about it, taking candy—or any other sweet from a baby—is never as easy as the old cliché implies. The three-month old just graduating to solid foods opens his mouth eagerly for sweet tapioca, and snaps it shut when the spinach heads his way. We all seem to have an innate need for the sweeter things in life.

Once the "sweet tooth" was a blessing. When our ancestors were hunter-gatherers millenia ago, it was the sweet tooth that led them to naturally supplement their diet of game with berries and other fruits. Without the vitamins and minerals these foods added to their menus, they might not have survived, and we might not be here today.

But the sweet tooth is no longer a blessing. In fact, there are those nutrition experts who call it a curse. It misleads us into craving those widely available sweets—candy, cake, soft drinks, and the like—that, unlike the natural treats our ancestors enjoyed, are almost totally void of nutrition. (Fortunately for early man, Twinkies and Ring Dings didn't grow on trees.) These experts urge a sharp reduction in the national intake of sugar, presently a whopping 120 pounds per person per year.

Cutting down on sugar may seem the unkindest cut of all. But for more than 10 million Americans who suffer from diabetes mellitus, and for an unknown number of hypoglycemics, it is a necessity. Because of defects in the way these people metabolize glucose (the form in which all sugars and starches enter the blood stream) the consumption of this seemingly innocent substance poses a serious threat to life and health.

Diabetes is both the most common and puzzling of the disorders that affect the functioning of the human endocrine system, that network of glands controlling a multitude of complex and interrelated bodily functions. The mechanisms of diabetes are not fully understood, but it is known that the condition involves an inability to properly utilize the carbohydrates, or sugars and starches, taken into the body. The unused carbohydrates, in the form of glucose, pile up in the blood. An early symptom reflective of the defective carbohydrate metabolism of diabetes is hyperglycemia, or high blood sugar.

The problem may begin in childhood or adolescence (the more severe form of the disease) or in adulthood (most commonly after the age of forty) and the tendency toward the development of the disease is often inherited. Depending upon its severity, diabetes may or may not be treated with insulin (which lowers the blood sugar) or other pharmaceutical agents; but the most common denominator in therapy is always dietary. With the help of diet—and often medication—the diabetic must try to maintain blood sugar at relatively constant levels, safely within the normal range, throughout the day.

While the diabetic tends toward hyperglycemia (higher than normal levels of sugar in the blood), the symptoms that a hypoglycemic individual suffers during an attack are the result of lower-than-normal levels of sugar in the blood stream. Though a popular topic in the media in recent years, the actual incidence of hypoglycemia is unknown. Many cases go undiagnosed, while many others are diagnosed (often self-diagnosed) incorrectly. Some experts believe that cases of hypoglycemia are very rare; others believe that almost everyone suffers from this condition at one time or another.

Though a long string of causes, both psychological and physiological, have been suggested for this disorder, an attack of hypoglycemia can be brought on, paradoxically, by the intake of too much sugar. The blood sugar will rise initially, as you might expect. In response, the pancreas produces an excess of insulin which serves to burn the sugar quickly, resulting in an extreme drop in blood sugar. In these cases of "food-reactive" hypoglycemia, an attack may occur two to six hours after eating a meal or snack excessively high in starch or sugar, and expresses itself in symptoms such as nervousness, weakness, headache, inability to concentrate, palpitations, and hunger. The treatment, not surprisingly, is dietary.

Though the diet therapy for both hypoglycemics and hyperglycemics—long-term, often lifetime, partial, or total abstinence from sugar—may seem worse than the diseases themselves, it can in reality allow for a very palatable diet. In fact, you may discover when you entertain one of the millions of Americans presently on a low-sugar diet, that this particular food regimen is a very easy one with which to comply.

Low Sugar Basics

The first thing you've got to remember about your diabetic or hypoglycemic guests is that if they're to regulate their blood sugar levels, they must have their meals on time. While other guests may be able to sit around sipping cocktails while they wait for late dinner guests to arrive, these special guests should not. So if dinner isn't being served immediately, make certain there are substantial low-sugar hors d'oeuvres available for your guests. (See the cocktail section of Menus for Guests on Low-Sugar Diets, and serve some of the items included instead of the meal's first course.) If the delay is unplanned, serve the planned first course in the living room. Have on hand a very nutritious beverage, such as milk, in case your guest requests one. If your guest is coming for the weekend, be sure that snacks are available throughout the day in addition to the three meals you ordinarily serve: a bowl of nuts and fruit in the guest room, a pitcher of juice in the refrigerator, a basket of pretzel sticks on the coffee table. Also be sure that an adequate breakfast, high in protein, is served.

The cocktail party may also present other problems for your low-sugar guest. Most can have no beer or wine; many can have no alcoholic beverages at all. Some diabetics, however, are permitted small quantities of distilled liquor: whiskey, gin, vodka, and scotch, so be sure to ask your guest in advance. For guests who can't handle alcohol, prepare one or more of the non-alcoholic beverages for low-sugar dieters (*D*), pages 545 to 552. Also have on hand low-carbohydrate mixers, such as tomato or vegetable juice, club soda or seltzer (the latter contains no salt), diet quinine water, and other diet soft drinks. Some guests may also be able to have fruit juices, particularly grapefruit or orange juice.

The diabetic diet varies from the typical American diet in that it contains virtually no sucrose (ordinary sugar) or other refined sweeteners. Refined sweeteners are almost pure carbohydrate (sugar is 99 percent carbohydrate as compared to an apple, which is 14 percent, and green beans, which are 7 percent) and are thus difficult for those with faulty carbohydrate metabolisms to handle.

At one time, the diabetic diet was limited in total carbohydrates. Now the trend is to prohibit sucrose and other concentrated simple carbohydrates, such as glucose and fructose, and to limit other simple carbohydrates: dried and fresh fruit, fruit juices, and milk—which contains milk sugar. These quick-energy foods are digested and absorbed in minutes and can cause a rapid rise in blood sugar. But complex carbohydrates, mostly starches (breads, grains, pastas, beans, root vegetables, and peas), are no longer limited to the extent that they once were, since they are digested more slowly than simple carbohydrates. Whole grains may be particularly useful to the diabetic, since recent studies show that certain types of fiber may delay carbohydrate absorption.

Some diabetics may still be on a low-carbohydrate diet, but the American Diabetes Association now recommends a diet that is 50 to 60 percent carbohydrate. They find this diet, with an emphasis on complex carbohydrates, is more effective at controlling blood sugar than the limited-carbohydrate diet.

A similar trend is seen in the dietary treatment of hypoglycemics. Though some still recommend a low-carbohydrate diet for those with low blood sugar, more and more experts are suggesting that a diet low in simple concentrated sweets and other simple concentrated carbohydrates and high in complex carbohydrates is more useful in controlling this condition. Nathan Pritikin is one of the proponents of the high complex carbohydrate diet.

Calories are often regulated on the diabetic diet in order to help the diabetic maintain or reach ideal weight. Obesity makes diabetes more difficult to control, and increases susceptibility to other health problems such as heart disease.

For many diabetics portion size is strictly controlled; thus how food is served is vital. These individuals learn to gauge the proper amount of meat, vegetable, or starch they can take at each meal or snack. You can help them by preparing foods that can be taken in small portions, and by allowing guests to help themselves. Avoid leaving serving dishes on the table; leave them instead on a buffet or warmer, so that seconds are out of sight, but available.

The foods that usually must be avoided on a low-sugar diet include:

- Table sugar, raw sugar, brown sugar, date sugar, honey, maple syrup, corn syrup, molasses

- Any of the following when prepared with any type of sugar:
  Jams, jellies, preserves
  Sweetened condensed milk
  Fruits, canned or frozen in syrup
  Soft drinks, fruit drinks, fruit punches, sweetened juices
  Cakes, cookies, pastries, candies, puddings, gelatins
  Ketchup (25 percent sugar), barbecue sauce, duck sauce, relishes, sweet pickles
  Sauces and gravies
  Breakfast cereals (some are more than 50 percent sugar)
  Salad dressings (some Russian and French dressings are ⅓ sugar)
  Whipped toppings, non-dairy creamers
  Canned and instant soups, bouillon cubes
  Convenience foods (instant, canned, dehydrated, frozen)
  Breads, crackers, baked goods

Practically all commercially prepared foods, savory and sweet, contain some sugar. It is frightening to consider just how much sugar we pump into our blood streams unawares; it is even more alarming for the diabetic and hypoglycemic.

Diabetics, because they are highly susceptible to heart and blood vessel disease, are often advised to limit fat and cholesterol intake, too. To be on the safe side, avoid serving foods high in cholesterol and fat, and keep cooking fats to a minimum.

Questions to Ask the Low-Sugar Guest

1. *Must you limit fruit, fruit juices, dried fruit, and milk?* These foods are limited on many low-sugar diets. If your guest's diet is limited, avoid recipes which are not recommended for those who must limit their intake of simple carbohydrates. Use the minimal amount of fruits and fruit juices—usually suggested in low-sugar (*D*) alternatives—called for in a recipe. Reduce or eliminate from recipes dried fruits, such as raisins and dates, concentrated fruit juices, and so on. If additional sweetening is needed, use the artificial sweetener of your guest's choice. Limit milk to no more than one cup per meal, in cooking or for drinking, per guest. For guests who need not limit simple carbohydrates, you may use all low-sugar (*D*) recipes.

2. *Is your diet limited in complex carbohydrates such as rice, beans, potatoes, and bread?* Though the trend is away from limiting these

foods, your guest may still be restricted. If so, simply omit one starch from your menu or serve smaller portions of each. Don't serve starchy foods with protein foods. For example, don't put the veal stew on the rice, or the chicken cacciatore on the pasta. Serve each dish separately, allowing your guest to take as much or as little as is appropriate. If your guest need not limit complex carbohydrates, you may use the Pritikin (*P*) menus, which tend to be high in complex carbohydrates and sugar-free, as well as the low-sugar (*D*) menus and recipes.

3. *Must you limit saturated fats and cholesterol?* If your guest is on a limited saturated fat and cholesterol diet, use low-sugar (*D*) recipes that are also low in cholesterol (*LCh*). Use the variations for *LCh* diets as well. All Pritikin (*P*) recipes are also suitable.

4. *Are you permitted any alcoholic beverages or wines in cooking?* Most diabetics cannot drink wine or beer, but some are permitted small quantities of distilled liquor. But for the drinker and non-drinker alike, it is important to provide a selection of non-alcoholic beverages, including seltzer, club soda, vegetable or tomato juice, and citrus juices. You may also offer some of the non-alcoholic drinks for low-sugar dieters in our beverage recipe section, pages 545 to 552. If wine is not permitted in cooking, make the parenthetical substitutions suggested for the diabetic diet (*D*), usually juices or stock. The guest on a hypoglycemic diet may not be allowed alcoholic beverages, but will probably be permitted dry wine in cooking, as long as the alcohol is well-evaporated. Provide a selection of non-alcoholic beverages for your hypoglycemic guest, too. And for both types of low-sugar dieters, provide appropriate snacks along with the drinks.

5. *Is your salt intake limited?* It is for many diabetics. If it is for your guest, use recipes suitable for both diabetics (*D*) and low-salt dieters (*LS*). Make the parenthetical alterations suggested for moderate salt restriction. If your guest is more severely restricted, and allowed only 1,000 milligrams of sodium per day or less, read about salt-restricted diets in Chapter Four.

6. *Are you permitted to use fructose? If so, how much?* Some diabetics may be permitted limited use of fructose (fruit sugar), as may some hypoglycemics. If so, you can leave this often optional ingredient in.

7. *Do you use artificial sweeteners? Saccharine? Sorbitol?* If your guest uses saccharine, have it available for sweetening tea and coffee. You may also use it in recipes calling for fructose or small amounts of sugar. If sorbitol is used, you can serve ice creams or other sweets containing it. Since it is a carbohydrate, its use may be limited.

8. *Do you use aspartame (APM)?* This new artificial sweetener marketed as NutraSweet™ or Equal™ by G.D. Searle and Co., is ideal for diabetics and hypoglycemics because it is not a carbohydrate as is sorbitol, but a protein compounded of two amino acids. APM can be used in coffee or tea, as well as in beverages and desserts, but not in baking or cooking. It can, however, be stirred into sauces at the very end of cooking. It cannot be used for those on low phenylalanine diets (those with PKU—phenylketonuria).

Low-Sugar Shopping

As the marketplace stands now, low sugar shopping is definitely a case of "let the buyer beware." Be wary, for instance, of labels that proclaim "no sugar added." Although the label must speak the literal truth—that is, no table sugar can be added to a product thus labeled—it may not be telling the whole story. The product may contain honey, molasses, or some other form of sugar just as forbidden on a diabetic or hypoglycemic diet. "Dietetic" on the label, too, may mislead. Dietetic means simply that it is suitable for some kind of special diet, and not necessarily a diabetic one. Thus, a box of cookies labeled "dietetic" could be low in salt but loaded with sugar. Even "diabetic" may not be much help to a low-sugar shopper. Although such a product will be free of sugar, it may contain artificial sweeteners that your guest doesn't use.

As usual, you will have to label read your way through the aisles. First of all, be sure that products you buy contain no form of sugar, including sucrose, glucose, dextrose, maltose, corn syrup, corn sweeteners, honey, molasses, maple syrup, brown sugar, turbinado sugar, raw sugar, date sugar, cane sugar, lactose, fructose (unless your guest is permitted this sweetener), natural sweeteners, dextrins, high-fructose corn syrup, refiner's syrup, raisin syrup, invert syrup, or invert sugar. The ending "ose" is a good indication that the substance in question is a sugar.

When shopping, concentrate on these foods:

- Fish, poultry, lean meats
- Fresh or frozen vegetables
- Fresh fruits, especially melons, cranberries, rhubarb
- Frozen unsweetened fruits
- Canned fruits in unsweetened juices
- Unsweetened fruit juices (fruit "drinks" indicate that sugar has been added)

- Pickles (sour or unsweetened dill), olives
- Stocks, broths, bouillons, soups containing no sugar
- Coffee and tea
- Vinegar, lemon juice, herbs, spices, dry mustard, flavoring extracts for seasoning
- Artificially sweetened diet soda, jams, gelatins, cranberry sauce (if your guest uses artificial sweeteners)
- Unflavored gelatin
- Raisins, dates and other dried fruits (may be allowed in very small amounts, due to concentrated sweetness)
- Milk, buttermilk, cottage cheese (may be limited to some extent due to milk sugar; always buy low-fat varieties)
- Aged cheese (buy low-fat, low-cholesterol varieties)
- Yogurt (unsweetened, plain)

Low-Sugar Cooking

When cooking for the diabetic dieter, there are two important principles to remember: *reduce fat* and *eliminate sugar.* For the hypoglycemic dieter, *eliminate sugar* is your cardinal rule. The task of reducing fat begins in the supermarket and at the butcher. Buy low-fat dairy products and lean meat and poultry. Before you begin cooking, trim meat and poultry of all visible fat and remove poultry skins. Skim fat from stocks, drippings, gravies, and soups before serving. Limit use of egg yolks. Thicken sauces with a flour and water or cornstarch and water paste, or with arrowroot, instead of a flour-fat roux. Avoid frying, and sauté in a minimum of fat (as described in Recipe Glossary, page 154).

Limiting sugar in cooking may only require not adding refined sugars (see Low-Sugar Shopping) and not using products containing them. Or it may require strictly limiting all foods with concentrated sweetness, such as fruit juices, in addition to omitting sugars.

When your guest must limit all simple carbohydrates or foods with concentrated sweetness, try to think in terms of a "sweetness allowance." Allow up to one sweetness allowance (what the diabetic would call one fruit exchange) per guest per meal (see Sweetness Table on page 48). Some of your guests, diabetic and hypoglycemic, will be able to handle more than one sweetness allowance at a meal. You may increase amounts in the Table accordingly or stick to the safe and conservative quantities suggested.

Because the sweeter carbohydrates are limited on low-sugar diets, you will probably want to save the sweetness allowance for dessert instead of serving a sweet main course, soup, or salad dressing. If you want to add a touch of sweetness to a dish, however, you can use 1 to 2 teaspoons of apple, orange, or pineapple juice concentrate, without upsetting anyone's diet plan.

Desserts, of course, require more sweetening than that. This shouldn't present a major problem if you aim for a natural sweetness rather than the sticky, oversweetness characteristic of so many desserts. Your best sweetening agents are fruit juices and fruit juice concentrates. Use these in modest amounts, guided by the sweetness allowance equivalents if your guest's diet dictates these restrictions. You can also combine sweet ingredients to make one allowance, for example, 1 tablespoon raisins and ¾ tablespoon apple juice concentrate in a cupcake.

You can, if your guest approves and you like, use artificial sweeteners to augment sweetness in some dishes. Saccharine-type sweeteners can be used in baking and cooking, although many people object to the unnatural taste of foods baked with this product. Or, you can combine saccharine and apple juice concentrate or other natural sweeteners for a less artificial taste.

A newer sweetener, and one that promises some new horizons for low-sugar dieters is aspartame (APM), available from S.D. Searle in packets under the brand name Equal™. Packets are equal to two teaspoonfuls of sugar or two teaspoonfuls of apple juice concentrate. Tablets, equal to 1 teaspoon of sugar, are useful for sweetening coffee or tea. The product is compounded from two amino acids and is thus a protein rather than a carbohydrate, which makes it particularly suitable for the diet limited in carbohydrates. It does have some drawbacks, though: it isn't stable in cooking and it doesn't provide the bulk and texture sugar supplies in baking. But, it can be used successfully in ice creams, sorbets, souffles, mousses, puddings, and similar uncooked desserts. It can also be stirred into sauces, puddings, and fruit soups when cooking is completed. Because it is a new product, you will probably have to experiment with it a few times before you are ready to use it in cooking for guests.

Low-Sugar Menus

In general, menus for the low-sugar dieter should contain no concentrated simple carbohydrates (such as sugar, honey, maple syrup, corn syrup, or fructose, though your guest may be permitted to use small amounts of this last sweetener). And they should include no more than one sweet dish (usually dessert) that is the equivalent of a single permitted serving of fruit (see chart), unless your guest is permitted unlimited simple carbohydrates. Plan on plentiful amounts of complex carbohydrates (potatoes, rice, beans, peas, bread, and so on) served separately so that your guests can take as little or as much as their diets dictate.

The recipes below are relatively high in complex carbohydrates and low in simple carbohydrates and fat as recommended by the American Diabetic Association. They are fine for all low-sugar dieters though you may want to eliminate one carbohydrate dish from the menu you select when your guest is limited in all carbohydrates.

Sweetness Table (all fruit is unsweetened)

1 sweetness or fruit allowance usually = 1 small (2-inch diameter) apple = ½ cup unsweetened applesauce = ⅓ cup apple juice = about 1½ tablespoons apple juice concentrate = 2 medium apricots or 4 dried halves = ½ small banana = 1 cup blackberries, raspberries, or strawberries, or ⅔ cup blueberries = ½ 6-inch canteloupe = 10 large cherries = 2 dates = 2 large fresh figs or 1 small dried = ½ small grapefruit or ½ cup juice = 12 grapes or ½ cup grape juice = ⅛ medium honeydew = ½ small mango = 1 small orange or ½ cup juice = ⅓ medium papaya = 1 medium peach = 1 small pear = ½ cup pineapple chunks or ⅓ cup juice = 2 medium plums = 2 medium prunes dried = 2 tablespoons raisins = 1 large tangerine = 1 cup watermelon chunks.

Menus for Guests on Low-Sugar Diets

Breakfasts

I

Nut-Filled Baked Apples (480)
Mushroom-Pepper-Onion Scramble (52)
Herb Bread (11)

II

Raspberries in Orange Juice
Whole Wheat Buttermilk Pancakes (55), *Fruited Yogurt* (428)

Brunches

I

Cantaloupe, Lime Wedge
Spinach-Feta Quiche (60)

Oriental Salad (205)
Maple-Walnut Shreddies (522)

II
Grapefruit Juice, Lime Wedge
Savory French Toast (64), *Sour Cream*
Vegetarian Bacon Strips
Branberry-Nut Muffins (23)

Lunches
I
Mushrooms and Artichoke Hearts a la Grecque (174)
Italian Minestrone (88), *Grated Cheese*
Whole Wheat Italian Bread (15)
Cheese-Stuffed Pears (496)

II
Gazpacho Verde (78)
Salad Nicoise (246)
Whole Wheat French Bread (9)
Strawberry Sorbet (468), *Chopped Nuts*

Barbecues
I
Mushroom-Stuffed Zucchini (154)
Grilled Fish Steaks (406), *Anchovy Butter* (427)
Coal-Roasted Potatoes (415)
Coal-Roasted Zucchini (415)
Dilled Cucumbers (196)
Whole Wheat Italian Bread (15)
Marinated Melon Balls and Blueberries (488), *Fruited Yogurt* (428)

II
Antipasto Vegetables (161)
Grilled Garlic Chicken (403)
Coal-Roasted Corn on the Cob (415)
Middle Eastern Salad (203)
Fresh Fruit Salad (475)
Walnut Shreddies (522)

Cocktail Parties
I
Curried Soy Nuts (128)
Lomi Lomi Salmon (176)

Nutted Lo-Cheese Spread (113), *Mixed Crackers*
Vegetable Pâté (126)
Guacamole (109), *Crudités (383)*
Melon Sections
Non-Alcoholic Beverages

II
Soybeans, Seeds, and Nuts
Cheese and Nut-Stuffed Mushrooms (147)
Curried Mushroom Dip (104), *Crudités* (383)
Pesto Pâté-Stuffed Celery (119)
Caponata (102), *Melba Squares* (16)
Fresh Fruit Bowl
Non-Alcoholic Beverages

Dinners
I
Curried Pea and Avocado Soup (74)
Veal Tarragon with Brazil Nuts (329)
Steamed Broccoli (397)
Sunchoke Salad on Greens (220)
Nature-Sweetened Apple Strudel (542)

II
Baba Ghanoush (101), *Crudités* (383) *and Pita Bread Triangles*
Tunisian Chicken Breasts (313)
Middle Eastern Salad (203)
Nut Crescents (516)
Fresh Fruit

III
Pesto Pâté (118), *Melba Squares* (16)
Baked Trout with Filberts (292)
Mushrooms and Zucchini (388)
Mixed Greens, Vinaigrette
Airy Apple Parfait (434), *Sliced Almonds*

IV
Seviche (177)
Stuffed Chicken Breasts in Phyllo (302)
Stir-Fried Fresh Kale and Julienne Carrots (399)
Spinach, Endive, and Mushroom Salad (216)
Apricot Mousse (438)

Buffets

I

Mushroom-Almond Pâté (117)
Lemon Chicken with Mushrooms and Hazelnuts (308)
Whole Wheat Noodles and Cauliflower (359)
Steamed Asparagus Spears (397)
Tossed Green Salad, Light Vinaigrette (258)
Berry Pudding (439)
Almond Shreddies (522)

II

Cold Sesame Noodles and Bean Sprouts (169)
Tangerine Chicken (312)
Chinese Vegetables (382)
Bulgur-Tofu Salad (229)
Fresh Papaya, Mangos, and Pineapple
Macadamia Nuts

Suppers

I

Gazpacho Verde (78)
Thai Tuna Salad (248)
Pita Bread
Cantaloupe and Strawberries, Fruited Yogurt (428)

II

Stuffed Peppers (150)
Onion Bouillabaisse (95)
Sunshine Salad (222)
Whole Wheat French Bread (9)
Nut-Filled Baked Apple (480)

The Low-Salt Dieter

Do you remember pouring salt onto your palm as a child, then licking it off with unabashed eagerness? Noted epicurean, Craig Claiborne, recalls a similar ritual. Each Sunday, when his mother made ice cream, he would stand anxiously by, waiting for a bit of the rock salt that was packed with the ice around the canister to fall onto the newly-churned ice cream. "I would hastily scoop up a spoonful of the ice cream with the salt chunk, letting the salt melt slowly in my mouth after the ice cream was gone."

But for Craig Claiborne, as for millions of other Americans, that pleasure—and all others derived from salt—is no more. Salt, once so highly valued for its preserving qualities that salaries (from the Latin word for salt) were paid in it, is now considered a menace by most health authorities, particularly for those suffering from hypertension, or high blood pressure. Population studies have shown a very close relationship between high sodium intake (salt is sodium chloride) and high levels of hypertension: Eskimos consume 1 to 2 grams of salt a day and have a 1 to 2 percent hypertension rate; Americans eat about 7 to 10 grams a day and have a 15 percent high blood pressure rate; the Japanese ingest a whopping 40 to 50 grams a day and nearly half the population shows high blood pressure readings.

With some 23 million Americans suffering from hypertension or from other diseases related to salt intake, it's not unlikely that you'll find a low-salt dieter on your guest list. But, not to fret. As you'll discover, you can prepare some truly extraordinary culinary triumphs without once lifting a salt shaker.

Low-Salt Basics

Just about every food in its natural form contains some sodium, so a completely salt-free diet is an impossibility. The person on a salt-restricted diet is usually asked to reduce salt intake from the average 7 to 12 grams per day to anywhere from ¼ to 3 grams. In the less restricted diets, this is done by avoiding those foods that are heavily salted. In the more severely restricted diets, even foods that are mildly high in sodium in their natural form are prohibited.

In entertaining the low-salt dieter, it isn't necessary to be familiar with the various levels of sodium restriction. We think it's easier to simply avoid buying all very highly salted foods and to limit or avoid (according to your guest's personal requirements) those foods that are naturally moderately high in sodium. You'll find that following these guidelines will be relatively easy. Remember:

- Do not add salt in cooking or after cooking. Your guest should be the one to decide whether or not to salt, as well as how much, and this can be done at the table.
- Do not serve foods that are heavily salted,* such as:
  Potato chips, pretzels, salted nuts, salted crackers
  Pickles, relishes, olives, other foods packed in brine
  Soy sauce, Worcestershire sauce, steak sauce, prepared mustard, prepared horseradish, ketchup, chili sauce
  Sodium bicarbonate, baking powder, baking soda, self-rising flour
  Seasoning salts, garlic salt, onion salt, celery salt, MSG (monosodium glutamate)
  Bouillon cubes, canned soups, dehydrated soups, commercial gravies, sauces, or broths
  Baked goods (breads, cookies, cakes, crackers)
  Canned and frozen fish, shellfish, smoked fish
  Salted meats, cold cuts, franks, koshered meats
  Regular cottage cheese, pot cheese, farmer cheese, hard cheeses
  Commercial salad dressings, mayonnaise

* Many of these foods are available in unsalted, no-salt added, or low-sodium forms, and are permitted as such.

Canned vegetables and frozen vegetables with added salt (peas and lima beans are always salted)
Meat tenderizers, meat extracts
Buttermilk
Salted butter or margarine
Sauerkraut
Cooking wine (salt is added)
Soft drinks containing sodium

- Limit foods that are high in sodium naturally, or have moderate amounts of salt added to them; or if your guest's diet requires, eliminate them entirely from your menu plans. These include:

Milk (on most low-salt diets, milks are limited to 2 cups per day)
Ice cream, frozen yogurt, ice milk (include these in the milk allowance)
Meat and poultry (fresh or frozen), fish (fresh or unsalted canned)
High-sodium vegetables (1 serving total per day), including: artichokes, beets, beet greens, carrots, celery, celery flakes, chard, collards, dandelion greens, whole hominy, kale, mustard greens, parsley flakes, spinach, watercress, white turnips, turnip greens
Eggs (usually limited to 1 per day)
Fruit dried with sodium bisulphate

The most severely restricted low-sodium diets may limit the meat allowance to as little as 2 to 4 ounces per day (be sure to serve meat in small portions), permit only low-sodium milk and milk products (up to 2 cups per day), and restrict eggs to only three per week. Fortunately, you will rarely come across a guest on so limited a diet.

Questions to Ask Low-Salt Dieters

1. *Are you allowed up to one serving a day of vegetables naturally high in sodium (such as carrots and spinach) or must you omit these vegetables entirely?* If your guest is permitted these high sodium vegetables, you can include one or more of them in a meal, up to a total of ½ cup per person. In low-salt (*LS*) recipes that feature these vegetables, you'll have the choice of omitting the vegetable, reducing the quantity used, or substituting another lower-in-sodium vegetable.

2. *Are you permitted non-dietetic canned fish or must you stick to the dietetic low-sodium pack?* If your guest is allowed only dietetic canned fish, substitute accordingly in recipes.

3. *Are you permitted regular milk, or are you restricted to the low-sodium variety? How much of either are you allowed?* Use the milk your guest is permitted; generally use no more than 1 cup of milk per meal per person. Always use unsalted buttermilk and cheeses. Unsalted cottage and farmer cheeses are easy to find. Almost as available are unsalted domestic Cheddar and Swiss. Specialty stores carry unsalted imported cheeses. When milk is severely limited, avoid recipes not recommended for those restricted to low-sodium milk.

4. *Does your physician permit use of salt substitutes?* The low-sodium / high-potassium salt substitutes found in the supermarket and health food stores are good for both cooking and table use if your guest is permitted to use them. But beware—use this product only if your guest's physician permits. And then don't use more than recommended on the label. Overuse can lead to dangerous potassium overload.

5. *Are you limiting your cholesterol as well?* Since salt and cholesterol are both linked to heart disease, a low-salt dieter may very well be restricting his or her cholesterol, too. In that case, use recipes that are both low in salt (LS), and low in cholesterol (LCh). Most Pritikin recipes (P) are low in salt, fat, and cholesterol and would be suitable for the guest who is limiting all three. If you are using your own recipes, read the suggestions in Chapter Two, The Cholesterol-Cautious Guest.

6. *Are you permitted to drink wine?* If not, there are several nonalcoholic options listed in the beverage section (pages 545–552).

7. *Are you permitted wine in cooking?* Most guests will be. If not, substitute stock for wine in recipes calling for wine. But do *not* use cooking wines and sherries. These are salted products.

Shopping for the Salt-Restricted Dieter

In our salt-addicted society, most packaged goods, both sweet and savory, have salt added. But because our taste buds have become dulled by inundation with salt and sugar from an early age, we can't rely on them to tell us when salt has been added to a product or not. When sodium content is listed (such a listing may soon be mandatory) your supermarket mission will be easier. Look for quantities that are less than 10 milligrams per serving in most foods, up to 30 or 40 milligrams per serving in main course foods. When sodium content is not listed, however, look for forms of sodium listed as ingredients: salt, sodium, sodium proprionate, sodium bicarbonate, sodium bisulfate, and any other additive containing the word sodium in its name. The chemical symbol for salt, Na, also indicates that a product should be avoided. Even fruits and fruit juices can contain added sodium compounds.

Avoid, too, any of the foods listed as restricted under Low Salt Basics (pages 53–54). If you're going to be baking quick breads or cakes, pick up some low-sodium baking powder at a health food store.

Basically, stick to foods in their most natural form. Fresh mushrooms contain only 7 milligrams of sodium per cup, while canned mushrooms contain up to 150 milligrams. Steer away, too, from bakery and packaged baked goods, unless the package states, "no salt added." Again, don't let your taste buds decide. A Hostess Twinkie, which certainly doesn't taste salty on your tongue, contains nearly ¼ of the daily limit for low-salt dieters, or 240 milligrams of sodium. Artificially sweetened foods and beverages, such as diet sodas, sweetened with sodium saccharine, are packed with sodium. Even tap water may be a problem in some areas. If tap water in your city contains more than 2 milligrams of sodium per 100 milliliters, or if your water is treated with softening "salts," use a low-sodium bottled water for soups, sauces, and beverages when possible.

Of course, beware especially of foods that do taste salty; one pickle, for instance, can contain more than 1,000 milligrams of sodium, the full day's quota or more for many dieters. Convenience foods, though not appearing overly salty, can contain mammoth amounts of sodium, too. One brand of beef pot pie, for example, has 1,700 milligrams of sodium per serving.

Although the restrictions may seem overwhelming, there are an abundance of foods that can be served to all salt-restricted dieters, including:

- Pastas, rice, barley, oats, triticale, bulgur, buckwheat groats (kasha), and other grains
- Cereals with no added salt (check labels)
- Dried, but not canned, peas and beans
- Fresh, frozen, or canned fruits and fruit juices, sun-dried fruit
- All fresh vegetables not prohibited on your guest's diet (see Low-Salt Basics pages 53–54)
- All frozen vegetables not prohibited on your guest's diet and having no salt added (peas and lima beans are always salted)
- Low-sodium vegetable and tomato juices, sauces, and pastes

- Fresh fish or low-sodium canned fish (but not frozen)
- Oil, unsalted margarine, unsalted butter
- Lemon juice, vinegar, spices, dry mustard, herbs, bitters
- Wine, but not cooking wine
- Low-sodium seltzer or bottled water (club soda has salt added)
- Low-sodium cheeses (hard cheeses, cottage cheese, pot cheese, etc.), unsalted buttermilk, and whole and skim milk and cream. (These will be served in limited quantities according to your guest's dietary needs; for the rare guest on a severely limited diet buy low-sodium milk, such as Lonalac by Mead Johnson.)

Low-Salt Cooking

In cooking for the low-salt dieter, the first thing to do is to lock up your salt shaker, meat tenderizers, MSG, seasoning salts, soy sauce, and any salty seasoning you are accustomed to using. Your regular baking powder and self-rising flour, too, must be kept behind cupboard doors. That accomplished, everything else should be relatively easy, especially if you've shopped according to our suggestions.

In planning menus and in cooking, rely heavily on the multitude of unsalted seasonings, herbs, and spices that are the mainstay of gourmet cooking: garlic, leeks, onions, scallions, shallots, basil, dill, parsley, rosemary, tarragon, thyme—the list is virtually endless. Double the quantity of fresh mushrooms in a favorite recipe to double the flavor, without adding salt. Use a touch of sweetness, for instance apple juice, honey, fructose, or sugar to bring out the flavors in food, as salt usually does. Or use lemon or lime juice, plain, wine, or tarragon vinegars where the tang of salt seems needed, as in tomato sauces, gazpacho, and salad dressings. Lemon juice is good, too, in sweet and sour dishes, which are good choices for a salt-reduced diet because of their reliance on flavorings other than salt. Dry mustard and freshly grated horseradish (the prepared versions of both are highly salted), are also excellent low-salt seasonings. But don't stop there. Be adventurous; try seasonings you've never used before, including green peppercorns, hot chilies (fresh, not in brine or salted vinegar), cumin in salads, cinnamon on poultry. And be generous with wines (again, not cooking wines) in sauces, soups, gravies, and entrées.

Even highly flavored foods can be used as seasoning agents. Craig Claiborne, who recently converted to a lifetime low-salt diet, suggests using arugula, processed to smoothness, with or without garlic and watercress, as a salad dressing.

Favorite cake recipes will do just as well without salt; fruit juice can replace milk to further cut sodium content. If baking powder is called for, use the low-sodium variety. Breads suffer some when salt is omitted, but one or more of a variety of flavorful additions can greatly improve their sagging taste: sautéed chopped or raw onions, herbs, or additional sweetening. Because of their high sodium content, use of eggs should be limited in baking, and in all low-salt cooking.

If the drinking water in your home is artificially softened, use bottled water to prepare foods and beverages. Softened water is high in sodium.

Since meat, fish, and poultry may be limited on your guest's diet, prepare 3 to 4 ounce portions, allowing guests to help themselves. Always rinse fresh fish well in water since it may have been stored in salt water. And, use dairy products in moderate amounts in cooking.

When serving time arrives, tell your guest that you have added no salt in preparation. Provide salt and salt substitute so that guests can add their own, if desired.

Low-Salt Menus

Our low-salt menus are rather rigorous, catering to the more extreme, though not the most extreme, salt-restricted diets. For guests who are only mildly restricted, you can add, if you wish, a restricted vegetable or some cheese or milk to the menu. You can also substitute other low-salt recipes for the ones we've included on a particular menu.

The key to successful low-salt entertaining, though, is in being innovative and creative with your low-salt cooking. The more exotic the flavor and texture of a dish is, the less likely anyone will notice that the salt has been left out.

Menus for Guests on Low-Salt Diets

Breakfasts

I

Orange Muesli (35)
Whole Wheat Raisin Bread (21), *Honey-Tofu Spread* (547)

II

Blended Fruit Juice, Lime Wedge (562)
Orange Pancakes (57) *with Nuts and Raisins, Orange-Maple Syrup* (551)

Brunches

I
Marinated Melon Balls and Blueberries (488)
French Toast with Brandied Apples (62)
Cranberry-Nut Muffins (24)

II
Spiced Prunes and Oranges in Port (498)
Apple Pancakes (54), *Cinnamon Sugar*
Low-Sodium Cheese Wedges

Lunches

I
Blueberry Soup (68)
Viva la Salad (249)
Apple Bread (1), *Sweet Butter*
Mango Ice (460)
Lace Cookies (520)

II
Sunchoke Salad (220)
Lentil Soup with Chick Peas (89)
Cheese-Nut Bread (8)
Pears Baked in Red Wine (493)

Barbecues

I
Apple-Veal Balls (160)
Crumb and Nut-Stuffed Mushrooms (148)
Hawaiian Chicken Kabobs 405)
Coal-Roasted Potatoes (415), *Margarine and Chives*
Papaya-Avocado Salad (206)
Mango Ice (460)
Pecan Balls (521)

II
Curried Mushroom Dip (104), *Crudités* (383)
Gazpacho (77)
Grilled Stuffed Trout (409)
Coal-Roasted Zucchini and Onions (415)
Sunchoke-Zucchini Salad (221)
Garlic-Herb Bread (10)
Fresh Fruit Salad (475) *in Melon Basket*
Cookie Treats (532)

Cocktail Parties

I

Guacamole (109), *Crudités* (383)
Lomi Lomi Salmon (176)
Veal-Stuffed Prunes (151)
Hawaiian Chicken Kabobs (405)
Fresh Tropical Fruit Kabobs (474)
Pecan Balls (521)

II

Curried Mushroom Dip (104), *Crudités* (383)
Eggplant Caviar (106), *Salt-Free Crackers*
Lo-Cheese Fondue (112)
  French Bread (9)
  Apple Slices
  Crisp-Tender Vegetables (383)
Tuna Balls in Tomato Sauce (156)
Unsalted Nuts and Raisins

Dinners

I

Asparagus Vinaigrette (167)
Cold Poached Whole Fish (284), *Orange-Dill Sauce* (422)
Moroccan Rice (366)
Middle-Eastern Salad (203)
Herb Bread (11)
Strawberries Romanoff (499), *Whipped Cream and Slivered Almonds*

II

India Salad (199)
Chicken Curry (305)
Saffron Rice (371)
Chutney (273)
Minted Green Beans (386)
Curried Lentils (387)
Chapatis (7)
Gingered Fruit (473)
Date-Nut Crescents (515)
Orange Almond Semolina (449)

III

Apple-Squash Bisque (65)
Trout Sauté with Almonds, Pine Nuts, and Raisins (293)
Chive Rice (368)

Steamed Lemon Broccoli (397)
Mushroom-Pea Salad (204)
Praline-Baked Bananas (482)

IV
Apple-Wine Soup (66), *Yogurt and Cinnamon*
Halibut Linguata (279)
Parsleyed Yogurt Potatoes (362)
Green Beans Almondine (384)
Papaya-Avocado Salad (206), *Spicy Orange Dressing* (262)
Poires au Gratin (492)

Buffets
Veal-Stuffed Prunes (151)
Burgundy Chicken (300)
Parsleyed Noodles
Vegetables a la Grecque (178)
Peas a la Française (391)
Marzipan-Stuffed Pears (447)
Pecan Balls (521)

II
Antipasto Vegetables (161)
Stuffed Peppers (150)
Chicken Cacciatore (303), *Pasta Shells*
Italian Salad (200)
Garlic-Herb Bread (10)
Frittatine Zingarella (446)

Suppers
I
Mushrooms a la Grecque (173)
Onion Bouillabaisse (95)
Whole Wheat French Bread (9)
Baked Apples (479)

II
Peach Love Soup (79)
Brown Rice and Bean Salad (242)
Low-Sodium Cheese Wedges, Seedless Grapes, Apple Slices
Almond Cookie Thins (525)

The Vegetarian Guest

What do George Bernard Shaw, playwright and pacifist, and Adolf Hitler, dictator and mass murderer, have in common? Each was, during his adult lifetime, a practicing vegetarian. But what was in their day a rather unusual, widely unacceptable dietary pursuit, is today fast becoming a significant national nutritional trend. In recent years, more than 6 million vegetarian cookbooks have been sold, reflecting everything from a passing curiosity to a burning passion for the vegetarian way of life among Americans.

The reasons behind the decision to go vegetarian are as varied as the people who make that decision. For some, it's pure and simple economics: meat is just too expensive. For others—Seventh Day Adventists, for example, and to a lesser extent, Mormons and Jews—it's a religious imperative. For still others, it's the belief that eating meat makes humans bloodthirsty and warlike, though Hitler's adherence to a meat-free diet didn't make him any less thirsty for blood.

Health, pure and simple, is a powerful incentive, too, for going vegetarian. Many are concerned with the health of disadvantaged people the world over. They want to see grain crops used to feed hungry people instead of cattle; four pounds of grain can produce one 8-ounce steak or it can feed a hungry child for a week. Others are concerned with their own health, particularly since so many recent reports connect the consumption of flesh foods, most often beef and pork, with the two major killers in modern society: cancer and heart disease. Still others are concerned with, as vegetarian and Nobel-prize-winning author Isaac Bashevis Singer has pointed out, the chicken's health.

However, one really needs no reason at all to enjoy vegetarian cooking; it boasts some of the most delicious dishes in the culinary world. In fact, over the centuries many ethnic cuisines have developed meatless dishes, often because of the scarcity of meat, that easily rival their best meat efforts.

Vegetarian Basics

All vegetarians, as you might expect, exclude red meat from their diets. But there the homogeneity ends. Vegetarians come in several styles. The strictest do not consume any foods of animal origin, not even eggs or milk. Slightly less strict are the lacto vegetarians, who consume milk and milk products, but will not eat eggs, since eggs, unlike milk, have potential for life. The more liberal ovolacto vegetarians will eat both eggs and milk products, while abstaining from fish, red meat, and poultry. Borderline vegetarians (and there are a growing number of these) will eat fish, but not meat or poultry. All vegetarians will avoid animal by-products, such as beef or chicken fat, lard, and gelatin made from animal bones.

Though planning meals for vegetarians who eat dairy products and/or eggs is relatively easy, meals for strict vegetarians need to be planned with a bit of nutritional understanding. Animal proteins (meat, milk, eggs, and cheese) are complete proteins, containing all the amino acids necessary to sustain life. Vegetable proteins are incomplete, containing some, but not all, of the essential amino acids. For a strict vegetarian meal to contain the necessary complete protein, it must mix and match all of the amino acids in sufficient quantities. The easiest way to do this is to serve both a whole-grain cereal food, such as rice, barley, wheat, or rye, with a legume, such as beans, peas, or peanuts. Alternately, or in addition, you could serve soybeans, meat analogues, such as vegetarian sausage, vegetarian chicken, etc. made from soybeans, tofu (soybean curd), or chick peas, all sources of protein that are almost equal to animal protein. Nuts, particularly almonds, cashews, Brazil nuts, and walnuts, can also be used to improve the quality of a vegetarian meal.

Questions to Ask Your Vegetarian Guest

1. *Do you eat dairy products? Eggs?* If your guest eats neither, prepare any of the menus or recipes for strict vegetarians (*V*). If your guest eats both, use any of the menus and recipes for ovolacto vegetarians (*v*). And if your guest eats dairy products and not eggs, use any recipes for ovolacto vegetarians (*v*) that do not contain eggs, or any recipe for strict vegetarians (*V*).

2. *Do you eat fish?* (This question is appropriate only for ovolacto vegetarians.) If your guest does eat fish, you can serve any menus and recipes for strict vegetarians (*V*), for ovolacto vegetarians (*v*), for strict kosher (*K*), or for lenient kosher (*k*).

3. *Do you avoid additives of animal origin?* If the answer is yes, look for kosher certification when buying products which contain additives. For strict vegetarians, look for the additional word *pareve* which assures that none of the additives in a product are meat or milk derivatives. For ovolacto vegetarians, *pareve* or *dairy* will assure that there are no meat derivatives. Both, however, may contain egg or fish products, so do check the label.

4. *Do you prefer to avoid additives of any kind and eat only "natural" foods?* Many vegetarians do prefer to avoid foods contaminated with chemical additives. If your guest is one of them, refer to "The Natural Guest," in Chapter Ten.

5. *Do you prefer whole grains and other unprocessed foods?* If so, our recipes will in general be suitable. When a choice of flours or rice is given, select the whole grain alternative. If your vegetarian guest doesn't have a preference, use any grains you wish.

6. *Do you prefer to keep your meals low in refined sugar?* If so, use vegetarian recipes that are also suitable for diabetics (*D*), or for the weight-conscious guest (*LC*). Nearly all of our recipes, though, are low in refined sugar. Pritikin recipes contain no sugar.

7. *Are you concerned about excessive fats in your diet, particularly animal fats, like butter and cream?* If your guest is conscious of the fats he or she consumes, prepare ovolacto vegetarian (*v*) dishes that are also suitable for cholesterol-cautious dieters (*LCh*).

Shopping Vegetarian

Strict (V)
To the non-vegetarian, the supermarket seems a virtual wonderland of vegetarian goodies.

Alas, it isn't so, as a quick survey of the "vegetarian" labels on your grocer's shelves will clearly prove. There's lard in "them thar" chocolate cream wafers, beef fat in the ready-to-spread frosting, milk derivatives in the "non-dairy" creamer. You can't even rely on the products proclaimed "vegetarian" by their labels. Look closely, and you'll discover butter in the "vegetarian vegetable" soup, cheese in the frozen "vegetarian" lasagna, and milk derivatives in the "vegetarian" sausage.

In other words, shopping for the strict vegetarian will require an eagle-eye for ingredients of animal origin. The most obvious, of course, are milk, cheese, butter, eggs, yogurt, cream, lard, meat, fish, and poultry in their various, relatively unadulterated forms. Much less obvious, but just as carefully avoided by strict vegetarians, are milk derivatives, such as sodium caseinate, casein, lactose, whey, and lactic acid, gelatin (unless the label indicates that it has been derived from vegetable, not animal sources, which is rare), natural flavorings (the source of which is often animal), margarine (which usually contains milk or a milk derivative), and mayonnaise (which is always made from eggs).

Even some chemicals originate in the barnyard, and not in the laboratory, as one might suppose. These include propylene glycol, glycerines and glycerides (mono and di), and flavorings and emulsifiers. One way to assure that these and other chemicals are not of animal origin is to look for a *kosher-pareve* label on products that contain them (see Chapter Eight, Shopping Kosher). This certification will assure you that a foodstuff contains neither milk, milk products, meat, nor meat products, and it will be particularly helpful when buying products that often contain hidden milk and milk derivatives, such as margarine, non-dairy creamers, and candies. However, you'll have to check the ingredients on baked goods, salad dressings, and desserts that are certified kosher-pareve, because they often contain eggs.

Ovolacto (*v*)
Compared to shopping for the strict vegetarian, shopping for the ovolacto vegetarian guest (*v*) will be a breeze. Again, your best guide when avoiding products containing meat or fish will be a kosher certification. Any product which is labeled *kosher-dairy* or *kosher-pareve*

is suitable for the ovolacto vegetarian, as is any kosher certified product that doesn't list fish or meat among its ingredients.

Unfortunately, products won't always carry kosher certification. In those cases, you'll have to rely on your label-reading skills, screening the product for ingredients of meat origin, such as the glycerides and gelatins mentioned in Shopping Vegetarian: Strict. Meat, meat products, meat fats, and, of course, fish products should also be avoided.

The dairy case is a fine place to find ovolacto proteins and trimmings. But, buy only kosher cheeses or those labeled as containing no rennet (available in health food stores).

For all vegetarians—strict, ovolacto, and everyone in between—fruits and vegetables (fresh, frozen, and canned) are good purchases. So are grains in all forms (except, of course, when mixed with animal products, as in casseroles), such as rice, beans, peas, triticale (a high protein hybrid grain), cereals, pastas, and nuts.

Cooking Vegetarian

Although there are many pitfalls to avoid when shopping for vegetarians, you can virtually do no wrong when it comes to cooking for them. As long as your ingredients have been carefully selected, you can prepare them in almost any way you see fit, from boiling to barbecuing, from steaming to sautéing. Just be certain to use the appropriate shortenings in your cooking: oil or pareve margarine for the strict vegetarian; oil, butter, or kosher margarine for the ovolacto vegetarian.

You can, of course, stick to typically and obviously "vegetarian" dishes when entertaining your vegetarian guests, but you'll cause more of a culinary sensation if you attempt a little food fakery. For example, to achieve a creamy texture in soups and sauces that must be free of dairy products, substitute one of the following: tofu pureed in water or stock, soy milk, stock blended into a roux of flour and oil, or instant mashed potato flakes blended into liquid. (Non-dairy creamers can, of course, be used if there is no objection to their ingredients.) To obtain a meaty texture in sauces, casseroles, and lasagnas, freeze tofu for one week or longer, defrost it, and crumble it, browning it, if desired, before adding it to the dish. Texturized vegetable protein may also be used as a meat substitute.

Other vegetarian cooking tricks include creating a sour cream-free dip with pureed tofu and your favorite seasonings. Make a "cream" pie by pureeing tofu with fruits or other flavorings, plus the sweeteners of your choice. Use fruit juices instead of milk in baking, and in cereals and desserts, for example orange juice in a carrot cake, or apple juice in a pudding. Serve sorbets and ices instead of ice creams for summer desserts.

Strict Vegetarian Menus

These menus are balanced to combine legumes, cereals, and nuts to insure that your guest won't leave your table deficient in nutrients—or hungry.

Ovolacto Vegetarian Menus

These menus contain both egg and milk products, but no meat or fish. They are suitable for ovolacto vegetarians, as well as for lenient kosher dieters (*k*). Ovolacto vegetarians can also be served any dishes that are suitable for strict vegetarians (*V*).

Menus for Guests on Ovolacto Vegetarian Diets

Breakfasts

I
Fresh Berries with Creme Fraîche or Sour Cream
Mozzarella Omelet (49)
Whole Wheat Italian Bread (15), *Sweet Butter*

II
Marinated Pineapple (487)
Whole Wheat Buttermilk Pancakes (55), *Maple Syrup*
Vegetarian Sausage

Brunches

I
Blended Fruit Juice, Lime Wedge (562) *or*
Champagne and Orange Juice
French Toast with Brandied Apples (62)
Vegetarian Sausage
Cheesecake (441)

II
Cheese-Stuffed Pears (496) *or Nectarines* (491)
Spinach-Mozzarella Crepes (45)

Crusty Whole Wheat Italian Bread (15)
Cranberry Crunchies (513)

Lunches

I

Mixed Greens, Italian Dressing (257)
Pasta del Sol (336)
Italian Bread (15)
Pears Baked in Red Wine (493)

II

Peach Love Soup (79)
Spinach-Feta Quiche (60)
Sliced Avocado and Tomato on Greens
Cranberry-Carrot Cake (504)

Barbecues

I

Guacamole (109), *Crudités* (383) *and Tortilla Chips*
Veggieburgers (413) *on Buns*
Vegetable Slaw (224)
Mustard-Dill Potato Salad (232)
Fruit-Nut Sundae (472)
Carob Brownies II (510)

II

Mushroom-Almond Pâté (117), *Mixed Crackers*
Grilled Herbed Eggplant (411)
Grilled Curried Eggplant (412)
Vegetable Sate (414)
Bulgur-Tofu Salad (229)
Wilted Spinach and Nut Salad (218)
Whole Wheat Pita Bread
Strawberries Romanoff (499), *Fruited Yogurt* (428)

Cocktail Parties

I

Cheeseball (114), *Wheat Crackers*
Spiked Tofu Zucchini Dip (122), *Crudités* (383)
Pesto Pâté-Stuffed Celery (119)
Cheese and Nut-Stuffed Mushrooms (147)
Open Zucchini Sandwiches (141)
Cheese-Prune Kabobs

II

Spinach-Feta Strudel (143)
Guacamole (109), *Tortilla Chips and Crudités* (383)
Mushroom-Almond Pâté (117), *Sesame Crackers*
Rice-Stuffed Vine Leaves (153)
Baked Mushroom Squares (134)
Fruit and Cheese Platter

Dinners

I

Apple-Wine Soup (66)
Individual Roulades (341)
Five-Grain Pilaf (369)
Steamed Lemon Broccoli (397)
Boston Lettuce and Hearts of Palm Salad (193)
Date-Nut Pie (536)

II

Cream of Hazelnut Soup (87)
Nut Loaf (351), *Cheese Sauce* (419)
Zucchini Rice (372)
Watercress-Apple Salad (225)
Poires au Gratin (492)

III

Mushroom-Onion Soup (91)
Stuffed Vegetarian Cabbage a la Cranberries (354)
Baby Belgian Carrots (378)
Stir-Fried Green Beans (398)
Sunshine Salad (222)
Nature-Sweetened Apple Strudel (542)

IV

Pesto Pâté (118)
Pasta with Peas, Mushrooms, and Pine Nuts (339)
Spinach-Mushroom Sformato (340)
Arugula Salad (188)
Orange Slices with Ricotta (451)
Lace Cookies (520)

Buffets

I

Italian Minestrone (88), *Whole Wheat Breadsticks*
Broccoli Lasagna (332)

Vegetarian Sausage Bread (20)
Italian Salad (200)
Pears Caramel Flambé (494)
Lace Cookies (520)

II
Stuffed Baby Eggplants (345)
Falafel Pie (347), *Tahina Dip* (123)
Lemon Broccoli with Pistachios (375)
Middle Eastern Salad (203)
Date-Nut Crescents (515)
Seedless Grapes with Rum and Yogurt (485)

Suppers
I
Mushrooms a la Grecque (173)
Broccoli Bread Soup with Cheese (94)
Watercress-Apple Salad (225)
Cranberry-Carrot Cake (504), *a la Mode*

II
Cream of Tomato Soup (93)
Crown of Noodles and Spinach, Creamed Mushroom Sauce (334)
Carrot and Zucchini Sticks
Strawberry-Yogurt Pie (540)

Menus for Guests on Strict Vegetarian Diets

Breakfasts
I
Fresh Berries, Slivered Almonds
Homemade Granola (32), *Mixed Fruit Juices and Sliced Bananas*
Whole Wheat Raisin Bread (21), *Honey-Tofu Spread* (547)

II
Macédoine of Citrus and Banana Slices (477)
Hot Bulgur Cereal (29) *with Coconut, Seeds, and Raisins*
Oatmeal Bread (17), *Peanut-Apple Butter* (546)

Brunches
I
Blended Fruit Juice, Lime Wedge (562)
Cornmeal-Baco Fritters (31), *Orange-Maple Syrup* (551)
Carrot Cake (503)

II
Macédoine of Winter Fruits (476), *Chopped Nuts*
Fruited Millet (33), *Applesauce*
Oatmeal Bread (17), *Honey-Tofu Spread* (547)
Cinnamon-Raisin Coffee Cake (506)

Lunches
I
Baked Tofu (355), *Teriyaki Dipping Sauce* (124)
Cold Sesame Noodles and Bean Sprouts (169)
Fresh Pineapple

II
Chilled Gazpacho (77), *Celery Swizzle-Stick*
Viva la Salad (249)
Whole Wheat Raisin Bread (21), *Honey-Peanut Butter Spread* (545)
Peaches Caramel Flambé (494)

Barbecues
I
Teriyaki Dipping Sauce (124), *Crisp-Tender Vegetables* (383)
Grilled Tofu Teriyaki (410)
Vegetable Sate (414)
Chutney Rice (365)
India Salad (199)
Fresh Fruit Kabobs (474)
Shreddies (522)

II
Chilled Gazpacho (77)
Grilled Curried Eggplant (412)
Brown Rice and Bean Salad (242)
Coal-Roasted Zucchini and Carrots (415)
Vegetable Slaw (224)
Whole Wheat Pita Bread
Watermelon
Date-Nut Bars (514)

Cocktail Parties
I
Seasoned Popcorn (131)
Curried Soy Nuts (128)
Tofu Tidbits (159), *Teriyaki Dipping Sauce* (124)
Mushroom-Vegetable Strudels (142)

Tahina Dip (123), Pita Bread and Black Olives
Rice-Stuffed Vine Leaves (153)
Peppery Chick Peas (130)
Walnut-Stuffed Prunes
Date-Nut Crescents (515)

II

Toasted Nuts and Seeds with Raisins
Tofu Tidbits (159), *Cumberland Sauce* (420)
Stuffed Peppers (150)
Eggplant Caviar-Stuffed Cherry Tomatoes (107)
Mushroom-Almond Pâté (117), *Melba Squares* (16)
Artichoke Hearts a la Grecque (178)
Seasonal Fruit Platter

Dinners

I

Rice-Stuffed Vine Leaves (153)
Lentil Soup with Chick Peas (89)
Stuffed Eggplant (345)
Minted Green Beans (386)
Spinach-Apple Salad (215)
Pita Bread
Date-Nut Crescents (515)
Orange Almond Semolina (449)
Fresh Fruit Salad (475)

II

Leeks Vinaigrette (172)
Individual Roulades (341), *Mushroom Sauce* (424)
Steamed Lemon Broccoli (397)
Sunshine Salad (222)
Nectarine Sorbet (467)
Lace Cookies (520) *and Shreddies* (522)

III

Cold Sesame Noodles (169)
Chinese Vegetables (382)
Beancurd and Chinese Mushrooms (344)
Cucumber Sticks Oriental (194)
Marinated Pineapple (487)
Almond Nut Cookie Thins (526)

IV

Cream of Hazelnut Soup (87)
Nut Loaf (351), *Mushroom Sauce* (424)

Brown Rice
Peas a la Française (391)
Pepper Salad (207)
Apple Pie (535)

Buffet

I

Vegetables a la Grecque (178)
Falafel Pie (347), *Tahina Dip* (123)
Ratatouille (392)
Moroccan Rice (366)
Spinach-Apple Salad (215)
Date-Nut Pie (536)

II

Mushrooms a la Grecque (173)
Flageolets au Gratin (348)
Okra and Tomatoes (389)
Spinach and Red Pepper Salad (219), *Sweet and Sour Dressing* (272)
Onion-Walnut Loaves (18)
Praline-Baked Bananas (482)
Date-Nut Crescents (515)

Suppers

I

Vegetarian Chili (357)
Whole Wheat Italian Bread (15), *Margarine*
Mexican Salad (202)
Carob Brownies II (510)

II

Chilled Avocado-Tomato Puree (67)
Brown Rice and Bean Salad (242) *on Mixed Greens, Tomato Garnish*
Sesame Breadsticks
Peach Sorbet (465)
Pecan Balls (521)

The Pritikin Proselyte

They say there's nothing worse than a reformed sinner, and reformed sinners are precisely what most Pritikin dieters are. The "sin" was eating the typical American diet. The "reform" is their conversion to the Pritikin diet and life-style.

The most ardent of such conversions take place at the mecca for Pritikin proselytes, the Pritikin Longevity Center in Santa Barbara, California. But millions more take place at home, with the guidance of Nathan Pritikin's best-selling bibles, *The Pritikin Program for Diet and Exercise,* and *The Pritikin Permanent Weight Loss Manual,* or through his growing network of workshops across the country.

Because of the extremes to which Pritikin dieters voluntarily take healthy eating, having one to a dinner party can be something like having a temperance crusader over for drinks. Nathan Pritikin himself admits that his followers make difficult—sometimes impossible—guests, and that many hosts and hostesses might just prefer to ignore the rigid guidelines he sets when entertaining such friends. Pritikin's philosophical advice to his dieters: "Find new friends."

Just what is this diet that is capable of breaking up friendships? Basically, it turns the typical American diet completely upside down and inside out. Instead of the average 120 pounds of table sugar consumed per capita by Americans each year, the Pritikin dieter is permitted *no* table sugar at all. Fat, another traditionally overused American staple and a potential health hazard, is another Pritikin taboo. In all its forms—oil, butter, margarine, lard, even non-stick sprays—it is strictly prohibited. Salt, the condiment most maligned by medical authorities, yet most abused by a majority of Americans, is not eliminated entirely from the Pritikin program, but is drastically reduced. On the Pritikin hit list, as well, are a number of other American dietary standbys, including those once termed "health foods," such as cheese, meat, nuts, and eggs. Favorite beverages, such as caffeinated coffee and tea, hot chocolate, and most alcoholic drinks are also shot down by Pritikin.

Foreign though the Pritikin diet is to Americans raised on bacon and eggs, it closely parallels the diets eaten in underdeveloped countries, where the degenerative diseases that are primary killers in America are virtually unknown. And though the evidence is certainly not yet conclusive, it at leasts suggests that a Pritikin diet could be life extending.

Actually, sacrifices made by the tastebuds in the name of a longer life need not be great, at least not as long as creativity is substituted for prohibited favorites. To that end, our Pritikin recipes should stimulate both your imagination and your guests' appetites.

Pritikin Basics

Once you've decided to undertake entertaining a Pritikin dieter, you may find that the nearly uncompromising rigidity of the program makes it easier to prepare for than most other special diets. Since so many staple foods and standard methods of food preparation are taboo on Pritikin, a good many of your menu-planning and cooking decisions will be made for you. You won't need to agonize, for instance, over which shortening to use in your baking; no shortening is permitted. Nor will you need to choose between deep-frying and sautéing when preparing potatoes; neither method is acceptable.

In fact, the most effective way of familiarizing yourself with the Pritikin diet isn't with a list of "permitted" foods, but rather with one of those forbidden. These include:

- All fats and oils: butter, margarine, lard, vegetable oils, hydrogenated vegetable fats, such as Crisco or Spry, meat drippings, chicken fat, lecithin
- Fatty poultry (duck and goose) and all poultry skins

- Fatty fish, including sardines, mackerel, tuna or salmon in oil, and shrimp
- Fatty meats, such as bacon, spare ribs, sausage, frankfurters, luncheon meats, salami, bologna, heavily marbled steaks, full-fat hamburgers, organ meats; all smoked, charbroiled, and barbecued meats
- All dairy products that are more than 1 percent fat, such as whole milk, 2 percent milk, creams, cream cheese, sour cream, yogurt made from whole milk, most cheeses, and all foods made with these products
- Egg yolks or products containing egg yolks; fish eggs, including caviar
- All nuts except chestnuts; all seeds except, in small quantities, as garnishes
- Avocados and olives
- All sweeteners, refined or artificial, including sugar: white, brown, turbinado, and raw; honey, maple syrup, corn syrup, fructose, saccharin, corn or natural sweeteners, glucose, dextrose, dextrin, and all products containing these sweeteners, such as breads, breakfast cereals, cakes, cookies, fruit (canned and frozen), fruit butters, juices, or syrups, jams and jellies, ketchup, and liqueurs. (The list of products containing sweeteners is, of course, nearly endless. A quick survey of your grocer's shelves will prove that.)*
- Wheat germ; baked goods containing wheat germ, soy flour, bleached flours, fats, oils, sugars, or egg yolks. Products made with refined unbleached flours are limited
- Excess salt, that is, more than 3 to 4 grams per day. This means that soy sauce, pickles, most commercial condiments, such as seasoned salt, Worcestershire sauce, salad dressings, and MSG are severely limited. The restriction, however, is less severe than for the low-salt dieter
- Beverages containing alcohol, except for limited amounts of dry white wine in cooking, and an occasional glass of white wine at dinner; those containing sugar, such as soft drinks and punches; artificial sweeteners, such as diet sodas; and caffeine, such as coffee, tea, chocolate, and colas
- Additives of all kinds to be avoided whenever possible.
- Excess protein—meat, fish, poultry, egg whites—limited to 10 percent of diet

* For more information on avoiding sugar when shopping, see Chapter Three, Low-Sugar Shopping.

Questions to Ask Your Pritikin Guest

1. *Are you on the weight-loss program, or the longevity program?* If your guest is on the weight-loss program, use Pritikin (*P*) recipes that are also appropriate for the weight-conscious dieter (*LC*).

2. *Do you adhere to the diet rigidly, or do you "cheat" occasionally?* If your guest admits to a little social straying from the program, you may want to add a few "forbidden" foods to your meal, but put them on the side, not in the dishes themselves. Have on hand vinegar *and* oil for the salad, black olives on the relish tray, and slivered almonds to sprinkle on the dessert. That way your Pritikin guest can decide for him or herself just how much he or she wants to stray. If, however, your Pritikin guest is ordinarily lenient about the diet, you may add 1 tablespoon of oil or sugar in recipes where Pritikin variations rule them out.

3. *What kind of beverage do you drink after your meals?* Pritikin doesn't recommend regular coffee or tea. He remains neutral on the issue of decaffeinated coffees and teas. Nevertheless, your guest may drink them. Or, he or she may prefer linden tea, or the Chinese teas containing no tannin that Pritikin does recommend. Also suitable: Pritikin drinks in the beverage recipe section.

4. *Can you have wine with dinner?* Nathan Pritikin, an apparently reasonable man when it comes to setting the limits, permits a single glass of wine at dinner for his followers who are in good health. If your guest can't have wine, provide mineral water or seltzer (salt-free), with a twist of lemon or lime, unsweetened fruit juices, or iced bottled or tap water. Beware, however, of tap water that contains more than 2 milligrams of sodium per 100 milliliters and most artificially softened water. They contain significant quantities of salt.

Pritikin Shopping

Now that you know what's prohibited on the Pritikin diet, you may be wondering what point there is in going to the market at all. (What, after all, could be left to buy?) But read on, and you'll discover that while filling your shopping cart for the Pritikin dieter can't exactly be a fly-through-the-aisles proposition, it can, with a little time and concentration, be possible.

The most difficult part of your shopping mission will be label reading. Pritikin staples will include:

- Fresh fruits and vegetables, except avocados
- Fresh fish, poultry, lean veal and beef, with an emphasis on the first two
- Whole grain breads made without fat or sugar (i.e., Pritikin bread, most whole wheat pita breads, sourdough breads)
- Whole grain flours, brown rice, whole grain cereals
- Eggs (you will be using only the whites)
- Sapsago (green) cheese and cheeses of up to 1 percent fat by weight (low-fat cottage cheese, pot cheese, hoop cheese)
- Skim milks, yogurts, and buttermilks of no more than 1 percent fat
- Linden tea or Chinese teas without tannin
- Condiments such as mustard, vinegar, capers, dill pickles (but not sweet pickles), peppers, pimientos, and other vegetables packed in vinegar; salt-reduced or regular soy sauce; lemons and limes; dry white wines for cooking

Pritikin Cooking

Just as you'll have to set aside many of the ingredients in your pantry when preparing for the Pritikin dieter, you'll also need to abandon temporarily some of your favorite cooking techniques such as frying and barbecuing. Since shortening is prohibited, sautéing must be done in a non-stick pan with the assistance of stock or other fat-free liquids. Baking and browning must also be done in non-stick pans, without greasing or non-stick sprays. (See page 154 of the Recipe Glossary for more on fat-free sautéing and browning.)

Adapting your own recipes for Pritikin guests may be possible if you can eliminate or find substitutes for all added fat, sugar, and egg yolks. Fat is easiest to drop from a recipe when it is used for sautéing or browning; it is often difficult to eliminate entirely from cakes, breads, and cookies. Sugar can be replaced in many instances by apple juice concentrate, but if the texture of a cookie or cake depends on sugar, switch instead to another recipe. (For more tips on sugar-free cooking, see Chapter Three.) We have found, too, that whole eggs can be replaced successfully by two egg whites in many breads, cakes, crepes, and fritters. If, however, you are going to put recipes through drastic transformations so that they will conform to Pritikin standards, we recommend that you try out the revised dishes before serving them to guests.

Pritikin Menus

Planning meals for Pritikin dieters requires emphasizing the salads, vegetables, and grains and playing down the proteins that usually form the centerpiece of your meals. However, if you are reluctant to serve non-dieters such a spartan meal, you have the option of passing them regular salad dressing, butter, and sugar, as well as extra meat, fish, or poultry.

Menus for Guests on Pritikin Diets

Breakfasts

I

Blended Fruit Juice, Lime Wedge (562)
Orange Muesli (35)
Fresh Summer Fruit
Fruited Yogurt (428)
Irish Soda Bread (14)

II

Macédoine of Winter Fruit (476)
Hot Bulgur Cereal (29), *Scoop of Hoop Cheese*
Cranberry-"Nut" Muffins (25), *Unsweetened Apple Butter*

Brunches

I

Fresh Melon Balls and Blueberries, Lime Wedge
French Toast with Berry Sauce (63)
Cheesecake (441)

II

Baked Apples (479)
Herbed Mushroom Angel Crepes (43), *Broccoli Sauce* (417)
Sliced Tomatoes and Basil
Orange-Oat Cake (508)

Lunches

I

Chilled Gazpacho (77), *Celery Swizzle-Stick*
Pasta Primavera with Buttermilk Dressing (338)
Mixed Greens, Light Vinaigrette (258)
Orange Slices with Hoop Cheese (450)

II
Chilean Fish Stew (278)
Whole Wheat Italian Bread (15)
Mexican Salad (202)
Pears Baked in White Wine (493)

Barbecues
I
Tahina Dip (123), *Crudités* (383)
Chicken Breasts in Foil with Nectarines (402)
Curried Potato-Apple Salad (231)
Vegetables a la Grecque (178)
Whole Wheat Italian Bread (15)
Fresh Fruit Salad (475) *in Melon Basket*
Cinnamon Shreddies (522)

Cocktail Parties
I
Mushroom "Nuts" (129)
Air-popped Popcorn
Peppery Chickpeas (130)
Eggplant Caviar-Stuffed Cherry Tomatoes (107)
Salmon Mousse I (287), *Melba Squares* (16)
Mock Guacamole (115), *Crudités* (383)
Fresh Pineapple Chunks

II
Peppery Chickpeas (130)
Caponata (102), *Melba Squares* (16) *and Raw Fennel Strips*
Antipasto Vegetables (161)
Tuna Balls in Tomato Sauce (156)
Open Zucchini Sandwiches (141)
Melon Cubes with Lime Dip (489)

Dinners
I
Creamless Zucchini Soup (83)
Chicken Breasts Florentine (306)
Arugula-Apple Salad (189), *Sweet and Sour Dressing* (272)
Whole Wheat Italian Bread (15)
Peach Sorbet (465)

II
Cheese-Stuffed Snow Peas (152)
Yucatecan Fish (295)

Brown Rice
Watercress, Orange, and Fennel Salad (227)
Whole Wheat Italian Bread (15)
Apricot Mousse (438)

III
Asparagus with Mushroom Sauce (163)
Apple-Stuffed Chicken Breasts (299)
Five-Grain Pilaf (369)
Steamed Lemon Broccoli (397)
Dark Mixed Greens with Beets and Onions (191), *Sweet and Sour Dressing (272)*
Orange Sorbet Supreme (464)

IV
Bean Sprouts Teriyaki with Raisins (168)
Scarborough Fair Chicken (311)
Whole Wheat Noodles and Cauliflower (359)
Watercress, Mushroom, and Tomato Salad (226)
Peasant Rye Bread (19)
Berry Pudding (439), *Lime Sauce* (429)

Buffets
I
Eggplant Caviar-Stuffed Cherry Tomatoes (107)
Fish Paprikash (282)
Parsleyed Yogurt Potatoes (362)
Herbed Vegetable Salad (198)
Steamed Shoestring Carrots and Zucchini, and Whole Green Beans (397)
Peasant Rye Bread (19)
Nature-Sweetened Apple Strudel (542)
Grape Clusters

II
Tahina Dip (123), *Crudités* (383)
Baba Ghanoush (101), *Whole Wheat Pita Bread Triangles*
Chicken with Chick Peas (304)
Stuffed Baby Eggplants (345)
Brown Rice and Triticale Pilaf (363)
Middle Eastern Salad (203)
Whole Wheat Pita Bread
Fresh Fruit Kabobs (474)
Date-"Nut" Pie (536)

Suppers

I

Onion Bouillabaisse (95)
Whole Wheat French Bread (9)
Wine-Poached Fruit (478)
Shreddies (522)

II

Gazpacho Verde (78)
Salad Nicoise (246)
Whole Wheat French Bread (9)
Strawberry Sorbet (468)

The Guest on The Milkless Diet

Beef Stroganoff. Fettucini Alfredo. Pizza. Creme caramel. Peach Melba. Cheesecake. Each easily ranks among the world's most celebrated culinary triumphs. And each, because it contains one seemingly innocuous ingredient—one of Mother Nature's own most celebrated triumphs—is also capable of making millions of people physically ill.

The ingredient: Milk. The symptoms it can produce in those millions of unfortunates: gas, bloating, indigestion, and cramping that can range from mildly uncomfortable to acute.

Lactose intolerance, the chronic, incurable disorder that makes digesting milk and milk products, and foods containing them, such as pizza and cheesecake, painfully difficult, is surprisingly common. Its roots are ancient, dating back, in fact, to early evolution. In the days before the domestication of animals, human milk consumption ended with weaning from the mother's breast. The body's logical evolutionary response was to slow down the production of lactase, the enzyme needed to break down lactose (milk sugar), as one progressed from infancy through adulthood.

Today, millions of Americans, particularly those of Oriental, African, or Mediterranean descent, still experience a drop in production of lactase as they approach adulthood. When they consume at one sitting more lactose (in milk or its close relatives) than their bodies have the lactase to break down, they suffer the painful consequences.

The lactose-intolerant individual can often tolerate small quantities of milk or milk products, but those allergic to milk can't have even the smallest drop of milk in any form.

Should a milk-intolerant or milk-allergic friend appear on your guest list, don't despair. You can serve them meals that lack in milk, but abound in all the qualities that make food good: taste, texture, variety.

Milkless Basics

The likelihood of a lactose intolerant individual having a reaction to milk depends on the amount and the form ingested. While Jack may be able to comfortably handle one or two glasses of milk at a sitting, Jill may not be able to tolerate a single sip. She may, however, be able to enjoy a hunk of Cheddar cheese without fear of stomach rebellion.

In general, the closer in form a dairy product is to milk, the more likely it will cause digestive trouble in the lactose intolerant. Therefore, milk, cream, ice cream, ice milk, cottage cheese, processed cheese foods, and foods containing these dairy products or milk derivatives, such as whey, milk solids, or lactose, are often prime enemies. On the other hand, dairy products such as aged cheese and fully-processed* yogurt, which have been fermented (a process which changes the offending lactose to lactic acid), may not disturb the lactose-sensitive stomach at all. Butter, too, can usually be handled. But reactions vary so much from one sufferer to another that only your guest can tell you, from his or her own past experience, just how milkless your cooking must be.

If your guest's diet is milkless because of an allergy to milk protein or another milk component, his dietary prohibitions may be extreme. Since allergic reactions are not dose-related, even the smallest amount of milk might trigger an allergic response ranging in severity from sniffles, or itching and hives, to headache, vomiting, or diarrhea, and, in rare cases, deadly systemic reactions. An allergic guest, therefore, may have to steadfastly avoid milk in any form, including all

* Some producers have taken to adding milk to their yogurts; these yogurts are not suitable for the lactose intolerant.

milk, milk products, and all milk derivatives. Again, ask your guest before you begin to plan your menu.

Questions to Ask Your Milk-Sensitive Guest

1. *Are you allergic to milk, or are you lactose intolerant?* Your vigilance in avoidance of milk, milk products, and derivatives will depend on the answer to this question.

2. *Must you avoid all dairy products? If not, which specifically must you avoid?* All of our milkless (*ML*) recipes and menus, as well as recipes and menus featuring meat or poultry are totally milk-free, and suitable for any milkless dieter. If your guest can handle one or two dairy products without difficulty, you may add them to meals if you wish. If your guest must avoid milk in any form or quantity, because of allergy or lactose-intolerance, please read this Chapter very carefully, especially Shopping Milkless.

3. *Do tiny amounts of lactose, as might be found in a milk-based additive, bother you?* If yes, look for the word *pareve* on questionable items.

Shopping Milkless

You'll have no trouble, of course, avoiding milk in its most obvious forms when shopping for your milk-sensitive guest. But when it comes to ferreting out the hidden milk, you'll need to break out your trusty magnifying glass, and do some serious label-reading. You'll discover that a very large percentage of processed foods, including breads, cakes, desserts, instant dinners, sauces, candies, even franks and cold cuts, contain some form of milk, whether non-fat milk solids, milk protein, lactose, sodium caseinate, whey, cream, or yogurt.

To simplify the screening process, the American Digestive Disease Society's national vice president, Jane Gross, recommends looking for the word *pareve* or *parve* on a product's label. This word, which for kosher shoppers identifies a product as neutral, containing neither meat nor dairy products, is also a valuable tool in shopping for the milkless dieter. It's particularly useful in identifying milkless margarine (most margarines contain milk or milk derivatives), nondairy creamers (again, many contain milk derivatives, often lactose itself), artificial sweeteners, candies, and cakes. Kosher meat products (sometimes labeled *fleishig*) will also always be milk-free.

As it is for strict vegetarians, tofu is a perfect base for a variety of "mock," yet delicious, dishes. It can replace sour cream in a dip, cheese in a pie, cream in a soup, ricotta in manicotti. It's one of the most versatile milkless ingredients you can drop into your shopping cart.

Cooking Milkless

Cooking procedures for milkless meals need not differ from the ones you ordinarily use, as long as your ingredients are appropriately milk-free. You can, however, expand your basic milkless repertoire with these simple tricks:

- To make a "cream" sauce, use stock and pureed potatoes, or stock and pureed tofu
- Add 1 tablespoon of a non-dairy creamer (pareve certified) to sauces for a creamy touch. We don't recommend more because the majority of non-dairy creamers are loaded with sugar, saturated fats, and chemicals. Pureed tofu can often work just as well, and is a whole lot more wholesome
- Use fruit juices in baking and desserts to replace milk; you'll find the extra flavor and sweetening power an added plus. Of course, choose a juice that complements the other ingredients in the dish
- Use sorbets and ices instead of ice creams and sherberts
- Serve non-dairy creamer (pareve certified) with coffee and tea. Or, serve lemon and lime wedges, or orange juice concentrate, with tea
- Use fruit juices instead of milk in cold or hot cereals, waffles, pancakes, crepes. Or, use stock in savory stuffed crepes

Milkless Menus

Try to plan milkless menus around cuisines that are traditionally either partly or completely milkless, such as Chinese, Japanese, Thai, Indian, Soul, and Jewish, instead of around cuisines that revolve around milk products, such as French and Italian. Meat or poultry main courses made without milk are found in most cuisines, of course, and they can easily be the focus of a milkless meal. Desserts, vegetarian meals, and breakfasts and brunches, where milk, cream, and cheeses are often central to the dishes being prepared, are more of a challenge. But as you can see from our menus, it can be a very satisfying one.

We've included fewer menus for milkless dieters than we have for most other special diets because so many of our other menus are also suitable for milkless meals. In fact, any menu which includes meat or poultry in our cookbook may be served to a milk-sensitive guest; they're all milkless. We didn't include a barbecue menu, because traditional barbecue fare—anything from shish kabob to pure meat hamburgers and hot dogs to grilled steak or chicken—can constitute a problem-free meal for the milk-sensitive guest.

Menus for Guests on Milkless Diets

Breakfasts

I
Fresh Melon Balls and Blueberries, Lime Wedge
Orange Pancakes (57), *Orange-Maple Syrup* (551)
Breakfast Sausage

II
Spiced Prunes and Oranges in Port (498)
Poached Eggs on Peas Portuguese (53)
French Bread (9)

Brunches

I
Marinated Mango (486)
Mushroom-Zucchini Omelet (50)
Whole Wheat Italian Bread (15)
Orange-Oat Cake (508)

II
Orange Muesli (35)
Kippered Herring with Onions (283), *Baked Potato*
Black Bread
Banana Muffins (2)

Lunches

I
Chilled Avocado-Tomato Puree (67)
Thai Tuna Salad (248)
Pita Bread
Cantaloupe-Strawberry Sorbet (462)

II
Hot Spiced Tomato Juice (557)
Veal Tarragon with Brazil Nuts (329)

Fluffy White Rice (370)
Spinach-Apple Salad (215)
Light Baklava (541)

Barbecues
Any meat-based or strict vegetarian (V) barbecue would be appropriate.

Cocktail Parties
I
Macadamia Nuts
Lomi Lomi Salmon (176)
Teriyaki Dipping Sauce (124), *Crisp-Tender Vegetables* (383)
Hawaiian Chicken Kabobs (405)
Hawaiian Meatballs, Sweet and Sour Sauce (155)

II
Baba Ghanoush (101), *Crudités* (383), *and Pita Bread Triangles*
Tahina Dip (123), *Pita Bread Triangles*
Veal-Stuffed Prunes (151)
Rice-Stuffed Vine Leaves (153)
Apple-Veal Balls (160)
Avocado-Citrus Platter

Dinners*
I
Apple-Wine Soup (66)
Cold Glazed Chicken Breasts, Nuts and Duxelles Stuffing (297)
Gourmet Rice Salad (234)
Cold Asparagus Vinaigrette (167) *with Sliced Tomatoes*
Plums in Port (497), *Sliced Almonds*

II
Leeks Vinaigrette (172)
Lemon Chicken with Mushrooms and Hazelnuts (308)
Five-Grain Pilaf (369)
Sunchoke-Zucchini Salad (221), *Mixed Greens*
Orange Sorbet Supreme (464)
Lemon Cookie Thins (530)

III
Asparagus Pepperonata (164)
Garden Italian Chicken (307) *Over Pasta*

* Any meat-based or strict vegetarian (V) dinner would be appropriate.

Mixed Greens, Italian Dressing (257)
Marzipan-Stuffed Pears (447)
Almond Cookie Thins (525)

Buffets

I

Cold Sesame Noodles (169)
Tangerine Chicken (312)
Fluffy White Rice (370)
Chinese Vegetables (382)
Bok Choy Salad (192)
Fresh Pineapple Chunks
Fortune Cookies

II

Whole Artichokes (162), *Garlic Mayonnaise* (255)
Cassoulet (323)
Portuguese Salad (209)
Whole Wheat French Bread (9)
Wine-Poached Fruit (478)

Suppers

I

Apple-Wine Soup (66)
German Tuna Salad (245)
Red Cabbage Salad (212)
Peasant Rye Bread (19)
Cassis Sorbet (457)
Cranberry-Carrot Cake (504)

II

Guacamole (109), *Tortilla Chips*
Chili Con Carne (324), *Chopped Onions*
Crusty Bread
Margarita Ice (463)
Mexican Coffee

The Kosher Guest

"Hey, Charlie," the stocking-capped thug mumbles suspiciously to his burly companion-in-crime as they attempt a midnight bank break in, "Something ain't kosher here."

At a corporate meeting, the chairman of the board solemnly reads a report, and raises his eyebrows ominously, causing the others to quake in their plush leather chairs. "I'm sorry, gentlemen," he declares in clipped aristocratic tones, slamming the report in front of him, "but something just isn't kosher here."

By the middle of this century, the word kosher, once exclusive property of the Jewish vocabulary, was becoming an accepted part of the rest of society's vernacular. At about the same time, "kosher" began dropping out of the vocabulary of many American Jews—and out of their life-style.

In the eighties, *kosher* is still frequently-used Americanese. But instead of continuing to drop out of style, a kosher diet is becoming increasingly popular with the new generation of American Jews. The reasons are varied for this return to roots. For some, it's a reverence for life, the humanist belief that killing, even for food, shouldn't be done casually. Kosher slaughtering, as strictly regulated today as it was a thousand years ago, is designed to bring the least possible pain or discomfort to the animal. For other Jews, keeping kosher is a way of building structure into their helter-skelter twentieth-century existences, a way of developing and maintaining self-discipline. They can't eat what they want, when they want it, and that puts them at least one notch above wild beasts.

Though Jewish scholars don't consider the dietary laws to be health laws, some people still adhere to them because they believe that kosher is clean or healthy. And, sometimes it is. An Israeli diplomat friend likes to tell the story of an African tour with other diplomats. Everyone else in the group, he relates, came down with intestinal disorders. "I stuck to my kosher diet," he says with a smile, "and I was fine."

Of course, there are Jews who keep kosher for purely religious reasons; they feel that by following biblical commandments, they imbue their own lives with holiness. Eating becomes for them more than a way of satisfying hunger or staying alive; it is a way of reaching a higher level of existence.

Maybe your guests subscribe to none of these rationales. Perhaps they keep kosher for Mom and Dad's sake, or for their grandparents, or because that's the way they were raised. Eating kosher food might be as natural to them as brushing their teeth. Or, it's their way of remembering their heritage, a reminder that comes at least three times a day.

As different as the reasons people keep the dietary laws are the ways they keep them. You may count several kosher friends among your acquaintances, and very likely no two keep kosher in exactly the same way, especially when eating out. They may all keep separate dishes for meat and milk at home, and buy only kosher meat, but one may eat anything at all away from home, with total disregard of dietary observance. Another may eat only fish and dairy products away from home and avoid non-kosher meats, pork products, and shellfish. Still another may eat anything but the prohibited species. And another will eat nothing but cold salad on a paper plate when dining out.

Your guests aren't practicing different religions when they observe dietary laws in such diverse ways. They are simply following different interpretations (sometimes their own) of the laws laid down in the Bible. As with the United States Constitution, the Hebrew Bible has been interpreted in various ways by people in different times. From it, rules are derived for a way of life that has changed over millenia, and yet has remained unchanged.

Kosher Basics

Whatever the reasons or the ways in which your guests keep kosher, the biblical foundations of their practice are the same. The Bible specifically points out that certain species of fowl, beast, and sea creatures are forbidden. Included in this list:

- All shellfish and all fish that do not have fins and scales, such as shark, porpoise, catfish
- All animals that do not both chew the cud and have cloven hoofs, such as pigs, camels, horses, rabbits
- Owls, eagles, and all other birds of prey

But the dietary laws, at times followed, to some extent, by non-Jews, including Muslims and Seventh Day Adventists, go beyond proscribing certain animals. First of all, any animals eaten must be ritually slaughtered in a humane way; kindness to animals is a strict biblical commandment. Secondly, the blood must be drained from the animal by soaking and salting, because the Bible states: . . . Only flesh with the life thereof, which is the blood thereof, shall you not eat. (Gen. 9:14). The Bible makes it clear that permitting the eating of flesh foods at all is merely a concession to the human lust for meat, and like all lusts, has to be rigidly controlled to avoid abuse.

Milk and meat foods are never mixed in kosher cooking in deference to another Biblical injunction: "Thou shalt not seethe a kid in its mother's milk." (Exod. 23:19, 34:26; Deut. 14:21). This humane law, which ran counter to a pagan fertility rite of the time, has developed into a highly detailed separation of milk and meat meant to assure that no young animal is ever cooked in the milk of its mother. Poultry is classified as meat, too, even though birds do not produce milk, simply because poultry and meat are often difficult to distinguish from each other.

Because of these complicated laws, it's advisable for the inexperienced to avoid serving meat dishes when entertaining a kosher guest. Thus, we've kept our kosher guest menus completely meatless (with the exception of one barbecue).

A special note on Passover. On Passover, the festival of freedom, observant Jews and even many who aren't kosher the rest of the year, avoid eating bread and other leavened products in memory of the unleavened bread eaten on the night of the Hebrews' hurried departure from Egypt. In traditional homes, separate (or sometimes, newly koshered) sets of dishes and flatware, pots and pans, utensils, and appliances are used to assure that not a drop of leaven from everyday dishes makes its way into Passover meals. The process, as you can imagine, is rather complicated, but one that becomes routine for the experienced. For the inexperienced, however, turning a kitchen kosher-for-Passover for a single meal can be nearly impossible. For that reason, many strict Passover observers will not eat in a non-kosher home during the eight-day (seven, in Israel) festival.

If you do have occasion to entertain someone who is observing the Passover holiday, you can serve kosher-for-Passover wines (they come in dry as well as sweet varieties), nuts (except peanuts) in the shell or roasted nuts that have kosher-for-Passover certification (U P, KP, or Kosher for Passover), macaroons or other kosher-for-Passover baked goods, matzah prepared especially for Passover, as well as sodas, candies, cheeses, milks, creams, and yogurts that are certified kosher for Passover. Use disposable dishes and utensils. Some (you can ask if your guest is among these) will also be willing to enjoy salads, tuna fish that is certified for Passover and served with Passover mayonnaise or dressing, raw vegetables and fresh fruit served on paper plates. Many varieties of salad dressing are available with Passover certification; ordinary oils and vinegars cannot be used. Also prohibited: pastas, grains of all kinds (except for rice for Jews of Eastern backgrounds), cereals, peas and beans, all baked goods not specially prepared for Passover, and all grain-based liquors.

Questions to Ask the Kosher Guest

1. *Will you eat dairy or fish meals cooked and served in a non-kosher home?* This question will immediately separate your potential kosher guests into two categories: the strict kosher guest (*K*) who will not eat food cooked in your home, regardless of how kosher the ingredients are, and the lenient kosher guest (*k*), who will, if the ingredients are kosher. We've prepared recipes and menus for each.

2. *Do you accept all kosher certifcation labels? If not, which ones do you approve of, and which ones should I avoid?* As you will see in our Kosher Shopping section, there are many different kosher certification symbols. Stick to the ones of which your guest approves.

3. *Is there a kosher bakery in town that you use? Or may I ask a rabbi to suggest one (if your guest is a stranger in town)?* Your guest may or may not have a preferred bakery. If not, there are almost always

packaged baked goods with kosher certification available. Depending upon your guest's orientation, he or she may accept a bakery approved by an Orthodox or Conservative rabbi.

4. *Will you eat any kind of cheese or only kosher cheese? Is there any particular brand you would recommend?* If your guest is one of the kosher adherents who avoids cheeses made with rennet, a curdling agent that is occasionally a meat by-product, look for cheese that is certified kosher. If kosher cheese is impossible to obtain in your area, just skip this food. Most of our kosher menus are cheeseless.

5. *Will you drink any kind of wine or only kosher wine?* Some kosher people will drink only wine that is made under rabbinical supervision. Though a wide variety of kosher table wines (Carmel, Kedem, Manischewitz, and others) are available in most major cities, they may be difficult to obtain in smaller towns (see Shopping for the Kosher Guest). Many people who avoid non-kosher wine also avoid non-kosher grape products, including jellies, juices, and punches. Check with your guest if you plan to serve any of these. Incidentally, since brandy and many liqueurs have grape wine bases, they fall into the same category as wines.

6. *Will you eat food prepared by Jews on the Sabbath?* If your guest doesn't eat food prepared during the twenty-five-hour period from just before sundown on Friday night until dark on Saturday night, and you're entertaining on a Saturday night, see "Preparing Food for Saturday Night." If you're not Jewish, the question is irrelevant.

7. *Can I purchase fresh fish from anywhere I wish? If not, is there a kosher fish market you recommend? Do you put any limitations on frozen fish? Is there a brand you prefer?* Most guests who eat fish in restaurants will have no qualms about eating fish you buy at a non-kosher fish market. If frozen fish is the only fish available in your area, and your guest has no limitations, use any permissible frozen fish. Otherwise, follow your guest's recommendations.

8. *Do you drink ordinary milk or only certified milk?* The vast majority of kosher adherents will drink any milk. If your guest drinks only kosher milk, ask where you can obtain it if you plan to serve it.

For the strict kosher guests who have already said that they won't eat food *cooked* in your house, add the following question:

9. *Will you eat cold foods like salads, tuna fish, and packaged kosher cake served on my dishes?* Many will, and do the same thing in restaurants. In that case, follow the strict kosher (*K*) menus and recipes, and use your regular dishes and silverware, as long as you're careful not to

cook *anything*. If the answer to your question is no, ask your guests if they will eat these cold foods on paper plates with disposable flatware. If they will, you can follow the suggestions for Cooking Kosher: Strict, page 99. It's a rare guest who will be more strict than that. But if you come upon someone who obviously won't eat a meal in your home, and you'd still like to entertain him or her, extend an invitation for a drink and some nuts, raisins, and other kosher snack foods (see Shopping Kosher).

Shopping for the Kosher Guest

At one time it was easy to shop kosher. You could buy fresh fruits and vegetables, eggs, milk, and meat from a kosher butcher. But, it wasn't very satisfying; only fresh, uncooked foods were available to the shopper. Today, the endless array of kosher products makes shopping more satisfying, but, alas, more complicated. Even in isolated towns, there are packages and boxes and cans with labels that indicate rabbinical supervision during the preparation of the product inside. But the symbols that represent supervision vary; some indicate stricter supervision than others. Some kosher guests will accept foods marked with a *K*. Others, unless they know of and are satisfied with the supervising rabbi, will not eat *K* foods. They prefer the symbols that indicate a particular rabbi or organization. And some kosher guests will accept all kosher supervision. The most common symbols and the organizations that issue them are:

- Ⓤ Joint Kashruth Commission of the Union of Orthodox Jewish Congregations
- Kosher Supervision service of New Jersey
- Ⓚ Organized Kashruth Laboratories, Rabbi Bernard Levy
- Kashruth Commissions of the Rabbinical Council (Vaad Harabonim) of New England
- K Kosher Overseers Association
- Kₒ Ko Kosher Service
- Dr. J. H. Ralbag

Always look for the symbol on the label before purchasing a product, even if you've seen a symbol on the product before. Policies alter, ingredients change, and what was kosher last year may not be today. (It may be helpful to know that the A & P chain of supermarkets carries a very wide variety of kosher store brand items.) In addition to kosher certification, some products will also have some indication on the label as to whether they contain dairy products, meat products, or are neutral (pareve):

- Products which contain dairy products may be marked: *Dairy, Milk,* or *KM*
- Products which contain meat products may be marked: *Meat,* or *Fleishig* (the Yiddish word for meat)
- Products which contain neither dairy products nor meat may be marked: *Pareve* or *parve*

Not all products are so labeled, so you will frequently have to check ingredients. For all of our meatless menus and recipes, select products labeled *dairy* or *pareve.* For the one meat barbecue menu and for guests who are joining you for dessert and may have had a meat meal recently (traditional Jews wait one to six hours after eating meat before eating dairy products), select items that are pareve. The coffee creamer, if any is used, must be pareve, too.

While you will be looking for the word "kosher," or for a symbol that tells you a product is kosher, you will want to avoid the words: "Kosher-style." Unless the product is certified kosher, this phrase is meaningless. Kosher-style pastrami, or pickles, or steaks (as Debbie Reynolds found out) are *not* kosher. Nor is food purchased at kosher-style take out places.

Here's what to look for in selecting kosher foods:

Fresh Foods. As with most special diets, the closer you stick with natural foods, the less likely you are to make a mistake. Fresh fruits and vegetables of any kind are kosher. They need no certification or rabbinical supervision. The same goes for eggs, unadulterated salt, sugar, natural coffee, or frozen fruits or vegetables to which nothing has been added. If something is added—chemical additives, margarine, butter, or just about anything else—check for a kosher symbol. Most fruit and vegetable juices are available with kosher supervision labels.

Dairy Products. Most observers of dietary laws will drink any fresh milk, though some require a specially supervised milk called Chalav Yisrael. Most other dairy products require a kosher label; cottage cheese, yogurt, margarine, butter (unless it is completely additive-free), cream cheese, and sour cream can be found with the appropriate symbol. Many major national and local brands carry certification on such products. Ice cream and frozen yogurt, too, need to be certified kosher, and many brands are. Cream and half-and-half, if they are natural (nothing is added to them), require no label. Hard cheeses should be labeled kosher when guests so request.

Baked Goods. Unless you live in a major city, it may be difficult to find a kosher bakery. If you aren't going to bake your own bread—and for the strict kosher guest (*K*), you can't—look for breads that are certified kosher. Most pita breads and many rye breads are. A few major manufacturers produce kosher cookies, but because most have mixed lines, combining both kosher and non-kosher cookies, you must be careful to look for a label on each and every box you buy. All baked goods, including breads, crackers, and cookies, may be pareve or dairy unless a meat meal is or has been served within the last few hours, in which case they must be pareve. A few of the more popular cake mixes are certified kosher, but because of their high sugar, fat, and chemical additive-content, we recommend their use only as a last resort or emergency measure.

Snack Foods. Like baked goods, pretzels, potato chips, corn chips, and other snack foods require, and often carry, certification. Nuts that are unflavored and unroasted, in or out of the shell, need not be certified, but those that are seasoned, roasted, or dry roasted must be; most are.

Cereals, Pastas, and Grains. A virtually problem-free category, no matter how small your town or local market. Cereals, both hot and cold, and uncooked macaroni products almost always carry kosher certification. Rice, beans, and peas rarely do, but plain they are accepted by all but the strictest of kosher adherents without certification.

Seasonings, Spices, and Herbs. Again, the more natural the product in question is, the more likely it is to be kosher. Herbs and spices, fresh or dried, require no kosher label unless they have been adulterated in some way, as when onion is sautéed, or chemicals have been added. Seasoning salts, and flavoring extracts, such as vanilla, require certification; but salt, sugar, and flour that contain no additives at all do not. You'll find most of the seasonings and flavorings already in your pantry, are probably suitable for kosher cooking.

Shortenings. Margarine needs a kosher label, as does butter that isn't completely pure. Lard and other meat-derived fats are, of course, not kosher. Vegetable oils almost always carry certification.

Prepared Foods. If it's been prepared, it's no longer natural and requires kosher certification. Some prepared foods, such as mustards, ketchups, Worcestershire sauce, vinegars, pickles, vegetarian vegetable soups, salad dressings, and mayonnaise, are easily available with a kosher label; others, such as prepared frozen vegetables, dinners, meats, fish cakes, and instant casserole dinners are rarely certified and are therefore not usable. This is just as well, since their high salt, sugar, and additive levels make them unsuitable choices for most diets.

Fish. Fresh fish won't need a label, though some guests may prefer fish purchased in a market that doesn't sell non-kosher fish. Some may prefer that frozen fish carry kosher certification; few brands do.

Most important in buying fish for kosher guests is knowing kosher fish from the non-kosher varieties. One gracious Southern hostess, who went out of her way not to serve pork to her kosher guest—Rabbi Herb Tarr, author of *Heaven Help Me, The Conversion of Chaplain Cohen* and other best-sellers—unwittingly served him just as big a no-no—shellfish. To avoid such a dietary *faux pas,* check the following list before serving fish to your kosher guests.

Permitted fish, according to the Bible, must have both scales and fins. Popular fish falling under that category include: anchovies, bass, bluefish, butterfish, carp, cod, flounder, fluke, grouper, haddock, halibut, herring, mackerel, pike, porgy, salmon, sardines, shad, smelts, snapper, sole, tile fish, trout, tuna, weakfish, and whitefish.

Forbidden fruit of the sea include: blowfish, clams, crab, catfish, eel, frogs, lobster, octopus and squid, oyster, porpoise, scallops, shrimp, snail, shark, turtle, and whale.

Controversial fish, accepted by some kosher adherents and rejected by others, include sturgeon and swordfish. If you are thinking of serving either one (or buying sturgeon caviar) check with your guest first.

Canned or bottled fish, including tuna, sardines, salmon, and herring, should carry kosher certification; many brands do.

Wines and Liquors. Most distilled liquors (scotch, rye, vodka, gin, bourbon, etc.) and beers can be used without kosher certification. Most mixers and soft drinks, incidentally, do have certification. Bottled waters don't need it. Buy any you like. But, if your guest drinks only kosher wines, then select from among the ever-growing varieties, both domestic and imported from Israel, France, and Italy, now being sold in most liquor stores. Wine-based brandies and liqueurs will also require certification; in addition to those available from Israel, the entire Leroux line of liqueurs and brandies is certified by the Union of Orthodox Rabbis

If you can't find any kosher wines in your community, chances are your guest doesn't drink wine very often, and won't miss it. If you do have the time and inclination, you might try ordering some from your local liquor store.

Cooking Kosher

Lenient

Once you've done the shopping for your lenient (*k*) guest, the rest is relatively easy. Kosher cooking, contrary to popular belief, isn't much different from any other kind of cooking. As long as you avoid forbidden foods, and don't mix meat with milk, you can use just about all of your favorite cooking techniques, from broiling and baking to basting, sautéing, and deep-frying. Be sure, however, to discard eggs with blood spots.

Strict

For the strict kosher guest (*K*), you won't be cooking at all. You'll be combining cold, raw, or prepared kosher foods that you have purchased. The only complication will be if your guest won't eat the food when prepared in and served on your dishes. In that case, prepare salads and other cold foods in a disposable plastic or paper bowl, or a brand new bowl that you haven't yet used. Any slicing or cutting can be done with a brand new paring knife, or a plastic one; if mashing or stirring is necessary, purchase a new stainless fork. Serve the meal on paper plates, with disposable flatware, and hot and cold cups for beverages. One plus: you'll have the easiest post-party clean-up ever.

Preparing for Saturday Night. Because the twenty-five hours from Friday just before sundown to Saturday at nightfall encompass the Sabbath for observant Jews, they may object to eating food prepared by other Jews during that period. If you are entertaining guests who feel that way, do all of your preparations for your dinner party either before sundown on Friday, or after dark on Saturday night. All shopping, too, must be done either before or after the Sabbath.

Kosher Menus: Lenient (k)

These menus include a wide variety of meatless meals to serve your kosher guests. You can also select menus and recipes from our strict kosher (*K*), strict vegetarian (V), and ovolacto vegetarian (*v*) sections, or substitute your own meatless favorites.

Kosher Menus: Strict (K)

Our strict kosher menus differ from the other menus in the book because most of the dishes suggested in them are either commercially prepared or ready-to-eat. When breads or cookies or crackers are called for, use bakery or packaged varieties that are certified kosher by an authority your guest finds acceptable. Prepared salads like sweet-and-sour cabbage, pickled beets, three-bean salad, and others are available with kosher certification, and are also called for in some of the menus. Herring comes in a jar; the smoked salmon can come packaged, frozen, or fresh, purchased from an approved kosher appetizing store. Salad dressings can be made at home as long as they are uncooked and contain no non-kosher ingredients; many bottled dressings are also available with kosher certification.

Menus for Guests on Lenient Kosher Diets

Breakfasts

I

Marinated Mango (486)
Homemade Granola (32)
Banana Bread (2), *Maple-Whipped Cream Cheese* (549)

II

Macédoine of Winter Fruit (476)
Mushroom Omelet (51)
Whole Wheat Italian Bread (15)
Cheesecake (441)

Brunches

I

Cold Spiced Tomato Juice (557), *Lemon Wedge*
Mushroom-Zucchini Quiche (59)
Whole Wheat French Bread (9), *Sweet Butter*
Strawberries Romanoff (499)

II

Cheese-Stuffed Pears (496)
Curried Salmon Kedgeree (285)
Spinach Salad (214)
Orange Biscuits (27)

Lunches

I

Gazpacho Verde (78)
Salmon Mousse I (287), *Avocado Sauce* (416)
Sweet and Sour Cucumber Salad (195)
Mustard-Dill Potato Salad (232)
Whole Wheat French Bread (9)
Peaches Caramel Flambé (494), *Vanilla Ice Cream*

II

Mushroom-Onion Soup (91)
Spinach-Mozzarella Crepes (45)
Watercress-Apple Salad (225)
Plums in Port (497)

Barbecues

I

Vegetable Sate (414)
Grilled Halibut Teriyaki (408)
Green Rice Salad (235)
Bok Choy Salad (192)
Fresh Tropical Fruits

II

Antipasto Vegetables (161)
Grilled Stuffed Baby Salmon (409)
Coal-Roasted Onions and Potatoes (415), *Buttermilk-Chive Dressing* (252)
Tossed Greens, Vinaigrette
Marinated Melon Balls and Blueberries (488)
Orange Cookie Thins (531)

Cocktail Parties

I

Mixed Nuts and Raisins
Mushroom Ambrosia (175)
Lomi Lomi Salmon (176)
Vegetable Pâté (126), *Melba Squares* (16)
Eggplant Caviar (106), *Black Bread*
Creamy Avocado Dip (103), *Crudités* (383)
Fresh Pineapple

II

Seasoned Popcorn (131)
Tuna Tapenade (125), *Zucchini Rounds* (383)

Spinach-Stuffed Mushrooms (149)
Mushroom-Almond Pâté (117), *Whole Wheat Crackers*
Tofu Tidbits (159), *Tartar Sauce*
Tahina Dip (123), *Crudités* (383)

Dinners

I

Mushrooms a la Grecque (173)
Trout Sauté with Almonds, Pine Nuts, and Raisins (293)
Chive Rice (368)
Buttered Broccoli Spears
Filbert Meringues Hélène (445)

II

Alu Gobi (373)
Tandoori Fish (291)
Chutney (273)
Gingered Carrots (379)
Raita (210)
Chapatis (7)
Mango Ice (460)
Gingered Fruit (473)

III

Whole Artichokes (162), *Garlic Mayonnaise* (255)
Herbed Salmon Steaks (280)
Broccoli with Capers (374)
Baked Potatoes, Buttermilk-Chive Dressing (252)
Mayo-Cucumber Mousse (184) *on Shredded Greens*
Orange Sorbet Supreme (464)
Pecan Balls (521)

IV

Leeks Vinaigrette (172)
Baked Fish Fillets in Mustard Sauce (276)
Glazed Carrots, Turnips, and Peas (380)
Pepper Salad (207)
Pears Caramel Flambé (494)
Lace Cookies (520)

Buffets

I

Herring in Mustard Sauce (277)
German Tuna Salad (245)

Red Cabbage Salad (212)
Peasant Rye Bread (19)
Cherry Tomatoes
Fresh Cherries in Kirsch (483), *Whipped Cream*
Nature-Sweetened Apple Strudel (542)

II
Stuffed Peppers (150)
Chilean Fish Stew (278)
Whole Wheat Italian Bread (15)
Spinach Salad (214)
Orange Slices with Ricotta (451)

Suppers
I
Cold Peach Love Soup (79)
Salad Nicoise (246)
Wheat-Dill Biscuits (28)
Honeydew Melon, Lime Wedge

II
Portuguese Salad (209)
Onion Bouillabaisse (95)
French Bread (9)
Apple Pie (535)

Menus for Strictly Kosher Guests

Breakfast
I
Orange Slices Sprinkled with Dried Coconut
Muesli (34), *Fresh Fruit*
Whole Wheat Bagels and Cream Cheese

II
Blended Fruit Juice, Lime Wedge (562)
Orange Muesli (35)
Cinnamon Raisin Bread, Maple-Whipped Cream Cheese (549)

Brunch
I
Strawberries and Bananas with Sour Cream or Yogurt, Brown Sugar
Israeli Buffet: Hard-Cooked Eggs, Sardines, Sliced Onions, Tomatoes,

Cucumbers
Fresh Rye Bread, Butter or Margarine
Pecan Coffee Cake

II
Macédoine of Citrus and Banana Slices (477), *Slivered Almonds*
Gefilte Fish with Horseradish Mayonnaise (274), *Hard-Cooked Egg Garnish*
Sliced Tomato, Cucumber, and Zucchini
Peppery Chick Peas (130)
Sliced Challah, Sweet Butter
Assorted Muffins

Lunch
I
Vegetable Juice, Celery Swizzle-Stick
Fresh Fruit Platter
Cottage Cheese
Fruited Yogurt (428)
Melba Toasts
Danish Pastries

II
Marinated Mango (486)
Salad Nicoise (246)
French Bread
Ice Cream-Rum Ball (459)

Barbecue*
I
Chopped Egg Salad with Walnuts, Wheat Tams
Guacamole (109), *Crudités* (383)
Kosher Hot Dogs on Buns, Mustard
Coal-Roasted Sweet Corn (415), *Margarine*
Sauerkraut and Sour Pickles
Choice of Prepared Salads
Fresh Fruit Salad (475) *in Melon Basket*
Kosher Marshmallows to Toast

* If you can obtain an inexpensive brand new grill and your guests agree, you can actually serve a real barbecue to your strictly kosher guests. If hot dogs are served, you'd have to be certain there are no milk products in any other food at the meal. If a new grill isn't a possibility, serve any other strict kosher menu.

II
Sour Cream-Onion Dip, Crudités (383)
Grilled Salmon or Halibut Steaks Teriyaki (408)
Coal-Roasted Potatoes (415), *Sour Cream and Chives*
Vegetable Slaw (224)
Sliced Tomatoes, Italian Dressing
Ice Cream-Cookie Sandwiches
Fresh Fruit

Cocktail Parties

I
Assorted Pretzels
Israeli Tahina or Hummous Dip, Crudités (383) *and Pita Bread Triangles*
Herring Tidbits in Wine Sauce
Anchovy and Sardine Butter Canapés (138) *on Melba Rounds*
Cream Cheese and Black Olives Wrapped in Smoked Salmon Slices
Raisin-Nut Farmer Cheese (120), *Assorted Crackers*

II
Mixed Nuts
Soy Nut-Peanut-Raisin Mix
Guacamole (109), *Crudités* (383)
Gefilte Tidbits, Cocktail Sauce
Lomi Lomi Salmon (176)
Cream Cheese and Capers Wrapped in Smoked Salmon
Fresh Fruit with Kosher Cheese Rounds
No-Bake Fruit-Nut Balls (518)

Dinners

I
Israeli Hummous and Tahina, Pita Bread Triangles
Crudités (383), *Lemon Pepper*
Dilled Salmon on Avocado Half-Shell (244)
Sesame Breadsticks
Spinach Salad (214)
Bakery Rugelach
Ice Cream

II
Chilled Tomato Juice, Lime Wedge
Curried Tuna Nestled on Mango Slices (243)
Melba Toasts
Middle Eastern Salad (203)

Walnut-Stuffed Dates
Sabra Sundaes (469)

III
Avocado and Papaya Slices, Vinaigrette
Smoked Salmon with Capers on Black Bread, Lemon Wedge, and Black Pepper
Sliced Canned Potatoes, Italian Dressing (257)
Sliced Tomatoes and Cucumbers, Parsley Garnish
Tropical Ice Cream Balls (471)
Thin Butter Cookies

IV
Mushroom Ambrosia (175)
Whole Smoked Whitefish, Lemon Wedges
Mexican Salad (202)
Wholegrain Flatbread, Sweet Butter
Seedless Grapes and Orange Slices Sabra (484)
No Bake Fruit-Nut Balls (518)

Buffets
I
Smoked Salmon with Lemon, Capers, and Black Bread
Smoked White Fish Garnished with Olives, Sliced Onion, and Cherry Tomatoes
Assorted Bagels, Butter-and-Chive Cream Cheese
Spinach Salad (214)
Fresh Fruit Salad (475)
Mixed Nuts

II
Smoked Salmon-Avocado Canapés (140)
Antipasto Platter: Tuna Chunks, Sardines, Cheeses, Hard-Cooked Eggs, Olives, Green Pepper, Onion, and Tomato Slices, Marinated Mushrooms, Italian Dressing
Italian Bread, Sweet Butter
Marinated Melon Balls and Blueberries (488)

Suppers
I
German Tuna Salad (245)
Black Bread, Sweet Butter
Prepared Red Cabbage Salad
Melon Wedge, Lime Garnish

II
Cashew–Raisin–Wheat Chex Mix
Tuna Hawaiian on Greens (247)
Sesame Pita Bread
Tropical Ice Cream Balls (471)

The Bland Dieter

The bland dieter may be one of the least "bland" people you know: a successful playwright, for instance, whose irregular hours and eating habits have led to a case of colitis; or a fashion designer, whose drive for success has recently driven her to the hospital with an ulcer. You'd hate to scratch such dynamic friends off your guest list. But still, you sense that pitchers of milk and bowls of mashed potatoes don't quite qualify as elegant party fare.

Fortunately for all bland dieters—and for all of those who have them to dinner—there are culinary options outside of mashed potatoes and milk. The comically pathetic image of a harried executive downing his prescribed glass of milk with a grimace, then guiltily sneaking a few forbidden gulps of whiskey from a bottle in his locked desk drawer is rather outdated. Executives still get ulcers, and are still forbidden their whiskey when they do. But the humbling milk-to-coat-the-stomach regime is less frequently part of what their doctors order, except, perhaps, during early convalescence days in the hospital. Even the all-soft, textureless, and often, flavorless diet (until recently the mandatory life sentence passed upon sufferers of digestive diseases) is beginning to lose favor in the medical community.

In fact, a lot of doctors today are beginning to think that the typical American diet is *too* bland. It's too full of refined flours and sugars, along with over-processed, overcooked foods. They charge that such bland diets are responsible for more digestive diseases than they could ever cure. And to prevent digestive problems, they recommend the very opposite dietary course: a high fiber diet. Some even recommend that kind of diet for those already stricken.

But even within modern medical circles, old treatments, including those for ulcers, gall bladder disease, colitis, diverticulitis, and other diseases of the digestive tract, die hard. It's not at all unusual for a host or hostess to discover that someone on his or her guest list is on a bland diet, or one of the other traditional dietary treatments. Since, as you will see, there are many dietary variations on the bland theme, it will be important to find out which your guest subscribes to. From there, serving him or her should be easy and delicious. Bland recipes need be bland only by medical definition.

Digestive Disease Diet Basics

The liberal approach to diet for digestive disorders is simple and straightforward: avoid foods that you can't tolerate. For some, that might mean anything fried. For others, anything containing onions or garlic is avoided. For still others, a particular spice can't be eaten. For that reason, guests following a liberalized dietary regimen are relatively easy to feed.

Guests with digestive disturbances may be on a six-small-meals-a-day routine, as six small meals are easier for their tender systems to handle than three large ones. Keep that in mind when you have such a dieter as a house guest. Include afternoon, and late-night snack breaks in your meal planning, or give guests the key to the larder, being certain, of course, that it's well-stocked with foods that are compatible with their dietary needs. When the invitation is for dinner, and you're planning a lengthy pre-dinner cocktail time, serve hors d'oeuvres that your guest can nibble on as a sort of mini-meal. Then, when dinner is presented, keep it relatively light, considering the food served previously as the first course. If guests stay on for a long period following dinner, have another snack ready to serve. If you prefer, save dessert for a little later.

Since the sensitive digestive system may not react well to large quantities of very cold or very hot foods, especially liquids, serve chilled soups cool, not icy cold, and hot soups less than boiling hot.

Don't put ice in a beverage unless it's requested. Ice cream can be served because it has time to melt before being swallowed; frozen ices should be allowed to thaw a bit before serving. Hot beverages, too, can be allowed to stand briefly before serving.

More than particular food or temperature extremes, mental and emotional stress can provoke digestive problems. Strive to create a relaxed, pleasant atmosphere for your guests. Orchestrate your meal in slow tempo, serving courses at a leisurely pace, allowing time for thorough chewing of food. If possible, see that mealtime discussions stay away from the controversial and the political. Keep any background music soft and soothing, avoiding disco or rock beats during the meal itself.

If you are serving a mixed buffet, and not all the food served is suitable for your guest, ask if he would like you to fill a plate for him. Not only will that offer keep confusion to a minimum; it will spare a guest who has recently been very ill the sight of food which, even visually, may be unsettling.

The guest with a digestive disorder may have a problem that requires not only dietary, but emotional support and understanding. He may have to visit the bathroom often, or for long periods of time. If there is a bathroom which is far from the entertaining area, where your guest won't be interrupted, tell him about it privately. Don't fuss if he disappears from the table or the living room for extended periods.

The food you will serve your guest will vary greatly depending on the diet he is on. If your guest has only a few sensitivities, you can leave those foods off the menu entirely, or offer alternatives. Among the most common problem foods are alcohol, black pepper, red pepper (cayenne), chili pepper or powder, nutmeg, cloves, onion, garlic, coffee, tea, colas, and fried or rich foods. Raw fruits, often melon, or vegetables, often cucumber, cabbage, or radishes, may be difficult for your guest to stomach as well.

The origins of the traditional bland diet date back to the first century, when Celsus ordered smooth diets free of acrid foods for ulcer sufferers. In the seventeenth century, milk became popular for ulcer treatment. In this century, the bland diet has been used in the treatment of many digestive disorders, as well as following surgery. Although it is becoming increasingly accepted that ulcer patients and others do just as well on less-restricted diets as on the bland regimen, many people are still saddled with the later. Your guests may start on a bland diet in the hospital, continue on it during convalescence, and then progress to a "diet as tolerated."

The traditional bland diet usually prohibits:

- Coffee, tea, cola, and other beverages containing caffeine
- Alcoholic beverages
- Carbonated beverages
- Fried foods or fatty, rich foods
- Fried, highly seasoned, pickled, or smoked meats (such as franks, bacon, sausage, cold cuts), and tough cuts of meat
- Soups and gravies made with meat or meat extract, and meat stocks or broths
- Bouillon cubes or gravies containing meat extracts
- Raw, smoked, and highly-seasoned fish; fried or fatty fish such as sardines
- Sharp, strongly flavored, and spicy cheeses
- Raw vegetables; strong flavored or gas-forming vegetables, such as broccoli, Brussels sprouts, cabbage, cauliflower, cucumbers, garlic, onions, peppers, radishes, turnips, dried beans and peas, even when cooked
- Seeds, skins, or tough, fibrous parts of *any* vegetable
- Raw fruit, except ripe bananas and avocados; dried fruit, including raisins
- Skins and seeds of any fruit, raw or cooked, including berries
- Coarse or whole grains, including brown or wild rice and bran; cereals and baked goods that contain them
- Nuts and seeds, and foods or breads that contain them
- Commercially or home-prepared foods containing any of the above
- Commercial salad dressings; mineral oil
- Excessively sweet or rich desserts, including sweet rolls, pies, pastries, cakes
- Very hot or very cold beverages and soups
- Spices and spicy condiments, particularly garlic, peppers, onions, mustard, pepper sauces, nutmeg, cayenne, horseradish, ketchup, pickles, vinegar, olives

In early convalescence, vegetables and fruits may have to be strained and/or pureed, and meats ground. Milk may be limited. All vegetables should be well-cooked.

Your guest's diet may not be nearly as limited as we've suggested; the questions you ask him will help to determine his individual prohibitions. Still, you're not likely to go wrong if you follow this rather rigid diet plan, unless your guest is on a low-residue diet, which is more rigid still. Similar to the bland diet in that it prohibits fried foods, uncooked cereal, bran, raw fruits and vegetables, skins, seeds, nuts, strong spices, and condiments, the low-residue diet restricts, too, foods which leave large amounts of residue in the digestive tract. Usually prohibited are:

- All raw fruits, including banana and avocado
- Spinach and squash, and sometimes potato (even when cooked)

Usually limited are:

- Milk products, except for cottage cheese
- Fats, except in small quantities
- All liquids, particularly during meals

Fortunately, the low-residue diet is not without its virtues. Unlike those following a bland diet, a low-residue dieter may be allowed:

- Soups with meat or meat bases
- Coffee, tea, and non-iced carbonated beverages
- Seasonings, in moderation

Yet another diet that a guest with digestive problems may be following is one of those recommended by the American Digestive Diseases Society. The diet may be:

- Bland, eliminating excess spices, fatty and rich foods, and such scratchy items as nuts and seeds
- Soft, eliminating coarse textured (tough meats) and very fibrous foods, particularly raw fruits and vegetables
- Low residue, eliminating whole grains, bran, and vegetables and fruits that are not well-cooked and small textured (cut up or chopped)

These diets break down the traditional bland diet into smaller units tailored to an individual patient's needs.

Questions to Ask Guests on a Bland Diet

1. *Are you on a traditional bland or low-residue diet?* If your guest's diet is traditional, simply follow the prohibitions set out in Bland Basics. All the menus and recipes for bland (*B*) dieters will be suitable

for one or the other of these diets, or both. The recipes calling for meat extractives or broth are generally not suitable for those on a traditional bland diet, while those containing milk are usually inappropriate for those on a low-residue diet. Some milkless recipes are suitable for either dieter, as well as those who are milk sensitive. If your guest is on one of the ADDS diets—bland, soft, or low residue—you can use any of the bland (*B*) menus and recipes in this book. Feel free to add to them any foods or seasonings that are not restricted in your guest's regimen. If your guest isn't on either of these diets, ask which foods he or she cannot tolerate. The following questions will aid in your menu planning.

2. *Must you avoid fried foods?* If the answer is yes, you may use any recipe in this book—none employ frying.

3. *Must you avoid fatty foods?* Many people, particularly those with gall bladder problems, cannot tolerate fat. For such guests, most bland (*B*) recipes will be suitable; use the lowest quantity of fat called for. When sour cream is called for, substitute pureed low-fat cottage cheese or low-fat yogurt, or buttermilk as appropriate. Stick to other low-fat dairy products and to lean meats, poultry, and fish. Avoid nuts, avocados, olives, salad oils and dressings containing them, as well as commerical baked goods and desserts. When a guest has no other dietary prohibitions, you may also use Pritikin (*P*) recipes or any other recipe that contains no fat.

4. *Whole grains?* More and more bland diets permit whole grains, particularly when the grains are finely ground. (But breads with seeds may be taboo.) For diets that don't, substitute refined flours and grains (eg: white rice) in recipes calling for whole grains.

5. *Coffee, tea, caffeinated beverages?* In some cases, weak tea or coffee with milk may be permitted in small quantities. If not, see the variety of non-caffeinated beverages in the beverage recipe section, pages 545 to 552.

6. *Alcoholic beverages?* Your guest may be permitted a well-diluted cocktail or wine with meals. If not, see the variety of nonalcoholic beverages at the end of the recipe section, pages 545 to 552.

7. *Wine in cooking?* Some bland dieters may be allowed this luxury on occasion. If your guest isn't, use bland (*B*) diet substitutions instead.

8. *Meat stocks or meat extractives?* If your guest cannot tolerate these, substitute VEGETABLE STOCK (B) (98).

9. *Milk or milk products?* If milk or milk products are limited or prohibited, select recipes and menus suitable for milkless (*Ml*) diets. If other bland restrictions apply, select recipes that are both Milkless (*Ml*) and bland (*B*). If milk products are limited but not prohibited, avoid recipes that are based on them, such as cream sauces, creamed soups, cheese casseroles, souffles, and ice cream cakes. When possible, substitute milkless variations in recipes, using stocks, or fruit or vegetable juices when appropriate instead of milk or cream.

10. *Are there any vegetables (raw or cooked) that you must avoid?* If you know which vegetables you plan to serve, you can ask if those are permitted and how they must be cooked. Eliminate from your menu any that are prohibited on your guest's diet.

Our bland (*B*) vegetable recipes will be suitable for most guests with digestive problems. If raw vegetables are prohibited, salads and crudités are obvious menu outcasts. In some cases, shredded lettuce and diced tomato, skin and seeds removed, may be permitted. Feel free, in any case, to use raw vegetables of any kind as garnish; no one need eat them.

11. *Are there any fruits (raw or cooked) that you must avoid?* If you know which ones you plan to serve, just ask if they are acceptable to your guest. Our bland (*B*) fruit recipes will be suitable in most cases. Many dieters can tolerate raw bananas and avocados.

12. *Must all your vegetables and fruits be peeled and seeded?* Often these extra steps are necessary in preparing produce for guests with digestive disturbances, even when a food, tomatoes, for example, can be tolerated raw. Fruits with seeds, such as strawberries and blackberries, can pose a particular problem and are best avoided.

13. *Must vegetables and/or fruits be pureed?* Most people, even on a traditional bland diet, can eat well-cooked fruits and vegetables without pureeing and straining, at least once convalescence is past. If your guest cannot, then puree fruits or vegetables in a blender, processor, or food mill. If necessary, strain to remove seeds and/or skins.

14. *Can you eat beef, veal, lamb, poultry, and fish?* Generally, meat from lean, tender cuts of beef, veal, or lamb and non-fatty fish and poultry (turkey and chicken) are well-tolerated. White meat poultry is preferable to dark and skin should be avoided completely.

15. *Must you avoid very hot and very cold foods?* Proceed according to your special guest's needs.

16. *Which spices or herbs must you avoid?* Eliminate from recipes any your guest names. Substitute an herb or spice your guest can tol-

erate. If you are planning to use an unusual spice, ask your guest about it specifically.

Shopping Bland

Even when your guest is on the most stringent of bland diets, your shopping cart needn't go empty to the checkout. Choose from the following often easily-tolerated foods, and expand or reduce the list according to your guest's specific tolerances:

- Asparagus tips, beets, carrots, green beans, mushrooms, pumpkin, spinach, squash, tomatoes, white and sweet potatoes. Buy vegetables fresh, frozen, or canned; fresh and frozen may have to be well-cooked and pureed
- Apples, applesauce, apricots, avocados, bananas, peaches, pears, fresh, frozen, or canned. Fresh and frozen fruit may have to be well-cooked, and in some cases, pureed. Canned crushed pineapple and stewed, pureed prunes may be permitted, too
- Fruit juices as permitted
- Milk, cream, yogurt, cottage and cream cheeses, very mild American or Swiss cheeses unless dairy products are restricted. Buy low-fat products as a rule, but especially if fats are restricted
- Tender cuts of beef, lamb, veal (ground if necessary); chicken, turkey, and organ meats as permitted
- Non-oily or fatty fish, such as sole, haddock, halibut, perch, flounder, bass, brook trout; tuna or salmon canned in water, if permitted
- Vegetable oils, butter, margarines, as permitted
- Gelatin, puddings (custard, tapioca), frozen yogurts, ice cream, and ice milk (unless milk products are limited or prohibited), water ices and sherberts, all without nuts, fruits, seeds, or skins
- Simple baked goods that are not overly rich or sweet, and contain no nuts, seeds, or raisins; plain cakes or cookies (sponge cake, sugar cookies); enriched white bread, soda crackers, rusks and zweiback, egg matzo, hard or soft rolls; refined cereals (ready-to-eat or cooked), such as cream of wheat, farina, corn flakes; white rice, macaroni, noodles, spaghetti; fine whole wheat or rye products without seeds, if permitted
- Eggs as permitted
- Seasonings such as lemons, lemon juice, paprika, cinnamon, mace, allspice, parsley, dill, sage, thyme, salt

If fats are limited, read shopping directions in Chapter Two, which explain how to avoid fat in the supermarket. Convenience foods, as is usually the case in shopping for problem guests, will present the biggest challenge of your shopping expedition. You'll want to avoid products in which fat of any kind (shortening, oil, lard, butter, cream, beef fat, chicken fat) is near the top of the ingredient list. And, of course, you'll avoid convenience foods that are fried, or that contain any of the restricted foods. You'll have to look out, too, for the generic word "spices" or any individual prohibited spices, particularly black pepper, cayenne, nutmeg, cloves, and chili powder and pepper. Avoid also products containing chocolate, cocoa, and coffee. In baked goods, watch out for coarse whole grains, bran, cellulose, or other fibrous foods when shopping for guests who can't tolerate these ingredients.

Cooking Bland

If your guest is on a liberal diet for treatment of a digestive disorder, and must abide by only a few restrictions, your work in the kitchen needn't stray far from the routine. In many cases, however, you will have to alter your usual methods of food preparation. You won't be able to stir-fry vegetables to a crispy turn; instead you'll have to cook them with minimal or no fat to a very tender stage.

The best methods of cooking vegetables for the bland diet are pressure cooking, microwaving, baking, waterless cooking, and, as a last resort, boiling. Tender vegetables, cut into small pieces, can be steamed. If you're serving a mixed group of guests, you may want to remove some of the vegetables when they are still crisply *al dente,* and continue cooking the rest for your bland dieter.

Fruits, too may have to be soft-cooked for the bland guest. Both vegetables and fruits may have to be stripped of skins and seeds, and in some cases, pureed and/or strained. Cutting fruits or vegetables into small pieces before cooking will speed preparation time. Fruit juices, too, should be strained if your guest's diet requires it.

While it may sometimes be necessary to overcook vegetables and fruits, casseroles, breads, or meats that are overbaked or over-roasted may turn out too crisp, crusty, and hard for the bland dieter. Keep careful track of cooking time.

Because frying is an unacceptable form of food preparation for the bland dieter, all paraphernalia of frying—woks, deep fryers, frying pans—will have to be temporarily retired. Fortunately, as any low-fat dieter will tell you, there is virtually nothing that can't be either broiled, baked, roasted, steamed, or poached. No- or low-fat sautéing, as described in the Recipe Glossary (page 154) will be useful in preparing foods for those who must seriously restrict fats. When gravies and sauces cannot be based on meat drippings or juices, vegetable stock, milk, fruit, or tomato juice can be substituted as permitted and appropriate. For those who are allowed meat extractives, skim fat well from drippings and stocks before making sauces and gravies. Soups, too, should be skimmed.

Garlic, onions, and pepper are usually taboo seasonings. Season, instead, to a delicate tastiness with modest amounts of salt, lemon juice, herbs, and mild spices.

Bland Menus

There are many diets for treating those with digestive problems. Among the traditional diets, the bland and the low residue are the most frequently prescribed. The bland permits milk, raw banana, and avocado, but no meat extractives; the low residue limits milk, prohibits all raw fruit including bananas and avocados, as well as cooked spinach and squash, but permits meat extractives. Some of the menus that follow are appropriate for both bland and low-residue dieters, but others are for one or the other. The latter are so labeled. In some of the following menus, we've given choices of bland or low-residue dishes, and, again, these are labeled. An extra pair of menus are provided for the time when friends may be on a very rigid convalescence diet.

Though our menus for other special diets may be, to a certain extent, interchangeable, those for bland diets are distinctly different from the rest. Raw vegetable salads, for instance, are never found on them; citrus juices, which may offend empty stomachs, are not offered as a first course. Keep in mind, however, that menus suggested here reflect some of the more rigid dietary guidelines that might be prescribed. For less restricted diets, feel free to add foods that are not included on our menus, but that your guest can tolerate.

Menus for Guests on Bland Diets

Early Convalescence

I

Puree Mongole (81), *Lemon Wedge*
Individual Apple-Veal Loaves (322)
Dutchess Potato Nests (361)

Tomato Aspic (186)
Orange Almond Semolina (449)

II
Cream of Asparagus Soup (84) (*B*)
or
Creamless Asparagus Soup (86) (*Low Residue*)
Cottage Cheese and Noodle Bake (333) (*B*)
or
Rice and Ground Meat Bake (325) (*Low Residue*)
Beet Aspic (180)
Fluffy Apple Mousse (456)

Breakfasts
I
Cream of Wheat with Pureed Apricots, Apricot Garnish
Poached Egg on Toasted English Muffin

II
Sliced Bananas (*B*)
or
Sliced Cooked Peaches
Buttermilk Pancakes (56), *Orange-Maple Syrup* (551) (*B*)
or
Orange Pancakes (57), *Orange-Maple Syrup* (551) (*Low Residue*)

Brunches
I
Grape-Apple Juice
Mushroom-filled Angel Crepes (42), *Cheese Sauce* (419) (*B*)
or
Orange Pancakes (57), *Maple-Whipped Butter* (550)
Banana Bread (2), *Apple Butter-Tofu Spread* (548)

II
Puree Mongole (81)
Bland Fish Kedgeree on Spinach (286) (*B*)
Crisp White Rolls, Sweet Butter
Peach Cobbler (452)

Lunches
I
Quick Cool Borscht (71), *Sour Cream*
Avocado-Halibut Salad (237) (*B*)
or

Halibut and Peach Salad (241)
French Bread (9)
Fruit Pudding (440)

II (B)
Cream of Asparagus Soup (84), *Croutons*
Macaroni and Peas au Gratin (335)
Tomato-Avocado Aspic (187)
Baked Apple Slices (481)

Barbecues
I
Cool Creamless Asparagus Soup (86) *in Mugs* (*Low Residue*)
Lean Beef Patties with Sautéed Mushrooms (401)
Burger Buns
Coal-Roasted Potatoes (415)
Coal-Roasted Green Beans (415)
Sweet-and-Sour Beets (190)
Apple-Banana Mold (435) (*B*)
or
Apple-Peach Mold (436)
Bland Cookie Thins (528)

II
Tomato Juice, Lemon Wedge
Grilled Halibut Steaks (406)
Macaroni a la Russe (230) (*B*)
Tender Asparagus Tips
Carrot-Prune Cake (505), *a la Mode* (*B*)

Cocktail Parties
I (B)
Pretzel Sticks
Salmon Mousse II (288), *Melba Toast Points* (16)
Fish Cocktail (170), *Creamy Avocado Dip* (103)
Spinach-Stuffed Mushrooms (149)
Angel Eggs I (132)
Canapes on White I (135)

II
Pretzel Sticks
Mushroom Rollups (139)
Apple-Veal Balls (160)
Honeyed Chicken Nuggets (157)

Canapés on White II (137)
Angel Eggs II (133)

Dinners

I (*Low Residue*)
Halibut and Peach Salad (241), *Finely Shredded Lettuce*
Veal Prince Orloff's Smarter Brother (328)
Dutchess Potato Nests Filled with Baby June Peas (361)
Beet Aspic (180)
Parkerhouse Rolls
Fruit Pudding (440)
Almond Cookie Thins (525)

II (*B*)
Cream of Spinach Soup (85)
Stuffed Fillets in Cheese Sauce (289)
Buttered Noodles
Green Beans au Gratin (385)
Tomato Aspic (186), *Avocado Garnish*
Farina-Banana Pudding (444)

III (*B*)
Spinach-Stuffed Mushrooms (149)
Salmon Mousse II (288)
Cold Parsleyed Yogurt Potatoes (362)
Asparagus Tips, Easy Hollandaise (423)
Apricot Mousse (438)

IV (*Low Residue*)
Creamless Asparagus Soup (86)
Chicken Breasts with Mushrooms (301)
Fluffy White Rice (370)
Glazed Carrots and Peas (380)
Tomato Aspic (186)
Juice-Poached Apples and Pears (478)
Vanilla Bland Cookie Thins (524)

Buffets

I (*B*)
Cool Fruit Soup (76)
Cold Poached Bass (284), *Creamy Avocado Dip* (103)
Macaroni a la Russe (230)
Carrot-Prune Cake (505), *a la Mode*

II
Apple-Veal Balls (160)
Chicken Noodle Bake (310)
Glazed Carrots and Peas (380)
Sweet-and-Sour Beets (190)
Fluffy Apple Mousse (456)
Vanilla Bland Cookie Thins (528)

Suppers
I
Cream of Tomato Soup (93) (*B*)
or
Warm Puree Mongole (81) (*Low Residue*)
Crown of Noodles and Spinach, Creamed Mushroom Sauce (334) (*B*)
or
Chicken Noodle Bake (310) (*Low Residue*)
Asparagus Tips, Lemon Garnish
Carrot-Prune Cake (505)

II (*B*)
Turban of Fish with Spinach Sauce (294)
Vegetables a la Russe (223)
Peach Cobbler (452)

The Other Special Guests

There are a lot of people who have dietary problems that aren't part of major national trends, or who have religious prohibitions that aren't widely known. Howard, for example, normally the nicest of Mr. Nice Guys, becomes as grouchy as any grinch when he eats chocolate. It would be folly, therefore, to serve him Black Forest Cake. Then there's Walter, who recently discovered that he's a victim of the "rich man's disease," gout, greatly limiting what he can eat. And Helena and Jimmy, a young Greek Orthodox couple, cling to the traditions of Wednesday, Friday and Lenten fasts, which surprises those who thought that the Greek Orthodox Church abandoned the meatless days when the Roman Catholic Church did.

If you're expecting a guest in an unusual dietary category—allergic, religious, medical, or even dental—you may find just the tricks for entertaining him or her right here.

The Allergic Guest

A person can become sensitized to a food the first—or the fiftieth—time he eats it. And once sensitization has occurred, even the tiniest amount of the food can cause an allergic reaction ranging from mild (mental depression, hives, runny nose, stomach cramps) to life-threatening (breathing difficulties, circulatory collapse, shock). If you know that your guest is allergic to a particular food, of course, don't serve it. "Are you allergic to any foods" is always a good question to ask guests in advance of a dinner party. That way, you'll know not to serve chocolate mousse when Howard comes to dinner. And more importantly, you won't risk the danger of an unsuspecting guest partaking of a strawberry sorbet that also contains cantaloupe, to which he is severely allergic.

Fortunately, omitting an allergy-triggering food from your menu won't, in most cases, cause much disruption. There are also good substitutes for most troublesome foods, as you can see below.

Chicken. For those allergic to chicken, plan on serving meat, fish, or vegetarian-based meals. Watch out for chicken broths and chicken fat (they are often found in prepared foods) if your guest is also allergic to them. Chicken may also turn up an ingredient in terrines, pâtés, pot pies, and in some cases, ready-made rice and macaroni dishes; be sure to read labels.

Chocolate. This common allergy often affects those who have been lifetime chocolate lovers. Chocolate's presence is usually obvious and easy to avoid, but it may be hidden in pumpernickel bread, honey cakes, Mexican and other savory sauces, and mocha-flavored products. Inspect labels for cocoa, cocoa butter, chocolate liqueur, and chocolate proper. An excellent substitute for this favorite ingredient in cooking and baking is carob. Though the taste is not precisely the same, it is similar. Carob's virtues include its lower-than-chocolate calorie count and fat content. Unsweetened carob powder can be substituted for unsweetened cocoa in nearly any of your favorite recipes, and especially in brownies. Carob candy bars, readily available in supermarkets and health food stores, can also be used shredded as a dessert garnish, or melted in a sauce.

Citrus Fruits. A guest may be allergic to just oranges, just grapefruits, or to all citrus fruits. In desserts, substitute a citrus fruit or juice that your guest is not allergic to, or use pineapple, apple, or cranapple juices. Avoid recipes that depend on the unique flavor of a citrus fruit (i.e., Orange Slices with Ricotta or Key Lime Pie). In sauces, marinades, salad dressings, and sweet and sour dishes, vinegar to taste can often replace lemon or lime juice. Watch for hidden citrus fruit, juice, oils, extracts, essences, or rind in steak sauce, barbecue sauce, candies, cakes, and other desserts.

Cottonseed. Though you're not likely to be serving cottonseeds, you must be aware that cottonseed oil is a very common ingredient in prepared foods and in liquid vegetable oils. Check labels. When type of vegetable oil isn't specified, play it safe and bypass the product.

Cucumber. A fairly common allergy. Use zucchini rounds instead of cucumber in salads or as garnishes. Cucumber is rarely hidden in foods, though it may be found in some dips and salad dressings.

Eggs. Eggs may be difficult to leave out of many recipes. But good meals can be prepared without them. All of our strict vegetarian (*V*) recipes and menus are eggless, and may be used for guests who are allergic to eggs. In shopping, be particularly thorough when reading labels on prepared foods, such as mayonnaise, fried or breaded foods, baking powders, cake, bread, cookie mixes, ready-prepared baked goods, and ice cream, which often contain egg whites or yolks, or albumin, which is present in egg whites. When eggs are called for in breading, substitute an appropriate liquid, such as milk, apple juice concentrate, tomato juice, honey, or water. Eggs can't be arbitrarily dropped from cookie, bread, and cake recipes; look, instead, for recipes that are already eggless.

Fish or Seafoods. While it's relatively easy to avoid serving fish and seafood in entrées and appetizers, it's not always so easy to spot hidden fish in unexpected places like Worcestershire sauce, salad dressings (especially Caesar and Green Goddess), and certain sauces, such as Sauce Verte and Sauce Nantua. If your guest is allergic to seafood and can't eat meat or poultry, vegetarian meals should be served.

Fruits. Many people are allergic to one or more types of fruit. Substitutions can be made in our recipes or in your favorites as follows: for strawberries, substitute raspberries or blackberries, as long as they don't cause problems, too; for mangoes, substitute papaya, cantaloupe, honeydew, or another melon; for cantaloupe, use papaya, mango or peaches; for bananas, in recipes for baked, sautéed, or fried bananas, substitute pears or apples, adding extra sweetening; in recipes calling for mashed banana as a sweetnener, substitute apple juice concentrate to taste.

Gluten. The guest on the gluten-free diet has to avoid everything avoided by the wheat-allergic guest (see page 160), except for wheat gluten-free bread, which is permitted. They must also avoid oats, barley, buckwheat, and rye. Substitutions should be made only with corn or rice flours (see table, page 160). Ground nuts can also be used in tortes and cookies. This special diet should not present a problem at most meals: the main course, as long as it isn't breaded or stuffed, will usually be gluten-free. So will vegetables and salads, as long as they aren't topped with ready-made dressings (these may contain wheat derivatives), or breaded. Potatoes or rice make good gluten-free side dishes. And desserts can easily be egg- or milk-based instead of pastry-based. Serve sorbets, homemade ice cream, poached fruit, souffles, and mousses.

Milk. All recipes and menus for the milk-sensitive (*Ml*) guest are suitable for a guest who is allergic to milk. Read Chapter Seven for tips on serving.

Mustard. No mustard on the boiled beef, of course, or on sandwiches. But watch out, too, for less obvious mustard presence, as in salad dressings, mayonnaise, and prepared convenience foods. Horseradish substitutes well for mustard in many recipes.

Nuts. Though they may very well be a cook's best friend by adding taste and texture to many foods, they may also be your guest's worst enemy. Instead of topping desserts for a nut-allergic guest with slivered almonds, use a Grape Nuts topping. In tortes and cakes, use wheat germ or finely ground whole wheat matzo instead of ground nuts. Raisins and other dried fruits can take the place of nuts in baked goods, and sliced water chestnuts or slivers of Jerusalem artichoke (sunchoke) can stand in for nuts in meat, fish, and poultry dishes. In vegetable dishes, such as string beans almondine, and in salads, substitute croutons, Chinese noodles, bacon bits, or water chestnuts for nuts.

Oatmeal. Oatmeal is frequently found in cereals, cookies, cakes, and crumb toppings, and is the main constituent of mueslis and granolas. In some cases, wheat germ or wheat flakes can take the place of oatmeal, but there will be differences in taste and texture. It's better to use recipes that are oat-free to start with when cooking for an oatmeal-allergic guest.

Onions and Garlic. These cooking staples can unfortunately cause allergic reactions or a great deal of digestive distress in some people. If your guest can't tolerate these ubiquitous seasonings, you may serve any recipes suitable for bland (*B*) dieters, without worrying about other bland prohibitions, such as herbs, spices, whole grains, or vegetables.

Pork. You wouldn't serve pork chops, of course, to a guest who is allergic to pork. But neither should you serve pork products, such as ham, bacon, pork sausages, some franks, cold cuts, and luncheon meats. In recipes, substitute bits of veal for bits of pork (as in fried rice), beef fry (a bacon-like product made from beef) or imitation bacon bits for the real thing in quiches and salads, and veal, beef, or vegetarian sausage for the pork varieties. Kosher sausage is a safe bet.

Rye. This grain, too, is a common allergen. It is, of course, the main constituent of rye bread, but it can also be found in pumpernickel and other mixed-grain breads. Check labels. In baking, wheat or other flours can be substituted in the proportions shown in the table on page 180.

Spicy Foods. While spicy foods don't usually cause allergic rections, they can cause digestive distress. All of our bland (*B*) recipes avoid spices, and can be safely used when serving spice-sensitive guests. Herbs are tasty substitutes for spices in many dishes.

Wheat. Because wheat in many forms is added to so many different kinds of foods, this is a difficult, though not impossible, allergy to deal with. To begin with, bread made from white or whole wheat flour is taboo. But the list of forbidden foods continues far beyond this. Most breads, including commercial ryes, pumpernickels, and corn breads, contain wheat in some form. So do almost all instant soups, dips, sauces, and ready-to-eat, dehydrated, canned, and frozen foods. Wheat can also be found in malted milk, Postum, Ovaltine, beer, ale, and some instant coffees; salad dressings (particularly thick ones), mustards, bouillon cubes, and seasoning mixes; croquettes, dumplings, fritters, waffles, pancakes, crepes; canned chili con carne and stews; meatballs, meatloaf, sausages, hot dogs, cold cuts and luncheon meats; cream sauces, creamed soups, vegetables prepared in cream sauce or au gratin; pretzels, chips, and other snack foods; kasha, pasta, noodles, and spaetzle; breaded chicken, veal, and fish; bread stuffings, cereals, cake, bread, and cookie mixes, commercial ice creams, ice cream cones and wafers, candies. Read all labels carefully, avoiding any product containing: wheat, wheat starch, unidentified starches, wheat germ, gluten, wheat gluten, or bran. In preparing foods at home, refer to page 180 for flour substitutions and amounts. Use pastas made with Jerusalem artichoke flour, or rice, barley, beans, or potatoes, instead of wheat. Do not use triticale; it's a wheat hybrid. In selecting breakfast foods, look for cereals that contain no wheat, such as oatmeal and some rice and corn cereals. Try crepes, waffles, and pancakes made with rice flour. Sprinkle vegetables with grated cheese instead of bread crumbs to obtain the au gratin effect. Thicken soups, sauces, and gravies with potato starch, cornstarch, or arrowroot. For desserts, make pie crusts with chopped nuts and oats, wheatless tortes with hazelnuts and eggs, homemade ice creams or sorbets. For breading, use ground nuts, grated cheese, crushed oat, rice, or barley cereals, and/or rye flour or corn meal. For snack foods, use nuts (check to be sure that no wheat products have been added, as in dry-roasted nuts), potato chips, corn chips (if no wheat has been added), and crudités with homemade dip. Instead of bread-based stuffings, use rice or vegetable stuffings.

The Guest with Gout

You don't have to have royalty to dinner to find a guest who has gout. This affliction, often associated with good living and rich foods, is quite common among middle-aged commoners right here in the United States. Attacks can be extremely painful, "the highest pain," according to first-century B.C. Roman statesman and writer Cicero. And though medication is given for gout, diet must also be controlled. The foods that are most likely to be prohibited include:

- Liver, kidneys, sweetbreads, brains, and other organ meats
- Anchovies, sardines, herring, fish roe, caviar
- Meat extracts, consommé, meat stocks and broths, gravies

Foods most often limited to one serving total per day include:

- Meat, fowl, fish, and seafood (except those noted above, which are prohibited)
- Lentils, beans, peas
- Yeast
- Whole grains
- Asparagus, cauliflower, mushrooms, and spinach

Foods that can be served freely to those with gout include:

- Vegetables not listed above and fruits
- Milk, cheese, eggs
- Refined grain products
- Sugar and sweets
- Vegetable soups

Fat is also limited on a gout diet, and liquids, especially water, are to be taken in abundance. If you're entertaining the guest with gout, stick to recipes low in fat (most recipes in this book are), always using the minimum amount of fat called for. Substitute vegetable stocks for meat stocks, and avoid prohibited foods entirely. Serve permitted meat, fish, and fowl in small portions, and avoid the vegetables that are to be limited. Serve a soda or other quick-bread made from refined flour instead of a whole-grain yeast bread. Vegetarian (*V* or *v*) menus and recipes are particularly suitable for the guest with gout, as long as you omit restricted vegetables and whole grains. Many of the kosher menus (*k*), with their emphasis on fish and dairy products, are also very appropriate. As for beverages, tea and coffee are usually permitted, as is alcohol. But because of the necessary high fluid intake, also keep a pitcher of iced water on the table at mealtime.

The Guest with Kidney Stones

Though kidney stones may be tiny—no more than a few millimeters in size—they can cause very great pain. Montaigne termed it "agony." Fortunately, dietary treatment can sometimes prevent recurrence. Your guest's restrictions will depend upon the kind of stones he has had in the past.

If the stones were primarily calcium phosphate, then his intake of foods rich in calcium and phosphorus are probably limited. The foods you should try to avoid when feeding such a guest would include: cheese (except cottage cheese, pot cheese, and hoop cheese), organ meats, fish roe (caviar); game meats; sardines; many green leafy vegetables (beet, mustard, and turnip greens, spinach, collards, chard); dried beans, peas, lentils, and soy beans, rhubarb; whole grains, self-rising flour, oatmeal, brown and wild rice, bran, wheat germ, cereals except rice or corn varieties; packaged cake mixes and desserts made with milk and eggs, including most cakes except angel cake; carbonated drinks; cocoa and chocolate; nuts and peanut butter; seasonings having a calcium or phosphate base. Milk is usually limited to 1 cup per day, but in severe cases may be eliminated entirely. For such guests, those milkless (*Ml*) or milk limited (*B*-low residue) recipes and menus that do not contain any of the above restricted foods will be suitable. Fish, veal, and beef are fine to serve, as are refined grains (white rice, white bread), root vegetables (carrots, potatoes, turnips), and legumes (green beans) and members of the cabbage family (broccoli, cauliflower, Brussels sprouts, etc.). Fruit desserts, many pies and pastries made without milk, and ices and sorbets make excellent finales to meals. Carob can substitute for chocolate and cocoa in such desserts. And popcorn can replace the nuts at cocktail time.

For the guest with kidney stones who is on an alkaline ash diet, you will want to serve plenty of vegetables and fruit, and to limit (though not omit) meats, fish, fowl, eggs, and cereals. This sort of meal is easy to plan even using your usual menus. Just be sure that your first course is vegetarian (EGGPLANT CAVIAR (106), WHOLE ARTICHOKE (162), or STUFFED MUSHROOMS (145) for example), that your main course (it can be meat, fish, or poultry) is served in a way that makes taking small portions easy, that you serve plenty of vegetables and salad on the side, and a potato instead of a grain (rice or pasta, for example). Dessert should be fruit rather than flour-based.

If, on the other hand, your guest is on an acid ash diet, you will have to do just the opposite: emphasize meats, fish, fowl, eggs, and cereals, and limit fruits and vegetables. So you can start with a liver pâté or a fish cocktail, and move on to a meat, fish or fowl main course served with pasta, rice, or kasha. Don't omit the vegetable and salad, but be sure these items can be taken in small quantities. For dessert, think of cakes, pies, or cookies, as well as egg-based dishes such as mousses, Bavarians, meringues, or tortes.

On both alkaline and acid ash diets, milk is usually limited to one pint a day, so avoid serving a cream soup followed by a cheese-filled fish roll, and an ice cream dessert. Try to keep the milk-cheese total for any one meal under one cup per person.

The Lenten (or Friday) Fast Guest

Roman Catholics still give up meat on specified days of Lent, and some, out of habit, on Friday. If your guest is among them, you can serve any of our vegetarian (*v* or *V*) or kosher (*K* or *k*) recipes or menus. Many members of the Greek Orthodox Church observe a number of fast days during the year. Some fast days are meatless; fish and dairy products are permitted. Others are more strict; all meat, fish, poultry, eggs, and dairy products are prohibited. Most Wednesdays and Fridays are meatless and there are major fast periods before Easter and Christmas. Be sure to check with Greek Orthodox guests in advance and then prepare accordingly. On meatless fast days, you can serve any of our kosher (*K* or *k*) or vegetarian (*V* or *v*) recipes or menus. On the strict fast days, stick to our strict vegetarian (*V*) menus and recipes.

The Macrobiotic Dieter

There are ten different macrobiotic diets, based on an interpretation of Zen Buddhism by Ohswara. They range from Diet No. Minus 3, which allows ten percent cereals, thirty percent vegetables, ten percent soups, thirty percent animal products, fifteen percent salads and fruits, and five percent desserts, to the Diet No. 7, which is one hundred percent cereals. The latter diet has been condemned by the AMA Council on Foods and Nutrition as a threat to human health; if followed for prolonged periods of time, it can prove lethal. But if your guest is on it, you can serve a mixture of steamed brown rice, triticale, soy beans, bulgur, or kasha, cooked with nothing added, and served with sea salt or soy sauce on the side. If you are entertaining other guests in addition, this can be served as a side dish for them, accompanying the rest of the meal. For those on the less stringent macrobiotic diets, prepare fish, vegetables, rice, or other grains as a main course, seasoning with sea salt or tamari. Avoid all artificial additives (see the Natural Guest) and heavy spices. Additional seasonings can be added at the table by those who wish them. Our strict vegetarian (*V*) dishes using tofu are suitable for some macrobiotic diets, but check with your guest about seasonings or spices that you plan to use. For dessert, offer fresh fruit, which your guest may or may not eat.

The Mormon Guest

The doctrines, principles, and practices of the Church of Jesus Christ of the Latter-Day Saints include a code of health that counsels against the use of tobacco, alcoholic beverages, tea, and coffee. The use of wholesome herbs, grains, and fruits are emphasized. If practicing Mormons are invited to your home, have a selection of non-alcoholic and non-caffeinated beverages available before and during the meal and at cocktail parties (see beverage section, pages 545 to 552). Stress whole grains and fresh fruits and vegetables in your meal planning. Our cholesterol conscious (*LCh*), vegetarian (*V* and *v*), and kosher (*K* and *k*) menus would be suitable for Mormon guests, who tend to avoid red meat.

The Muslim Guest

The Koran, like the Bible, sets down some basic dietary laws. Thus, observant followers of Islam abstain from eating "swine" products (pork, bacon, ham, lard, etc.), and eat only meat which has been properly slaughtered and drained of blood. Kosher meat and poultry fulfill these requirements and are appropriate for serving the Muslim guest. If kosher meat is unavailable, stick to our non-meat menus and recipes (*V, v, K, k,* and some *LC, LCh, D, LS, and P*). Alcohol is also avoided by strict Muslims, so you will want to offer some alternatives, such as those found in the beverage recipe section (pages 545 to 552). If wine is called for in a recipe, you can use the bland (*B*) or low-sugar (*D*) alternatives, substituting stock, juices, or water for the wine or liqueur.

The Natural Guest

To some people, eating "naturally" is very nearly a religion; the words "chemical" or "additive" cause them to shudder. And, if you studied the plethora of strange additives turning up in foods today, you'd probably shudder, too. Still, "natural" doesn't necessarily mean safe. The word on a food package is legally meaningless. And even foods that are "natural" and "additive-free," aren't necessarily harmless. "Natural" eggs, butter, and cream have been implicated in the development of heart disease, "natural" sugar in tooth decay and degenerative diseases, spinach in infant illness. Milk, salt, and liver can cause illness when consumed in excess. And some foods in their natural state are poisonous in any dose (varieties of mushrooms and raw soybeans, for example).

Just as "natural" isn't always safe, neither are all chemicals automatically harmful. Acetone, acetaldehyde, and ethyl caproate are all natural components of the innocent strawberry. Some chemicals are beneficial, for instance ascorbic acid (vitamin C). Some, like arsenic, are lethal. Others are extracted from natural sources: sodium caseinate from milk, lecithin from soybeans. Still others are synthesized in the laboratory from a wide variety of organic and inorganic materials. Some 200,000 new chemicals appear in the scientific literature each year; ever-growing numbers are being added to foods as preservatives and to improve texture, taste, or color. Some of these additives have already been proven hazardous to human health; still others have not yet been well-tested enough, according to some authorities, to be declared safe for human consumption. And while these controversies continue, millions of us consume these chemicals daily.

For the guest who isn't willing to take the risk that the chemicals in his or her food are the safe ones, confine your shopping to the produce department (fresh fruit and vegetables), the butcher and the fish market (avoiding meat and fish that have been smoked, or otherwise preserved), and the dairy case (but watch out for chemical preservatives in butter, cream, and cheeses).

A visit to the frozen foods section of your supermarket is possible, as long as you stick to fruits, vegetables, ice creams, and ice milks that are additive-and-preservative free. Fresh nuts are fine, also, as are cereals and grains in their dry state: oats, bulgur, triticale, brown rice, beans, peas, buckwheat groats (kasha), and so on. Most ready-to-serve cereals, both cold and hot, are packed with additives, so read labels carefully. And don't let a "no preservatives" banner fool you; the product in question may contain stabilizers, colorings, and flavorings. An "all natural" product may be free of chemical additives, yet contain sugar or honey, which to many "natural" guests are as unacceptable as chemicals. "Natural flavor" doesn't mean that the product doesn't contain unnatural ingredients. In general, if you discover an ingredient in a product that you can't pronounce or identify, you're probably better off not serving it to a natural guest.

The health food store is a good source of additive-free foods, but even there you've got to read your labels. You'll probably be able to find some excellent breads, soy sauce (tamari), margarine, cereals, dried fruit, salad dressings, fruit and nut butters, rice, and other grains processed or prepared without chemical additives.

But even if you go back-to-basics in your marketing, you still aren't home-free. In the kitchen, you've got to be extra careful to scrub pesticides and other chemicals from fruits and vegetables. Use either dish detergent or vinegar on your produce, rinsing carefully. (This is a practice which some medical authorities believe should be adopted by everyone.) You will also have to put to temporary rest many of your usual condiments, including ketchup, bouillon cubes, Worcestershire sauce, and seasoning salts, many of which contain unnatural additives.

Virtually all of the recipes in this book are natural enough for your natural guest. The exceptions are those few recipes that call for Worcestershire sauce or mayonnaise. Omit these ingredients, or substitute their "natural" counterparts, which are available in health food stores or in the health food section of your supermarket.

The Pregnant Guest

The old adage is true: the pregnant woman is eating for two. If she's your guest for a meal or weekend, be sure she has plenty of nutritious foods to choose from. Virtually all the *Special Guest* recipes are good for the pregnant guest with the exception of the very occasional recipe that is high in sugar and those designed for bland diets containing no roughage. Though the pregnant woman should avoid junk food and the empty calories of sugar, she can eat almost anything else that doesn't disagree with her. But the more nutritious the food, the better. Lean toward whole grains in baking and in breakfast foods. Have skim milk on hand; she doesn't need the added calories of milk fat. Fried and fatty foods may also provide more calories as compared to nutritive value than are necessary. Fish and poultry are particularly good main courses, and vegetables, salads, and fruits are valuable accompaniments, rich in vitamins, minerals, and fiber.

Though salt is rarely restricted in pregnancy these days, alcohol most certainly is. So have a supply of juices and other nutritious non-alcoholic beverages at the bar (see beverage recipes pages 545 to 552). Caffeine, too, may be limited, so serve non-caffeinated beverages instead of, or as well as, coffee.

The Nursing Mother Guest

Because the nursing mother is supplying food to her child as well as nutrients for her own body, she needs a highly nutritious diet. If you're entertaining her, you should have few problems in planning the menu (most *Special Guest* recipes are suitable) as long as you check in advance to see if there are any specific foods that seem to bother her or baby. Often gassy foods such as cabbage or Brussels sprouts do. And alcohol may be limited. So, have a selection of non-alcoholic beverages available (see beverage recipes). The nursing mother needs plenty of fluids. Coffee and tea may also cause distress, so have some alternatives on hand (see beverage recipes pages 545 to 552).

Guests With Teeth and Gum Problems

Though we usually associate loss of teeth and severe gum problems with old age, many millions of Americans have lost all of their teeth by the age of thirty-five. Millions more have temporary or permanent teeth or gum problems that prevent them from munching on corn-on-the-cob or raw fruits and vegetables. For those guests, think soft. *Al dente* pastas and crisp, stir-fried vegetables will prove inedible, as will any but the most tender cuts of beef and lamb. Hard breadsticks will languish, but soft Parkerhouse rolls won't. Fresh fruit salad will be left on plates; poached fruit will be eaten.

For such guests, most of our bland (*B*) recipes will be suitable.

However, don't forget that onions, garlic, and spices can be added to these recipes without concern, whenever desired. Soft whole grain breads and cereals can also be served, as can any vegetable which has been cooked until soft. Because variations in texture will be lacking for these dieters, concentrate instead on variations in flavor and color.

Everybody is Coming to Dinner

It's Aunt Edna's birthday, and you're planning a big dinner party in her honor. You've got to invite Uncle Fred, her adoring younger brother, high blood pressure and all, and, of course, Cousin Sara, with her diabetes. And how could you leave out your nephew and his new wife, who just converted him to vegetarianism? Short of retreating to an expensive restaurant (let the chef worry!) there seems to be no solution to the dizzying dilemma of how to feed your loveable but all-of-a-different-kind family.

Holiday and Celebration Basics

How can you please all of your guests all of the time no matter how many different diets they may be following? The trick is having something for everyone and freedom of choice. Have two or three different dips with the crudités; butter *and* margarine *and* vegetarian spread for the bread. If cocktails are being served, offer not only a selection of mixers, but of tasty non-alcoholic beverages as well. Such old standbys as tomato or vegetable juice, seltzer, and mineral waters have never been more popular.

At dinner, pass the trimmings separately: the gravy for the roast, the slivered almonds for the green beans, the dressing for the salad, the whipped cream for the dessert. The result? Guests who can't eat gravy won't have to surreptitiously brush it off their beef, and those who can't tolerate whipped cream won't have to dig beneath it to retrieve a few bites of the baked pear. When you can, offer alternatives, too, like lemon wedges and vinegar for the salad, sliced water chestnuts for the green beans, and ANGEL CREAM (543) for the pears.

Probably the single most useful serving device when entertaining a crowd of special guests is a salad bar. We're not talking about the kind you find in some restaurants that overflow with oily dressings and salads, but one that abounds with garden fresh raw vegetables, and a choice of dressings and toppings.

A similar opportunity for self-selection should come at the end of the meal. In addition to brewed coffee, offer caffeine-free coffee (preferably brewed), linden tea, or some other hot beverages (Recipes 552–556). A choice of sweeteners and coffee lighteners will also be appreciated: aspartame for diabetics, non-dairy creamers for vegetarians, skim milk for the dieter. If you can't resist serving a gooey dessert, fill a bowl with a variety of ripe, fresh fruit as well. Be sure to include a banana for the bland dieter, and something less caloric for the weight-watcher.

Questions to Ask Holiday Guests

1. *Do you allow a little leeway in your diet on the holidays, or at a party?* Most dieters who stray from the straight and restricted at all choose to do so at parties and celebrations. If your guest does, follow the requirements for his diet, but serve a few added goodies on the side. That way, he can choose to add them to his meal or not, as the holiday spirit moves him. If he doesn't like to, or, because of a serious medical condition, can't stray no matter what the occasion, try to stay away from the treats that will tempt. Follow the directions in the appropriate chapter.

(You will, of course, want to ask your dieting guests the questions listed in the chapters that apply to them.)

Shopping for the Holidays

How you shop for a holiday or celebration at which you expect one or more guests on special diets, depends upon their individual dietary needs. Read the appropriate chapters carefully before sallying forth with shopping list in hand. (If you're shopping for three or more different diets, perhaps you should have this book in the other hand.) Because our holiday recipes are geared for most diets, things shouldn't get too complicated or confusing.

Holiday and Celebration Cooking

In cooking for a variety of guests, use the preparation methods and ingredients suitable for the most extremely restricted of your guests. If you have low-cholesterol and calorie-counting dieters coming to dinner, use skim milks and low-fat cheeses in your recipes. If strict vegetarians are invited, cook the vegetables with a non-dairy (pareve) margarine. If Pritikin dieters are expected, sauté the onions in wine or stock, instead of oil. For diabetics, use the minimum amounts of sweetening agents called for in recipes and omit all sugar.

For tips on cooking for each special diet, see the appropriate chapter.

Holiday and Celebration Menus

Our mix and match holiday menus are the most expansive in the book, encompassing as many diets as possible, while trying to retain the festive atmosphere holidays and celebrations merit. And because they are festive, they are a little less stringent than most other of our menus. Of course, you can vary any menu according to the problem guests you're entertaining. It's unlikely that you will use every dish on these menus unless you've hit the jackpot and have invited guests on every one of our special diets. In most cases you will use the meat soup *or* the vegetarian soup, the Rice-Stuffed Phyllo Cumberland *or* the Stuffed Shoulder of Spring Lamb Cumberland, the Juice-Poached Fruit *or* the Fluffy Apple Mousse. Just check the diet codes on the recipes and select the appropriate dishes for your guest list.

In addition to the menus in this chapter, you'll find that many other menus in the book are adaptable to feeding a mixed crowd. Select a menu that will meet the needs of one of your special guests, and build from there. For example, if one of your guests is on a low-cholesterol diet, select a low-cholesterol (*LCh*) menu that you like. Then check the recipes on the menu to see if all are appropriate for your diabetic guest. In many cases, there will be plenty of overlap. If the given dessert isn't labeled (*D*) for diabetics, then substitute one that is, as long as it is also appropriate for your low-cholesterol dieter. If you're entertaining yet another problem guest, say a calorie counter, go over the menu once more. You may find that no additional changes are necessary. If something on the menu does, however, turn out to be unsuitable for your calorie-conscious guest, substitute again. This time, be sure the substitute recipe will be suitable for the low-cholesterol, diabetic, and the calorie-counting guest. Now that wasn't so difficult, was it?

Holiday Menus

Easter Brunch
Fresh Strawberries/ Sliced Bananas/ Sliced Cooked Peaches
Fruited Yogurt (428)
Orange Muesli (35)
Orange Almond Semolina (449)
Eggs Florentine (46)
Yolkless Florentine (47)
Broccoli Florentine (48)
Peel-and-Eat Easter Eggs
Whole Wheat Raisin Bread (21), *Margarine or Apple Butter*
White and Wheat Toast
Hot Cross Buns (13)

Easter Dinner
Fresh Steamed Asparagus (397), *Choice of Dressings*
Stuffed Shoulder of Spring Lamb, Cumberland (327)
Rice-Stuffed Phyllo Cumberland (353)
Minted Green Beans (386)
Tomato Aspic (186)
Salad Bar (228)
Easter Egg Ices (458)
Assorted Cookie Thins (524 to 531)
Shreddies (522)

Passover
Matzo
Gefilte Fish en Gelée (171), *Homemade Horseradish* (274)
Vegetarian Chopped Liver (127)
Chicken Soup, Matzo Balls (100)
Hot Garlic Borscht (70), *Boiled Potatoes*
or

Cabbage Borscht (73)
Roast Apricot Turkey (316), *Apricot-Matzah Stuffing* (319)
Apricot-Matzah Gâteau (343)
Tsimmes (395)
Steamed Lemon Broccoli (397)
Salad Bar (228)
Juice-Poached Fruit (478)
Fluffy Apple Mousse (456)
Date-Nut Bars (514)
Plain Sponge Cake

Shavuot
No-Yolk Challah (4)
Cool Fruit Soup (76)
Chilled Vegetable Juice
Selection of Blintzes and/or Crepes (36 through 45)
Sweet-and-Sour Beets (190)
Viva la Salad Bar (249)
Fruited Cheesecake (442)
Date-Nut Pie (536)
Apple-Peach Mold (436)

July-Fourth Barbecue
Tomato Juice Coolers, Lemon and Lime Wedges
Gazpacho (77)
Grilled Herbed Eggplant (411)
Grilled Stuffed Trout (409)
Grilled Fish Steaks (406)
Macaroni a la Russe (230)
Green Rice Salad (235)
Salad Bar (228)
Fresh Fruit Salad (475) *in Melon Basket*
Juice-Poached Fruit (478)
Patriots' Pie (537)
Angel Cake Slices

Jewish New Year
Raisin Challah (6)
Gefilte Fish en Gelée (171)
Vegetarian Chopped Liver (127)
Veal Roast, Minted Cranberry Glaze (330)
Minted Cranberry-Nut Loaf (352)
Tsimmes (395)

Cabbage au Pecans (377)
Steamed Shoestring Vegetables (397)
Date-Nut Crescents (515)
Nut Crescents (516)
Apricot Mousse (438)

Yom Kippur Eve
No-Yolk Challah (4)
Holiday Pâté (111), *Melba Squares* (16) *and Zucchini Rounds* (383)
Chicken Soup, Chicken Kreplach (99)
Cream of Hazelnut Soup (87), *Vegetarian Kreplach* (99)
Chicken Breasts with Mushrooms (301)
Tsimmes (395)
Green Beans au Gratin (385)
Tomato Aspic (186)
Apricot-Banana Mold (437)
Assorted Shreddies (522) *and Cookie Thins* (524 to 531)
Nature-Sweetened Apple Strudel (542)

Sukkot
Cranberry Challah (5)
Hot Apple-Wine Soup (66)
Mushroom-Onion Soup (91)
Stuffed Cabbage a la Cranberries (326)
Stuffed Vegetarian Cabbage a la Cranberries (354)
Baby Belgian Carrots (378)
Salad Bar (228)
Juice-Poached Harvest Fruit (478)
Apple Pies (535)

Thanksgiving Dinner
Mushroom-Onion Soup (91)
Roast Turkey with Apple-Champagne Sauce (315)
Chestnut-Apple Stuffing (320)
Mock Turkey in Phyllo (350)
Baby Belgian Carrots (378)
Brussels Sprouts with Chestnuts (376)
Sweet-and-Sour Onions (390)
Apple-Stuffed Yams (360)
Pumpkin Chiffon Pie (539)
Juice-Poached Fruit (478)
Cranberry Crunchies (513) and *Lemon Cookie Thins* (530)

Christmas Eve Supper
Veal and Turkey Pie (331)
Flageolets au Gratin (348)
Sweet-and-Sour Onions (390)
Tomato-Avocado Aspic (187)
Herbed Vegetable Salad (198)
Wheat and White French Breads (9), *Whipped Margarine*
Baked Apples (479)
Date-Nut Pie (536)
Fluffy Apple Mousse (456)

Christmas Brunch
Macédoine of Winter Fruit (476)
Sliced Bananas/ Sliced Peaches
French Toast with Brandied Apples (62)
Savory French Toast (64), *Sautéed Onions*
Curried Salmon Kedgeree (285)/ *Bland Salmon Kedgeree* (286)
Sliced Tomatoes
Irish Soda Bread (14), *Choice of Spreads*
Cranberry-Nut Muffins (24)

Christmas Dinner
Holiday Pâté (111), *Melba Squares* (16) *and Zucchini Rounds* (383)
Hot Avocado-Tomato Puree (67)
Roast Turkey with Apple-Prune Stuffing (317)
Glazed Apple Rings (432)
Glazed Chestnuts (433)
Apple-Prune Stuffed Phyllo Log (342)
Green Beans au Gratin (385)
Brussels Spouts with Chestnuts (376)
Sweet-and-Sour Onions (390)
Jersey Pepper Relish (275)
Holiday Fruitcake (507)
Apricot Mousse (438)
Lemon Cookie Thins (530)
Cranberry Crunchies (513)
Orange-Almond Semolina (449)
Hot Mulled Cider (554)
Hot Mulled Wine (555)

New Year's Buffet
Hot Mulled Wine (555)
Hot Mulled Cider (554)

or

Hot Wassail Bowl with Baked Apples (558)
Lo-Cheese Fondue (112)
  French Bread (9)
  Apple Slices
  Crisp-Tender Vegetables (383)
Holiday Pâté (111), *Melba Squares* (16) *and Vegetable Chips* (383)
Salmon Pâté (121), *Assorted Crackers*
Chilean Fish Stew (278)
Chilean Vegetable Stew (346)
Five-Grain Pilaf (369)
Fluffy White Rice (370)
Salad Bar (228)
Basket of Mixed Breads
Cranberry Crunchies (513)
Choice of Carrot Cakes (503 to 505)
Fluffy Apple Mousse (456)

Party Luncheon
Chilled Gazpacho (77)
Tomato Juice, Lemon Wedge
Fish Paprikash (282)
Tofu Paprikash (356)
Cottage Cheese and Noodle Bake (333)
Salad Bar (228)
Mixed Breads, Assorted Spreads
Fresh Fruit
Farina-Banana Pudding (444)
Carob Party Cake (502)

Dinner Party
Mushroom Rollups (139)
Herring Tidbits with Chopped Apple
Assorted Dips (103 to 125) *and Crudités* (383)
Seasoned Popcorn (131)
Herbed Fish Steaks (280), *Choice of Sauces*
Grilled Herbed Eggplant Steaks (411), *Choice of Sauces*
Five-Grain Pilaf (369)
Fluffy White Rice (370)
Medley of Steamed Vegetables (397)
Salad Bar (228)
Basket of Breads, Assorted Spreads
Fresh Fruit Bowl, Nuts in Shells

Apricot Mousse (438)
Shreddies (522) *and Lemon Cookie Thins* (530)

Cocktail Party
Seasoned Popcorn (131)
Unsalted Nuts and Raisins
Pretzel Sticks
Lo-Cheese Spread (113)
Assorted Dips (103 to 125), *Crudités* (383) *and Crackers*
Eggplant Caviar (106), *Dark Bread*
Holiday Pâté (111), *Crackers*
Selection of Stuffed Mushrooms (145 to 149)
Salmon Mousse II (288)
Party Punch (564)

Solving the Problem Guest and Glossary

The Special Guest Cookbook—dedicated to the proposition that no guest need go home hungry—is a different kind of cookbook. And its recipes, from concept to format—because they're designed to meet a dizzying range of dietary requirements—are different, too. Even the practiced chef will need to do a little preparatory reading before heading for the chopping board.

First, we suggest that you acquaint yourself thoroughly with the individual dietary guidelines of the problem guest you are about to entertain by reading the appropriate chapters. Then, familiarize yourself with the following symbols, which will appear in recipes throughout the book, indicating the diets each recipe is suitable for, and the changes that might be necessary for a particular diet:

Weight Conscious	LC
Cholesterol Cautious	LCh
Low Sugar (Diabetic/ Hypoglycemic)	D
Low Salt	LS
Vegetarian, Strict	V
Vegetarian, Ovolacto	v
Pritikin (low salt, no fat, no sugar)	P
Milkless	M1
Kosher, Strict	K
Kosher, Lenient	k
Bland (Colitis, Ulcer Gall-bladder, etc.)	B

The recipes and menus for these diets lean towards the stringent because in most cases that's safest. But as dietary needs vary from dieter to dieter, so can the recipes. Your guest may be on only a mildly salt-restricted diet, for instance. In that case, though we've suggested removing the high-sodium celery from the holiday stuffing when serving low-salt dieters, you can leave it in.

Of course, what's good for the goose on a bland diet, may very well spell dietary disaster for the gander who's watching her calories. And if you're going to have both these problem guests to a single dinner party—and don't relish the idea of preparing separate meals for each—some accommodations must be made. That's why we've made the Special Guest recipes so versatile. They are easily adaptable to several special diets. When a recipe must be adapted for a particular diet by a change of ingredients or quantities, such a change will be noted within parentheses. Variations, whether for varying dietary requirements, or just for variety's sake, will follow the basic recipe.

In all of the recipes, yields and cooking times are approximate, as appetites, ingredients, oven temperatures, and tastes can vary.

Words in **bold face** within a recipe are defined and explained in our Recipe Glossary, as are several other ingredients and terms. Read through the glossary *before* you start cooking, in order to avoid mid-recipe confusion and delay.

Recipes are numbered for easy reference and when they are referred to in other recipes, they are CAPITALIZED and followed by the appropriate reference number.

Recipe Glossary

Additive. Many people, including those not on special diets, prefer to avoid as many artificial additives as possible. If you or your guests are among these people, read labels carefully for such ingredients as artificial flavors, colors, stabilizers, emulsifiers, thickeners, preservatives, and so on (see "The Natural Guest" in Chapter Ten).

P: Whenever possible, use foods that contain no additives.

V and *v:* Avoid using products containing additives of questionable origin, e.g.: natural flavorings, monoglycerides, diglycerides, and stabilizers. The "pareve" label on products certified kosher indicates that the additives are not derived from milk or meat products.

K and *k:* Using only products with kosher certification assures that any additives are kosher.

Apple Juice. More flavorful, and certainly more nutritious than the traditional water-sugar syrup combinations used in cakes, desserts, fruits, and sauces, apple juice makes a frequent appearance in Special Guest recipes.

D: Use may be limited.

Apple Juice Concentrate (Frozen concentrated apple juice, unsweetened). A very nearly perfect sweetener, it's natural, doesn't send blood sugar soaring as quickly as table sugar, glucose, corn syrup, or honey do, and is lower in calories than these refined sweeteners. Apple juice concentrate can replace sugar ounce for ounce in many recipes, though occasionally we add 1 tablespoon of sugar or fructose for a sharper sweetness, or to help egg whites retain their stiffness. When it's called for in recipes, use it undiluted, and defrosted.

D: Use may be limited.

Aspartame (APM). This new artificial sweetener may bring about a revolution in the diet-foods industry. Marketed as Nutrasweet™ or Equal ™by G.D. Searle and Co., it is likely to pick up a good part of the sweetening trade formerly held by saccharine. According to the manufacturers, it has been shown in testing to have no adverse effects. Since it is a protein compound rather than a carbohydrate (as is sorbitol which is now widely used to replace saccharine), it is ideal for use by diabetics and hypoglycemics. Its very low calorie count makes it suitable for use in weight-loss diets. Though it is not stable in cooking, it can be used in beverages and added to uncooked foods as well as stirred into foods after cooking. *Caution:* it should not be used for those on low-phenylalanine (PKU) diets. You may want to check with your guest in advance about use of APM.

LC: Useful.

D: Useful.

Baking Powder. This baking aid is high in sodium (salt). Therefore, we suggest the use of low-sodium baking powders for salt-restricted baking. Use 1½ times the amount called for of ordinary double-acting baking powder. If low-sodium baking powder is called for and you wish to substitute double-acting, reduce the quantity by one-third.

LS: Use low-sodium baking powder.

P: Use baking powder that does not contain aluminum.

Baking Soda. Even higher in sodium than baking powder, of which it is an ingredient, baking soda is prohibited on salt-restricted diets.

LS: Use of baking soda is prohibited.

Bread, Bread Crumbs, Breadsticks, and Crackers. Whole-grain baked goods are packed with flavor, fiber, and nutrition. We highly recommend their use. Aside from flours, breads contain other ingredients, many of which may be restricted or prohibited on special diets. Read lists of ingredients carefully to screen the product for a particular diet. The type of bread or bread crumbs used in a particular recipe will depend upon the diet for which it is being prepared. When bread crumbs are called for, do not use commercial crumbs. Recipes are calculated for fresh bread (unless otherwise stated) that has been crumbed in the blender or processor.

LC: Use breadstuffs in limited quantities; favor those that are high in fiber (whole grains, bran), and low in fats, sugars, nuts.

LCh: Use breads made with polyunsaturated fats (liquid vegetable oils), rather than with partially or totally hydrogenated vegetable fats or animal fats, or use breads that are completely fat free. "Vegetable shortening" usually means hydrogenated (hardened) fat.

D: Use breads made without refined sweeteners, including sugar (white, brown, raw, or turbinado), corn syrup, honey, dextrose, glucose, fructose, and molasses (see Chapter Three for additional list).

LS: Use breads made without ordinary baking powder, baking soda, or any other form of sodium, such as sodium propionate, sodium benzoate, sodium alginate, sodium citrate, sodium acetate, disodium phosphate, monosodium glutamate, and, of course, table salt.

V: Use breadstuffs made without animal products: milk or milk derivatives, such as lactose, casein, whey, or butter, eggs, lard or other animal fats, gelatins, animal-based monoglycerides and/or diglycerides. The word *pareve* on the label assures the absence of meat and dairy by-products, but not of eggs.

v: Breads used may contain butter, eggs, milk, or other dairy products, but not lard, chicken fat, or other meat by-products.

P: Use whole grain breads whenever possible; all breads must be made without refined sugars (see Chapter Three, "Low-Sugar Shopping"), shortening of any kind (oil, margarine, lard, etc.), and contain little or no salt. Read list of ingredients carefully, and try to avoid *additives.* Pritikin himself puts out an excellent bread marketed in health-food stores that is designed for those following his diet.

Ml: Use breads made without dairy products, such as milk, cheese, butter, yogurt, and sour cream. Look for the word "pareve."

K and *k:* Use breads carrying one of the approved kosher symbols (see Chapter Eight), or purchase bread from a baker certified kosher by a rabbi acceptable to your guest. With meat meals, bread should be pareve.

B: Use breads made without whole grain flours, wheat germ, or bran, and with only moderate amounts of fats and/or sugars. Some bland dieters may be permitted fine-textured or regular whole grain breads.

Butter. Because it is high in fat, cholesterol, and calories, butter isn't often recommended for special diets, though butter enthusiasts will assert that it is unbeatable in certain dishes and at the table. When we do use butter in Special Guest recipes, we use it sweet and unsalted, and preferably without preservatives or other additives. At the table, its fat, cholesterol, and calorie contents can be reduced by whipping 2 parts butter with 1 part water in processor or blender until the mixture is light and fluffy.

LC: Use sparingly because of high calorie count.

LCh: Use rarely, if at all, because of high cholesterol content.

D: Use sparingly because of calories, fat, and cholesterol.

LS: Use unsalted butter.

P and *V:* Use of butter is prohibited.

Ml: Use may be prohibited.

K and *k:* Use butter with kosher certification, or with no additives.

B: Use of butter may be limited.

Buttermilk. There's buttermilk and there's buttermilk. And for many special diets, the best buttermilk is the low-fat variety. Check nutrition labels for milk that is no more than 1 to 1.5% milk fat. Otherwise, you may end up with high-fat buttermilk.

LC, LCh, D, B: Use low-fat buttermilk.

LS: Use low-fat buttermilk with no added salt. Some salt-restricted dieters may be permitted limited amounts of salted buttermilk.

P: Use "non-fat" buttermilk or buttermilk with no more than 1 percent fat.

V: Use of buttermilk is prohibited.

Ml: Use of buttermilk may be prohibited.

Cake and Cookies. Same rules apply as for breads.

Cottage Cheese. Not the diet miracle many believe it to be, regular cottage cheese contains as many calories as ice cream. Low-fat cottage cheese, preferably containing 1 percent fat or less, is the cheese of choice for many special diets.

LC, LCh, D: Use low-fat cottage cheese.

LS: Use low-fat cottage cheese. Most salt-restricted dieters must limit daily consumption of cottage cheese and other dairy products; those under moderate to severe restrictions are limited to low-sodium or unsalted cottage cheese.

v, K, k: Use cottage cheese labeled with an accepted kosher symbol (see Chapter Eight.)

P: Use 100 percent uncreamed cottage cheese, such as dry curd cottage cheese or hoop cheese.

B: Use low-fat cottage cheese; use of dairy products may be limited.

Cheese, hard. High in both fat and salt, these cheeses are avoided in many special diet recipes, except in small quantities. In general, it is wise to use cheeses with a fat (milkfat or butterfat) content less than 20 percent, though many of us can afford to make exceptions once in a while. Low-fat (as low as 4 or 5 percent fat), low-cholesterol, and low-salt cheeses are becoming easier to find. Keep in mind that: 1) low-cholesterol cheeses use oils to replace some of the fat, and are not usually lower in calories than high-cholesterol cheeses, and 2) part-skim milk cheeses are not always low in fat.

LC: Use low-fat cheese in moderation; avoid using high-fat cheeses except in small quantities, as when sprinkling on a bit of grated cheese.

LCh: Use only low-cholesterol cheeses in small quantities.

D: Use low-fat and low-salt cheeses whenever possible.

LS: Use low-fat cheeses when possible. Most salt-restricted dieters must limit daily consumption of cheese and other dairy products; those on moderately to severely restricted diets are limited to using low-sodium or unsalted hard cheeses.

V: Use of all cheese is prohibited.

v: Use all cheeses, except those containing meat or fish; some vegetarians may only eat cheese made without animal derivatives, (for example, rennet). Find these in health food stores, or use kosher cheeses.

P: Use only sapsago, or "green cheese." One must acquire a taste for this pungent cheese.

Ml: Use of cheese may be prohibited.

K: use only kosher cheeses.

k: Use kosher cheese if guest requests, otherwise use any cheese made without meat.

B: Use mild American or mild Swiss cheese; some bland dieters may be permitted other cheeses. Other bland dieters may be allowed only limited quantities of dairy products.

Crackers. See Bread.

Eggs. A subject of heated controversy, eggs stubbornly refuse to get out of the kitchen. Whenever possible, using the American Heart Association's Prudent Diet Guidelines, we've avoided the use of egg yolks in our recipes. In most cases, two egg whites are used to replace one whole egg. If a guest is not specifically restricted, use your discretion when cooking with eggs.

LC: Use yolks sparingly; yolks have most of the calories.

LCh and *D:* Use yolks sparingly, yolks have all of the cholesterol.

LS: Use eggs sparingly, both whites and yolks. Many salt-restricted dieters must limit consumption of eggs to one daily or three per week. Eggs, especially the whites, are naturally high in sodium.

V: Use of eggs is prohibited.

v: Some vegetarians use dairy products, but no eggs.

P: Use only egg whites.

B: Use yolks sparingly.

Flour. Nutritionally speaking, it is wise to use whole grain flours in baking. When using white wheat flour, we recommend the unbleached variety. When flour type is not specified in a recipe, you may use all white, all whole wheat, or any combination of the wide variety of flours available in your supermarket or health food store (see our flour substitution table). Most special diets permit a wide freedom of choice, with these exceptions:

P: Use of whole grains is preferred; use of wheat germ prohibited.

B: Use of whole grains and coarse textured flours is often prohibited.

Fructose. This fruit sugar has no magical properties, but it does have slightly more sweetening power per teaspoon, and thus per calorie, than does regular table sugar. Therefore you may use slightly less of it than you would use of sugar in your favorite recipes. Special diet guidelines:

LC: Use fructose only in small amounts.

D: Use of fructose may be prohibited, or permitted in very small amounts.

P: Use of fructose is prohibited.

Fruit: We recommend using fresh fruit in recipes unless otherwise indicated. If you wish to substitute, use unsweetened frozen or unsweetened canned, packed in water or juice. Almost everyone on your guest list can enjoy fruit prepared in any manner, with these exceptions:

LC: Use high-calorie fruits sparingly.

D: Use dried fruits (raisins, dates, prunes, etc.), and other fruits with concentrated sweetness sparingly.

P: Use of avocados is prohibited; use dried and other fruits with concentrated sweetness sparingly.

B: Tolerances vary widely, depending on the individual and/or the stage of convalescence (see Chapter Nine); many bland dieters are allowed skinless fruits cooked until very soft. Others may only have pureed cooked fruit. Still others can have selected raw fruits.

Gelatin. Use unflavored, unsweetened gelatin.

V and *v:* Use gelatin of vegetable, not animal origin.

K and *k:* Use gelatin that is certified kosher (see Chapter Eight).

Herbs and Spices. The best way to enhance food being prepared for most special diets is to add herbs and spices. Use them freely. Dried herbs and spices may be used in all recipes, unless otherwise specified. Fresh parsley is called for in all recipes. If other fresh herbs are available, however, by all means use them to taste.

LS: Do not use seasoned salts, vegetable salts (celery, onion, or garlic), flavor enhancers (such as Accent, monosodium glutamate, or MSG), celery, onion, or parsley flakes.

P: Use white pepper instead of black.

B: Tolerances to spices and herbs vary according to the individual. Most commonly prohibited are black and chili pepper, mustard seed, cloves, and nutmeg.

Hoop Cheese. Recommended by Pritikin, this whey-based cheese is wonderfully creamy and tasty. Use it as a low-fat, low-salt substitute for cottage cheese, pot cheese, or ricotta.

V: Use of all cheese is prohibited.

Ml: Use of hoop cheese may be prohibited.

Lemon Juice and Lime Juice. These excellent flavor-suppliers are very useful in special diet cooking, particularly for low-salt and low-calorie dieters. Use only freshly squeezed juices.

Margarine. Contrary to popular belief, it's not the perfect substitute for butter. High in fat, and often containing several additives, margarine nevertheless has its place in special diet cooking.

LC: Use the smallest amount of any kind of shortening called for. Diet-style margarine is not made for cooking, and best used only as a spread.

LCh and *D:* Use margarine with a high polyunsaturated-to-saturated fat ratio. Look for 4 to 2 ratio or better on nutrition label. Use of polyunsaturated oil is preferable, when appropriate.

LS: Use unsalted margarine, preferably with a high ratio of polyunsaturated to saturated fats.

V and *Ml:* Use margarine labeled *pareve,* meaning it contains no dairy or meat products.

v: Use any margarine with kosher certification.

P: No margarine (or fat of any kind) is permitted.

K and *k:* Use any margarine certified kosher. With meat meals, use only pareve margarine.

B: Use only limited amounts of margarine.

Mayonnaise. Commercial mayonnaises contain eggs, sugar, and salt, and are therefore unsuitable for several special diets. Mayonnaises made without these ingredients are available in health food stores, and, increasingly, in supermarkets.

LC: Use any mayonnaise in very limited quantities or use SOYO-NAISE (264).

LCh: Use commercial mayonnaise in very limited quantities, or use yolkless mayonnaise, or SOYO-NAISE.

D: Use mayonnaise made without sugar or honey; use in limited quantities.

LS: Use mayonnaise made without salt.

V: Use of mayonnaise made with eggs not permitted; use SOYO-NAISE.

P: Use SOYO-NAISE or other mayonnaise-like product made without oil, yolks, sugar, and salt.

K and *k:* Use only mayonnaise with kosher certification.

B: Use in limited amounts mayonnaise made without mustard and pepper.

Milk. Recipes in this book almost invariably call for skim or evaporated skimmed milk. For most special diets these are preferable to the popular low-fat (2 percent fat, 99 percent fat free, and so on) milks and to whole milk. In general, the American Heart Association recommends the lower fat and skimmed milks for everyone.

LC, LCh, P: Use skim, evaporated skim, or instant non-fat dry milk.

D: Use of milk may be limited due to milk sugar content; use low-fat milks.

LS: Use low-fat and skim milks when possible; many salt-restricted dieters must limit daily consumption of milk and other dairy products; those under severe restriction are limited to low-sodium milk.

V: Use of milk is prohibited.

Ml: Use of milk is prohibited or limited.

B: Use low-fat, skim, evaporated skimmed, or instant non-fat dry milk; use of dairy products may be limited.

Non-Stick. SilverStone™-lined cookware is excellent for special diet food preparation because it allows fats to be reduced or eliminated in many cooking procedures. The use of a non-stick spray further enhances the qualities of this cookware. When our recipes call for non-stick pans, use them if you have them, with a non-stick spray, except as noted below. If you don't have non-stick pans, use a non-stick spray on your regular pans.

v: Use only sprays labeled kosher, dairy, or pareve.

V and *Ml:* Use only sprays labeled both kosher and pareve.

K and *k:* Use sprays with kosher certification; for meat meals, use only sprays labeled pareve.

P: Using non-stick cookware is virtually a necessity because non-stick sprays—as well as shortening of all kinds—are prohibited.

Oats. Use rolled oats or slow-cooking oats, uncooked, in recipes calling for oats. In a pinch, you can substitute quick-cooking oats, but the results will not be quite the same.

B: In many cases use of oats is prohibited.

Oil. Recommended in many special diets because it is higher in polyunsaturated fats than are butter and margarine, oil can be used as a shortening in most recipes.

LC: Use minimum quantities of oil (and all other fats).

LCh and D: Use pure vegetable oils that are high in polyunsaturates (e.g.: safflower, corn, sunflower, sesame, soybean, cottonseed). Avoid palm and coconut oils. Limit use of peanut and olive oils.

LS, V, v, Ml, B: Use any pure vegetable oil.

P: Use of all oils is prohibited.

K and *k:* Use any pure vegetable oil with kosher certification.

Orange Juice Concentrate. (Frozen concentrated orange juice, unsweetened). Useful for imparting a rich natural orange flavor to foods and baked goods. Use undiluted and defrosted.

D: Use may be limited.

Pepper. Useful for adding flavor to almost any savory dish, peppercorns come in black, white, and green. We suggest using freshly ground pepper in all recipes calling for pepper.

P: Use white pepper only.

B: Use of pepper is generally prohibited.

Pineapple Juice Concentrate (frozen concentrated pineapple juice, unsweetened). Good for Oriental cooking or other dishes where a pineapple flavor is desired, this juice adds sweetness and good taste without adding refined sugar. Use undiluted and defrosted.

D: Use may be limited to small amounts.

Pot Cheese. Like cottage cheeses, pot cheeses can vary in fat content. In general, it is sensible for everyone to use the lower-fat cheeses when possible.

LC, LCh, D: Always use low-fat pot cheese.

LS: Use unsalted low-fat pot cheese when possible. Many salt-restricted dieters must limit daily consumption of cheese and other dairy products; those under severe restriction are limited to low-sodium or unsalted dairy products.

V: Use of pot cheese is prohibited.

Ml: Use of pot cheese may be prohibited or limited.

P: Use pot cheese with no more than 1 percent fat.

B: Use of pot cheese may be prohibited or limited; when permitted, use low-fat pot cheese.

Salt. Most of our special-diet recipes call for "salt to taste." In general, we try to keep salting down, since overconsumption is associated with high blood pressure. In recipes where salt is omitted for dietary reasons, we suggest you taste as you would for salt and then add wine vinegar, lemon juice, bitters or additional herbs or spices if more flavor is needed (see Chapter Four). Salting in moderation is permitted in special-diet cooking, with these exceptions:

LS: Omit salt in cooking for those on salt-restricted diets. Provide salt (and salt substitute, if permitted) at the table.

P: Omit salt in cooking; low-salt soy sauce or small amounts of regular soy sauce may be substituted.

Sauté. Basically, all our recipes call for low or no-fat sautéing, processes that work well when **non-stick** cookware and/or **non-stick** sprays are used.

Low-fat sautéing. 1) Spray the pan with a **non-stick** spray; 2) Heat pan over moderate heat; 3) Add a minimal amount of shortening (as little as ½ teaspoon may be enough); 4) Heat shortening and coat pan; 5) Add food to be sautéed; 6) Stir or shake pan frequently over medium low heat until stage called for in recipe is reached. If recipe merely says *sauté,* cook until ingredients are soft and golden.

No-fat sautéing. 1) Spray pan with a **non-stick** spray if possible; if not, a **non-stick** pan is necessary; 2) Heat pan over moderate heat; 3) If spray is not used, add 1 or 2 tablespoons of dry **wine, stock,** or water; 4) Add ingredients to be sautéed; 5) Stir almost constantly over medium low heat. If ingredients seem to be sticking, add additional wine or stock. Cook to stage called for in recipe or until ingredients are soft.

No-fat browning. 1) Spray pan with a **non-stick** spray if possible; if not, a **non-stick** pan is necesary; 2) Heat pan over moderate heat; 3) Add ingredients to be sautéed; 4) Stir constantly over medium high heat until ingredients (usually onions) begin to brown; 5) Lower heat and add 2 tablespoons *wine* or *stock* or water; 6) Continue cooking, stirring frequently, until ingredients are soft.

P: Use no spray or shortening; use non-stick pan.

Soy Sauce. Commercial soy sauce often contains sugar, colorings, and preservatives. Soy sauce without these additives, often called tamari, is available in health food stores.

D: Use soy sauce that does not contain sugar.

LS: Use of soy sauce is prohibited.

P: Use low-salt soy sauce or small amounts of regular soy sauce, preferably additive-free.

Stock. One of the most valuable aids in preparing food for special diets, homemade stock is better than water in soups, sauces, main and side dishes, and even in place of oil in salad dressings. All stocks should be very well skimmed of fat. Our stock recipes and variations are suitable for all diets indicated.

LC: Use homemade meat, chicken, fish, or vegetable stock as desired. Commercial stocks or bouillons may be used.

LCh: Use homemade meat, chicken, fish, or vegetable stock as desired. Do not use commercial stocks containing hydrogenated shortening or animal fats.

D: Use homemade meat, chicken, fish, or vegetable stock made without sugar. Do not use commercial stocks, broths, soup mixes, or bouillons made with sugar or other sweeteners. (Many are!)

LS: Use homemade meat, chicken, fish, or vegetable stock made without added salt. Do not use commercial stocks, broths, soup mixes, or bouillons made with salt or other forms or sodium (careful—some bouillon cubes are 50 percent salt!).

V: Use homemade vegetable stock made without meat, fish, or dairy products. Or, use commercial stocks or bouillons that contain no dairy or animal products or are labeled kosher and pareve, and contain no fish.

v: Use homemade vegetable stock made without meat or fish products. Or, use commercial products that contain no animal products or are labeled kosher and dairy or pareve, and contain no fish.

P: Use homemade meat, chicken, fish, or vegetable stock made without sugar, salt, or fat. Do not use commercial products.

Ml: Use homemade meat, chicken, fish, or vegetable stock made without dairy products. Or, use commercial stocks that contain no dairy products or are labeled kosher and pareve or meat.

K: Do not use homemade stocks. For meals containing no meat or poultry, use commercial stocks, broths, soup mixes, or bouillons labeled kosher and dairy or pareve.

k: Use homemade fish or vegetable stock, or use commercial products labeled kosher and dairy or pareve.

B: Stock used depends upon type of diet. Some bland dieters can't have meat stocks. In most cases, bland stocks should be made without onions, garlic, and pepper.

Sugar. Special diet or not, most people could do with less of this nonnutritive substance. Little is called for in our recipes.

LC: Use sugar in limited quantities, as it adds only calories to your menu.

LCh: Use sugar in limited quantities, since sugar consumption has been linked to a heart attack-related blood fat: triglycerides.

D: Use of sugar, glucose, corn syrup, honey, and all refined sugars is prohibited. Some diabetics may be permitted to use small amounts of fructose, and most will be allowed small quantities of unsweetened fruit juice concentrate. When they are not, substitute the new sweetener, aspartame, made from proteins, not carbohydrates, except in cooking or baking.

V and *v:* Some vegetarians limit all refined foods, including sugar.

Unsweetened. When a recipe calls for fruit or juice, or any other product that is unsweetened, check the label to be sure that no sugar (sucrose), corn syrup, glucose, honey, corn or natural sweeteners, fructose, turbinado sugar, or other refined sweeteners are added. Unsweetened fruit juice is a good packing for fruit. Water is much less tasty.

Vegetables. Use fresh vegetables when possible in problem guest recipes. Frozen may be substituted, but watch out for hidden additives like salt (found in peas and lima beans), and fats (found in seasoned vegetables). Fresh vegetables can be widely used for most special diet guests, with the following exceptions:

LS: Use of vegetables naturally high in sodium (see Chapter Four) is limited. Do not use canned or frozen vegetables with added salt.

B: Use of strongly flavored vegetables may be prohibited (see Chapter Nine for a list of these vegetables). All vegetables for bland dieters must be well cooked; for some dieters they must be pureed.

Wine. Wines are excellent flavor enhancers in foods, and many special diets permit their use.

LC: Use dry wines, and be sure they are simmered for several minutes to cook off the alcohol and its calories.

D: Use of wines is usually prohibited, even in cooking. Use of wine vinegar may also be prohibited.

LS: Use of cooking wines with added salt is prohibited.

P: Use only dry white wines; other dry wines (rosés and sherries) may be used sparingly.

K and *k:* Some kosher guests drink only kosher wines. Such wines are widely available, though dry wines may be harder to obtain. These guests may also drink only kosher liqueurs and brandies, when these have a wine base. Use only kosher wine vinegar and grape juices for these guests.

B: Use of wines is usually prohibited. Vinegar and wine vinegar are also prohibited.

Yogurt. Like milk and cottage cheese, yogurts can be low or moderately high in fat and calories. Look for yogurts labeled *low-fat, non-fat,* or made from skim milk. Lowest in fat are homemade yogurts made from instant non-fat dry milk. Low-fat yogurts are suitable for all diets except:

V: Use of yogurt is prohibited.

Ml: Use of yogurt may be limited or prohibited.

B and *LS:* Use of yogurt may be limited.

RECIPES

Breads, Muffins, and Biscuits

(1)

Apple Bread

9 x 5 x 3-inch loaf *LCh, LS, v, Ml, k*

Cream together until light and fluffy:

¼ cup **margarine** or **butter***
¼ cup brown **sugar**

Beat in:

2 *eggs* (*LCh:* use 4 egg whites; if diet both *LCh* and *LS:* use 1 egg plus 2 whites)

In another bowl, sift together:

2 cups **flour**
1 teaspoon cinnamon
1½ teaspoons **baking powder** (*LS:* use 2¼ teaspoons low-sodium **baking powder**)

(*Recipe continued on next page*)

Add the dry ingredients to the creamed ingredients, beginning and ending with the dry, alternately with mixture of:

¼ cup **apple juice**
¼ cup **apple juice concentrate**

Stir in:

1 cup coarsely chopped apples
1 cup coarsely chopped nuts
1 teaspoon grated lemon rind

Pour batter into a **non-stick** 9 x 5 x 3-inch loaf pan. Bake in preheated 350° F oven for 40 to 50 minutes, or until loaf pulls away slightly from sides of pan, and toothpick inserted in center comes out clean. Cool bread in pan for 5 minutes, then turn out onto rack to cool.

* Ingredients and utensils in boldface are referred to in the Glossary.

(2)

Banana Bread or Banana Muffins

1 9 x 5 x 3-inch loaf or 18 to 24 muffins — *LC, LCh, D, LS, V, v, Ml, k, B*

Tip: 1¾-inch slice of 2 small or 1 large muffin is equal to 1 (*D*) sweetness allowance.

Mash together, or process in blender:

3 very ripe bananas equal to about 1½ cups puree
1 teaspoon **lemon juice**

Combine in large bowl:

2 tablespoons **margarine,** melted, or 2 tablespoons **oil**
⅓ cup **apple juice concentrate**
¼ cup **apple juice**
1 tablespoon **orange juice concentrate**

Stir to mix. Combine in another bowl:

1½ cups whole wheat **flour** (*B:* use white **flour**)
½ cup wheat germ (*B:* use white **flour**)
1 teaspoon **baking powder** (*LS:* use 1½ teaspoons low-sodium **baking powder**)

Stir the dry ingredients and the bananas into the liquid to make a thick batter. If desired, stir in:

¼ to 1 cup raisins, chopped dates, or other dried fruit (*LC* and *D:* use ¼ cup; *B:* omit)

¼ to 1 cup toasted nuts and/or seeds (*D:* use 1 cup; *LC* and *B:* omit)

Transfer batter to a **non-stick** 9 x 5 x 3-inch loaf pan. Bake at 375° F for 30 to 45 minutes or until inserted knife comes out clean. Or spoon batter into **non-stick** muffin tins and bake for 20 to 25 minutes.

(3) *LIGHT BANANA BREAD*

LC, LCh, D, LS, v, Ml, K

Follow recipe for BANANA BREAD (**2**). Fold batter into 2 stiffly-beaten egg whites before baking.

(4)
No-Yolk Challah

2 small loaves or 1 large — *LC, LCh, D, LS, v, P, Ml, k, B*

Tip: Bake same day or store in freezer for freshest challahs.

Sift into a large bowl:

3 cups **flour**

1 to 3 teaspoons **salt** (LS: omit; P: reduce to ½ teaspoon)

Make a well in center of flour and add:

1 envelope dry active yeast

2 tablespoons **apple juice concentrate,** lukewarm

1 cup lukewarm water (or 1 cup lukewarm **apple juice** for sweeter bread)

Cover and let stand in a warm place for ½ hour. Add and beat well with electric mixer or by hand:

3 large or 4 medium **egg** whites (*LS:* use 3 medium whites plus 1 tablespoon **apple juice**)

½ cup lukewarm water

1 cup **flour**

Make a ball with dough, cover, and let stand in warm place for 2 hours or more, until doubled in bulk. For 1 large challah, divide

(*Recipe continued on next page*)

dough in 3 parts. For 2 smaller ones, divide into 6. Knead each part on floured board with floured fingers until smooth enough to roll. Roll into strips 1 to 1½ inches thick. Pinch together one end of each three strips. Braid. Pinch ends together. Place loaf or loaves on **non-stick** cookie sheet. Let stand ½ hour. Brush with:

1 **egg** white, lightly beaten *or* **apple juice concentrate** (*LS:* use apple juice concentrate)

Sprinkle loaves with:

Sesame or poppy seeds

Bake 15 minutes in preheated oven at 400° F. Reduce temperature to 350° F and bake 30 to 45 minutes longer or until nicely browned on top and bottom. (Lift bottom to check.) Smaller challahs need less time.

(5) *CRANBERRY CHALLAH*

LC, LCh, LS, v, P, Ml, k

To NO-YOLK CHALLAH (4) dough, or your favorite homemade or defrosted frozen dough, add 1 cup cranberries, simmered for 2 minutes with ½ cup **apple juice concentrate,** soaked for 5 minutes more, then drained thoroughly. Cranberries can be worked into dough as strips are being rolled.

(6) *RAISIN CHALLAH*

LC, LCh, LS, v, P, Ml, k

Proceed as for CRANBERRY CHALLAH (5), using ½ cup raisins instead of cranberries.

(7)

Chapatis

About 24 chapatis *LC, LCh, D, LS, V, v, P, Ml, k, B*

Tip: Best baked 1 hour before serving, but can be baked ahead and reheated

Fill a small bowl with cold water and keep it next to you as you work. Combine in another bowl:

1 pound (4 cups) whole wheat **flour** (*B:* use unbleached white)
¼ teaspoon **salt** (*LS:* omit)

Add and blend well with hands or spatula:

1¼ cups water, or enough to form a semi-firm dough

When dough comes away from sides of bowl, sprinkle it with a few drops of water, cover with a damp cloth, and let rest for 15 minutes. Knead dough until smooth, dampening hands with water as you work to prevent sticking. Cover dough and let rest for another 5 minutes. Dough may be tough—don't panic—as long as it is smooth surfaced. Cover dough and let rest another 5 minutes. Lightly flour working surface and have ready next to it:

½ cup whole wheat **flour** (*B:* use unbleached white)

Divide dough into 24 golf-ball-sized portions. Flatten each ball into a disc ½- to ¾-inch thick. Dip both sides into flour and roll out ⅛ inch thick. Place one at a time on ungreased griddle or **non-stick** skillet. Cook for 30 seconds, then turn and cook another 30 seconds. Excess flour will burn, so wipe pan between batches. Place each chapati under broiler on aluminum foil for one minute to crisp and puff up. (It will deflate again once taken out of broiler.) Repeat with remaining balls of dough. Do not refrigerate dough; it will become difficult to work with. You may, however, refrigerate baked chapatis, and reheat before serving.

(8)

Cheese-Nut Bread

2 loaves *LCh, D, LS, v, k*

Combine in a large bowl of electric mixer:

2 cups unbleached white **flour**
3 cups whole wheat **flour**

Remove 1½ cups of this mixture and combine with:

2 teaspoons **salt** (*LS:* omit)
2 packages active dry yeast

Return this mixture to the center of the flour in the bowl. Heat in a saucepan over low heat until liquid is very warm:

1 cup water
½ cup **apple juice concentrate**
¼ cup **margarine** or **butter**

(Recipe continued on next page)

1 cup low-fat **cottage cheese** (LS: use **hoop cheese** or unsalted **cottage cheese**)

Gradually add this liquid to the center of the flour mixture. Beat at medium speed for 2 minutes, scraping bowl occasionally. Add:

2 **eggs** or 4 **egg** whites (*LCh:* use egg whites; *LS:* use whole eggs; if diet both *LCh* and *LS:* use 1 whole egg and 2 whites)

½ cup unbleached white **flour**

Beat at high speed for 2 minutes, scraping bowl occasionally. Stir in:

¾ cup rolled **oats**

Add if needed to make a soft dough:

½ cup unbleached white **flour** or more

Turn out onto lightly floured board. Knead until smooth and elastic, about 8 to 10 minutes. Place in an oiled bowl, turning to grease all over. Cover tightly with foil and a dish towel. Set bowl in warm place until doubled in bulk, about 1 hour. Punch dough down. Turn out onto lightly floured board. Knead in:

¾ cup chopped pecans

Divide dough in half. Shape each half into a loaf and place in 2 small 8½ x 4½-inch loaf pans. Or shape into 2 small rounds and place in greased 8-inch cake pans. Brush tops of loaves lightly with:

Melted **margarine**

Let rise again, covered with a towel, in a warm place until doubled, about 1 hour. Bake at 375° F for 35 to 40 minutes or until loaves are nicely browned and bottoms sound hollow when tapped.

(9)

French Bread

3 small loaves or 2 longer ones — *LC, LCh, D, LS, V, v, P, Ml, k, B*

Tip: Using 1½ cups unbleached all-purpose or bread **flour,** and 2½ cups whole wheat **flour** makes a light and yet hearty loaf.

Combine in a large bowl, blending:

¼ cup lukewarm water

1½ envelopes active dry yeast

Add, stirring in:

4 cups unbleached all-purpose or bread **flour** or 4 cups whole wheat **flour,** or any mix of the two (B: use white only)

1¼ cups lukewarm water

1 to 3 teaspoons **salt** (*LS:* omit; *P:* use 2 teaspoons **soy sauce**)

Blend until mixture comes away from sides of the bowl. Turn dough out onto a lightly floured board. Knead lightly and shape into a ball. Lightly flour and return to lightly floured mixing bowl. Cover and let stand in a warm place for 1½ to 2 hours, or until double in bulk. Turn out onto lightly floured board and knead again for 1 minute. Shape into a ball and dust with flour, returning to lightly floured bowl. Cover and let rise in a warm place once again, until double in bulk, about 1½ hours. Punch down again and knead for several minutes on the lightly floured board. Divide dough into 2 or 3 portions. Roll each out into a long, rectangular shape with a rolling pin. Then roll up into a long, thin loaf, and place on a lightly floured baking sheet or into a long French bread baking tin. Cover with a towel, and return to warm place until again double in bulk. Preheat oven to 425° F, and place pan of hot water below shelf bread will be placed on in oven. Use very sharp razor blade to slash the breads diagonally with 3 or 4 parallel gashes. Place immediately in the oven and bake for 30 minutes. Reduce oven heat to 400° F and bake for 10 minutes longer, or until bread is golden brown and sounds hollow when bottom is tapped.

(10)

Garlic-Herb Bread

Enough for 1 small loaf *LCh, D, LS, V, v, Ml, k*

Melt in small saucepan:

2 tablespoons **margarine** or **butter** (*LS:* use unsalted)

Stir in:

1 medium to large garlic clove, crushed
½ teaspoon oregano
½ teaspoon finely minced dried parsley, or 1 tablespoon fresh
½ teaspoon basil

Warm mixture at very low heat to blend flavors, stirring constantly. Do not allow it to burn. Brush mixture on both cut surfaces of:

1 small ITALIAN BREAD **(15),** cut lengthwise (*LS:* prepare without salt; permissible store-bought **bread** may be substituted)

Close bread and wrap in aluminum foil. Bake at 325° F for 15 to 20 minutes, or until bread is well heated and crusty.

(11)

Herb Bread

2 long loaves *LC, LCh, D, LS, V, v, P, Ml, k*

Prepare 1 whole wheat or 1 white ITALIAN **(15)** or FRENCH BREAD **(9)** recipe (*LS* and *P:* prepare without salt). Add to dough before kneading one of the following mixtures:

½ teaspoon marjoram or basil and
½ teaspoon thyme and
1 tablespoon fresh chopped parsley and
½ teaspoon oregano *or*
1 teaspoon rosemary and
¼ teaspoon thyme and
1 teaspoon sage and
1 tablespoon chopped fresh parsley *or*
2 teaspoons dill *or*
Your favorite combination of herbs

If you use fresh herbs, triple the quantities called for above. Bake according to basic bread recipe.

(12) *SESAME HERB BREAD*

LC, LCh, D, LS, V, v, P, Ml, k

Prepare **HERB BREAD (11)** as above, pressing ⅓ cup sesame seeds into bottom of loaves

(13)

Hot Cross Buns

14 to 18 buns *LC, LCh, D, LS, V, v, P, Ml, k, B*

Heat to boiling:

½ cup **apple juice**
½ cup orange juice

Add and stir to dissolve:

½ cup **apple juice concentrate**
1 tablespoon **margarine** or **butter** (*P:* omit)

¼ teaspoon cinnamon
⅛ teaspoon nutmeg (*B:* omit)
¼ cup currants or raisins (*B:* use peeled, diced fresh apple)
2 tablespoons diced sun-dried apples, apricots, peaches, pears, or pineapple (*B:* omit)

Cool.

Combine:

1 package active dry yeast
2 tablespoons lukewarm water (105° to 115° F)

Add cooled juices and fruit to yeast mixture. Stir in:

1⅔ cup sifted **flour**
1 teaspoon grated lemon rind

Knead in to make a soft dough:

1 cup or more of additional **flour**

Form into a ball and place in an oiled (*P:* omit) bowl, turning to grease all sides. Cover and place in a warm place to rise to double in bulk. This will take about an hour. Punch down on a floured board and form into small balls. Place these, well-spaced, on **non-stick** baking sheets. Cover and allow to rise in a warm place until again about doubled. Bake in a preheated oven at 425° F for 15 to 20 minutes. Decorate, if desired, with a traditional cross or other design made from a mixture of:

⅓ cup confectioners' **sugar***
1 tablespoon lemon juice
¼ teaspoon vanilla

* The sugar decoration on this holiday recipe can be omitted or simply brushed off by low sugar dieters (*D*).

(14)

Irish Soda Bread

1 round loaf *LC, LCh, D, v, P, k*

Combine in saucepan over low heat and cook for 10 minutes:

½ cup currants or raisins (*D:* omit or reduce to ¼ cup)
3 tablespoons water
2 tablespoons **orange juice concentrate**

Meanwhile, sift together into a bowl:

1¾ cups unbleached white **flour**
1 teaspoon **baking soda**

(*Recipe continued on next page*)

1½ teaspoons low-sodium **baking powder**
1 teaspoon cream of tartar

Add and mix well the raisins with cooking liquid and:

2 cups whole wheat **flour**

Make a well in the middle of the dry ingredients and pour in:

1½ cups low-fat **buttermilk**

Work milk into flour quickly and transfer to a lightly floured board. Knead dough lightly for 30 seconds and form it into a ball. Transfer to a **non-stick** pie tin sprinkled with:

Cornmeal

Flatten into a 1-inch round. With a razor or sharp knife, mark off wedge-shaped pieces on top of round, ¼-inch deep. Bake in a preheated 350° F oven for 35 minutes or until bread is golden and edges pull away from sides of pan. Cool on wire rack before serving.

(15)

Italian Bread

2 large or 3 medium loaves *LC, LCh, D, LS, V, v, P, Ml, k, B*

Tip: 3 cups whole wheat flour and 2 to 2½ cups unbleached bread flour make a light yet hearty loaf.

Combine to soften:

1 envelope active dry yeast
¼ cup warm water (110° to 115° F)

Let stand 5 to 10 minutes. Meanwhile, put into a large bowl:

1¾ cups warm water
1 tablespoon **salt** (*LS:* omit; *P:* use 1 tablespoon **soy sauce**)

Blend in:

3 cups sifted **flour**

Stir softened yeast, and add to flour-water mixture, blending well. Measure:

2 to 2½ cups sifted **flour**

Add about half the additional flour to the yeast mixture and beat until very smooth. Blend in enough of the remaining flour to make a soft dough. Turn mixture out onto lightly floured surface. Allow to rest 5 to 10 minutes. Knead 5 to 8 minutes, until smooth and elastic. Add additional flour only if necessary. Shape dough into smooth ball, and place in a deep oiled bowl (*P:* omit oil), turning ball so all surfaces are greased. Cover with waxed paper and a towel, and let stand in warm place (about 80° F) until doubled in bulk, about 1½ to 2 hours. Punch down. Knead on lightly floured surface, about 2 minutes. Divide into 2 equal balls. Let stand covered 10 minutes. Roll eac' ball of dough into a 14 x 9-inch rectangle. Roll up tightly into a long, slender loaf. Pinch ends to seal. If desired, press into bottoms of loaves:

¼ cup sesame seeds (*B:* omit)

Place loaves on **non-stick** or greased baking sheet. Cover loaves loosely with a towel, and set in warm place until doubled in bulk. Meanwhile, preheat oven to 425° F. Place a large pan of boiling water on bottom of oven before placing bread in to bake. Bake bread for 10 minutes at 425° F, then reduce temperature to 350° F and bake another hour, or until golden brown.

(16)

Melba Rounds, Squares, or Points

32 rounds or squares *LC, LCh, D, LS, V, v, P, Ml, k, B*

Trim crusts from:

8 slices **bread**

With rolling pin, flatten bread. Cut slices into squares or points or, using cookie cutter, into rounds. Place on ungreased cookie sheet and bake in preheated oven at 250° F for 1 hour. Turn carefully with fingers or wooden tongs and bake for about 1 hour longer. Cool on wire racks.

(17)

Oatmeal Bread

2 small loaves *LCh, D, LS, V, v, Ml, K, k*

Combine in large bowl:

1½ cups rolled **oats**
2 cups boiling water

Stir and cool. Add:

1 cup unbleached or whole wheat **flour**
1 envelope active dry yeast

(*Recipe continued on next page*)

Place in warm, draft-free place, and allow to rise, uncovered, until double in bulk. Punch down, and work into dough:

¼ cup wheat germ
1 cup whole wheat **flour**
2 teaspoons **salt** (Opt.; *LS:* omit)
2 tablespoons **oil**
½ cup **apple juice concentrate** or honey (*D:* use juice concentrate)

Blend in, until stiff dough is formed:

1½ to 2 cups unbleached or whole wheat **flour**

Turn out on floured board and knead, adding additional flour if necessary, until smooth and elastic, about 10 minutes. If desired, work in:

½ cup raisins (*D:* use ¼ cup)

Divide dough in half, placing each in small, **non-stick** 4½ x 8½-inch loaf pan, and allow to rise, uncovered, until double in bulk. Preheat oven to 350° F. Brush tops of loaves with:

Beaten **egg** whites (*LS* and *V:* Brush with **margarine** or **apple juice concentrate**)

Sprinkle with:

Sesame seeds

Bake loaves for 35 to 55 minutes, or until loaf is golden, and bottom sounds hollow when tapped. Turn out onto wire racks and cool before slicing.

(18)

Onion-Walnut Loaves

4 small rounds *LCh, D, LS, V, v, Ml, k*

Sift into warm bowl:

4½ cups unbleached **flour**
2 to 3 teaspoons **salt** (*LS:* omit)

Stir in:

½ cup wheat germ

In small bowl, combine:

½ cup warm water (105° to 115° F)
2 envelopes active dry yeast

Stir to dissolve yeast, and add:

2 tablespoons **sugar** (*D:* use **apple juice concentrate,** warmed)

Make a well in the center of the flour mixture. Pour in the yeast mixture and:

¼ cup **oil**

1¾ cups warm water

Knead until a smooth, springy ball of dough is formed—about 10 minutes. Leave covered in a warm place to rise 2 hours. Punch down the dough, and blend in:

½ cup coarsely chopped walnuts

¾ cup finely chopped onion

Shape dough into 4 rounds, and set on a greased baking tray. Allow to rise for 45 minutes. Bake at 400° F for 45 minutes, or until loaves sound hollow when bottoms are tapped. Turn out onto wire racks, and cool before slicing.

(19)

Peasant Rye

2 medium loaves *LC, LCh, D, LS, V, v, P, Ml, k*

In large mixing bowl, put:

2¼ cups warm water or potato water (105° to 115° F)

Dissolve in the water:

2 packages active dry yeast

Stir in to make a spongey batter:

2 cups whole wheat **flour**

1 cup all-purpose unbleached **flour**

⅓ cup **apple juice concentrate,** defrosted to room temperature

Beat by hand or with mixer for several minutes. Cover and let rise in warm, draft-free place for 40 minutes. Stir into batter:

1 cup unprocessed **bran**

½ cup rolled **oats**

2 or 3 teaspoons **salt** (*LS:* omit; *P:* substitute 2 teaspoons **soy sauce**)

Work in to make sticky dough:

1½ cups dark or light rye **flour**

Turn out onto surface generously dusted with:

Whole wheat **flour**

Knead for 10 minutes, working in additional flour as needed to make

(*Recipe continued on next page*)

dough stiff but elastic. Transfer to oiled bowl (*P:* omit oil) and cover with damp cloth. Let rise in warm, draft-free place until doubled, or about 1 to 1½ hours. Oil medium-sized loaf pans or a large baking sheet (*P:* use **non-stick** pans). Punch down dough and shape into 2 loaves. Roll in:

Rolled **oats**

Place in baking pans or on sheet. Cover and let rise again until doubled, about 45 minutes. Preheat oven to 350° F. Bake until well browned, about 45 minutes.

(20)

Vegetarian Sausage Bread

8 servings *LCh, D, v, k*

In large **non-stick** skillet, heat:

1 tablespoon **oil**

Sauté in skillet over low heat for 1 minute:

2 small garlic cloves, minced

Add and sauté for 2 minutes over low heat, stirring frequently:

8 vegetarian sausage links, cooked according to package directions and crumbled

Stir in and continue to sauté for 5 minutes longer, stirring frequently:

½ cup chopped red pepper or pimiento
2 tablespoons chopped fresh parsley
1 tablespoon basil
1 tablespoon oregano
⅛ teaspoon cayenne pepper
Salt to taste
Pepper to taste

Stir in to blend well:

6 tablespoons grated **cheese**

Set filling aside.

Combine in small bowl:

½ cup lukewarm water
1 package active dry yeast
½ tablespoon brown **sugar**

Dissolve yeast and sugar, letting stand until frothy.

Combine in large bowl:

2 cups whole wheat **flour**
2 **egg** whites, lightly beaten

2 tablespoons **oil**
½ teaspoon **salt**

Knead for 3 or 4 minutes until dough is elastic. Cover and set in a warm place to rise until double in bulk. Meanwhile, cut into small cubes and set aside:

8 to 12 ounces part-skim mozzarella (*LCh:* use low-cholesterol **cheese**)

Turn dough out onto lightly floured board and punch down. Roll out to ⅛-inch thickness. Cut into 6-inch rounds by placing a 6-inch saucer face down on the dough and cutting around it with a sharp knife. On one half of each round place ½ cup of the filling plus one eighth of the mozzarella cheese. Fold unfilled side of round over filled side, pinching the edges and sealing with:

1 lightly beaten **egg** white

Place sausage breads on **non-stick** baking sheet and bake in preheated oven at 325° F for 15 minutes or until nicely browned. Serve hot.

(21)

Whole Wheat Raisin Bread

2 9 x 5-inch loaves *LC, LCh, D, LS, V, v, P, Ml, k*

Tip: ⅛ loaf is equal to 1 (*D*) sweetness allowance

In large mixing bowl, combine and set aside:

½ cup **apple juice concentrate**
¼ cup brown **sugar** (*D* and *P:* use **apple juice concentrate**)
1 tablespoon cinnamon
2 teaspoons **salt** (*LS* and *P:* omit)

In another bowl, combine until yeast dissolves:

3 cups warm water (110° to 115° F)
2 packages active dry yeast

Add yeast to large mixing bowl mixture and beat at low speed, or by hand, until well blended. Gradually add, beating at medium speed and scraping sides of bowl occasionally:

6 cups whole wheat **flour**

Then stir in:

½ cup wheat germ (*P:* use whole wheat **flour**)
½ cup **bran**
1 cup unbleached **flour**

(*Recipe continued on next page*)

Add additional flour if needed to make a medium-firm dough. Turn out onto floured board and knead in:

¾ cup sunflower seeds, shelled (*P:* omit; *D:* increase to 1 cup)
2 cups **raisins** (*D:* reduce to 1 cup)

Knead until dough is smooth and elastic, adding additional flour if needed. Place in a deep oiled bowl, turning to grease all over (*P:* omit oil). Cover and let rise in a warm place until doubled in bulk, about 1½ hours. Punch down dough. Turn out onto floured board and form into 2 loaves. Place in greased or **non-stick** pans (*P:* use **non-stick**). Cover and let rise until doubled in warm place about 1 hour. Bake at 350° F for 50 minutes, or until nicely browned. Cool on wire racks.

(22)

Bran Muffins

12 to 16 muffins *LC, LCh, D, LS, v, k*

Tip: 1 large muffin is equal to 1 (*D*) sweetness allowance.

In small saucepan, simmer 5 minutes over low heat, stirring occasionally:

½ cup raisins (*D:* use ¼ cup raisins)
2 tablespoons **apple juice concentrate**
1 tablespoon **orange juice concentrate**

Combine in mixing bowl and blend thoroughly:

2 cups whole wheat **flour**
1½ cups **bran**
1¼ teaspoons **baking soda** (*LS:* use 3 teaspoons low-sodium **baking powder**)
½ cup coarsely chopped walnuts (*LC:* omit)

Beat together in separate bowl:

2 cups **buttermilk** (*LS:* use 1 cup **skim milk** plus 1 cup orange juice)
½ cup **apple juice concentrate**
2 egg whites, slightly beaten
2 tablespoons **margarine,** melted and cooled

Combine dry and liquid ingredients, blending thoroughly in a few strokes. Fold in raisins with cooking juice. Fill 12 to 16 **non-stick** muffin tins or paper muffin cups in regular tins to ⅔ full. Bake in preheated 350° F oven for about 20 to 25 minutes, or until nicely browned.

(23)

Branberry-Nut Muffins

12 to 16 large muffins *LC, LCh, D, LS, v, k*

Tip: 1 large muffin is equal to 1 (*D*) sweetness allowance.

In small saucepan, simmer over low heat 10 minutes or until tender, stirring occasionally:

- 2 cups raw cranberries
- ½ cup **apple juice concentrate**
- 2 tablespoons **orange juice concentrate**

Set aside. Combine in mixing bowl:

- 2 cups whole wheat **flour**
- 1½ cups **bran**
- ½ cup broken walnut pieces
- 2 teaspoons **baking powder** (*LS:* use 3 teaspoons low-sodium **baking powder**)

Beat together in separate bowl:

- 2 cups skim **milk** (*LS:* use 1 cup **milk** plus 1 cup orange juice)
- ½ cup **apple juice concentrate**
- 2 **egg** whites, slightly beaten
- 2 tablespoons unsalted **margarine,** melted and cooled

Combine dry and liquid ingredients, blending thoroughly with a few strokes. Fold in cranberries with cooking juice. Fill 12 to 16 **non-stick** muffin tins or paper muffin cups in regular tins to ⅔ full. Bake in preheated 350° F oven for 20 to 25 minutes, or until nicely browned on top.

(24)

Cranberry-Nut Muffins

12 muffins *LC, LCh, D, LS, v, Ml, k*

Tip: 1 large muffin is equal to 1 (*D*) sweetness allowance.

Combine in mixing bowl:

- ½ cup whole wheat **flour**
- ½ cup **bran**

(*Recipe continued on next page*)

½ cup **oats**
½ cup broken walnut pieces or sliced almonds
¼ cup wheat germ
½ teaspoon cinnamon

Stir to blend ingredients well. In separate bowl, combine:

2 apples, peeled and chopped
½ cup raw cranberries

Stir in:

½ cup plus 2 tablespoons **apple juice concentrate**
½ cup **apple juice**

Combine wet and dry ingredients, and stir to blend well. Do not over mix. Fold in:

3 **egg** whites, beaten until stiff

Turn batter into **non-stick** muffin tins or muffin papers in any tins. Bake in preheated 400° F oven for 20 to 25 minutes, or until toothpick inserted in center of muffin comes out clean.

(25) *CRANBERRY "NUT" MUFFINS*

12 muffins *LC, LCh, D, v, P, Ml, k*

Proceed as in CRANBERRY-NUT MUFFINS (**24**); omit wheat germ, increase **oats** to ¾ cup; omit nuts, use Grape Nuts instead.

(26)

Granola Muffins

12 to 16 muffins *LC, LCh, D, LS, v, k*

Tip: 1 large muffin is equal to 1 (*D*) sweetness allowance.

In small saucepan, simmer 5 minutes over low heat, stirring occasionally:

½ cup raisins (*D:* use ¼ cup raisins)
2 tablespoons **apple juice concentrate**
1 tablespoon **orange juice concentrate**

Set aside. Combine in mixing bowl and blend thoroughly:

2 cups whole wheat **flour**
1½ cups HOMEMADE GRANOLA (**32**) (or unsweetened store-bought)

1¼ teaspoons **baking soda** (*LS:* use 3 teaspoons low-sodium **baking powder**)
¼ cup chopped nuts (*LC:* omit)

Beat together in separate bowl:

2 cups **buttermilk** (*LS:* use 1 cup skim **milk** plus 1 cup orange juice)
½ cup **apple juice concentrate**
2 tablespoons unsalted **margarine,** melted and cooled
2 **egg** whites, slightly beaten

Combine dry and liquid ingredients, blending together thoroughly with a few strokes. Fold in raisins with cooking juices. Fill 12 to 16 **non-stick** muffin tins or paper muffin cups in regular tins to ⅔ full. Bake in preheated 350° F oven for about 20 to 25 minutes, or until nicely browned.

(27)

Orange Biscuits

12 2-inch biscuits *LCh, LS, D, V, v, Ml, k*

In a bowl, sift together:

1⅓ cups **flour**
1 tablespoon **sugar** (*D:* omit)
2½ teaspoons **baking powder** (*LS:* use 3¾ teaspoons low-sodium **baking powder**)
¼ teaspoon **salt** (*LS:* omit)

Add:

⅔ cup wheat germ
1½ teaspoons grated orange rind

Add, and cut in with pastry blender or two knives until mixture resembles meal:

5 tablespoons **margarine** or **butter**

Stir in:

½ cup **orange juice concentrate,** plus water to make ⅔ cup (*D:* use 1 tablespoon **apple juice** in addition)

Form a smooth, soft dough, adding more water if necessary. Turn out onto lightly floured board, and knead 30 seconds. Roll out ¾-inch thick and cut 2-inch rounds with biscuit cutter or with rim of glass. Arrange biscuits on baking sheet, and bake in top third of preheated 425° F oven for 10 to 15 minutes, or until puffed and golden.

(28)

Wheat-Dill Biscuits

12 biscuits *LC, LCh, D, LS, v, k*

Sift together into a bowl:

⅔ cup white **flour**

¾ teaspoon **baking soda** (*LS:* use 1¾ teaspoons low-sodium baking powder)

¾ teaspoon **salt** (*LS:* omit)

Blend well into flour mixture:

⅓ cup wheat germ

1 teaspoon chopped fresh dill

Add, and cut in with pastry blender or two knives until crumbly:

2 tablespoons unsalted **margarine** or **butter**

Add:

1 **egg** white, slightly beaten

2½ tablespoons evaporated skimmed **milk**, or enough to form a smooth, soft dough)

Turn out on lightly floured board, and knead 30 seconds. Roll out ½-inch thick and cut out 1½-inch rounds with a biscuit cutter, or with the rim of a glass. Arrange biscuits on baking sheet and bake in top third of preheated 425° F oven for 8 to 12 minutes, or until golden.

FLOUR EQUIVALENTS

Table I

*1 cup white all-purpose **flour** equals:*

*1 cup plus 2 tablespoons coarsely ground whole-wheat **flour***

*1 cup finely ground whole-wheat **flour** (also called graham **flour**)*

*1¼ cups rye **flour***

*1 cup less 2 tablespoons rice **flour***

1 cup cornmeal

*13/16 cup gluten **flour***

*⅝ cup potato **flour***

*½ cup barley **flour***

*¼ cup buckwheat plus ¾ cup all-purpose **flour***

*2 tablespoons soy flour plus ⅞ cup all purpose **flour***

*1⅓ cups rolled **oats***

*⅓ cup wheat germ plus ⅔ cup all-purpose **flour***

Cereals

(29)

Hot Bulgur Cereal

4 to 6 servings *LC, LCh, D, LS, V, v, P, Ml, k*

Combine in saucepan:
¾ cup bulgur wheat
2 cups water
Salt to taste (*P* and *LS:* omit)

Cover and bring to a boil. Cook over medium heat, stirring frequently, for 5 minutes or until liquid is absorbed and bulgur is tender. Stir in:
1 tablespoon **margarine** (Opt.; *P:* omit)

If orange flavor is desired, stir in:
⅓ cup **orange juice concentrate**

Serve cereal with a choice of any of the following, passed separately:
Chopped apricots, raisins, dates, or other dried fruit
Sunflower seeds, chopped toasted nuts

(*Recipe continued on next page*)

Shredded **cheese**
Shredded apple
Cinnamon
Cream, **milk,** or skim **milk** (unless cereal is orange flavored)
Low-fat **cottage, pot,** or **hoop cheese** (*LS:* use unsalted **cheese**)

(30) *HOT BULGUR CEREAL WITH RAISINS AND CINNAMON*

4 to 6 servings *LCh, LS, V, v, P, Ml, k*

Add to bulgur wheat and water before preparing HOT BULGUR CEREAL (**29**):

¼ cup **apple juice concentrate** and ¼ to ½ cup raisins
Sprinkle with cinnamon to taste before serving.

(31)

Cornmeal-Baco Fritters

4 servings *LCh, D, V, v, Ml, k*

Combine in saucepan:

2¼ cups water
1½ cups cornmeal
Salt to taste

Stir until smooth. Bring to a boil and cook, stirring, for 3 to 5 minutes, or until mixture is very thick. Stir in:

3 tablespoons imitation bacon bits

Turn mixture into a small **non-stick** loaf pan, spreading it to fill pan evenly. Chill for 1 hour or longer. Unmold and slice. Heat in **non-stick** skillet over medium heat:

1 teaspoon **oil** or more, as desired

Fry slices in oil until golden brown on both sides. Serve hot with:

Maple syrup *or*
ORANGE MAPLE SYRUP (**551**)

(32)

Homemade Granola

About 5 cups *LC*, LCh, D, LS, V, v, P, Ml, k*

Tip: ¾ cup serving equals 1 (*D*) sweetness allowance.

Spread in **non-stick** baking pan, 9 x 11-inches or larger:
3 cups rolled **oats** (*P:* increase to 3½ cups)
Toast in preheated oven at 350° F for 10 minutes.
Combine in a small saucepan and bring to a boil, simmering over low heat for 5 minutes:
½ cup **apple juice concentrate** or ¼ cup **apple juice concentrate** plus ¼ cup **orange juice concentrate** (*D:* use ¼ cup **apple juice** plus ¼ cup orange juice)
½ cup raisins (*D:* reduce to ¼ cup or omit)
Add to toasted oats, and blend well with liquid from raisins:
¼ to ⅓ cup **apple juice concentrate** to taste
½ cup wheat germ (*P:* use **bran**)
¼ cup unsalted soy nuts (*P:* use Grape Nuts)
¼ cup sliced almonds *or* chopped walnuts (*P:* omit)
2 tablespoons sesame seeds (Opt.)
2 tablespoons sunflower seeds (Opt.; *P:* omit)
1 teaspoon cinnamon or to taste
Continue baking at 300° F for 20 minutes. Stir once or twice during baking.
Add raisins and stir to blend well. Press mixture firmly into pan and bake another 5 minutes. Cool and store in tightly-covered container.
Serve with one or more of the following, depending upon diet:
Milk, plain yogurt, FRUITED YOGURT (**428**), juice
Use as a topping for ice cream, frozen yogurt, cottage cheese, yogurt, or fruit.
Use as a substitute for part of flour in cookies, cakes, breads.

* Because of its relatively high calorie count, weight watchers should use granola only in small amounts.

(33)

Fruited Millet

2 servings *LCh, LS, V, v, P, Ml, k*

Combine in saucepan:
- 2 cups orange juice
- ½ cup millet

Bring to a boil; lower heat and simmer for 25 minutes or until liquid is almost absorbed. Add:
- ¼ cup raisins or chopped dates

Continue cooking for 5 minutes, or until liquid is absorbed and millet is tender. If millet is not tender enough, add a bit more juice or water, and cook a little longer. Stir in:
- ¼ cup chopped nuts or seeds (*P:* omit)
- 1 tablespoon grated orange rind

Serve hot or cold at breakfast, brunch, or as a dessert. If desired, vary as follows, depending upon guest's diet:
- Fold in 1 cup **unsweetened apple sauce**
- Stir in 1 cup low-fat **buttermilk** (*LS:* use unsalted buttermilk)
- Top with whipped cream or FRUITED YOGURT **(428)** or ANGEL CREAM **(543)**

(34)

Muesli

4 to 6 servings *LCh, LS, D, v, K, k*

Combine in bowl:
- 2 cups rolled **oats**
- ½ cup wheat germ
- ¼ cup nuts (sliced almonds, chopped walnuts or pecans)
- ¼ cup raisins (*D:* omit or pass separately)
- ¼ cup chopped dried fruit (dates, apricots, apples, peaches, prunes, etc.) (*D:* omit or pass separately)

Twenty minutes before serving, add:
- 2 apples, peeled and grated
- 1 teaspoon **lemon juice** (Opt.)

Sliced ripe bananas or other fresh fruit (*D:* pass separately)
Skim **milk**, whole **milk,** or cream (according to diet) to thoroughly moisten

Let stand for 15 to 20 minutes.

(35)

Orange Muesli

4 servings *LC, LCh, LS, V, v, P, Ml, K, k*

Combine and let soak for at least 1 hour:

2 cups orange juice
1½ cups rolled **oats**

When ready to serve, stir in:

1 naval orange, peeled, sectioned, and cut up (reserve 4 pieces for garnish)
1 banana, sliced
4 dates, pitted and sliced
¼ cup raisins
¼ cup almonds (*LC* and *P:* omit)
1 apple, cored, pared and sliced

Serve cold, garnished with orange sections.

Crepes

(36)

Standard Crepe

10 to 12 crepes *D, LS, v, k, B*

Tip: Allow 30 minutes to 1 hour preparation time for batter to settle.

Combine in blender and blend until smooth:

2 **eggs**
2 **egg** whites
½ cup **milk**
½ cup water
3 tablespoons **butter** or **margarine**
¾ cup unbleached white or whole wheat **flour**
½ teaspoon **salt** (*LS:* omit)

Let batter stand for 30 minutes to 1 hour. Heat **non-stick** crepe pan or skillet over medium-high heat. When water droplets sprinkled on its surface dance about, the pan is ready for the batter. Pour ⅛ cup batter for a 7-inch pan (more or less for pans of other sizes) into pan and quickly spread over entire bottom. Pour off any excess batter. For filled crepes, it is only necessary to brown one side. Fill unbrowned side. For blintzes, and other crepes that will be baked or fried after cooking, fill the browned side. For crepes to be used later, turn baked crepes onto wax paper sheet. Add another sheet of wax paper before adding additional layers of crepes. If you are going to use crepes immediately, stack and keep covered and warm.

(37)

Angel Crepes

10 to 12 crepes *LC, LCh, D, LS, v, P, k, B**

Tip: Allow 1 hour preparation time for batter to settle.

Combine in blender and process until smooth:

- 1½ cups skim **milk**
- ¾ cup low-fat **buttermilk** (*LS:* use unsalted buttermilk)
- 1½ cups whole wheat **flour** (*B:* use white flour)
- 1 tablespoon **baking powder** (*LS:* use 1½ tablespoons low-sodium **baking powder**)
- ½ teaspoon **salt** (*LS* and *P:* omit)

In large mixing bowl, beat with electric mixer until stiff:

- 2 large **egg** whites (*LS:* use 1 whole egg and beat lightly)

With mixer still at high speed, add milk-flour mixture, beating for a few seconds until well blended. Let mixture stand for 1 hour. Stir before using. Heat **non-stick** omelet or crepe pan. Pour about ½ cup of batter into pan quickly turning pan to allow batter to cover entire bottom of pan. When bottom of crepe is golden brown, turn pan over and drop crepe onto sheet of waxed paper. In some cases, you may want to brown both sides of crepe, second side lightly.

VARIATION: Add to batter, one of the following (except *B*):

- 1 tablespoon minced chives
- 2 tablespoons sautéed onions
- 1 tablespoon chopped parsley

* If milk is restricted, this recipe isn't appropriate.

(38)

Sweet Angel Crepes

10 to 12 crepes *LC, LCh, D, LS, v, Ml, P, k, B*

Tip: Allow 1 hour preparation time for batter to settle.

Combine in blender and process until smooth:

1¼ cups skim **milk,** or half **milk** and half water, or all juice (*D:* use milk and water; *LS* and *Ml:* use all juice)
1 tablespoon **apple juice concentrate**
1 teaspoon vanilla extract
1 cup whole wheat **flour** (*B:* use white)
1 tablespoon wheat germ (*P:* use bran; *B:* use **flour**)
2 tablespoons water

Beat mixture into:

2 stiffly beaten **egg** whites

Prepare crepes according to basic ANGEL CREPE **(37)** recipe.

VARIATION: Use basic ANGEL CREPE **(37)** recipe, adding to blender:

2 tablespoons **apple juice concentrate**

Reduce skim milk to 1¼ cups. Cook crepes according to basic recipe.

(39)

Orange Crepes

10 to 12 crepes *LC, LCh, D, LS, v, P, Ml, k*

Tip: Allow 1 hour preparation time for batter to settle.

Combine in blender and process until smooth:

¼ cup **orange juice concentrate**
1 cup water
1 cup whole wheat **flour**
1 tablespoon wheat germ or **bran** (*P:* use **bran**)
1 tablespoon **apple juice concentrate**

Process until smooth, then beat quickly into:

2 stiffly beaten **egg** whites

Let batter stand for 1 hour. Stir before making crepes. Proceed as for ANGEL CREPES **(37)**.

(40)

Cheese Blintzes

10 to 12 blintzes *LC, LCh, D, LS, v, Ml, P, k, B*

Tip: Allow 1 hour for crepe batter to settle.

Prepare:
 1 recipe SWEET ANGEL CREPES (**38**)
Process in blender until smooth:
 1½ cups low-fat **pot cheese** or **hoop cheese** (*LS:* Use hoop cheese or unsalted pot cheese; *Ml:* use 1¼ cups pureed soft tofu)
 2½ tablespoons **apple juice concentrate** or to taste
 ¾ teaspoon vanilla or almond extract
Fill each prepared crepe with some of the cheese mixture. Fold up bottom of crepe, then fold over ends. Roll and tuck in top side. Bake in 350° F oven for 20 minutes or until golden brown. Or, if desired, pan fry in **non-stick** skillet, greasing the pan, if diet permits with:
 1 to 3 teaspoons **margarine** or **butter**
Serve with choices of topping such as:
 Yogurt or sour cream
 BERRY SAUCE (**431**)
 FRUITED YOGURT (**428**)
 Unsweetened applesauce

(41) *BLUEBERRY BLINTZES*

LCh, LC, D, LS, v, P, Ml, k

Prepare:
 1 recipe SWEET ANGEL CREPES (**38**)
Fill with:
 1 recipe BERRY FILLING (**430**)

(42)

Mushroom-Filled Angel Crepes

4 servings *D, v, k, B*

Tip: Allow 1 hour for crepe batter to settle.

Prepare:
1 recipe ANGEL CREPES (**37**) or STANDARD CREPES (**36**)
Melt in **non-stick** skillet over medium heat:
1 tablespoon **margarine** or **butter**
Sauté in skillet until soft:
1 pound fresh mushrooms, washed, stems trimmed, sliced
Sprinkle over mushrooms:
1 tablespoon **flour**
Stir to blend well for 2 minutes over medium-low heat, stirring constantly. Gradually add:
½ cup skim **milk** (*B:* use **stock** if milk products limited)
Cook and stir until the mixture has come to a boil, and is smooth and thickened. Stir in:
¼ cup sour cream
Salt to taste
Pepper to taste (*B:* omit)
Keep filling warm until ready to use. Fill crepes, and serve, if desired, with:
CHEESE SAUCE (**419**) (*B:* omit if milk products are restricted)

(43)

Herbed Mushroom Angel Crepes

4 to 6 servings *LC, LCh, D, LS, v, P, k*

Tip: Allow 1 hour in preparation time for batter to settle.

Prepare:
1 recipe ANGEL CREPES (**37**)
Heat in **non-stick** skillet over medium flame:
½ to 1 tablespoon **oil** or **margarine** (*P:* omit)
Sauté in skillet until just softened:

1 cup chopped shallots or scallions, white parts only
Add and continue sautéing:
4 cups finely sliced mushrooms
⅓ cup sherry or dry white **wine** (*P:* use white **wine**, *D:* use **stock**)
2 teaspoons tarragon *or* thyme
½ cup finely chopped parsley
In a small cup, blend together until smooth:
2 tablespoons **flour**
½ cup water
When mushrooms are softened, add the flour mixture to the skillet, blending it in until smooth. Cook over low heat for 2 minutes. Add and cook, stirring, until smooth:
1 cup **stock**
Season with:
Salt to taste (*P* and *LS:* omit, use **wine** vinegar to taste if desired)
White **pepper** to taste
Fill crepes with mushroom mixture, sprinkling if desired with:
Pine nuts (*P:* omit)
Fold crepes. Serve warm with:
BROCCOLI SAUCE (**417**)

(44)

Mushroom-Rice Angel Crepes

4 servings *LCh, D, v, k, B*

Tip: Allow 1 hour preparation time for batter to settle.

Prepare:
1 recipe ANGEL CREPES (**37**)
Melt in large **non-stick** skillet over medium heat:
1 tablespoon **margarine** or **butter**
Sauté in skillet for 1 minute:
1 medium garlic clove, minced (*B:* omit)
1 tablespoon minced shallots or scallions, white part only (*B:* omit)
Add and **sauté** over low heat until just soft (*B:* very soft):
1 pound mushrooms, washed, stems trimmed, sliced
1 tablespoon dried tarragon *or* dill, to taste

(*Recipe continued on next page*)

Sprinkle over mushrooms:

1 tablespoon **flour**

Stir to blend well; continue stirring 2 minutes longer. Add, over medium-low heat, stirring constantly:

½ cup skim **milk**

Continue stirring over medium-low heat until mixture is smooth and slightly thickened. Fold in:

3 cups cooked brown rice (*B:* use white rice)

Season, if desired, with:

Salt to taste

Pepper to taste (*B:* omit)

Keep filling warm until ready to use. Fill crepes when ready to serve, and pass separately, if desired:

CHEESE SAUCE (**419**) (*B:* if milk products are restricted, use WARM SPINACH VICHYSSOISE SAUCE (**92**))

(45)

Spinach-Mozzarella Crepes

6 to 12 crepe servings — *v, k*

Prepare and let batter stand for 1 hour.

1 recipe STANDARD CREPES (**36**) or ANGEL CREPES (**37**)

Meanwhile, heat in **non-stick** saucepan over medium flame:

2 tablespoons **butter** or **margarine**

Sauté in the saucepan:

2 tablespoons finely chopped onion

Stir in to make a roux:

3 tablespoons **flour**

Mix well, and continue cooking over low heat until mixture just begins to turn golden. Gradually add:

3 cups scalded **milk** or scalded skim **milk**

Cook mixture, stirring vigorously with a wire whisk, until it is smooth. Stir in:

Sprig parsley

3 white peppercorns

Pinch nutmeg (Opt.)

¼ teaspoon **salt** or to taste

Cook sauce slowly, stirring frequently, for 30 minutes, or until it is reduced by about one-third. Strain through fine sieve. Set aside. In a bowl, combine, blending well:

1⅓ cups chopped cooked spinach, drained well
1 cup part-skim ricotta
4 tablespoons grated **cheese**
2 **eggs** plus 2 whites, lightly beaten
Salt and **pepper** to taste

Set aside.

Make crepes. Divide spinach filling among crepes. Fold sides of each and then roll. Place crepes in a **non-stick** flameproof baking dish and top with the sauce.

On sauce, arrange:

½ pound mozzarella **cheese,** thinly sliced

Bake at 375° F for 10 to 15 minutes, or until cheese is melted. Slip dish under the broiler for 2 to 4 minutes, or until cheese is melted and lightly browned.

Eggs

(46)

Eggs Florentine

4 servings ***LC, LCh, LS, k, v, B***

Prepare:

1 recipe CREAMED SPINACH (**393**) (*LS:* use CREAMED BROCCOLI (**394**))

In **non-stick** skillet, melt over medium heat:

1 tablespoon unsalted **margarine**

Add and stir to blend well for 3 to 4 minutes:

2 tablespoons **flour**

Add gradually over medium heat, stirring constantly:

1 cup skim **milk** (*LS:* use ¾ cup **stock** plus ¼ cup **milk**)

Continue to cook over low heat, stirring constantly, until sauce thickens. Add and stir until melted:

2 tablespoons grated parmesan **cheese** (*LCh:* use low-cholesterol cheese; *LS:* use low-sodium cheese; *B:* omit, unless permitted)

2 tablespoons grated Gruyère **cheese** (*LCh:* use low-cholesterol

cheese; *LS:* use low-sodium cheese; *B:* use 2 tablespoons mild American cheese if parmesan permitted; otherwise, use ¼ cup mild American cheese)

Season as desired with:

Salt to taste (*LS:* omit)

Cayenne pepper to taste (*B:* use ⅛ to ¼ teaspoon paprika)

Poach:

4 eggs

Arrange CREAMED SPINACH in shallow **non-stick** baking dish. Top with poached eggs. Pour prepared cheese sauce over eggs. Sprinkle with:

¼ cup **bread** crumbs

Brown quickly under hot broiler and serve garnished, if desired, with:

Fresh parsley sprigs

(47) *YOLKLESS FLORENTINE*

LCh, D

Prepare as for EGGS FLORENTINE (**46**) substituting 1 or 2 poached egg whites for each whole egg.

(48) *BROCCOLI FLORENTINE ON TOAST*

LC, LCh, D, LS, v, k*

Prepare sauce with CREAMED BROCCOLI (**394**) as for EGGS FLORENTINE (**46**), but omit eggs. Serve on:

Toast points (see **bread**)

* When eggs are severely restricted on the low-salt diet.

(49)

Mozzarella Omelet

3 servings *LCh, v, k,*

In a bowl, beat lightly together:

6 **eggs** (*LCh:* use egg substitute equal to 6 eggs)

¼ cup chopped Italian parsley

(*Recipe continued on next page*)

2 tablespoons water
½ teaspoon **salt**
Pepper to taste

In omelet pan, heat over medium flame:

2 tablespoons **butter** or **margarine**

Pour in egg mixture and cook it, lifting the cooked portions as they become firm and letting the liquid egg run under them. Continue until omelet is almost set. Arrange over half the omelet:

¼ pound part-skim mozzarella **cheese**, thinly sliced (*LCh:* use low cholesterol **cheese**)

Put the pan under a hot broiler for 2 to 3 minutes to melt cheese. Fold omelet in half over cheese and slide onto serving dish.

VARIATION: Add with cheese:

1 thinly sliced apple *or*
2 ripe bananas, sliced

(50)

Mushroom-Zucchini Omelet

3 servings *LC, LCh, v, k, Ml*

Prepare eggs as MOZZARELLA OMELET (**49**), but instead of cheese filling use the following: Heat in skillet over medium flame:

1 tablespoon **oil**

Sauté in oil for 2 minutes:

2 scallions, thinly sliced

Add and continue sautéing until vegetables are softened:

1 cup sliced zucchini
1 cup sliced mushrooms

Season with:

⅛ teaspoon tarragon or to taste
Salt and **pepper** to taste

This filling does not need to be placed under broiler. Merely fold omelet and serve.

(51) *MUSHROOM OMELET*

LC, LCh, v, k, Ml

Prepare eggs as MUSHROOM-ZUCCHINI OMELET (**50**). Instead of zucchini, add 1 additional cup mushrooms.

(52)

Mushroom-Pepper-Onion Scramble

2 servings *LC, D, v, Ml, k*

Lightly beat together:
- 2 **eggs**
- 4 **egg** whites
- 1 tablespoon **milk** or water (*Ml:* use water)
- **Salt** and **pepper** to taste

Heat in **non-stick** skillet over medium flame:
- ½ tablespoon **margarine** or **butter**

Sauté in skillet until softened:
- ½ cup chopped onion

Add and continue sautéing:
- ½ cup diced green pepper

When peppers are softened, add:
- ½ cup sliced fresh mushrooms

Sauté mushrooms for another 3 minutes or until just softened. Remove vegetable mixture from skillet and wipe pan with paper towel. Add additional **non-stick** spray or:
- ½ tablespoon **margarine** or **butter**

Add egg mixture to skillet over medium heat. Allow to set slightly, pulling set edges inward and letting raw egg flow out. Spread vegetable mixture over the surface of the egg and continue scrambling to desired doneness.

(53)

Poached Eggs on Peas Portuguese

4 servings *D, v, Ml, k*

In a **non-stick** skillet, heat:
- 1 tablespoon **oil** or **margarine**

Sauté in skillet:
- 1 onion, chopped
- 1 carrot, chopped
- 1 garlic clove, minced

(*Recipe continued on next page*)

Stir into vegetable mixture:

⅔ cup **stock,** vegetable or chicken
½ pound fresh tomato, or ½ cup canned
¼ teaspoon basil
¼ cup chopped fresh parsley
¼ teaspoon Worcestershire sauce (*v:* omit, substitute steak sauce)
Salt to taste
Pepper to taste

Simmer mixture for 5 minutes. Then add:

3 cups fresh or frozen green peas

Cook covered for 20 minutes (15 if frozen peas are used). With the back of a spoon, make 4 indentations in pea mixture. Into each indentation, carefully drop, without breaking yolk:

1 **egg** (total of 4 eggs)

Season eggs with salt and pepper to taste.
Cover and cook for another 2 to 3 minutes, or until egg whites are set.

Pancakes and Quiches

(54)

Apple Pancakes

6 10-inch pancakes *LC, LCh, LS, v, P, k*

Tip: Allow 1 hour of preparation time to allow batter to settle.

Combine in blender and process until smooth:

1 cup skim **milk**

¾ cup low-fat **buttermilk** (*LS:* use **unsweetened** applesauce)

3 tablespoons **apple juice concentrate**

1½ cups whole wheat **flour**

1 tablespoon low-sodium **baking powder**

1 teaspoon cinnamon or to taste

Beat until stiff:

4 large **egg** whites (*LS:* whip 2 whites, add 2 yolks to batter)

With mixer still at high speed, add milk-flour mixture, beating for a

(*Recipe continued on next page*)

few seconds until batter is well blended. Let stand for 1 hour. Meanwhile, thinly slice:

4 MacIntosh or Courtland apples (about 3 cups), peeled and cored

Combine in **non-stick** skillet:

3 tablespoons **apple juice concentrate**
3 tablespoons **lemon juice**
½ teaspoon cinnamon
½ teaspoon brown **sugar** (*P:* omit)
¼ teaspoon **margarine** (*P:* omit)

Bring mixture to a simmer and add apples; simmer until apples are just softened. With slotted spoon remove apples from liquid and set on plate.

Combine in small saucepan and bring to a boil, simmering for 5 minutes:

⅓ cup raisins or chopped dates
⅓ cup **apple juice**

When batter is ready, heat heavy **non-stick*** skillet. Stir batter several times and pour ⅓ cup batter over bottom of pan, spreading evenly. Arrange about ⅙ of apples over batter. Sprinkle with some raisins and, if desired,

Chopped nuts (*P* and *LC:* omit)

Cover evenly with another ⅓ cup batter. Let pancake cook over medium heat for 2 to 3 minutes, or until bottom is lightly browned. Loosen edges with pancake turner and slip onto large plate. Respray pan with **non-stick** spray or wipe with oiled paper towel. Invert pancake into pan and cook second side until it, too, is lightly browned. Keep warm while preparing 5 or more other pancakes similarly. If diet permits, pancakes may be spread with:

Melted **butter** or **margarine**
Cinnamon **sugar**

* See WHOLE WHEAT BUTTERMILK PANCAKES (**55**) for directions for "greasing" pan for Pritikin dieters.

(55)

Whole Wheat Buttermilk Pancakes

3 to 4 servings *LC, LCh, D, LS, v, P, k*

Tip: Allow 1 hour preparation time for batter to settle.

Combine in blender and blend until smooth:
- 1 cup low-fat **buttermilk** (*LS:* use unsalted buttermilk)
- 1 teaspoon **apple juice concentrate**
- 1 cup whole wheat **flour**
- 1 tablespoon wheat germ (*P:* use 1 additional tablespoon **flour** instead)

Stir in:
- 2 teaspoons **baking powder** (*LS:* use 1 tablespoon low-sodium **baking powder**

In mixer bowl, beat until stiff:
- 2 large **egg** whites (*LS:* use 1 whole **egg**, lightly beaten)

Quickly beat in the buttermilk-flour mixture. Let batter stand for 1 hour.
Heat a **non-stick** sprayed* skillet or griddle to moderate temperature. Stir batter and pour onto skillet to make pancakes of the desired size. When surface of pancake begins to bubble and underside is nicely browned, turn, cover, and brown the other side.

VARIATIONS: Add sliced almonds, chopped pecans or walnuts, or raisins and chopped nuts to batter. (*P:* omit nuts)
Serve with:
- ORANGE MAPLE SYRUP (**551**) *or*
- FRUITED YOGURT (**428**) *or*
- BERRY SAUCE (**431**)

* Nathan Pritikin's recommendation to those following his diet is to grease the pan for pancakes this way: Dab a bit of oil on a paper towel, rinse the towel in water, wring out, and wipe surface of skillet or crepe pan. Reuse the towel whenever greasing is needed, but do not add more oil to it.

(56) *BUTTERMILK PANCAKES*

LC, LCh, D, LS, v, k, B

Substitute unbleached white **flour** for both the whole wheat **flour** and wheat germ in the recipe for WHOLE WHEAT BUTTERMILK PANCAKES (**55**).

(57) *ORANGE PANCAKES*

LC, LCh, LS, v, P, Ml, k, B

In WHOLE WHEAT BUTTERMILK PANCAKES **(55),** or BUTTERMILK PANCAKES **(56),** substitute 1 cup orange juice for **buttermilk.** Add 1 tablespoon orange rind (*B:* omit).

(58)

Quiche Crust

One 9 to 10-inch quiche crust *LCh, D, LS, V, v, Ml, k*

Combine in mixing bowl, and stir well:

¾ cup unbleached white **flour**

¾ cup wheat germ

Add:

6 tablespoons unsalted **margarine,** chilled

Cut shortening into flour with pastry blender or two knives until particles are the size of large peas. Add:

3 tablespoons ice water

Mix only enough to moisten ingredients. Turn dough onto floured board or waxed paper. Pat dough quickly into a flat, round ball, dust top with flour, and roll a circle ⅛-inch thick. Avoid over-handling dough. Transfer dough to quiche pan. Flute edges, and line crust with waxed paper, adding a handful of beans, peas, or rice (raw) to prevent crust from buckling during baking. Bake 8 to 10 minutes in preheated 425° F oven. Remove waxed paper and weights. Crust is now ready for filling.

(59)

Mushroom-Zucchini Quiche

6 servings *LCh, D, v, k*

In large, **non-stick** skillet, heat:

1 tablespoon **margarine**

Stir fry in margarine over low heat for 1 minute:

1 teaspoon minced garlic

Add to skillet and **sauté** for 5 minutes, stirring occasionally:

3 cups sliced fresh mushrooms

3 cups coarsely match-sticked zucchini

Remove from heat. Combine in large mixing bowl:

1 cup semi-sharp Cheddar **cheese** (*LCh* and *D:* use low-cholesterol or skim-milk cheese)

1 cup **pot cheese** (*LCh* and *D:* use low-fat pot cheese)

3 **egg** whites, slightly beaten

¼ cup evaporated skimmed **milk**

Add skillet mixture to cheeses in mixing bowl. Stir to blend well. Season to taste with:

Salt

Pepper

Set filling aside while preparing:

1 recipe QUICHE CRUST (**58**)

Pour filling into prepared crust, and bake in preheated 425° F oven for 1 hour, or until toothpick inserted into center comes out clean but not dry, and top is golden brown. Allow quiche to set for 10 to 15 minutes before cutting.

VARIATION: (*LC*) Prepare crustless quiche using low-fat cheeses.

(60)

Spinach-Feta Quiche

6 servings *LCh, D, v, k*

In large **non-stick** skillet, heat over medium flame:

½ to 1 tablespoon **margarine**

Sauté in margarine for 1 minute:

1½ teaspoons minced garlic

Add and continue to sauté about 5 minutes:

½ cup finely chopped red onion

⅓ cup finely chopped fresh dill or 1 tablespoon dried dill

¼ cup finely chopped fresh parsley

2 small scallions, thinly sliced

2 tablespoons finely chopped shallots

Add to skillet and stir until heated through:

1 10-ounce package frozen chopped spinach, cooked

(*Recipe continued on next page*)

Remove from heat. Combine in large mixing bowl:

2 cups low-fat **cottage cheese** or **hoop cheese**
½ pound feta **cheese,** crumbled
4 **egg** whites, slightly beaten

Add skillet mixture to cheese in mixing bowl. Stir to blend well. Season to taste with:

Salt (usually not necessary; depends on type of feta cheese used)
Pepper

Set filling aside while preparing:

1 recipe QUICHE CRUST (**58**)

Pour filling into prepared crust. Bake at 425° F for 1 hour, or until toothpick inserted into center of quiche comes out clean but not dry. Allow quiche to set 10 to 15 minutes before cutting.

(61) *SPINACH-CHEESE QUICHE*

LCh, D, v, k

Prepare SPINACH-FETA QUICHE (**60**) filling as above, substituting 6 to 8 ounces low-cholesterol **cheese** for feta cheese, plus **salt** to taste.

(62)

French Toast with Brandied Apples

6 slices *LC, LCh, D, LS, v, P, Ml, k, B*

Heat in **non-stick** skillet over medium flame:

1 teaspoon **margarine** (*P:* omit)
1 teaspoon **oil** (*P:* omit)

Add to skillet:

2 cups finely sliced apple (*D:* use 1½ cups apples plus ½ cup sliced almonds)
2 tablespoons **apple juice concentrate**
2 tablespoons apple brandy or other brandy or liqueur (*P* and *B*: use **apple juice concentrate;** (*D:* use 2 teaspoons brandy or rum extract)
1 teaspoon grated orange rind (*B:* use ¼ teaspoon orange extract)

Coat apple well with juice-brandy mixture, and **sauté** until the apples are nicely glazed but not mushy. Keep warm. Combine in bowl and beat with wire whip until light:

2 tablespoons skim **milk** *or* 1 tablespoon orange juice and 1 tablespoon **apple juice** (*Ml:* use juice; *D:* use milk)
2 large **egg** whites (*LS:* use 1 whole egg)
2 teaspoons **apple juice concentrate**

Pour mixture into flat baking pan. Arrange in pan to soak:

6 slices **bread**

Let bread stand until all liquid is absorbed, at least 1 hour. Heat **non-stick** skillet. Add, if desired, and heat:

1 teaspoon **margarine** (*P:* omit)
1 teaspoon **oil** (*P:* omit)

Fry the bread until it is nicely browned on both sides. Serve hot with warm brandied apples.

(63) *FRENCH TOAST WITH BERRY SAUCE*

LC, LCh, D, LS, v, P, Ml, k

Prepare French toast according to FRENCH TOAST WITH BRANDIED APPLES (**62**). Omit brandied apples, serve instead with BERRY SAUCE (**431**).

(64)

Savory French Toast

4 to 6 slices *LC, LCh, D, v, P, Ml, k*

Heat in a **non-stick** skillet over medium flame:

1 tablespoon **oil** (*P:* omit)

Sauté in skillet until golden brown:

⅓ cup finely chopped onions or scallions or shallots

Combine in bowl and beat with wire whip until light:

¼ cup skim **milk** (*Ml:* use **stock**)
2 large **egg** whites
¼ teaspoon **salt** (*P:* use **soy sauce**)
Dash white **pepper** to taste
Dash onion powder to taste

Stir in the sautéed onions. Pour mixture into flat baking pan. Arrange in pan to soak:

4 to 6 slices **bread**

(*Recipe continued on next page*)

Let stand until all liquid is absorbed, depending on thickness of bread, about 1 hour. Heat **non-stick** skillet. "Fry" bread until it is browned on both sides.

VARIATION: Sauté 1 cup onions, reserve ⅔ cup as topping when serving French toast.

Soups

(65)

Apple-Squash Bisque

8 servings *LC, LCh, D, LS, v, P, k*

Tip: Prepare early enough for soup to chill thoroughly.

In medium saucepan, combine and simmer, covered, 5 minutes or until vegetables are tender:

2 apples, preferably Granny Smith, peeled, cored, cut in eighths
1 large zucchini, unpeeled, sliced (about 2 cups)
1 onion, sliced (about 1 cup)
1 cup vegetable **stock**
¼ teaspoon dried leaf marjoram, crushed
½ teaspoon **salt,** or to taste (*LS:* omit)
⅛ teaspoon **pepper,** or to taste (*P:* use white)

(*Recipe continued on next page*)

Pour half of mixture into an electric blender and process until smooth. Repeat with remainder of mixture. Stir in:

1 cup vegetable **stock**
1 cup skim **milk**
½ cup evaporated skimmed **milk**
2 tablespoons **orange juice concentrate** or to taste

Cover mixture and chill several hours or overnight. Serve very cold. To each serving, add:

1 dollop of low-fat **yogurt** (about ½ cup in all)
A sprinkle of shredded apple (about 1 unpeeled apple)

(66)

Apple-Wine Soup

4 to 6 servings *LC, LCh, LS, V, v, Ml, k*

Tip: May be served hot or cold.

Combine in saucepan and bring to a boil:

3 cups **apple juice**
6 cups peeled, cored, and sliced apples
1 lemon rind, thinly sliced
6 tablespoons dry white **bread** crumbs
1 cinnamon stick

Simmer for 5 minutes. Add and simmer for 5 minutes more:

2 cups dry red **wine**

Remove lemon rind and cinnamon stick and discard. Puree apple mixture in blender and stir in:

3 tablespoons **lemon juice**
3 tablespoons currant jelly or **apple juice concentrate**

Return to saucepan and simmer over medium heat until heated through, and jelly is dissolved.
Sprinkle with cinnamon and serve.

VARIATIONS: Pass separately any of the following the diet permits:

Yogurt
Whipped cream
Sour cream

(67)

Chilled Avocado-Tomato Puree

4 servings *LCh, D, LS, V, v, Ml, k, B**

Combine in blender and process until smooth:

1 cup mashed avocado pulp
1 cup tomato juice (*LS:* use low sodium tomato juice)
1 cup **stock**
½ teaspoon mashed garlic (Opt.; *B:* omit)
1 teaspoon minced fresh basil (Opt.)

Salt to taste, if needed (*LS:* use **lemon juice** to taste)
Chill. Serve sprinkled with:

Finely minced parsley *or*
Chopped chives (*B:* omit)

* Except low residue diet.

(68)

Cold Blueberry Soup

6 to 8 servings *LC, LCh, LS, v, P, k*

In a saucepan, stir together and let stand 5 minutes:

1½ tablespoons quick-cooking tapioca
¾ cup water

Bring to a boil and cook, stirring, until the mixture is clear, about 6 to 8 minutes. Stir in:

1½ cups **unsweetened** grape juice
1½ cups **unsweetened** pineapple juice
⅛ to ¼ cup **apple juice concentrate** to taste
2 tablespoons grated lemon rind
2 tablespoons **lemon juice**
¼ teaspoon cinnamon, or to taste

Cook mixture over low heat, stirring occasionally, for 10 minutes. Cool. Stir in:

2 cups fresh blueberries, washed and picked over
⅓ cup sour cream or low-fat **yogurt** or **buttermilk** (*LC, LCh,* and *P:* use **yogurt** or **buttermilk**)

(*Recipe continued on next page*)

¼ cup cherry brandy (Opt.; *LC:* use 1 teaspoon brandy extract; *P:* omit; see **wine**)

Blend the mixture in a blender in batches until smooth. Chill, covered, for at least 4 hours.

(69)

Cold or Hot Borscht

8 to 12 servings *LC, LCh, D*, V, v, P, Ml, k, B*

Combine in large soup pot:

2 bunches beets, trimmed, peeled, and grated
2 teaspoons sour salt or 3 tablespoons **lemon juice** (*P:* use juice) or to taste
¾ cup **apple juice concentrate,** or to taste
3 quarts water
Salt to taste (*P:* omit)

Bring to a boil and simmer for 20 minutes or until beets are tender. Serve hot, or thoroughly chilled, with:

Boiled potatoes
Sour cream, if permitted

* Except those limited in simple carbohydrates such as fruit.

(70) *GARLIC BORSCHT*

LC, LCh, D, V, v, P, Ml, k

Add to BORSCHT **(69),** at beginning of recipe:

1 garlic clove, mashed

Remove garlic clove before serving borscht.

(71)

Quick Cold Borscht

4 to 5 servings ***LC, LCh, V, v, P, Ml, k, B***

Combine in blender and puree in batches:
2 16-ounce cans sliced beets, with liquid
1 to 2 tablespoons **sugar** (*P:* use **apple juice concentrate**)
2 tablespoons **lemon juice** or ⅛ teaspoon sour salt (citric acid crystals)

Transfer mixture to a saucepan and bring to a simmer, simmering for 5 minutes. Chill. Serve cold, but not icy, with:
Boiled potatoes
Dollops of sour cream or low-fat **yogurt** (*LC, LCh,* and *P:* use **yogurt;** *V* and *Ml:* omit; *B:* omit or pass separately if milk products are restricted)

(72)

Frozen Borscht Sherbet

4 to 5 servings ***LC, LCh, V, v, P, Ml, k***

Freeze BORSCHT (**71**) to mushiness, stirring, to break up ice crystals, every 15 minutes. Serve mushy in sherbet glasses.

(73)

Cabbage Borscht

4 to 5 servings ***LC, LCh, D, LS, V, v, P, Ml, k***

In large non-stick pot, heat over medium flame:
½ tablespoon **oil** (*P:* omit)

Sauté in skillet until golden and soft:
2 medium onions, very thinly sliced

(*Recipe continued on next page*)

Add to onions, sautéing briefly:
  6 cups shredded red cabbage
Then add and bring to a boil:
  1 cup **apple juice** (*D:* reduce to ½ cup)
  3 cups **stock**
Simmer for 10 minutes. Season as needed with:
  Salt (*P* and *LS:* omit)
  Pepper (*P:* use white)
  Lemon juice *or* **wine** vinegar to taste

(74)

Curried Pea and Avocado Soup

4 servings *LCh, D, LS, v, k*

In **non-stick** saucepan, heat:
  1 tablespoon **butter** or **margarine**
Sauté in saucepan until soft:
  ¼ cup finely chopped onion
  1 tablespoon curry powder
Add:
  2 cups fresh or frozen green peas (*LS:* use fresh peas)
  1 teaspoon chervil
  Salt to taste (*LS:* omit)
  Pepper to taste
  2 cups **stock**
Simmer, covered, for 10 to 20 minutes or until peas are very tender. (Less time needed for frozen peas.) Transfer peas and liquid to blender. Add:
  1 cup avocado pulp
Puree mixture until smooth. Return to saucepan and stir in:
  ¾ cup skim **milk** (*LS:* use ½ cup **milk** plus ½ cup **stock**)
  ¼ cup evaporated skimmed **milk** (*LS:* omit)
Heat soup, stirring occasionally, until warm but not boiling. Adjust seasoning. Serve warm, or chill and serve very cold. Garnish with:
  Thin slices of avocado

(75)

Creamy Pea and Avocado Soup

4 servings *LCh, D, LS, v, B**

Omit onion and curry powder in recipe for CURRIED PEA AND AVOCADO SOUP **(74).** Simply combine cooked or canned peas with chervil, avocado, and vegetable **stock.** Puree, and add milks. Serve warm or cool.

* Except low-residue diet.

(76)

Chilled Fruit Soup

About 4 cups *LC, LCh, LS, V, v, P, Ml, k, B*

Combine in saucepan and bring to a simmer:

4 cups mixed peeled, pitted, and sliced fruit (*B:* use permitted fruit)
2 cups **apple juice**
1 cinnamon stick
1 whole clove (*B:* omit)

Cook until all fruit is tender. Remove and discard cinnamon stick and clove. Puree soup and cool. Add:

2 tablespoons **lemon juice**

Taste soup for sweetness. If needed, add:

Apple juice concentrate to taste

Chill thoroughly before serving (*B:* serve cool).

(77)

Gazpacho

6 servings *LC, LCh, D, LS, V, v, P, Ml, k*

Combine in blender, in batches if necessary:

2 16-ounce cans tomatoes in puree (*LS:* use canned tomatoes with no salt added or 4 cups fresh chopped tomatoes)
1 8 to 8½-ounce jar pimiento
2 cucumbers, peeled, seeded, and sliced
2 medium green peppers, seeded and sliced
1 large red onion, quartered
5 tablespoons **wine** vinegar or to taste
1 tablespoon **oil** (*P* and *LC:* omit)
Salt to taste (*LS* and *P:* omit)
Tabasco to taste

Combine in large bowl or pitcher and chill thoroughly before serving with one of the following garnishes:

Bread croutons
Diced onions or peppers
Seedless grapes

(78)

Gazpacho Verde

4 servings *LC, LCh, D, LS, v, P, k*

In blender, puree:

1 cup vegetable **stock**
½ cup low-fat **yogurt**
2 small cucumbers, peeled, seeded, and chopped
1 medium green pepper, cored, seeded, and chopped
2 garlic cloves, chopped
1 tablespoon chopped onion
4 to 6 tablespoons white **wine** vinegar or to taste
White **pepper** to taste
Salt to taste (*LS* and *P:* omit)

Chill well. Garnish before serving with:

Seedless green grapes *or*
Red and/or green pepper, finely chopped

(79)

Peach Love Soup

2 servings *LCh, LS, v, k*

Puree in blender or processor:
1 cup sliced fresh peaches or **unsweetened** frozen or canned
¼ cup sherry or cherry **wine**
¼ cup **apple juice**
Pour into saucepan and add:
½ cup **apple juice**
Simmer for 10 minutes. Add:
1 tablespoon sour cream (*LCh* and *LS:* use 1 tablespoon low-fat **yogurt** or **buttermilk**)
Cool. Add:
2 tablespoons sour cream (*LCh* and *LS:* use 2 tablespoons low-fat **yogurt** or **buttermilk**)
Dash cinnamon to taste

(80) *STRAWBERRY LOVE SOUP*

2 servings *LCh, LS, v, k*

Substitute strawberries for peaches in PEACH LOVE SOUP **(79)**.

(81)

Puree Mongole

2 servings *LC, LCh, D, V, v, P, Ml, k, B*

Combine in blender, pureeing until smooth:
1½ cups tomato juice
1 cup canned peas, drained
Add:
Lemon juice to taste
Salt to taste (*P:* omit)
White **pepper** to taste (*B:* omit)
Serve cool in glasses or warm in bowls. Garnish with:
Lemon wedges

(82)

Zucchini Soup

8 to 10 servings *LC, LCh, D, v, P, k*

Scrub, trim, and thinly slice:
1 pound zucchini (about 4 cups)
Thinly slice:
2 large yellow onions (about 2 cups)
2 green peppers (about 1 cup)
In a large, **non-stick** soup pot, heat:
1 tablespoon **butter, margarine,** or **oil** (*P:* omit)
Add the onions and green peppers, and **sauté,** stirring, until onions are soft, but not brown, about 10 minutes. Add the zucchini and:
1 cup water or vegetable **stock**
1 garlic clove, finely chopped
Salt to taste (*P:* omit)
Pepper to taste (*P:* use white)
Cover and cook over high heat for 3 to 5 minutes, stirring occasionally. Reduce heat to medium and cook covered about 5 minutes. Uncover and let part of the liquid evaporate. Remove from heat. Stir in:
⅓ cup finely chopped fresh parsley
⅓ cup finely shredded fresh basil, or 1 teaspoon dry
1 tablespoon chopped tarragon, or 1 teaspoon dry
Transfer mixture to a processor or blender, in batches. Puree. There should be about 2 cups. Pour into a bowl and cool. Add:
½ cup evaporated skimmed **milk**
2 cups low-fat **buttermilk**
1 tablespoon **lemon juice**
½ teaspoon **apple juice concentrate**
¼ teaspoon Worcestershire sauce (*v:* use steak sauce; *P:* use **soy sauce**)
2 teaspoons finely chopped dill
Check seasonings, and adjust. Serve warm or chill for 2 to 3 hours or more. When ready to serve, sieve or chop fine:
2 hardboiled **egg** whites
Mince:
¼ cup parsley
¼ cup chives
Sprinkle each portion with a little egg white and about 1 teaspoon each of parsley and chives.

(83)

Creamless Zucchini Soup

6 to 8 servings *LC, LCh, D, Ml, V, v, P*

Instead of milk and buttermilk, add ½ cup pureed tofu and 1 cup chicken **stock** to ZUCCHINI SOUP (**82**) recipe. Substitute chicken **stock** for the 1 cup of vegetable **stock.** (*V:* use vegetable **stock,** substitute steak sauce for Worcestershire, and omit egg white garnish.)

(84)

Cream of Asparagus Soup

4 servings *LC, LCh, D, v, k, B**

Melt in small saucepan over low heat:
 1 tablespoon **margarine**
Remove from heat and blend in:
 2 tablespoons **flour**
Return to heat and cook, stirring, for 3 minutes over very low heat.
Add gradually, stirring constantly:
 2 cups skim **milk**
Continue stirring over low heat until mixture thickens. Set sauce aside. Puree in blender:
 1 10-ounce can asparagus tips with liquid
Add asparagus puree to sauce, blending thoroughly. Simmer for 3 minutes, stirring frequently.
Taste for seasoning. If needed, add:
 Salt to taste
 White **pepper** to taste (*B:* omit)
Serve warm with, if desired:
 Bread croutons

* For milk-restricted dieters, use CREAMLESS ASPARAGUS SOUP

(85)

Cream of Spinach Soup

4 servings *LC, LCh, D, v, k, B**

Follow recipe for CREAM OF ASPARAGUS SOUP (**84**), but substitute 2 cups cooked spinach for asparagus.

* For milk-restricted dieters, use WARM SPINACH VICHYSSOISE

(86)

Creamless Asparagus Soup

4 servings *LC, LCh, D, V, v, Ml, B*

Follow recipe for CREAM OF ASPARAGUS SOUP (**84**), but substitute 2 cups **stock** for the skim **milk.**

(87)

Cream of Hazelnut Soup

6 to 8 servings *LCh, D, V, v, P, Ml, k*

In large, **non-stick** skillet, heat:
 1 tablespoon **margarine** or **butter**
Sauté in skillet until vegetables are softened:
 2 carrots, peeled and chopped finely
 2 celery stalks, chopped
 1 garlic clove, minced
 1 leek, chopped, or 2 medium scallions, thinly sliced, white parts only
 ⅔ cup finely chopped hazelnuts
Blend in, until smooth:
 2 tablespoons **flour**

Cook mixture, stirring for 2 minutes longer. Add:

8 cups **stock**
2 bay leaves

Bring mixture to a boil, stirring, and simmer for 1 hour, stirring occasionally. Strain soup through a cheesecloth-lined colander, into a saucepan. Add:

1 cup evaporated skimmed **milk** (*V* and *Ml:* use ¼ pound pureed tofu plus ½ cup water)
1 tablespoon **margarine** or **butter,** cut into pieces
⅔ cup finely chopped toasted hazelnuts
Salt to taste
Pepper to taste (*P:* use white)

Heat soup, stirring, but do not boil. Serve warm.

VARIATION: Puree strained vegetable-nut mixture and return to soup.

(88)

Italian Minestrone

8 servings *LCh, D, V, v, P, Ml, k*

Cover with water to 1 inch above top:

1 cup dried baby lima beans

Bring to a boil, and simmer for 1 hour. Meanwhile, heat in **non-stick** skillet:

1 tablespoon **oil** (*P:* omit)

Sauté in skillet until golden:

1 large onion, sliced
2 garlic cloves, minced
½ cup sliced or diced celery

Drain lima beans and combine in large soup pot with onion mixture and:

1 can chick peas, drained
2 carrots, peeled and sliced, or diced
1 zucchini, scrubbed, and sliced or diced
1 potato, peeled and diced
1 28 or 29-ounce can crushed tomatoes
2 tablespoons chopped parsley

(*Recipe continued on next page*)

2 teaspoons **salt** (*P:* omit)
½ teaspoon **pepper** (*P:* use white)
2 quarts water

Simmer for 1 hour and 10 minutes. Fifteen minutes before serving, add:

1 package frozen peas
1 cup small pasta (elbows, shells, etc.)
1 cup Savoy cabbage, shredded
1 tablespoon fresh basil

Bring soup back to boil, and simmer for 15 minutes. Serve immediately. If desired, pass separately:

½ cup grated **cheese**

(89)

Lentil Soup with Chick Peas

8 to 10 servings *LCh, D, LS, V, v, P, Ml, k*

Soak together overnight or 8 hours:

1 cup dried chick peas
½ cup dried black beans

Drain beans and place in large, heavy pan with:

1 cup dried lentils
8 cups water *or* **stock**

Bring to a boil and simmer covered over low heat 1 to 1½ hours or until beans, peas, and lentils are tender. While beans are cooking, heat in a small, **non-stick** skillet:

½ to 1 tablespoon **oil** or **margarine** (*P:* omit)

In skillet, **sauté** until golden brown:

½ cup chopped onions

Add onions to soup. Stir in:

½ teaspoon paprika
½ to 1 teaspoon crushed caraway seeds, to taste
Salt to taste (*LS* and *P:* omit or use wine vinegar to taste)
Pepper to taste (*P:* use white)
1 16-ounce can tomatoes in juice, chopped coarsely (*LS:* use unsalted canned or 2 cups fresh, chopped)

Add water if necessary. Simmer 5 minutes. Serve hot.

(90)

Lentil Soup with Spinach and Prunes

8 to 10 servings *LCh, LS, V, v, P, Ml, k*

Combine and cook over low heat for 1 hour:

9 cups water or **stock**
2 cups lentils
Salt to taste (*LS* and *P:* omit)

Meanwhile, heat in **non-stick** skillet over medium flame:

1 to 2 tablespoons **oil** (*P:* omit)

Sauté in skillet until lightly browned:

1 medium onion, sliced

Add onion to lentils and continue cooking for 1 hour more. Then add:

¾ pound fresh spinach, washed and chopped, or 1 10-ounce package frozen chopped spinach, partly thawed (*LS:* omit if prohibited)
2 cups **stock**
20 pitted and quartered prunes

Cook 15 minutes more. Stir in:

2 tablespoons **lemon juice**
Salt to taste (*LS* and *P:* omit; add additional **lemon juice** if desired)
Pepper to taste (*P:* use white)

Serve soup hot.

(91)

Mushroom-Onion Soup

4 to 6 servings *LC, LCh, D, LS, V, v, P, Ml, k*

Heat in **non-stick** skillet:

½ to 1 tablespoon **oil** (P: omit)

Sauté in skillet until brown:

4 medium onions, preferably Bermuda, chopped

(*Recipe continued on next page*)

Blend in well:

1 tablespoon **apple juice concentrate**

Continue sautéing over medium low heat for another 3 minutes. Stir in and continue sautéing for another 3 minutes:

2 cups sliced fresh mushrooms

Blend in:

½ cup dry white vermouth or dry white **wine** (*D:* omit if prohibited)

Cook for another minute. Transfer mixture to saucepan. Add:

5 cups **stock**

Simmer for 10 minutes. Taste for seasoning, add:

Salt to taste (*LS* and *P:* omit)

Pepper to taste (*P:* use white)

Serve warm. If desired pass separately:

Grated **cheese** (*P, V,* and *Ml:* omit)

(92)

Warm Spinach Vichysoisse

4 servings *LC, LCh, D, V, v, Ml, k, B**

Puree in blender or food processor until smooth:

1 10-ounce package frozen chopped spinach, cooked

1 8-ounce boiled potato, peeled

Transfer to medium saucepan. Add:

2 cups **stock**

1 teaspoon **salt** or to taste

Pepper to taste (*B:* omit)

Cook over low heat for 10 minutes, stirring occasionally.

VARIATION: To make a sauce, use only 1½ cups stock.

* Except low residue diet.

(93)

Cream of Tomato Soup

4 servings *LC, LCh, D, LS, v, k, B**

In saucepan, melt over low heat:
1 tablespoon **margarine**
Add to margarine and blend over very low heat for 3 minutes:
2 tablespoons **flour**
Gradually blend in over low heat:
1¾ cups skim **milk** (*LS:* use 1 cup **milk** plus ¾ cup low-sodium tomato juice)
Continue cooking over low heat, stirring constantly, until thickened.
Stir in until smooth:
3 cups tomato juice (*LS:* use low-sodium juice)
4 tablespoons tomato paste (*LS:* use low-sodium paste)
Salt to taste (*LS:* use ¼ teaspoon oregano plus ¼ teaspoon basil plus 1 teaspoon **apple juice concentrate**)
Continue cooking over low heat for 5 minutes, stirring frequently.
Serve soup warm with, if desired:
Bread croutons

VARIATION: Serve a la mode, with small scoop of low-fat **cottage** or **pot cheese** (*LS:* omit).

* Do not serve to low-residue or milk-restricted dieters.

(94)

Broccoli Bread Soup with Cheese

6 to 8 servings *LCh, v, k*

Heat in large **non-stick** skillet over medium flame:
1 to 2 tablespoons **oil**
Sauté in the oil:
6 medium onions, thinly sliced
3 garlic cloves, minced

(*Recipe continued on next page*)

When onions are golden, stir in to glaze:
  1½ teaspoons brown **sugar** or **apple juice concentrate**
When onions are nicely glazed, add:
  1 large bunch broccoli, chopped, or 2 10-ounce packages frozen chopped broccoli
Continue **sautéing** until broccoli is tender-crisp. Season with:
  Salt to taste
  Pepper to taste
  Nutmeg to taste
Prepare **non-stick** casserole. Combine in bowl:
  ½ pound Swiss **cheese**, grated (*LCh:* use low-cholesterol **cheese**)
  ½ pound Cheddar **cheese,** grated (*LCh:* use low-cholesterol **cheese**)
Count out:
  12 slices of whole-wheat **bread** (about ½ pound)
Layer bottom of casserole with 4 slices. Spread with layer of ⅓ of broccoli mixture. Sprinkle with layer of ⅓ of cheese.
Add 2 more layers of bread and cheese. Pour over all:
  2 quarts boiling vegetable **stock** or vegetarian beef-flavored broth
Taste for seasoning. Brown in oven at 375° F for 10 minutes.

(95)

Onion Bouillabaisse

6 to 8 servings *LC, LCh, D, LS, P, Ml, k*

Heat in large, **non-stick** kettle:
  1 to 2 tablespoons **oil** (*P:* omit)
Add and **sauté** slowly for 5 minutes without browning:
  1 cup sliced onions
  1 cup sliced leeks, white part only, or an additional ¾ cup onions
  5 garlic cloves, mashed or minced
Stir in and cook 5 minutes more:
  2 to 3 cups chopped fresh tomatoes or 1¼ cups drained canned tomatoes (*LS:* use fresh or unsalted canned)
  2 tablespoons tomato paste (*LS:* use unsalted paste)
Add:
  2½ quarts water
  ½ cup celery, sliced (*LS:* omit)

4 ½-inch strips orange rind
6 parsley sprigs
1 teaspoon chopped fresh fennel
2 bay leaves
½ teaspoon saffron (opt.)
½ teaspoon thyme
½ teaspoon basil
⅛ teaspoon fennel seeds
¼ teaspoon **pepper** (*P:* use white)
Salt to taste (*LS* and *P:* omit)
3 to 4 pounds fish bones, heads, and trimmings

Bring to a boil and cook uncovered at slow boil for 45 minutes. Strain and season to taste. If you are not serving the soup within half an hour, let stand and cool uncovered, then refrigerate. Half an hour before serving, heat in **non-stick** skillet:

½ to 1 tablespoon **oil** (*P:* omit)

Sauté in skillet:

3 large onions, thinly sliced

When onions are soft, and slightly browned, stir in:

½ tablespoon **apple juice concentrate** *or* brown **sugar** (*D* and *P:* use **apple juice concentrate**)

Cook over medium heat, stirring constantly, until onions are caramelized. Meanwhile, bring stock to a boil. Wash and sort into firm and tender-fleshed varieties:

6 to 8 pounds of assorted lean fish

Add caramelized onions to stock along with firm-fleshed fish and:

1 cup dry white **wine** (*D:* omit if prohibited)

Cook fish for 5 minutes at a rapid boil. Add tender-fleshed fish and cook for another 5 minutes or until all fish has turned opaque. Transfer fish to serving platter with a slotted spoon. Add a ladleful of soup. Arrange around fish:

6 to 8 rounds of garlic-toasted French **bread** (*LS:* use GARLIC HERB BREAD **(10)**)
Parsley to garnish

Taste soup; adjust seasoning. Transfer to a tureen or serving bowl. Guests can assemble their own selections of fish, soup, and toasted bread.

(96)

Fish Stock

About 2½ quarts *LC, LCh, D, LS, P, Ml, k*

Combine in large stock pot:

3 to 3½ pounds fish bones, trimmings, and heads (gills removed)
2 onions, sliced
2 ribs celery, sliced (*LS:* omit)
6 sprigs parsley
2 tablespoons **lemon juice**
1 teaspoon thyme or tarragon
3 quarts water
Salt to taste (*P* and *LS:* omit)

Bring mixture to a boil and cook at simmer, covered, for 25 minutes. Add and cook for 5 minutes more:

4 sprigs dill

Strain stock through cheesecloth-lined colander. Chill and remove any fat.

(97)

Chicken Stock

About 3 quarts *LC, LCh, D, LS, P, Ml, k, B*

Combine in large stock pot:

4 pounds chicken bones with some meat on them, and, if available, chicken giblets
2 onions, chopped (*B:* omit)
3 garlic cloves, mashed (*B:* omit)
2 leeks, sliced (*B:* omit)
3 carrots, diced (*LS:* use 1 carrot)
3 ribs celery, sliced (*LS:* omit)
6 sprigs parsley
1 parsnip, sliced (*LS:* use 3 parsnips)
1 bay leaf
1 sprig thyme or ½ teaspoon dried thyme
12 peppercorns (*P:* use white peppercorns; *B:* omit)

1 tablespoon **lemon juice** or tarragon vinegar
4 quarts water
Salt to taste: (*P* and *LS:* omit)

Bring mixture to a boil and cook, covered, at simmer for 3 hours if unsalted, 2½ if salt has been added. Strain stock through cheesecloth-lined colander. Chill and skim off any remaining fat.

(98)

Vegetable Stock

3 quarts *LC, LCh, D, LS, V, v, P, Ml, k, B*

Tip: Long cooking is the key to strong flavor.

Combine in large stock pot:
2 onions, chopped (*B:* omit)
4 garlic cloves, mashed (B: omit)
2 leeks, chopped (*B:* omit)
3 carrots, diced (*LS:* use 1 carrot)
3 ribs celery, sliced (*LS:* omit)
6 sprigs parsley
1 parsnip, sliced (*LS:* use 3 parsnips)
2 to 3 sprigs fresh, or ¼ to ½ teaspoon dried thyme
1 bay leaf
2 tablespoons **lemon juice** or tarragon vinegar
10 peppercorns (*P:* white peppercorns; *B:* omit)
4 quarts water
Salt to taste (*P* and *LS:* omit)

Add miscellaneous permitted vegetable trimmings as available, except for cabbage family members such as broccoli or cauliflower. Good additions include:
Empty peapods
Mushroom stems
Asparagus ends
Iceberg or Boston lettuce

Cook stock, covered, at a simmer for 3 hours. Meanwhile, in a **nonstick** skillet, heat over medium flame (B: omit this step):
1 tablespoon **oil** (*P:* omit)

Sauté in skillet until golden brown:
2 cups onions, sliced

(*Recipe continued on next page*)

Strain stock and return to stock pot. Add the sautéed onions and simmer for another 20 to 25 minutes. Strain stock again, reserving onions for other cooking uses if desired.

(99)

Kreplach

50 to 60 kreplach *LC, LCh, D, LS, v, P, Ml, k*

In non-stick skillet, heat:
1 tablespoon **oil** (*P:* omit)
Sauté in skillet until slightly browned:
2 large onions, sliced
Grind together with:
¾ pound cooked turkey or chicken without skin (*v* and *k:* omit meat; use 3 cups cooked chick peas, drained)
Add to mixture:
2 **egg** whites
Salt to taste (*LS* and *P:* omit)
White pepper to taste
Set aside. Combine in a bowl:
1 cup water
½ teaspoon **salt** (*LS* and *P:* use onion powder)
Beat in:
2 **egg** whites (*LS:* use 1 whole egg)
Blend in 1 cup at a time, until a smooth dough is formed:
3½ cups **flour** or more
If dough sticks to hands, add more flour. Knead until smooth. Roll out to ⅛-inch thickness on floured board. Cut dough into squares. Place a dollop of filling on each. With floured fingers, fold into a triangle, pinching edges to close. Cook 5 to 6 kreplach at a time in:
Boiling salted water (*LS* and *P:* omit salt; if desired, add **lemon juice** or 1 whole onion, sliced, to water)
When kreplach rise to the top, they are ready. Remove from water with a slotted spoon, place in a colander, and rinse gently with cold water. Serve in soup, or as a side dish with **sautéed** fried onions, or tossed with margarine. (*v* and *k:* If desired, serve vegetarian kreplach with grated **cheese.**)

(100)

Matzo Balls

6 to 12 servings *LC, LCh, D, LS, v, P, Ml, k, B*

Tip: LS: limit to 2 matzo balls per person

Heat in **non-stick** skillet:
2 tablespoons **oil** (*P:* omit)
Sauté in skillet until golden brown:
1 onion, very finely chopped
Cool. Beat together the onions, oil, and:
3 **eggs** or 5 **egg** whites (*LC* and *LCh:* use whites; *LS:* use whole eggs; if diet both *LS* and *LCh:* use 1 whole egg and 3 whites)
Stir in:
⅞ cup matzo meal (or ¾ cup fine whole-wheat matzo crumbs plus ¼ cup matzo meal)
Gradually beat in:
⅜ cup seltzer (salt-free club soda) (*P:* increase to ½ cup)
Salt to taste (*P* and *LS*: omit)
White **pepper** to taste (*B:* omit)
Chill for at least 2 hours. With hands dipped in water, form dough into 12 balls. Drop into: simmering salted water or soup (*LS* and *P:* use unsalted soup or water to which 1 sliced onion has been added). Cook for 20 minutes. Serve with soup or as a side dish.

Hors d'Oeuvres and Appetizers

(101)

Baba Ghanoush

About 1½ cups *LC, LCh, D, LS, V, v, P, Ml, k*

Prick with a fork and bake on foil in preheated oven at 400° F for about 1 hour or until soft:

1 medium eggplant

Cool eggplant, halve, and scoop out pulp, discarding skins. Puree in blender or food processor. Add:

1 large garlic clove, chopped
2 tablespoons tahina
1 to 2 teaspoons **lemon juice,** or to taste
1 teaspoon **oil** (*P:* omit; otherwise: Opt.)
Salt to taste (*LS* and *P:* omit)

Chill. Serve garnished with:

Parsley sprigs
Lemon wedges
Black olives

As accompaniments:

Pita **bread** wedges
CRUDITÉS (**383**)

(102)

Caponata

6 to 8 servings *LC, LCh, D, V, v, P, k*

Heat in **non-stick** skillet:

2 tablespoons **oil** (*P:* omit; *LC:* reduce to 1 tablespoon)

Sauté in skillet until lightly browned:

1 large eggplant (about 1½ pounds) peeled and cubed

Remove eggplant from skillet with slotted spoon. Set aside. Add to skillet and sauté until soft and golden:

2½ cups sliced onions
1 cup sliced celery

Add:

1½ pounds tomatoes, peeled and chopped, or 1½ pounds canned tomatoes in puree
¼ cup tomato paste
2 tablespoons capers, drained
12 pitted black olives, sliced (*P:* use 2 tablespoons chopped pimiento)
2 tablespoons **apple juice concentrate**
½ cup **wine** vinegar
Salt to taste (*P:* omit)
Pepper to taste (*P:* use white)

Simmer for 10 minutes or until ingredients are well cooked and blended. Chill in refrigerator overnight. Serve as an appetizer with:

MELBA SQUARES (**16**)

(103)

Creamy Avocado Dip

About 1½ cups *D, v, k, B**

Puree in blender or food processor:

1 medium avocado, peeled and pitted
½ cup sour cream
½ cup low-fat **cottage cheese**

(*Recipe continued on next page*)

½ teaspoon **lemon juice**
½ teaspoon **salt** or to taste

Transfer to serving bowl and chill. Serve on:

MELBA SQUARES (**16**)

Or with:

CRUDITÉS (**383**) (*B:* omit)

* Except-low residue or milk-restricted diets.

(104)

Curried Mushroom Dip

Almost 3 cups *LC, LCh, D, LS, v, k*

Puree in blender or food processor:

2 cups chopped fresh mushrooms
1 cup low-fat **cottage cheese** (*LS:* use unsalted)
¼ cup sour cream (*LC* and *LCh:* use ⅓ cup low-fat **buttermilk**)
2 tablespoons curry powder or to taste
2 tablespoons almond butter (blanched almonds ground to paste in processor)
Salt to taste (*LS:* use ½ teaspoon **lemon juice**)

Transfer to serving bowl; chill. Garnish with:

Paprika
Mushroom slices

Serve with:

CRUDITÉS (**383**)
MELBA SQUARES (**16**) *or* **crackers**

(105)

Dilled Salmon-Avocado Spread

About 1½ cups *LC, LCh, D, Ml, k, B**

Puree in blender or food processor:

1 6 to 7-ounce can salmon, drained
1 medium avocado, peeled and pitted, cut into pieces

Lemon juice to taste
Fresh chopped dill to taste
Salt to taste
Chill. Serve with, according to diet:
CRUDITÉS (**383**)
Black or whole-grain **bread**
MELBA ROUNDS, SQUARES, OR POINTS (**16**)
Or use as filling for ANGEL EGGS (**132**)

* Except for low-residue diet, where avocado is prohibited.

(106)

Eggplant Caviar

About 1½ cups *LC, LCh, D, LS, V, v, P, Ml, k*

Prick with a fork and bake on foil in preheated oven at 400° F for one hour or until soft:
1 medium eggplant
Cool eggplant and scrape out pulp, discarding skins. Coarsely chop in blender or food processer. Add to eggplant and process quickly at medium speed:
1 medium onion, chopped
2 tablespoons tomato paste (*LS:* use unsalted paste)
1 tablespoon **lemon juice** or to taste
Salt to taste (*LS* and *P:* omit)
Pepper to taste (*P:* use white pepper)
Chill. Garnish if desired with:
Sliced black olives
Parsley sprigs
Serve with, according to diet:
Black **bread**
CRUDITÉS (**383**)

(107)

Eggplant Caviar-Stuffed Cherry Tomatoes

20 stuffed cherry tomatoes *LC, LCh, D, LS, V, v, Ml, k*

Prepare:

1 recipe EGGPLANT CAVIAR (**106**)

Cut tops from and scoop out insides of:

20 cherry tomatoes

Fill tomatoes with EGGPLANT CAVIAR. A very thin slice can be cut off the bottom of any tomato that will not stand up easily.

(108)

Gazpacho Dip

About 2⅓ cups *LC, LCh, D, LS, V, v, P, Ml, K, k,*

Combine in glass or stainless steel bowl or crockery:

1 cup cucumber, peeled, seeded, sliced, and chopped
½ cup tomato juice (*LS:* use low-salt tomato juice)
3 finely minced scallions
1 small garlic clove, finely minced
⅔ cup chopped or crushed fresh tomatoes
2 tablespoons **wine** vinegar
2 tablespoons tomato paste (*LS:* use unsalted tomato paste)

Stir well. Add:

Salt to taste (*LS* and *P:* use **wine** vinegar)
Pepper to taste (*P:* use white)

Refrigerate for at least 2 hours before serving to allow flavors to blend. Serve with, diet permitting:

CRUDITÉS (**383**)
Taco chips

(109)

Guacamole

4 servings *LCh, D, LS, V, v, Ml, K, k*

Peel, pit, and mash with a fork:
  2 medium, ripe avocados
Add and blend well:
  2 small tomatoes, peeled, seeded, and coarsely chopped
  3 to 4 tablespoons finely chopped Bermuda onion
  ¼ teaspoon garlic powder
  2 tablespoons **lemon juice**
  Dash tabasco or to taste (*LS:* use a dash)
  Salt to taste (*LS:* omit; increase **lemon juice** as needed)
Cover tightly and chill. Serve with any of the following, diet permitting:
  CRUDITÉS **(383)**
  Tortilla chips
  Crackers

(110)

Mild Guacamole

4 servings *LCh, D, v, Ml, K, k, B**

Peel, pit, and mash with fork:
  2 medium, ripe avocados
Mash in:
  1 hard-boiled egg white
Add to taste:
  Salt
  Lemon juice

* Except low-residue diet.

(111)

Holiday Pâté

1 4½ x 8½-inch loaf *LC, LCh, D, LS, V, v, P, Ml, k*

Tip: Prepare about 36 hours ahead

Place in refrigerator or freezer 1 loaf pan, 4½ x 8½ inches.
Measure and refrigerate:

1½ cups chick peas (canned or cooked according to package directions, and drained) (*LS:* use dried and prepare without salt)
½ cup soy beans (canned, or cooked according to package directions, and drained) (*LS:* use dried and prepare without salt)
½ cup chopped walnuts (*P:* use chopped roasted chestnuts)

Heat in a **non-stick** skillet over medium heat:

1 tablespoon **oil** (*P:* omit)

Sauté in skillet until golden:

2 teaspoons minced garlic
¾ cup chopped onions

Add and sauté until just tender:

2½ cups sliced fresh mushrooms
2 tablespoons dry white **wine** (except *D*), brandy (except *D* and *P*), vermouth (except *D*), *or* **stock**

Heat together in small saucepan, simmering for 3 minutes:

¼ cup dry white **wine** (*D:* if prohibited use **stock**)
1 teaspoon thyme
1 teaspoon savory

Remove from heat and stir in:

1 tablespoon **wine** vinegar (*D:* use tarragon vinegar)
1 teaspoon sautéd onion

Add this liquid mixture to mushrooms. Chill. Combine chilled mushroom mixture, beans, and nuts and chop finely in processor or blender in batches. Blend well. Refrigerate. Combine in small saucepan:

2 envelopes unflavored **gelatin**
¼ cup dry white **wine** (*D:* use **stock**)

Let stand 1 minute to soften. Heat to boiling, simmering for 3 minutes. Add:

2 cups **stock**
2 tablespoons **lemon juice**
1 teaspoon **apple juice concentrate**

Salt to taste (*P* and *LS:* omit; *LS:* if permissible, use salt substitute)
White **pepper** to taste

Chill gelatin mixture until it just begins to thicken. Meanwhile, cut tiny decorations with holiday motifs from any or all of the following:

Pimientos, olives, truffles
Egg whites
Peppers, cucumbers, carrots, parsley

Rinse chilled loaf pan in cold water and spread thin layer of gelatin over bottom and sides of pan. Refrigerate for a few minutes until firmly set. Arrange decorations by first dipping in gelatin mixture and then setting in place in gelatin layer. Refrigerate again to hold decorations in place. (If gelatin mixture begins to thin at room temperature, stir over ice until it is proper consistency.) When they are firmly set, add a second layer of gelatin to bottom and sides of pan. Chill this second layer until firm. Then add chilled pâté, spreading evenly. Heat remaining gelatin until just reliquefied. Pour into mold. Let set overnight.

To serve, unmold on:
Watercress or other greens

Garnish with:
Tomato wedges

Serve with:
Dark **bread,** thinly sliced, or **crackers**

(112)

Lo-Cheese Fondue

About 3 cups *LC, LCh, LS, v, k*

Rub a fondue pot or heavy saucepan with:
1 peeled, slashed garlic clove

Add to pot and bring to a simmer:
1½ cups dry white **wine**

Gradually stir in:
½ pound low-fat, low-salt **cheese,** grated
1 cup low-fat **cottage** or **hoop cheese** processed until smooth in blender (*LS:* use **hoop cheese** or unsalted **cottage cheese**)

(Recipe continued on next page)

Continue stirring over medium-low heat until all cheese is melted. In a measuring cup, combine until smooth:

1 tablespoon kirsch or other dry liqueur (See **wine**)
1½ teaspoons cornstarch

Stir cornstarch-kirsch mixture into cheese. Add to taste:

White **pepper**

Continue stirring over medium-low heat until mixture is thickened. Transfer pot to warming tray, alcohol light, or candle warmer, and serve with:

Par-cooked broccoli, cauliflower florets
Raw zucchini, cucumber slices, or mushrooms caps
Sliced apple
French **bread** chunks

(113)

Lo-Cheese Spread

About 1½ cups *LC, LCh, D, LS, v, k*

Combine in blender or processor:

¾ cup low-fat **pot cheese** or **hoop cheese** (*LS:* use **hoop** or low-salt **pot cheese**)
2 ounces low-fat, low-cholesterol Cheddar-type **cheese** (*LS:* use unsalted cheese)
3 scallions, sliced
1 tablespoon pimiento, chopped
1 teaspoon Worcestershire sauce (*LS:* omit; *v:* use steak sauce)
Freshly ground **pepper** to taste
⅜ teaspoon dry mustard

Blend until smooth. Combine in small saucepan:

1½ teaspoons **gelatin**
2 tablespoons dry white **wine** (*D:* use 5 teaspoons water plus 1 teaspoon brandy extract)

Blend and let stand for 1 minute. Then bring to a boil, stirring constantly. Blend gelatin mixture into cheese until smooth. Transfer cheese mixture to a bowl. Stir in:

2 tablespoons finely minced green pepper
2 tablespoons finely minced pimiento or red pepper

Transfer to a serving bowl and refrigerate until set, about 2 to 3 hours.

VARIATION: Stir in ¼ cup chopped walnuts before chilling (*LC:* omit).

(114)

Cheeseball

1 small ball or log *LCh, D, LS, v, k*

Combine in blender or food processor, processing until smooth:
6 ounces Cheddar **cheese** (*LCh:* use low-cholesterol cheese; *LS:* use low-sodium cheese)
¼ cup **pot cheese**
¼ cup chopped parsley leaves, tightly packed
¼ cup finely chopped onion, or to taste
1 to 2 teaspoons Worcestershire sauce, to taste (*LS:* omit; *v:* use steak sauce)
¾ teaspoon dry mustard
2 tablespoons unsalted **margarine,** melted
Add if needed to facilitate processing:
1 to 2 tablespoons **milk**
Turn mixture into bowl and blend in:
2 tablespoons chopped green pepper
2 tablespoons chopped red pepper
Chill for 30 minutes or until cheese mixture is moldable. Form into a ball or log and roll in a mixture of:
¼ cup finely chopped nuts
¼ cup finely chopped parsley
Wrap in waxed paper and chill until firm.
Serve with:
Crackers or **bread**

(115)

Mock Guacamole

About 2¼ cups *LC, LCh, D, V, v, P, Ml, k*

Combine in blender:
8 ounces tofu, soft style
5 ounces frozen chopped spinach, cooked, and squeezed dry
¾ cup chopped onion

(*Recipe continued on next page*)

2 medium garlic cloves
1 tablespoon **lemon juice**
¾ teaspoon **salt** (*P:* omit; add additional lemon juice to taste)
2 to 3 canned green chili peppers, chopped, optional
Dash of Tabasco or to taste

Blend until smooth, add:

¼ cup finely chopped red pepper

Serve with:

Crackers *or* CRUDITÉS **(383)**

(116)

Mushroom Pâté

About 2 cups *LC, LCh, D, LS, V, v, P, Ml, k, B*

In **non-stick** skillet, heat:

1 tablespoon **oil** (*P:* substitute 1 tablespoon dry white **wine**)

Sauté in skillet:

1 pound fresh mushrooms, finely chopped, excess moisture squeezed out
1 cup finely chopped scallions *or* shallots (*B:* omit)
2 teaspoons finely minced garlic (*B:* omit)

Cook until all moisture disappears. Remove from heat and season with:

Salt (*P* and *LS:* substitute 1 tablespoon **lemon juice**)
Pepper (*B:* omit; *P:* use white)

In a small saucepan, combine:

½ envelope unflavored **gelatin**
¼ cup dry white **wine** (*P*) or brandy (*D* and *B:* substitute tomato juice if wine prohibited)

Blend and let stand 1 minute to soften gelatin. Then heat to boiling. Remove from heat and stir into mushroom mixture. Pour into a small mold or bowl, **non-stick** treated. Chill until firmly set. Unmold and garnish with:

Watercress or parsley

(117)

Mushroom-Almond Pâté

About 2½ cups *LCh, D, LS, V, v, Ml, k*

Sauté and season mushrooms, scallions, and onions as for MUSHROOM PÂTÉ (**116**) recipe. Transfer to blender or processor and blend until smooth. Add:

½ cup finely ground almonds or walnuts

Proceed as for MUSHROOM PÂTÉ, adding gelatin-wine (or brandy) mixture, and chilling for several hours.

(118)

Pesto Pâté

1 1-quart ring mold *LC, LCh, D, v, k*

In blender or processor combine and puree:

1¾ cups loosely packed fresh basil
3 to 4 cloves garlic or to taste
½ cup pine nuts
½ cup water
⅔ cup grated **cheese** (*LC, LCh* and *D:* use low-cholesterol, low-fat cheese)
1 tablespoon **oil**

Divide pesto mixture in 3 parts.

Puree and combine with ⅓ of the pesto:

1½ cups chopped cooked spinach, squeezed dry
1 **egg** white

Add to taste:

Salt and **pepper**

Layer mixture evenly at bottom of **non-stick** 1 quart ring mold.

Puree and combine with ⅓ of the pesto:

1½ cups chopped cooked cauliflower, drained
1 **egg** white

Add to taste:

Salt and **pepper**

(*Recipe continued on next page*)

Spread mixture over spinach mixture.
Puree and combine with last ⅓ of pesto:
 1½ cups chopped cooked broccoli, drained
 1 **egg** white
Add to taste:
 Salt and **pepper**
Spread mixture over cauliflower mixture. Place ring mold in pan of hot water. Bake at 350° F for 40 minutes or until set. Chill in mold. Unmold and serve with:
 Crackers or dark **bread**

(119)

Pesto–Pâté Stuffed Celery

LC, LCh, D, v, k

Prepare PESTO PÂTÉ (**118**). Instead of unmolding, use to fill celery stalks or other vegetables.

(120)

Raisin-Nut Farmer Cheese

About 2½ cups *LCh, LS, v, K, k*

Blend together with fork until very smooth:
 3 tablespoons **apple juice concentrate**
 ½ cup raisins
 ½ cup coarsely chopped walnuts
 1 pound **farmer cheese** (*LS:* use unsalted **farmer cheese**)
 2 tablespoons sweet red **wine** or 2 tablespoons additional **apple juice concentrate**
 1½ tablespoons **orange juice concentrate**
 Cinnamon to taste *or* 1 teaspoon freshly grated orange peel
Place mixture on wax paper and roll into a log shape. Chill, wrapped in wax paper, for several hours. Garnish with:
 Chopped nuts
Serve with:
 Crackers

(121)

Salmon Pâté

About 1 cup *LCh, D, k, B*

Puree in blender or food processor:

1 7-ounce can salmon, drained
1 medium boiled potato, peeled
¼ cup chopped onion (*B:* omit)
2 tablespoons sour cream
2 tablespoons low-fat **cottage cheese**
2 tablespoons melted **margarine**
2 hard-boiled **egg** whites
Salt to taste

The following additions are optional:

¼ cup chopped fresh dill, added to processor
2 tablespoons chopped smoked salmon, stirred in (*B:* omit)

Transfer to serving dish and chill well. Serve with, depending on diet:

CRUDITÉS (**383**)
MELBA SQUARES (**16**)
Crackers

Or use as filling for ANGEL EGGS (**132**)

(122)

Spiked Tofu Zucchini Dip

About 1 cup *LC, LCh, V, v, k*

Combine in blender or processor and process until smooth:

½ pound tofu
1 small zucchini, peeled and sliced
2 tablespoons **mayonnaise** (*V:* leave out)
1 tablespoon dry vermouth (See **wine**)
1 tablespoon sweet vermouth (See **wine**)

Stir in well:

1 package dry onion soup mix

Let dip stand for 1 to 2 hours in the refrigerator. Serve with (depending on diet):

CRUDITÉS (**383**)
Chips

(123)

Tahina Dip

About 1¼ cups *LCh, D, V, v, P, Ml, k*

Puree in blender or food processor:

1 cup tahina (sesame paste)
1 to 2 tablespoons **lemon juice**
1 to 3 cloves garlic, sliced
Salt to taste (*P:* use ¼ teaspoon **soy sauce**)
¼ cup water or enough to bring to desired consistency

Serve with:

CRUDITÉS or CRISP TENDER VEGETABLES **(383)**

(124)

Teriyaki Dipping Sauce

About 1¼ cups *LC, LCh, D, V, v, Ml, k*

In small saucepan, combine:

¾ cup vegetable **stock** or water
3 tablespoons **apple juice concentrate**
2 tablespoons **soy sauce**
1 tablespoon thinly sliced scallion
1 tablespoon **orange juice concentrate**
1 tablespoon sherry **wine** (*D:* omit)
1 garlic clove, crushed
½ teaspoon grated ginger root or pinch ground ginger, or to taste.

Bring to a boil and simmer over low heat 20 minutes, stirring occasionally. Prepare paste of:

2 tablespoons vegetable **stock** or water
1 tablespoon cornstarch

Add cornstarch mixture to sauce and stir until sauce thickens and becomes translucent. Serve as dipping sauce with:

CRISP-TENDER VEGETABLES and CRUDITÉS **(383)**

(125)

Tuna Tapenade

About 1 cup *LCh, D, Ml, k*

In blender or processor, blend well:
1 6 to 7-ounce can tuna in water, drained
¼ cup pitted black olives
1½ teaspoons anchovy paste
1 tablespoon capers, drained
2 to 3 teaspoons **lemon juice**
1 tablespoon **oil** (Opt.)
2 tablespoons water, or to desired consistency
Fresh **pepper** to taste
Serve as a spread with:
CRUDITÉS (**383**)
MELBA SQUARES (**16**)
Or stuff mixture into:
ANGEL EGGS (**132**) *or*
Vegetables, such as cherry tomatoes, mushrooms, or zucchini

(126)

Vegetable Pâté

1 9 x 5-inch or 4 x 11-inch loaf *LC, LCh, D, v, k*

Tip: Prepare the day before

Bring to room temperature according to package directions:
1 package phyllo leaves (6 will be needed; refrigerate remainder)
Layer leaves in **non-stick** loaf pan, leaving ends to overlap sides of pan. Cover with damp dish towel to keep from drying out.
Combine in blender, processing until smooth:
½ cup evaporated skimmed **milk**
½ cup skim **milk**
¼ cup **flour**
3 **egg** whites
Set aside.

(Recipe continued on next page)

Combine in blender or processor, blending until fine but not pureed:

2 cups cooked spinach, pressed dry
¼ cup chopped onions
1 teaspoon thyme, or to taste

Stir ¼ of milk mixture into spinach, and add to taste:

Salt
Pepper

Spread spinach mixture evenly over phyllo leaves in bottom of loaf pan. Cover again with dish towel.

Combine in bowl:

2 cups finely chopped carrots
¼ cup pureed or very finely minced onions
¾ teaspoon nutmeg, or to taste
Salt to taste
White **pepper** to taste

Spread carrot layer evenly over spinach layer and recover with towel. Down center of carrot layer, arrange in one or two rows:

6 to 8 canned artichoke hearts, drained and sprinkled with lemon juice
or
6 to 8 whole mushroom caps sprinkled with lemon juice

Combine in blender or processor and chop finely:

2 cups chopped cooked broccoli or cut green beans, drained
¼ cup chopped onions
1 teaspoon minced garlic

Stir into broccoli (or bean) mixture, ¼ of milk mixture. Spread broccoli (or bean) mixture over carrot layer and artichokes or mushrooms. In **non-stick** skillet, heat over medium heat:

2 teaspoons **margarine, butter,** or **oil**

Add to skillet and **sauté** until golden brown:

⅓ cup chopped onions

Combine onions in blender or processor with:

2 cups parcooked cauliflower pieces, drained.

Add to cauliflower the remaining milk mixture plus:

1 teaspoon Sauté Onion
Salt to taste
White **pepper** to taste

Spoon cauliflower mixture over broccoli (or bean) layer. Smooth surface. Fold phyllo leaves over top mixture to enclose. Spread phyllo with:

2 teaspoons melted **margarine** or **butter**

Cover with wax paper and then with foil, crimped to seal at the edges. Set in larger pan of hot water (⅔ way up side of loaf). Set pans in oven and bake in preheated oven at 325° F for 1½ to 2 hours, or until set. Refrigerate in pan overnight. Unmold to serve.

(127)

Vegetarian Chopped Liver

6 appetizer servings or serve as spread

LC, LCh, D, LS, V, v, P, Ml, k

Heat in **non-stick** skillet over medium heat:
    ½ to 1 tablespoon **oil** (*P:* omit)
Sauté in skillet until well browned:
    2 large onions, chopped
    2 ribs celery, chopped (*LS:* omit)
Cool. Grind or chop together with:
    7 hard-cooked **eggs** *or* 10 hard-cooked **egg** whites (*LC, LCh,* and *P:* use whites only; *LS:* use 4 whole **eggs;** if diet both *LCh* and *LS:* use 2 whole **eggs** and 2 whites; *V:* use ½-pound tofu)
    1 cup walnuts (*P* and *LC:* use cooked lentils, chickpeas, or chestnuts)
    3 cups cut green beans, cooked crisp-tender
Season to taste with:
    Coarse **salt** (*LS* and *P:* omit)
    Pepper (*P:* use white)
Serve with:
    Bread or **crackers**
Or stuff in:
    ANGEL EGGS (**132**)

(128)

Curried Soy Nuts

1 cup seasoned nuts *LC, LCh, LS, D, V, v, Ml, k*

Melt in small, **non-stick** skillet:
  1 to 2 teaspoons unsalted **margarine**
Add:
  ¼ teaspoon curry powder
  ⅛ teaspoon **salt** (*LS*: omit)
Add and toss to coat:
  1 cup unsalted soy nuts
Cook over low heat for 2 to 3 minutes, shaking pan frequently.

(129)

Mushroom "Nuts"

LC, LCh, D, V, v, P, Ml, k

Drain, reserving liquid for future cooking:
  1 8-ounce can button mushrooms
Spread mushrooms on **non-stick** cookie sheet. Sprinkle with your choice of:
  Salt (*P:* omit)
  Garlic powder
  Onion Powder
  Chili powder
  Curry powder
  Season **salt** (*P:* omit)
Bake at 250° F for about 1 hour or until mushrooms are brown and completely dry. Turn once or twice during baking. Serve as "nuts" with cocktails.

(130)

Peppery Chick Peas

About 4 cups *LC, LCh, D, V, v, P, Ml, K*, k*

Heat in a saucepan, simmering for 3 to 4 minutes until heated through:

2 20-ounce cans chick peas

Drain thoroughly and heat for 1 or 2 minutes, shaking the pot vigorously to be sure all moisture is evaporated. Sprinkle peas with:

Salt to taste (*P:* omit)

Pepper to taste (*P:* use white)

* Heat open can in pot of boiling water.

(131)

Seasoned Popcorn

6 cups *LC, LCh, LS, D, V, v, P, Ml, k*

In small saucepan, melt over low heat:

1 to 2 tablespoons unsalted **margarine**

Add over very low heat, being careful not to let margarine burn:

¼ teaspoon cumin

⅛ teaspoon chili powder

¼ teaspoon **salt** (*LS:* omit)

or

¼ to ½ teaspoon curry powder

¼ teaspoon **salt** (*LS:* omit)

Cook over very low heat for two minutes longer to blend flavors. Drizzle over:

6 cups popcorn

Toss well. Popcorn can be stored in plastic bags in a cool dry place. *Note:* Air-popping is the lowest calorie method of making popcorn. (*LC:* Air-popped seasoned or unseasoned is preferable; *LS:* do not add salt; *P:* use only air-popped and do not add salt). Avoid using popcorn that comes with its own shortening—it's usually a high-cholesterol blend.

(132)

Angel Eggs I

20 angel eggs ***See fillings***

Slice in half lengthwise:

10 hard-boiled **eggs**

Scoop out the yolks and discard. Reserve the whites. Prepare choice of fillings:

EGGPLANT CAVIAR (**106**) (*LC, LCh, D, LS, V, v, P, Ml, k*)
TUNA TAPENADE (**125**) (*LCh, D, Ml, k*)
CREAMY AVOCADO DIP (**103**) (*D, v, k, B*)
SALMON PÂTÉ (**121**) (*LCh, D, k, B*)

Or prepare your favorite dip or spread. Fill egg whites. Garnish if desired and diet permits with:

Fresh parsley sprigs
Small, diamond-shaped pieces of pimiento or black olive
Black or stuffed-olive slices
Chopped fresh chives

(133)

Angel Eggs II

20 angel eggs ***See fillings***

Prepare eggs as in ANGEL EGGS I. Fill with choice of fillings:

EGGPLANT CAVIAR (**106**) (*LC, LCh, D, LS, V, v, P, Ml, k*)
TUNA TAPENADE (**125**) (*LCh, D, Ml, k*)
VEGETARIAN CHOPPED LIVER (**127**) (*LC, LCh, D, LS, V, v, P, Ml, k*)
DILLED SALMON-AVOCADO SPREAD (**105**) (*LC, LCh, D, Ml, k, B*)

Garnish as desired.

(134)

Baked Mushroom Squares

16 squares *LCh, D, LS, v, k*

Heat in **non-stick** skillet:

1 tablespoon **margarine** *or* **butter** *or* **oil**

Sauté in skillet until soft and golden:

2 cups sliced fresh mushrooms

In bowl, combine mushrooms with:

¼ cup **mayonnaise** (*LCh:* use low-cholesterol **mayonnaise;** *LS:* use low-sodium)

¼ cup grated **cheese** (*LCh* and *D:* use low-cholesterol low-fat **cheese;** *LS:* use unsalted)

¼ cup sour cream (*LCh* and *D:* use low-fat **yogurt)**

Set aside.

Flatten with a rolling pin:

8 slices whole wheat **bread,** crusts removed

Spread mushroom mixture on 4 of the slices and cover with remaining 4 slices, making 4 sandwiches. Cut each sandwich into 4 squares. Dip squares in a mixture of:

2 **egg** whites, lightly beaten (*LS:* use 1 **egg** white)

½ cup skim **milk** (*LS:* use water)

Then dip them in a mixture of:

¼ cup wheat germ

¼ cup whole wheat **bread** crumbs or matzo crumbs

¼ cup finely chopped nuts

2 tablespoons grated **cheese** (*LCh* and *D:* use low-cholesterol low-fat cheese)

Place squares on a **non-stick** baking sheet and bake at 400° F for 10 minutes or until crumb crust is nicely browned. Serve hot.

(135)

Canapés on White I

24 canapés *v, k, B**

Remove crusts from:
6 slices white **bread**
Cut into 24 rounds or squares. Lightly spread with:
Butter or **margarine**
Combine in blender or food processor, blending until smooth:
¼ cup whipped cream cheese (fat restricted: use **hoop** or low-fat **pot cheese**)
¼ cup chopped cooked spinach, squeezed dry
Dash nutmeg, or to taste (*B:* use allspice or omit)
Spread mixture on 8 of the rounds or squares. Garnish with:
Hard-cooked **egg** slices, or egg-white rings
Combine in blender, and process until smooth:
1 cup cooked or canned peas
2 tablespoons tomato juice
¼ cup whipped cream cheese (fat restricted: use **hoop** or low-fat **pot cheese**)
Add to taste:
Salt
Spread on 8 of the remaining rounds or squares. Garnish with:
A ring of tiny peas
Chop together:
⅓ cup cooked mushrooms
2 tablespoons sour cream
1 teaspoon very finely minced parsley
Salt to taste
Spread on remaining rounds. Garnish with:
Tiny button mushrooms
Dash of paprika

* Except low-residue or milk-restricted diets.

(136)

Canapé Whirls

24 to 30 canapés *v, k, B*

Using a rolling pin, roll the slices of bread in CANAPES ON WHITE I (**135**) recipe as thin as possible. Spread very thinly with **butter** or **margarine** and then spread each filling on 2 of the slices. Roll up as a jelly roll, and press edges to seal. Chill, seam side down, in refrigerator for several hours. To serve, slice and arrange flat on a platter.

(137)

Canapés on White II

24 canapés *LCh, D, Ml, k, B*

Follow recipe for CANAPES ON WHITE I (**135**), but substitute either or both of the following fillings:

Puree together:

1 3½-ounce can tuna, drained
1 small avocado (*low-residue:* use 8 ounces tofu)
1 tablespoon **lemon juice**

Garnish rounds with:

Slivers of avocado

Puree together:

1 3½-ounce can salmon, drained
1 tablespoon melted **margarine**
Lemon juice to taste

Garnish rounds with:

Slices of hard-cooked **egg**

(138)

Fish-Butter Canapés

24 to 36 canapés *D, Ml, K, k*

Mash together until well blended:
 ¼ cup softened **butter** or **margarine**
 2 teaspoons anchovy paste
 1 teaspoon **lemon juice**
Spread anchovy butter on:
 Crackers or MELBA ROUNDS (**16**) (*K:* use packaged crackers)
Garnish with:
 Sprigs of parsley
Arrange on serving platter.
Combine and mash until smooth:
 2 tablespoons softened **butter** or **margarine**
 ¼ teaspoon Worcestershire sauce
 4 skinless, boneless sardines
 ½ teaspoon **lemon juice** or to taste
Spread sardine butter on:
 Crackers or MELBA ROUNDS (**16**) (*K:* use packaged crackers)
Top with:
 Cucumber slices *or*
 Sprigs of dill
Arrange on serving platter.

(139)

Mushroom Roll-Ups

16 slices *LCh, D, LS, V, v, k, B*

In **non-stick** skillet, melt:
 1 tablespoon **margarine**
Sauté in skillet until soft:
 1 cup sliced fresh mushrooms
Crumb in blender or processor and set aside:
 1 slice **bread**
With rolling pin, roll flat:
 4 slices **bread,** crusts removed

Spread slices with:
 2 tablespoons sour cream *or*
 1 tablespoon softened **margarine** (*V* and *B* milk restricted: use **margarine**)
Sprinkle with:
 1 teaspoon finely chopped parsley
Spread with mushroom mixture. If desired, add:
 Salt to taste (*LS:* omit)
Roll up, pressing edges to seal. Dip in:
 1 beaten **egg** white
Then roll in reserved bread crumbs. Bake in preheated oven at 400° F for 10 minutes or until crumb crusts are golden brown. Slice each roll into 4 rounds. Serve warm.

(140)

Smoked Salmon-Avocado Canapés

12 canapés *Ml, K, k*

Arrange on platter:
 12 sesame rounds
Spread on each a very thin coat of:
 Mayonnaise
Pit, peel, and mash:
 1 small avocado
Spread a layer of avocado on each round.
Slice into 12 squares, placing one on each sesame round:
 ⅛ pound smoked salmon
Squeeze over each canapé a bit of:
 Lemon juice

(141)

Open Zucchini Sandwiches

1 dozen *LC, LCh, D, LS, V, v, P, Ml, k*

Combine in blender and puree:
¼ pound tofu, soft style
1 garlic clove, minced
1 tablespoon **lemon juice**
⅛ teaspoon dry mustard
1 tablespoon **apple juice concentrate**
Salt to taste (*LS:* omit; *P:* substitute ¼ teaspoon **soy sauce**)
Pepper to taste (*P:* use white)
Spread mixture on:
12 ½-inch slices of unpeeled zucchini
Sprinkle each open sandwich with:
Sesame seeds

(142)

Mushroom-Vegetable Strudel

3 strips of strudel *LC, LCh, D, LS, V, v, P, Ml, k*

Bring to room temperature according to package directions:
1 package of phyllo leaves
Chop finely:
1 pound fresh mushrooms
Squeeze out excess moisture in a towel. Set aside.
Heat in **non-stick** skillet over medium flame:
½ to 1 tablespoon **oil** (*P:* use 1 tablespoon dry white **wine**)
Sauté in skillet until softened:
½ cup finely chopped shallots, scallions, or onions
Add mushrooms and continue sautéing over low heat until all moisture has evaporated. Remove from heat.
Prepare:
½ cup whole wheat **bread** crumbs
Melt:
1 tablespoon **margarine** (*P:* use dry white **wine**)
1 tablespoon **stock**

Set aside.
Cut in strips and set aside 1 or more of the following:
- 1 14-ounce can, drained, or 1 10-ounce package frozen artichoke hearts thawed (*LS:* omit)
- 1 small zucchini
- 1 small carrot (*LS:* use whole green beans)

Carrots should be blanched for 1 minute in boiling water.
Count out:
- 9 phyllo leaves

Store remaining leaves in refrigerator. Cover 8 leaves with a damp towel. Spread 1 sheet of phyllo on another damp towel. Brush with margarine-stock mixture. Sprinkle with bread crumbs. Add another sheet and repeat. And a third. Then take ⅓ of mushroom mixture and spread in a line down long side of phyllo sheet. Arrange down center of mushrooms some of the vegetable strips or artichoke hearts. Roll up as for strudel and place on **non-stick** cookie sheet. Brush with margarine-stock mixture. Prepare 2 additional rolls using remaining ingredients. Bake at 400° F for 15 minutes or until golden. Slice and serve warm.

(143)

Spinach-Feta Strudel

3 to 4 strudel strips ***LC, D, v, k***

Bring to room temperature according to package directions:
- 1 package of phyllo leaves

In a large **non-stick** skillet, heat over medium flame:
- 1 tablespoon **margarine** or **oil**

Sauté in margarine:
- 1½ teaspoons minced garlic

Add, and continue to sauté over low heat for 10 minutes, stirring frequently:
- ½ cup finely chopped red onion
- 2 small scallions, thinly sliced
- ½ cup finely chopped fresh parsley
- ¼ cup finely chopped fresh dill or 1 tablespoon dried
- 2 tablespoons finely chopped shallots

(*Recipe continued on next page*)

Add to skillet and stir until heated through:
1 10-ounce package frozen chopped spinach, cooked and squeezed dry
Add and blend well:
½ pound feta cheese, crumbled
½ cup **bread** crumbs
2 **egg** whites, slightly beaten
Melt and set aside:
2 tablespoons **margarine**
Prepare and set aside:
½ cup **bread** crumbs
Count out:
9 strudel leaves
Store remaining leaves in refrigerator. Cover 8 leaves with a damp towel. Spread 1 sheet of phyllo on another damp towel. Brush with melted margarine. Sprinkle with bread crumbs. Add another sheet and repeat. Add a third sheet and repeat. Then take ⅓ of spinach-feta mixture and spread in a line down long side of phyllo sheet. Roll up as for strudel and place on **non-stick** cookie sheet. Brush with more of the melted margarine. Prepare 2 additional rolls using remaining ingredients. Brush each with melted margarine. Bake at 400° F for 15 minutes or until golden.
Slice and serve warm.

(144) *SPINACH-CHEESE STRUDEL*

3 to 4 strudels *LC, LCh, D, v, k*

Proceed as in SPINACH-FETA QUICHE (**143**), substituting 6 to 8 ounces low-cholesterol **cheese** plus salt to taste in place of feta cheese.

(145)
Stuffed Mushrooms

16 to 20 mushrooms *See fillings*

Wipe with damp paper towel and trim stems of:
1 pound large mushrooms, firm and white
Remove the stems.

In **non-stick** skillet, heat:

½ to 1 tablespoon **oil, butter** or **margarine** (Opt.; *P:* omit)
2 tablespoons **lemon juice**
1 tablespoon **stock** or dry **wine**
¼ teaspoon **salt** (*P* and *LS:* omit)
Several grinds of **pepper** (*P:* use white pepper)

Toss mushroom caps in skillet. Cover with round of wax paper and pan lid. Steam for 6 to 8 minutes or until mushrooms are tender, shaking the pan frequently. Let mushrooms cool. Fill with one or more of the following:

TUNA TAPENADE (**125**)
PESTO PÂTÉ (**118**)
LO-CHEESE SPREAD (**113**)

(146)

Baked Stuffed Mushrooms

16 to 20 mushrooms *LC, LCh, D, LS, V, v, P, Ml, k*

Wipe with a damp paper towel and trim stems of:

1 pound large fresh mushrooms, firm and white

Remove the stems and reserve for stuffing. Brush the caps with:

Lemon juice

Set aside until ready to fill. Prepare filling of choice.
In **non-stick** skillet heat:

½ to 1 tablespoon **oil, butter,** or **margarine** (*P:* omit)
1 tablespoon **stock** or dry **wine**
¼ teaspoon **salt** (*LS* and *P:* omit)

Toss mushrooms in skillet mixture and **sauté** for 3 minutes. Transfer with slotted spoon to a **non-stick** baking dish large enough to hold them in one layer. Arrange with open side up. Fill each with selected filling. Dot, if desired, with:

Butter or **margarine** (*P* and *LC:* omit)

Add to baking dish:

¼ cup dry white **wine** (*D:* use stock)
¼ cup water
1 tablespoon **lemon juice**

Bake in preheated oven at 350° F for 20 to 25 minutes or until tops are lightly browned. Serve warm.

(147)

Cheese and Nut-Stuffed Mushrooms

16 to 20 mushrooms *D, v, k*

Prepare BAKED STUFFED MUSHROOMS (**146**). To prepare filling, heat in **non-stick** pan over medium flame:

1 tablespoon **butter, margarine,** or **oil**

Sauté in pan:

2 shallots or 4 medium scallions (whites only), chopped

Add to pan and continue sautéing the reserved mushroom stems and:

3 tablespoons dry white **wine** (*D:* if prohibited, use 1 tablespoon tarragon vinegar)

Add and chop together in processor or blender:

¾ cup whole wheat **bread** crumbs
¼ cup wheat germ
¼ cup grated **cheese**
¼ cup chopped walnuts

VARIATION: Use filling to stuff: cherry tomatoes, small zucchini, baby eggplants, onions.

(148)

Crumb and Nut-Stuffed Mushrooms

16 to 20 mushrooms *LC, LCh, D, LS, V, v, P, Ml, k*

Prepare BAKED STUFFED MUSHROOMS (**146**). To prepare filling, heat in a **non-stick** skillet over medium flame:

½ to 1 tablespoon **oil** (*P:* omit)

Sauté in skillet:

2 teaspoons minced garlic
1½ cups finely chopped onion

When onions are softened, add:

½ cup chopped green and/or red pepper

Continue cooking until peppers are softened. Add chopped mushroom stems and cook for 3 or 4 minutes or until stems are softened. Remove from heat and stir in:

1 cup whole wheat matzo or unsalted **cracker crumbs**
2 tablespoons chopped pimiento
¼ **cup pine nuts** (*P:* use chopped roasted chestnuts)
2 tablespoons dry white **wine** (*D:* use **stock**)
2 tablespoons **wine** vinegar (*D:* use tarragon vinegar)
Salt to taste (*P* and *LS:* omit)
Pepper to taste (*P:* use white pepper)

Blend mixture well. Fill mushroom caps with mixture.

(149)

Spinach-Stuffed Mushrooms

16 to 20 mushrooms *v, k, B**

Clean and trim:

1 pound large mushrooms, firm and white

Remove and reserve stems. Prepare:

1 recipe CREAMED SPINACH **(393)**

In **non-stick** pan, heat:

1 teaspoon **margarine** or **butter**

Sauté reserved mushroom stems, chopped, in skillet until very soft. Add to CREAMED SPINACH along with:

2 ounces shredded or finely chopped **cheese** (*B:* use mild American)
½ cup **bread** crumbs
1 **egg** white, slightly beaten

Arrange mushrooms on **non-stick** baking sheet, open sides up, and stuff hollows with filling. Bake in preheated 350° F oven for 15 minutes, or until mushroom caps are soft.

* Except low-residue or milk restricted diets.

(150)

Stuffed Peppers

8 halves *LC, LCh, D, LS, V, v, P, Ml, k*

Peel and remove seeds and sinews from:
4 nicely shaped green or red peppers
Set aside.
In **non-stick** skillet, heat:
½ to 1 tablespoon **oil** (*P:* omit)
In skillet, **sauté** until golden:
2 cups chopped onions
2 teaspoons minced garlic
Add and cook for 2 to 3 minutes:
1 cup chopped fresh mushrooms
When mushrooms are softened, remove from heat and stir in:
½ cup whole wheat matzo or unsalted **cracker** crumbs
¼ cup pine nuts (*P:* omit)
2 tablespoons chopped pimiento
2 tablespoons dry white **wine** (*D:* if prohibited, use **stock**)
2 tablespoons **wine** vinegar (*D:* if prohibited, use tarragon vinegar)
Salt to taste (*P* and *LS:* omit)
Pepper to taste (*P:* use white)
Blend mixture well. Fill pepper halves with mixture and place in **non-stick** baking pan large enough to hold peppers in one layer. Add to pan:
2 tablespoons dry white **wine** (*D:* if prohibited, use **stock**)
1 tablespoon **wine** vinegar (*D:* if prohibited, use tarragon vinegar)
Bake in preheated oven at 350° F for 30 to 40 minutes, or until filling is nicely browned.
Serve hot or at room temperature.

(151)

Veal-Stuffed Prunes

8 servings *LCh, LS, Ml*

Tip: Veal mixture can also be made into meatballs or used to stuff eggplants, zucchini, or vine leaves (except *LS*).

Heat in **non-stick** skillet:
 2 tablespoons **oil**
Sauté in skillet until golden:
 1 large onion, chopped
Combine onions to form a smooth mixture with:
 ¾ pound ground lean veal
 1 cup walnuts, finely chopped
 ¼ cup raisins
 Salt to taste (*LS:* omit)
 Pepper to taste
Use mixture to fill cavities of:
 30 ready-to-eat pitted prunes
Place prunes in **non-stick** baking dish.
In a small bowl, combine:
 ¼ cup tomato sauce (*LS:* use unsalted sauce)
 1½ cups water
 3 tablespoons **lemon juice**
 ¼ cup **apple juice concentrate**
 1 teaspoon brown **sugar**
Pour mixture over prunes. Cover the dish and bake in a preheated oven at 350° F for 45 minutes.
Serve warm or at room temperature.

(152)

Cheese-Stuffed Snow Peas

25 to 30 stuffed snow peas *LC, LCh, D, LS, v, P, k*

Blanch for 1 minute in boiling water:

25 to 30 snow peas

With a sharp knife, gently split snow peas open on one side. Set aside while preparing filling.

Combine in blender or food processor:

1 cup **hoop cheese**

½ cup cooked chopped spinach, squeezed dry (*LS:* use chopped broccoli)

1 tablespoon chopped onion or shallot

½ teaspoon **soy sauce** (*LS:* omit)

Stir in:

2 tablespoons finely chopped red or green pepper

Fill snow peas and chill before serving.

(153)

Rice-Stuffed Vine Leaves

6 to 8 servings, or 30 to 40 hors d'oeuvres *LC, LCh, D, LS, V, v, P, Ml, k*

Tip: Use same filling for peppers, mushrooms, or tiny eggplants.

Combine in small saucepan and simmer for 5 minutes until raisins soften (*D:* omit this step):

½ cup **wine**

¼ cup **apple juice**

¼ cup water

½ cup white raisins

Carefully unfold and rinse in colander under cold water:

1 8-ounce jar vine leaves (*LS:* if unsalted vine leaves are not available, use small cabbage leaves softened in boiling water)

Heat in **non-stick** skillet:

1 tablespoon **oil** (*P:* omit)

Sauté in skillet until golden brown:

1½ cups chopped onion

Add and **sauté** for another 3 minutes, stirring constantly:

⅔ cup raw rice (*P:* increase to 1 cup)

Drain raisins. Measure liquid and add water to make 1⅓ cups. (*D:* use ⅔ cup water and ⅔ cup apple juice) Add raisins and liquid to skillet with:

½ cup pine nuts (*D:* increase to ¾ cup; *P:* omit)

Stir once with a fork, cover, and simmer slowly for 25 minutes or until all the liquid has been absorbed. Remove from heat and stir in:

1 tablespoon finely chopped parsley
½ teaspoon **salt** (*LS:* omit; *P:* use **soy sauce**)
Pepper (*P:* use white)
⅛ teaspoon cinnamon
2 small tomatoes, peeled, seeded, and chopped

Place a tablespoon of the rice mixture in the center of each vine leaf. Fold sides of each leaf; then fold up bottom of leaf. Roll up from bottom. Place each roll in a **non-stick** flameproof baking dish just large enough to hold all the stuffed vine leaves tightly packed in a single layer. Add to dish:

1 cup dry white **wine** (*D:* use **stock**)
2 tablespoons **lemon juice**
Water to almost cover

Place plate or other weight over vine leaves and cover baking dish. Bring to a boil over medium heat. Reduce heat and simmer for 50 minutes. Serve warm, at room temperature, or chilled.

(154)

Mushroom-Stuffed Zucchini

4 servings *LC, LCh, D, LS, V, v, P, Ml, k*

Scrub and slice in half lengthwise:

2 medium zucchini

Scoop out the centers with a melon scoop, leaving a ⅜-inch shell. Chop the scooped out centers with:

3 cups chopped fresh mushrooms
2 scallions, chopped fine

(Recipe continued on next page)

3 tablespoons **lemon juice**
3 tablespoons chopped red pepper or pimiento
3 tablespoons sunflower seeds (*P:* omit)

Blend mixture well. Add to taste:

Salt (*LS* and *P:* omit)
Pepper (*P:* use white)

Stuff mixture into zucchini halves. Chill. Slice to serve.

(155)

Hawaiian Meatballs, Sweet and Sour Sauce

LC, LCh, D, LS, Ml*

Combine in medium bowl, mixing until ingredients are well blended:

1 pound ground lean veal
2 slices **bread** crumbed in blender
2 **egg** whites (*LS:* use 1 whole **egg**)
1¼ teaspoons ground ginger
¼ cup minced green onion
¼ cup finely minced onion
¼ teaspoon garlic powder
2 teaspoons sherry **wine** (*D:* omit)

Shape into small balls. Bake on a **non-stick** baking sheet at 350° F for 15 to 20 minutes. Meanwhile, make paste of:

2 tablespoons cornstarch
½ cup chicken or vegetable **stock**
1 tablespoon **soy sauce** (*LS:* omit)

Combine in small saucepan:

1 cup chicken or vegetable **stock**
¼ cup thinly sliced scallions
½ cup **unsweetened** pineapple chunks
¼ cup chopped red pepper

Cover and simmer 5 minutes; add paste and:

¼ cup vinegar
½ cup pineapple juice
4 tablespoons **pineapple juice concentrate**
1 tablespoon sweet vermouth (see **wines**) (*D:* omit)

1 teaspoon brown **sugar,** packed tightly (*D:* use 2 tablespoons **apple juice concentrate**)
¼ teaspoon ground ginger or to taste

Simmer, stirring constantly, until sauce thickens. Serve with meatballs.

* Except those on diets limited in simple carbohydrates, such as fruit.

(156)

Tuna Balls in Tomato Sauce

25 tunaballs *LC, LCh, D, LS, P, Ml, k*

Prepare:
1 recipe TOMATO SAUCE (**425**)

Grind in blender or processor and transfer to mixing bowl:
1 6 to 7-ounce can chunk or solid white tuna in water, drained (*LS:* use low-sodium tuna if required)
1½ slices **bread**
¼ cup fresh parsley, loosely packed

Add to mixing bowl and stir to mix ingredients thoroughly:
1½ cups cooked brown rice
¼ cup chopped red pepper (or green if red unavailable)

In small saucepan simmer over low heat for 10 minutes:
¼ cup tomato juice (*LS:* use low-sodium juice)
1 teaspoon tomato paste (*LS:* use low-sodium paste)
1½ teaspoons oregano
1½ teaspoons basil
¼ teaspoon **salt** (*LS* omit; *P:* use **soy sauce**)

Add juice mixture to mixing bowl and stir to blend ingredients.

Add:
3 slightly-beaten **egg** whites (*LS:* use 2 whites plus 2 tablespoons water)
Salt to taste (*LS* and *P:* use **lemon juice** to taste)
Pepper to taste (*P:* use white **pepper**)

Stir to blend well. Shape into 2-inch balls. Arrange on **non-stick** baking sheet and bake in preheated oven at 325° F for 15 minutes or until lightly browned. Serve in TOMATO SAUCE as appetizers or as a main course with:
Pasta

(157)

Honeyed Chicken Nuggets

Servings vary *LC, LCh, LS, Ml, B*

Skin, bone, and cut into cubes the meat of:
2 whole chicken breasts (about 2 pounds)
Reserve bones for making **stock.** Dip chicken cubes in mixture of:
2 tablespoons honey
2 tablespoons **apple juice concentrate**
Roll cubes until covered in:
½ cup **bread** crumbs
Place breaded chicken cubes on a **non-stick** baking sheet. Ten minutes before serving, place in preheated 325° F oven and bake for 5 minutes. Turn and bake another 3 to 4 minutes, or until crumbs are nicely browned. Serve with a dip made of:
2 tablespoons honey
2 tablespoons **apple juice concentrate**
2 tablespoons **orange juice concentrate**

(158)

Indonesian Chicken Nuggets

6 to 8 appetizer servings *LCh, D, Ml*

Tip: Can be prepared ahead and baked just before serving.

Bone, skin, and cut into small cubes:
2 whole chicken breasts (about 2 pounds)
Reserve bones for making stock. Set chicken cubes aside.
Combine in blender and puree:
4 tablespoons **stock** *or* water
4 scallions, sliced
1 teaspoon minced garlic
1 teaspoon **soy sauce**
1 tablespoon **apple juice concentrate**
1 tablespoon **pineapple juice concentrate**
⅔ cup **lime juice**

Add and process until nuts are chopped fine:
1 cup roasted unsalted peanuts or walnuts
Divide mixture in half. Reserve one-half. To other half, add:
¼ cup wheat germ
Coat the chicken nuggets with this mixture, pressing it on all sides. Place nuggets on a **non-stick** baking sheet. Ten minutes before ready to serve, bake in a preheated 325° F oven for 5 minutes. Turn and bake for 3 to 4 minutes longer or until nuggets are crunchy on outside, but still tender inside. Serve hot with a dip made from the reserved sauce and:
2 tablespoons soft tofu, pureed

(159)

Tofu Tidbits

Servings vary *LC, LCh, V, v, Ml, k*

Combine in small dish:
⅓ cup **bread** crumbs
⅓ cup chopped walnuts (*LC:* omit; use additional ⅓ cup crumbs)
Dash **pepper**
Cut into 1-inch cubes:
1 pound firm tofu
Combine in small bowl:
1 tablespoon **soy sauce**
1 tablespoon honey
2 tablespoons **orange juice concentrate**
Dip tofu cubes first in orange juice mixture, then into crumbs, coating evenly on all sides. Bake on **non-stick** cookie sheet in preheated 400° F oven for 10 minutes. Turn and bake for another 10 minutes, or until brown on all sides. Serve with:
CUMBERLAND SAUCE **(420)**, made without currants or raisins
Or
Duck sauce

(160)

Apple-Veal Balls

15 meatballs *LC, LCh, D, LS, P, Ml, B*

In small **non-stick** skillet **sauté** over low heat, stirring occasionally, until just softened (*B:* until soft):

1 cup coarsely chopped apple
3 tablespoons **apple juice concentrate** (*D:* reduce to 1 tablespoon)
½ teaspoon thyme, crumbled
½ teaspoon **salt** (*LS* and *P:* omit)

Combine in large mixing bowl and mix thoroughly:

½ pound ground lean veal
½ cup **bread** crumbs
1 **egg** white, slightly beaten

Add apples to veal mixture. Stir to blend. Form into small meatballs. Arrange on **non-stick** baking sheet and bake in preheated oven at 325° F for 15 minutes or until golden brown and firm.

(161)

Antipasto Vegetables

12 appetizer servings *LC, LCh, D, LS, V, v, P, Ml, k*

Tip: Prepare a day ahead to allow time for marinating.

In a large saucepan, bring to a boil:

2 tablespoons **oil** (*P:* omit)
1 cup vegetable **stock**
¼ cup **wine** vinegar (*D:* use tarragon vinegar)
¼ cup **apple juice concentrate**
2 tablespoons dry white **wine** (*D:* omit)
1 teaspoon minced garlic
Salt to taste (*P* and *LS:* omit)
Pepper to taste (*P:* use white)

Add to this mixture and simmer for 5 minutes:

12 small white onions, peeled
1 small cauliflower, broken into small florets

In a large glass or earthenware bowl, combine:
- ½ pound small mushroom caps
- 2 green peppers, cut into strips
- 1 14-ounce can, drained, or 1 10-ounce package frozen and defrosted artichoke hearts (*LS:* omit)
- 18 black olives (*P* and *LS:* omit)

Pour marinade mixture with onions and cauliflower over these vegetables. Marinate for at least 24 hours in the refrigerator. Drain before serving. Arrange attractively on:
- Washed and crisped Romaine leaves

Garnish, if desired, with any of the following:
- Hard boiled **egg** slices or quarters
- Sliced pimientos
- Tomato wedges

(162)

Whole Artichokes

4 servings *LC, LCh, D, V, v, P, Ml, k,*

Wash and trim tops of heavy leaves and stems, from:
- 4 medium artichokes

Sprinkle cut edges with:
- **Lemon juice**

Place top down in glass, enamel, or stainless steel saucepan, with:
- 4 cups boiling water
- 1 tablespoon **lemon juice**
- 1 tablespoon **oil** (*P:* omit)
- 1 tablespoon **flour**

Bring water back to a boil and simmer, covered, for 20 to 40 minutes, or until artichokes are tender and leaves can be pulled off easily. Serve warm or cold with, depending upon diet:
- Melted **butter** *or*
- GARLIC MAYONNAISE (**255**) *or*
- GARLIC SOYO-NAISE (**267**) *or*
- LIGHT MUSTARD VINAIGRETTE (**260**)

(163)

Asparagus with Mushroom Sauce

4 servings *LC, LCh, D, LS, v, V, P, Ml, k*

Cook in boiling water until crisp tender:
1½ pounds asparagus, cleaned and trimmed
Set aside. Heat in **non-stick** skillet over medium flame:
½ to 1 tablespoon **oil** (Opt.; *P:* omit)
Sauté in skillet until golden:
1 large shallot (*or* 3 green onions), chopped
½ pound fresh mushrooms, cleaned and sliced
Add to skillet:
¾ cup vegetable **stock**
½ cup medium dry white **wine** (*D:* use 1 tablespoon vinegar and 3 tablespoons **apple juice** plus additional ¼ cup stock)
¼ teaspoon ground coriander
Salt to taste (*P* and *LS:* omit)
Pepper (*P:* use white pepper)
Blend together until very smooth:
2 tablespoons **stock**
1 tablespoon **flour**
Gradually stir this paste into the mushroom mixture, blending till smooth. Continue cooking, stirring constantly, for 3 or 4 minutes or until a thick sauce is formed.
When ready to serve, combine mushroom sauce and asparagus, and heat briefly. If desired, serve over:
Toast points

(164)

Asparagus Pepperonata

4 servings *LC, LCh, D, LS, V, v, P, Ml, k*

Heat in **non-stick** skillet over medium flame:
½ to 1 tablespoon **oil** (*P:* omit)
Sauté in skillet until softened:
2 medium onions, cut in chunks

Add:

1 red pepper, cut in chunks
1 green pepper, cut in chunks

Cover and cook 1 minute.
Uncover, add:

1 pound asparagus, cut in 1-inch lengths
1 tomato, cubed
2 tablespoons **wine** vinegar (*D:* if prohibited, use tarragon vinegar)
¼ teaspoon **salt** (Opt.; *P* and *LS:* omit)

Simmer 20 minutes or until liquid is somewhat thickened and vegetables are tender.

(165)

Zucchini Pepperonata

4 servings *LC, LCh, D, LS, V, v, P, Ml, k*

Substitute 5 cups sliced zucchini for asparagus in ASPARAGUS PEPPERONATA (**164**).

(166)

Pepperonata

4 servings *LC, LCh, D, LS, V, v, P, Ml, k*

Proceed as for ASPARAGUS PEPPERONATA (**164**), but omit asparagus and use instead 4 red and 4 green peppers.

(167)

Asparagus Vinaigrette

4 servings *LC, LCh, D, LS, V, v, P, Ml, k*

Steam over boiling water until tender:
1½ pounds fresh asparagus stalks, trimmed
Cool and arrange on serving platter. Drizzle with:
1 cup LIGHT MUSTARD VINAIGRETTE (**260**) (*LC, D, LS, P*)
or
1 cup regular vinaigrette
Serve at room temperature garnished with:
Sieved hard-cooked **egg** whites (*LS:* omit)
Lemon wedges
Cherry tomatoes *or* tomato slices *or* wedges

(168)

Bean Sprouts Teriyaki with Raisins

4 servings *LC, LCh, V, v, Ml, k*

In small saucepan, combine and simmer for 1½ minutes:
2 tablespoons **soy sauce**
1 small garlic clove, crushed
½ teaspoon grated ginger root
3 tablespoons **apple juice concentrate**
1 tablespoon medium dry sherry **wine**
¾ cup vegetable **stock**
1 tablespoon **orange juice concentrate**
Add and simmer for 5 minutes longer:
⅓ cup raisins
Combine:
1 tablespoon water
½ teaspoon cornstarch
Add to sauce, stirring over medium heat until thickened and translucent. Add:
5 cups bean sprouts, rinsed and drained
Toss to coat; serve at room temperature.

(169)

Cold Sesame Noodles and/or Bean Sprouts

4 servings *LC, LCh, D, V, v, Ml, k*

Heat in **non-stick** skillet over medium flame:
  1½ teaspoons **oil** (Opt.)
Sauté in skillet until soft:
  2 scallions
  1 teaspoon minced garlic
Blend in:
  2 tablespoons sherry **wine** (*D:* use 1 tablespoon vinegar)
  2 tablespoons **apple juice concentrate**
  2 tablespoons **pineapple juice concentrate**
  1 tablespoon **soy sauce,** or to taste
  1 tablespoon natural **unsweetened** peanut butter
  1 tablespoon sesame paste *or* 1 additional tablespoon peanut butter
  1 ½-inch slice ginger, mashed
  ⅛ teaspoon ground ginger
Cook, stirring frequently, for 3 minutes. Add and toss over low heat for 1 minute:
  ½ cup julienned seeded cucumber
Remove from heat; cool.
To serve, toss sauce thoroughly with:
  5 cups bean sprouts, steamed until just crisp tender, and cooled
  or
  8 ounces vermicelli or Chinese noodles, cooked, drained, rinsed, and cooled (*LCh* and *V:* do not use noodles with eggs)
  or
  2½ cups bean sprouts and 4 ounces of cooked noodles, tossed together
Sprinkle if desired with:
  Sesame seeds
  Sliced scallions
  Julienned cucumbers

(170)

Fish Cocktail with Creamy Avocado Dip

6 servings *LC, D, k, B**

Prepare and set aside:
1 recipe CREAMY AVOCADO DIP (**103**)
Divide into 6 sherbet or cocktail dishes:
3 cups poached firm-fleshed fish, in bite-sized chunks
Top each fish cocktail with a dollop of CREAMY AVOCADO DIP.
Garnish, as desired, with:
Slices of pimiento-stuffed olives
Lemon wedges
Fresh parsley sprigs

* Except low-residue diets.

(171)

Gefilte Fish en Gelée

10 to 12 appetizers *LC, LCh, D, LS, P, Ml, k, B*

Combine in a bowl and blend well:
1½ pounds ground white fish and yellow pike
1 onion, finely chopped (*B:* omit)
1 small carrot, finely chopped
2 **egg** whites, lightly beaten
2 tablespoons cold water
1 tablespoon matzo meal
Salt to taste (*LS* and *P:* omit)
White **pepper** (*B:* omit)
Form into a large loaf and wrap in:
Parchment paper
Place in large pot or fish poacher. Add to pot:
2 ribs celery, sliced (*LS:* use 1 rib celery)
3 **carrots**, sliced (*LS:* use 1 small carrot)

1 onion, sliced (*B:* omit)
Fish bones and heads, if available, wrapped in cheesecloth bag
Salt to taste (*LS* and *P:* omit)
White **pepper** to taste (*B:* omit)
Water to almost cover fish

Cover and simmer for about 1½ hours. Remove fish from liquid and chill. Strain fish stock and reserve. Cool ¼ cup in freezer. Combine ¼ cup cooled fish stock with:

1 envelope unflavored **gelatin**

Blend until smooth. Let stand 1 minute to soften gelatin. Heat to boiling ¾ cup of stock.

Stir boiling stock into gelatin mixture, until gelatin is completely dissolved. Cool and stir in:

6 tablespoons **mayonnaise** (*LC, LS, P,* and *D:* use SOYO-NAISE **(264)**)
4 teaspoons Dijon-style mustard *or* white horseradish (*LS:* use dry mustard to taste; *B:* omit)
4 teaspoons **apple juice concentrate**

Blend well and chill. When gelatin mixture is syrupy, remove chilled fish from refrigerator and spoon gelatin over. Return to refrigerator and chill until gelatin is set. Add 2 more layers of gelatin this way. Chill thoroughly. Combine 2 tablespoons cold stock with:

1 envelope unflavored **gelatin**

Blend until smooth and let stand 1 minute to soften. Heat ⅔ cup of stock to a boil and stir into gelatin mixture until gelatin is dissolved. Chill until syrupy. Meanwhile, cut decorative designs from:

Pimientos, green peppers, dill sprigs, egg whites, carrots from stock

When gelatin is ready, dip each piece into the gelatin and set in place in chosen design on fish. Refrigerate until design pieces are set. Brush with gelatin syrup to coat. Chill again. Repeat twice more until nice coating covers fish loaf. Chill fish loaf and remaining gelatin. Serve cold with cubes of gelatin as garnish.

(172)

Leeks Vinaigrette

5 to 6 servings *LC, LCh, D, V, v, Ml, k*

Carefully wash to remove sand and trim:

20 young leeks, root ends and green tops discarded

In a large kettle, bring to a boil:

3 quarts water

1 tablespoon **salt**

Add leeks and cook them for 30 minutes or until tender. Drain and cool under cold running water. Drain on paper towels for 5 minutes. Transfer to a shallow dish and let cool. Pour over leeks:

1 cup LIGHT MUSTARD VINAIGRETTE (**260**) *or*

1 cup regular ✓vinaigrette

Let marinate for 1 hour before serving. Garnish with:

Chopped parsley or

Sieved hard-cooked egg whites (*V:* leave out)

Lemon wedges

Cherry tomatoes or tomato slices or wedges

(173)

Mushrooms a la Grecque

4 to 6 appetizer servings *LC, LCh, D, LS, V, v, P, Ml, k*

In large saucepan combine:

2 large white or Bermuda onions (about 1 pound) peeled and cut into eighths, then separated into leaves

2 tablespoons fresh **lemon juice**

½ cup dry white **wine** (*D:* if prohibited, use additional stock)

1 tablespoon **oil** (*P:* omit)

½ cup vegetable **stock**

1 teaspoon ground coriander

1 teaspoon black peppercorns, crushed (*P:* use white)

3 large bay leaves

3 sprigs fresh thyme or ½ teaspoon dried

2 teaspoons **salt** (*LS:* omit; *P:* use ½ teaspoon **soy sauce**)

Bring these ingredients, covered, to a boil over high heat for two or three minutes. Add:

¾ pound fresh button mushrooms, or large mushrooms cut into quarters or eighths.

Bring to a boil again, cover, and continue boiling for another 1 or 2 minutes. Transfer to a covered bowl and cool. Mushrooms can be kept in the refrigerator for a week.

(174) *MUSHROOMS AND ARTICHOKES A LA GRECQUE*

8 to 10 appetizer servings *LC, LCh, D, V, v, P, Ml, k*

Follow recipe for MUSHROOMS A LA GRECQUE (**173**), doubling ingredients and adding with mushrooms: 2 14-ounce cans, drained or 2 10-ounce packages frozen and defrosted artichoke hearts.

(175)

Mushroom Ambrosia

6 servings *v, K, k*

Blend in bowl of electric mixer (*K:* mix by hand):

¼ cup sour cream
¼ cup **buttermilk**
½ cup **mayonnaise**
1 small garlic clove, crushed (*K:* use ⅛ teaspoon garlic powder)
1 tablespoon finely chopped fresh parsley
1 tablespoon white vinegar
1 tablespoon fresh **lemon juice**
2 teaspoons freshly chopped basil, or ½ teaspoon dried
1 teaspoon Worcestershire sauce (*v:* use steak sauce)
1 teaspoon Sherry **wine** and ¼ teaspoon salt, or 1 teaspoon cooking sherry
Dash **pepper**

Gently toss with:

1 pound washed, stemmed, and thinly sliced fresh mushrooms (reserve 8 to 10 slices for garnish)

Line large serving platter with:

Lettuce leaves

(*Recipe continued on next page*)

Mound mushroom mixture in center, garnish with reserved mushrooms and:

Parsley sprigs

(176)

Lomi-Lomi Salmon

4 appetizers *LC, LCh, D, LS, P, Ml, K, k*

Tip: Prepare day before serving

Combine in glass or earthenware bowl, blending well:

1 cup **lime juice**
4 scallions, very thinly sliced
2 tablespoons **apple juice concentrate**
Dash hot pepper sauce
Pinch **salt** (*LS* omit; *P:* use dash of **soy sauce**)

Carefully add:

½ pound fresh salmon, cubed
2 tomatoes, peeled, cubed, seeded, and diced
1 green pepper, diced

Marinate overnight, or until fish becomes opaque. Drain and shred fish. Arrange fish and vegetables on appetizer plates. Garnish with:

Parsley sprigs
Lime wedges

(177)

Seviche

4 to 6 servings *LC, LCh, D, LS, P, Ml, k*

Combine in glass bowl:

1 pound firm fleshed fish (sole, pompano, snapper), cut in 1-inch cubes
1 cup **lime juice**
½ cup chopped onion
1 tablespoon **apple juice concentrate**
1 whole clove garlic, peeled and slashed

⅛ cup chopped green chilies (*LS:* use fresh)
½ cup seeded, chopped tomato
½ to 1 teaspoon **salt** (*LS:* omit; *P:* omit and use ½ teaspoon **soy sauce**)
Dash cayenne
1 tablespoon minced fresh coriander, or ⅛ teaspoon dried
Pinch oregano
1 green pepper, sliced

Marinate mixture for 3 to 4 hours in the refrigerator. Serve fish drained over greens garnished with:

Onions
Tomatoes
Peppers
Avocado slices (*P:* omit)

(178)

Vegetables a la Grecque

6 to 8 servings *LC, LCh, D, LS, V, v, P, Ml, k*

Combine and tie in cheesecloth bag:

¼ cup coriander seed or 1 teaspoon ground coriander
1 tablespoon whole black **peppercorns** (*P:* use white)
4 springs fresh thyme, or 1 teaspoon dried
3 bay leaves
3 to 4 parsley sprigs

Combine in a medium bowl and set aside:

2 cups vegetable **stock**
½ cup dry white **wine** (*D:* if prohibited, use ⅓ cup **stock** plus 2 tablespoons vinegar)
2 tablespoons tomato paste (*LS:* use unsalted paste)
2 tablespoons **lemon juice**
Salt to taste (*P* and *LS:* omit)

In large pot, heat:

1 teaspoon to 2 tablespoons **oil** (*P:* use vegetable **stock**)

Lightly **sauté** in pot for about 3 minutes:

12 small boiling onions, quartered and separated into leaves

Add stock mixture and one of the following vegetables:

2 pounds zucchini, cut into thick slices *or*
2 pounds cauliflower, in florets *or*

(*Recipe continued on next page*)

2 pounds green beans, trimmed *or*
2 pounds fresh artichoke bottoms, rubbed with lemon and cut into wedges (*LS:* omit)

And, if desired:
4 medium fresh tomatoes, peeled, seeded, and coarsely chopped (Opt.)

If liquid in pot does not quite cover vegetables, add a bit more stock or water. Add the cheesecloth bag of spices and bring all to a rapid boil. Continue boiling for about 15 minutes (20 to 25 minutes for artichoke bottoms) or until vegetables are crisp tender. Discard spice bag. Cool. Serve at room temperature, drained and arranged on greens, if desired.

(179)

Zucchini, Tomato, and Basil Appetizer

4 appetizer or salad servings *LC, LCh, D, LS, V, v, P, Ml, k*

Heat in **non-stick** pan:
1½ teaspoons **oil** (*P:* omit)

Add and **sauté** until golden:
½ teaspoon minced garlic
1 tablespoon chopped fresh basil

Add, tossing well:
2 cups zucchini

Sauté until zucchini just begins to lose its opaqueness. Stir in:
1 tablespoon chopped fresh basil
Salt to taste (*P* and *LS:* substitute 1 tablespoon wine vinegar or to taste)

Arrange on individual plates or on serving platter:
3 tomatoes, sliced

Mound zucchini mixture in center of tomatoes. Chill. When ready to serve, garnish with:
Whole basil leaves

Pass separately:
Salt and **pepper**
Oil and vinegar
Grated **cheese**

(180)

Beet Aspic

4 to 6 servings *LC, LCh, V, v, P, Ml, k, B*

Drain and reserve liquid from:

2 16-ounce cans sliced beets

Measure ½ cup liquid and add to it:

2 envelopes unflavored **gelatin**

Blend and let stand 1 minute to soften.

Heat 1 cup of remaining liquid to boiling. Stir this liquid into the gelatin mixture until gelatin is dissolved.

Set aside 8 even slices of the canned beets. Put remaining beets and liquid in blender with:

3 tablespoons **lemon juice**

3 tablespoons **apple juice concentrate**

Puree until smooth. Stir in gelatin mixture, blending well. Pour half of this mixture into a 1-quart ring mold, chilled and rinsed in cold water. Refrigerate until aspic is set. Layer with:

3 hard-boiled **egg** whites, sliced into rings (*V:* leave out)

Add remaining gelatin mixture and chill until set. Unmold. Serve garnished with reserved beet slices and:

2 hard-boiled **egg** whites, sliced into rings (*V:* leave out)

(181)

Cucumber Mousse

4 servings *LC, LCh, D, LS, v, P, k*

Combine in small saucepan:

1 envelope unflavored **gelatin**

3 tablespoons **lemon juice** or **lime juice** or vinegar

1 tablespoon water

Let mixture stand for 1 minute to soften gelatin; then bring to a boil over medium heat, stirring constantly until gelatin dissolves. Remove from heat and add:

3 tablespoons **apple juice concentrate** (*D:* Reduce to 1 tablespoon or omit)

(*Recipe continued on next page*)

2 tablespoons grated onion
1 teaspoon dried dill or 2 tablespoons chopped fresh dill

Chill mixture until it begins to thicken.

Meanwhile, set on paper towels or in colander to drain:

1 cup peeled, seeded, and chopped cucumber

Beat thickened gelatin mixture until light and fluffy and gradually beat in:

½ cup low-fat **yogurt**

Fold in cucumber and:

Salt to taste (*P* and *LS:* omit)
White **pepper** to taste

Pour mixture into 4 individual molds, chilled and dipped in cold water.

(182) *RICH CUCUMBER MOUSSE*

4 servings *v, k*

Follow recipe for CUCUMBER MOUSSE (**181**), but substitute ½ cup whipping cream whipped until stiff for **yogurt.** Beat the gelatin mixture gradually into the whipped cream, then fold in cucumbers.

(183) *ANGEL CUCUMBER MOUSSE*

4 servings *LC, LCh, D, V, v, P, Ml, k*

Follow recipe for CUCUMBER MOUSSE (**181**), but substitute 1 egg white, beaten stiff with ⅛ teaspoon cream of tartar, for the yogurt. Beat gelatin mixture into egg whites, then fold in cucumbers.

(184) *MAYO-CUCUMBER MOUSSE*

4 servings *v, Ml, k*

Follow recipe for CUCUMBER MOUSSE (**181**), but substitute ¼ cup mayonnaise for the yogurt.

(185) *SOYO-CUCUMBER MOUSSE*

LC, LCh, D, LS, V, v, P, Ml, k

Follow recipe for CUCUMBER MOUSSE (**181**), but substitute ½ cup SOYO-NAISE (**264**) for yogurt.

(186)

Tomato Aspic

4 to 6 servings *LC, LCh, D, LS, V, v, P, Ml, k, B*

Tip: Prepare 3 to 5 hours in advance

Heat in saucepan, simmering uncovered for 10 minutes:
- 2 cups tomato juice (*LS:* use unsalted juice)
- 1 small bay leaf
- ½ teaspoon dried basil or ½ tablespoon chopped fresh
- 1 tablespoon cider vinegar or **lemon juice**
- ½ teaspoon **sugar** or **apple juice concentrate** (*D:* use juice concentrate)
- 1 tablespoon finely chopped parsley

Meanwhile, combine:
- 1 envelope unflavored **gelatin**
- ¼ cup tomato juice (*LS:* use unsalted juice)

Let stand 1 minute to soften gelatin. Strain heated tomato juice mixture. Taste for seasoning, adding:
- **Salt** to taste (*LS* and *P:* omit) *or*
- ½ teaspoon **soy sauce** (*LS:* use additional **wine** vinegar to taste)

Pour hot juice over softened gelatin, a little at a time, stirring to be sure all gelatin is dissolved. Pour into 3 or 4 cup mold, or into muffin tins for individual aspics, and chill until firm. Garnish with:
- Hard-boiled **eggs**
- Parsley
- Asparagus tips

VARIATION: Add to TOMATO ASPIC (**186**) any of the following as permitted by guests' diet:
- Tiny new peas
- Sliced avocado*
- Flaked fish
- Chopped onion and celery
- Chopped cucumber and green pepper

* Except low-residue diets.

(187) *TOMATO-AVOCADO ASPIC*

5 to 6 servings *LC, D, LS, V, v, Ml, k, B**

Follow recipe for TOMATO ASPIC (**186**), substituting 1½ envelopes of **gelatin** and adding 1 cup pureed avocado.

* Except low-residue diets.

Salads

(188)

Arugula Salad

4 servings *LC, LCh, D, LS, V, v, P, Ml, K, k*

Combine in large salad bowl:

1 head Boston or bibb lettuce, torn into bite-sized pieces
1 bunch arugula, torn into bite-sized pieces
1 small red onion, thinly sliced and separated into rings
12 cherry tomatoes
¾ cup chick peas, drained (*LS:* use unsalted canned or home-cooked prepared without salt)

Toss with:

ITALIAN DRESSING (**257**)

Serve immediately after tossing.

(189)

Arugula-Apple Salad

4 servings *LC, LCh, V, v, P, Ml, K, k*

Prepare:
1 recipe LIGHT VINAIGRETTE (**258**) (*K:* use bottled dressing)
Combine in salad bowl:
1 head Boston or bibb lettuce, washed, dried, and torn
1 bunch arugula, washed, dried, and torn
1 large or 2 small apples, cored and diced
When ready to serve, toss salad with LIGHT VINAIGRETTE or bottled dressing. Sprinkle with:
Toasted sesame seeds (*K:* use untoasted)

(190)

Sweet and Sour Beets

4 to 6 servings *LC, LCh, V, v, P, Ml, K, k, B*

Drain, reserving liquid:
2 16-ounce cans sliced, diced, or julienned beets
Measure ¼ cup of liquid and add to it:
3 tablespoons **orange juice concentrate**
1 tablespoon **apple juice concentrate**
2 tablespoons **lemon juice**
Salt to taste (*P:* omit)
Combine mixture with beets and marinate several hours. Serve chilled.

(191)

Dark Mixed Greens with Beets and Onions

4 to 6 servings *LC, LCh, V, v, P, Ml, k*

Dice finely:
3 large fresh beets, peeled
1 medium red onion
Marinate mixture in:
SWEET AND SOUR SALAD DRESSING (**272**)
Chill. When ready to serve, line salad bowl with:
Mixed dark greens, torn into small pieces
Arrange beets and onions on greens and toss to serve.

(192)

Bok Choy Salad

4 to 6 servings *LC, LCh, V, v, P, Ml, K, k*

Combine in bowl:
1 red pepper, sliced
1 green pepper, sliced
1 medium bunch bok choy, white parts only, finely sliced (reserve green leaves)
2 medium oranges, peeled and sliced
1 small zucchini, sliced
½ cup alfalfa sprouts, separated
In another small bowl, whisk together:
2 tablespoons **apple juice**
1 tablespoon vinegar
1 tablespoon **oil** (*P:* omit)
⅛ teaspoon dry mustard
1 teaspoon **apple juice concentrate**
½ teaspoon **soy sauce**
Refrigerate both bowls of ingredients until ready to serve. Before serving time, line a salad bowl with the reserved bok choy leaves. Just before serving, combine dressing and vegetable mixture, tossing lightly. Turn mixture into salad bowl and serve immediately.

(193)

Boston Lettuce and Hearts-of-Palm Salad

4 servings *LC, LCh, D, LS, V, v, Ml, k*

Combine in salad bowl:
2 heads Boston lettuce, washed, dried, and torn
2 cups sliced fresh mushrooms
1 15-ounce can hearts of palm, sliced in thin strips (*LS:* omit)
12 halved cherry tomatoes or 2 small tomatoes, cut into wedges
When ready to serve, toss with:
1 recipe GARLIC SESAME DRESSING **(256)**

(194)

Cucumber Sticks Oriental

4 to 6 servings *LC, LCh, D, V, v, Ml, k*

Place in bowl:
2 cucumbers, peeled, seeded, and cut into thin sticks
Add:
¼ cup vinegar
Let stand, covered, in refrigerator overnight. Drain off accumulated liquid, rinse, and squeeze dry.
Add to cucumbers:
2 tablespoons rice or cider vinegar
2 tablespoons **soy sauce**
2 tablespoons **apple juice concentrate**
⅛ teaspoon sesame seed **oil**
½ teaspoon ground ginger
¼ teaspoon dry mustard
Serve chilled.

(195)

Sweet and Sour Cucumbers

4 to 6 servings *LC, LCh, D, LS, V, v, P, Ml, K, k*

Wash, peel, and slice thinly:
 1 large or 2 small cucumbers
Sprinkle with:
 Salt (*P* and *LS:* sprinkle with vinegar)
Cover with a weighted plate. Set aside for 2 hours. Rinse and drain in colander, pressing out any excess juices.
Combine in small bowl, then add to cucumbers in glass bowl:
 ¼ cup vinegar
 1 teaspoon **sugar, apple juice concentrate,** *or* **aspartame,** to taste (*P:* use **apple juice concentrate;** *D:* use **aspartame**)
 ¼ teaspoon ground white **pepper**
 Salt to taste (*LS* and *P:* omit)
Chill for several hours.

(196) *DILLED CUCUMBERS*

4 to 6 servings *LC, LCh, D, LS, V, v, P, Ml, K, k*

Prepare cucumbers as for SWEET AND SOUR CUCUMBERS **(195).**
Along with vinegar, add:
 1 tablespoon chopped fresh dill or 1 teaspoon dried
Sweetening may be omitted if desired.

(197) *DILLED YOGURT CUCUMBER SALAD*

4 to 6 servings *LC, LCh, D, LS, v, P, K, k*

Prepare cucumbers as for SWEET AND SOUR CUCUMBERS **(195).**
After chilling, drain.
Add:
 ½ cup low-fat **yogurt**
 1 tablespoon sour cream (Opt.; *P:* omit)
 1 tablespoon chopped fresh dill or 1 teaspoon dried (Opt.)
Sweetening may be omitted if desired.

(198)

Herbed Vegetable Salad

6 to 8 servings *LC, LCh, D, LS, V, v, P, Ml, K, k*

In large salad bowl, combine:

1 small head romaine lettuce, torn into bite-sized pieces
2 cups broccoli florets
1 cup shredded cabbage
2 cups sliced fresh mushrooms
¼ cup chopped parsley
¼ cup chopped dill
2 medium tomatoes, cut in eighths
1 small zucchini, sliced thin
1 small cucumber, peeled and thinly sliced

Combine in small bowl, whisking together:

¾ cup LIGHT VINAIGRETTE (**258**) (*K:* use bottled)
¼ teaspoon garlic powder
¼ teaspoon cumin

When ready to serve, pour dressing over salad and toss well.

(199)

India Salad

6 to 8 servings *LC, LCh, D, LS, V, v, P, Ml, K, k*

Peel, seed, and dice:

2 large cucumbers

Peel and coarsely chop:

3 large firm tomatoes
1 large Spanish or Bermuda onion

Combine vegetables in a bowl or shallow dish and add:

½ cup **wine** vinegar (*D:* if prohibited, use other vinegar)
4 tablespoons chopped coriander leaves (cilantro) *or* ½ teaspoon ground coriander
½ to 2 green chili peppers, chopped and seeded (Opt.; *LS:* use fresh)

Sprinkle with:

¼ cup toasted, unsalted peanuts (*LC* and *P:* use 1 tablespoon sesame seeds)

(200)

Italian Salad

6 to 8 servings ***LCh, D, LS, V, v, P, Ml, k***

Arrange attractively in salad bowl:

1 small head leafy lettuce, torn in bite-size pieces
1 small head romaine lettuce, torn in bite-size pieces
1 cup chick peas, drained (*LS:* use chick peas with no salt added)
2 cups Italian green beans, cooked and chilled
3 to 4 fresh plum tomatoes, sliced
1 small zucchini, cut into match-stick pieces 1-inch long

In a small bowl, whisk together

¾ cup LIGHT VINAIGRETTE (**258**)
½ teaspoon oregano
Salt to taste (*LS* and *P:* omit)
Pepper to taste (*P:* use white)

When ready to serve, toss dressing with salad. Garnish, if desired, with:

12 small pitted olives (*LS* and *P:* omit)

If desired, pass separately when diets permit:

Grated **cheese**

(201)

Kensington Salad with Creamy Citrus Dressing

6 servings ***LC, LCh, D*, LS, v, P, k***

Blanch in boiling salted water over medium high heat until *al dente,* about 3 to 4 minutes:

1 pound green beans *or* Chinese long beans *or* sugar snap peas, cut into 2-inch lengths

Drain well. Transfer to a medium bowl and toss with:

2 tablespoons fresh lime juice

(*Recipe continued on next page*)

Cover and refrigerate. When ready to serve, combine in large salad bowl with:

1½ cups melon (cranshaw, honeydew, or cantaloupe), cut into 2-inch slices
2 cups loosely packed watercress, trimmed, cut into 2-inch lengths

Toss lightly with:

1 cup CREAMY CITRUS DRESSING (253)

Sprinkle with:

¼ cup walnut or pecan pieces, sliced almonds, or pine nuts (*LC* and *P:* use 1 tablespoon sesame seeds)

* Except those on diets restricted in simple carbohydrates, such as fruit.

(202)

Mexican Salad

4 servings *LC, LCh, D*, V, v, P, Ml, K, k*

Arrange in salad bowl:

1 head Boston or bibb lettuce
12 black olives, pitted and sliced (*P:* omit)
2 oranges, peeled and sliced
3 slices Spanish onion, separated into rings
1 green pepper, sliced into rings
8 strips of pimiento

Combine in small bowl and blend well:

¼ cup orange juice
2 tablespoons **wine** vinegar (*D:* if prohibited, use **lemon juice**)
2 teaspoons **oil** (*P:* omit)
¼ teaspoon dry mustard
¼ teaspoon onion powder
¼ teaspoon cumin
½ teaspoon coarse **salt** (*P:* omit)
Freshly ground black **pepper** (*P:* use white)

Pour dressing over salad when ready to serve. Toss well, until all vegetables are covered with dressing. Taste for seasoning. Add, if desired:

3 tablespoons pine nuts (*LC* and *P:* omit)

* Except those on diets restricted in simple carbohydrates, such as fruit.

(203)

Middle Eastern Salad

4 to 5 servings *LC, LCh, D, LS, V, v, P, Ml, K, k*

Combine in salad bowl:

2 cups peeled and finely diced cucumber
1 cup finely diced green and/or red pepper
3 tomatoes, peeled after dipping in boiling water for 1 minute, and cut into small cubes
½ cup finely diced onion
¼ cup chopped parsley

Combine in a small bowl:

1 tablespoon **wine** vinegar
1 teaspoon **lime juice**
1 teaspoon **lemon juice**
¼ teaspoon ground coriander
¼ teaspoon cumin

Whisk in:

3 tablespoons **stock** or **oil,** or combination (*LC* and *P:* use **stock**)
Salt to taste (*LS* and *P:* omit)
Pepper to taste (*P:* use white)

Blend dressing ingredients well and pour over chopped vegetables. Toss well and let marinate for at least 1 hour before serving.

(204)

Mushroom-Pea Salad

4 servings *LC, LCh, D, LS, V, v, P, Ml, K, k*

Combine in bowl:

1 cup sliced fresh mushrooms
½ cup fresh sweet peas
½ cup alfalfa sprouts, pulled apart after measuring
1 small head Boston or butter lettuce, washed and torn

(*Recipe continued on next page*)

Just before serving, toss well with:

½ cup LIGHT LEMON VINAIGRETTE DRESSING **(259)** (*K:* use bottled dressing)

Add:

Salt to taste (*P* and *LS:* omit)
Pepper to taste (*P:* use white)

(205)

Oriental Salad

6 to 8 servings *LC, LCh, D, v, P, k*

Combine in large bowl:

2 cups broccoli florets
1 cup finely diced carrots
1 cup finely diced green pepper
½ cup finely diced red pepper
1 cup bean sprouts, rinsed and drained
½ cup finely diced celery
¼ cup finely diced scallions
1 8-ounce can water chestnuts, sliced
20 snow pea pods, washed, trimmed, and parboiled for 1 minute

Combine in a small bowl:

¼ cup **pineapple juice concentrate** (*D:* reduce to 3 tablespoons)
1 cup low-fat **yogurt**
1½ tablespoons **soy sauce** (*P:* use 1 tablespoon)
¾ teaspoon dry mustard
½ teaspoon coriander
¼ teaspoon ground ginger
1 tablespoon **oil** (*P:* omit)

Combine vegetables and dressing, tossing well. Let marinate for 1 hour before serving. Garnish with:

Sesame seeds

(206)

Papaya-Avocado Salad

4 to 6 servings *LCh, D*, LS, V, v, Ml, K, k*

Combine in salad bowl and toss:

2 bunches watercress, washed, dried, and trimmed (*LS:* use Boston lettuce)

½ medium avocado, cut into 1-inch cubes

½ small papaya, cut into 1-inch cubes (melon or mango can be substituted)

Serve with:

LIGHT ORANGE VINAIGRETTE (**261**) *or*
SPICY ORANGE DRESSING (**262**)

* Except those on diets restricted in simple carbohydrates such as fruit.

(207)

Pepper Salad

4 servings *LCh, D, LS, V, v, Ml, K, k*

Place under hot broiler:

2 whole large red peppers

2 whole large green peppers

Char, turning frequently, until all sides are blackened. Remove from broiler carefully and peel under running water. Remove stalk, inner pith, and seeds. Slice peppers into strips. Place in paper toweling to allow any excess liquid to drain off. Transfer to a large glass bowl. In another bowl combine:

2 tablespoons **oil**

2 tablespoons **lemon juice** or white **wine** vinegar (*D:* use lemon juice)

Salt to taste (*LS:* omit)

Pepper to taste

Whisk mixture and pour over peppers. Cover and marinate in refrigerator 1 hour or more. Before serving, garnish with:

Chopped fresh parsley

(208) *PEPPER SALAD (LOW-FAT)*

4 servings *LC, P*

Follow recipe above, but substitute LIGHT VINAIGRETTE (**258**) for dressing.

(209)

Portuguese Salad

4 to 6 servings *LC, LCh, D, LS, P, Ml, K, k*

Combine in salad bowl:

1 apple, cored, and diced (*D:* use small apple, omit for those on diets restricted in simple carbohydrates)
1 small cucumber, peeled, seeded, and diced
1 green pepper, seeded and diced
1 red pepper, seeded and diced
2 medium tomatoes, seeded and diced
3 tablespoons chopped red onion
2 tablespoons diced pimiento

Combine in separate bowl and beat well:

1 teaspoon **oil** (*P:* omit)
2½ tablespoons **lime juice**
2 tablespoons **stock**
1 teaspoon **apple juice concentrate**
1 garlic clove, mashed
Salt to taste (*P:* add 1 teaspoon **soy sauce;** *LS:* omit **salt,** increase **apple juice concentrate** to 2 teaspoons)
Pepper to taste (*P:* use white)

Combine dressing with salad and marinate for 1 hour or more. When ready to serve, garnish with:

12 roasted, peeled, and sliced chestnuts
4 hard-cooked **egg** whites, diced (*LS:* omit)

(210)

Raita

4 servings *LC, LCh, D, LS*, v, P, K, k*

Combine in small bowl:
- 1½ cups low-fat **yogurt** (*LS:* reduce to 1 cup)
- 2 tablespoons sour cream (*P:* omit)
- 1 cup chopped fresh tomatoes
- 1 cup chopped cucumber, drained on paper towel
- 1 tablespoon finely chopped fresh coriander (cilantro)
- ½ teaspoon **sugar** or **apple juice concentrate** (*D* and *P:* use **apple juice concentrate**)
- ½ teaspoon garam masala *or* 1 teaspoon cumin
- 1 garlic clove, minced
- 2 tablespoons chopped onion
- **Salt** to taste (*LS* and *P:* omit)
- **Pepper** to taste (*P:* use white)
- ⅛ to ¼ teaspoon cayenne or red pepper

Toss well, garnish with:
- Tomatoes
- Chopped cucumber
- Coriander leaves

* Except those limited to low-sodium milk.

(211)

Radish and Walnut Salad

6 to 8 servings *LC, LCh, D, LS, V, v, P, Ml, K, k*

Combine in salad bowl and toss lightly:
- 2 quarts mixed greens, torn into bite-size pieces
- 2 cups sliced radishes
- ½ cup minced parsley

Just before serving, add:
- LIGHT VINAIGRETTE **(258)**
- **Salt** to taste (*P* and *LS:* omit)
- **Pepper** to taste (*P:* use white)

(*Recipe continued on next page*)

Toss. Add and toss again:
½ cup chopped walnuts (*LC:* use 2 tablespoons sesame seeds; *P:* use chick peas, halved)

(212)

Red Cabbage Salad

10 to 12 servings *LC, LCh, D*, LS, V, v, P, Ml, k*

In large **non-stick** pot, heat over medium flame:
½ tablespoon **oil** (*P:* omit)
In pot, **sauté** until softened:
2 medium onions, sliced
Add to pot:
1 small head red cabbage, shredded
1 cup **apple juice**
½ cup cider vinegar
⅓ cup **apple juice concentrate**
2 medium apples, peeled, cored, thinly sliced
Simmer, covered, stirring occasionally, for 1 hour and 15 minutes or until cabbage is soft.
Chill before serving.

* Except those on diets limited in simple carbohydrates, such as fruit.

(213)

Slender Slaw

4 to 6 servings *LC, LCh, D*, LS, V, v, P, Ml, k*

Combine in glass or earthenware bowl:
1 small head cabbage, shredded
1 green pepper, finely shredded
½ red pepper, finely shredded
2 carrots, finely shredded
3 scallions, chopped

In a small saucepan, whisk together:

⅓ cup cider vinegar
⅓ cup **apple juice**
⅓ cup water plus 2 tablespoons
3 tablespoons **apple juice concentrate**
1 teaspoon dry mustard
¼ teaspoon coriander

Bring mixture to a boil. Pour over the cabbage-vegetable mixture. Marinate for 12 hours. Serve cold.

* Except those on diets restricted in simple carbohydrates, such as fruit.

(214)

Spinach Salad

4 servings *LC, LCh, D, V, v, P, Ml, K, k*

Combine in a large salad bowl:

10 ounces fresh spinach, washed, stemmed, and torn
½ pound fresh mushrooms, sliced

Garnish with:

4 hard-boiled **egg** whites, sliced or chopped (*LS* and *V:* leave out)
2 tablespoons bacon-flavored soy bits (*P* and *LS:* use raisins)

When ready to serve, toss with a combination of:

1 tablespoon **oil** (*P:* omit)
2 tablespoons **lemon juice**
2 tablespoons vegetable **stock** or water
2 tablespoons dry white **wine** (*D:* use additional **stock**)
1 garlic clove, mashed
2 teaspoons **apple juice concentrate**
½ teaspoon dry mustard
Salt (*LS* and *P:* omit)
Pepper (*P:* use white pepper)

(215)

Spinach-Apple Salad

4 to 6 servings *LC, LCh, D, V, v, P, Ml, K, k*

Combine in salad bowl:
1 pound fresh young spinach, washed, dried, trimmed, and torn
2 MacIntosh apples, cored, and sliced thinly (*D:* omit for those on diets limited in simple carbohydrates)
1 cup sliced mushrooms
When ready to serve, toss with:
1 recipe CORIANDER DRESSING **(254)**
Garnish with:
¼ cup thinly sliced almonds (*LC:* pass separately; *P:* omit)
2 diced hard-cooked **egg** whites (*V:* leave out)

(216)

Spinach, Endive, and Mushroom Salad

4 to 6 servings *LC, LCh, D, V, v, Ml, k*

Blanch in boiling water for 1 minute:
2 Belgian endives
Transfer endives to a flameproof glass or enamel saucepan and add:
½ cup **stock**
3 tablespoons **lemon juice**
1 tablespoon **apple juice concentrate**
1 tablespoon **oil**
Salt to taste
Bring liquid to a boil and simmer, covered, for about 10 minutes, or until endives are just tender. Cool and separate leaves. Arrange in bowl with:
8 ounces washed and torn spinach leaves
2 cups sliced fresh mushrooms
¼ cup broken walnut pieces (*LC:* use 2 tablespoons)

When ready to serve, toss with:
- ½ cup LIGHT ORANGE VINAIGRETTE (**261**)

Garnish with:
- Hard-cooked **egg** whites, finely chopped (*V:* leave out)

(217)

Spinach-Peach Salad

4 to 6 servings *LC, LCh, D*, LS, V, v, Ml, K, k*

Combine in salad bowl:
- 1 pound fresh spinach, washed, dried, and torn
- 2 to 4 ripe peaches, peeled and sliced
- 1 scallion, finely sliced

When ready to serve, dress with a combination of:
- ½ cup LIGHT VINAIGRETTE (**258**) (*K:* use bottled dressing)
- ½ teaspoon dry mustard
- 1 teaspoon **apple juice concentrate**
- 1 tablespoon **lemon juice**

Toss lightly and serve immediately.

* Except those on diets restricted in simple carbohydrates, such as fruit.

(218)

Wilted Spinach and Nut Salad

4 servings *LC, LCh, D, v, k*

Tip: It is essential to use very fresh spinach leaves for this dish.

Wash and finely chop:
- 1½ pounds fresh, young spinach

Combine with:
- 1 small onion, finely chopped

Place in a saucepan. Cook over low heat until all the water clinging to the spinach leaves has evaporated. Add:
- 1 to 2 teaspoons **oil**

(*Recipe continued on next page*)

Toss for 2 minutes. Transfer to bowl, and add:

1 cup low-fat **yogurt**
½ teaspoon dried mint
¼ teaspoon **salt** (*LS:* omit)
Pepper to taste
1 clove garlic, crushed

Chill for two hours. Add, if desired:

1 teaspoon finely chopped fresh mint

Sprinkle with:

½ cup chopped walnuts (*LC:* use 2 tablespoons sesame seed)
¼ cup raisins (*D:* omit; *LC:* use 1 tablespoon raisins)

Serve chilled.

(219)

Spinach and Red Pepper Salad

4 to 6 servings ***LC, LCh, D, LS, V, v, P, Ml, K, k***

Combine in salad bowl:

1 pound fresh spinach, washed, trimmed, and torn (*LS:* use arugula or Boston or bibb lettuce)
2 red peppers, thinly sliced
1 8-ounce can water chestnuts, thinly sliced

When ready to serve, toss with:

LIGHT ORANGE VINAIGRETTE (**261**) *or*
SWEET AND SOUR DRESSING (**272**) (*K:* use bottled dressing)

(220)

Sunchoke Salad

4 to 5 servings ***LC, LCh, D, LS, V, v, Ml, k***

Combine in jar with tight-fitting lid and shake well:

¼ cup **apple juice**
2 tablespoons white **wine** (*D:* use **stock**)
2 tablespoons white **wine** vinegar (*D:* use tarragon vinegar)
1 tablespoon **oil**

½ cup finely chopped scallions
1 teaspoon tarragon, crumbled
Salt to taste (*LS:* omit)
Pepper to taste

Refrigerate for 1 hour or more.
Arrange on serving platter:

1 pound sunchokes (Jerusalem artichokes), washed, peeled, and cut into ⅛ x 1-inch matchsticks

Toss with dressing.

(221) *SUNCHOKE-ZUCCHINI SALAD*

4 to 6 servings *LC, LCh, D, LS, V, v, Ml, k*

Prepare dressing as for SUNCHOKE SALAD (**220**). Combine ½-pound match-stick–cut sunchokes with 2 cups of match-stick–cut zucchini.

(222) *Sunshine Salad*

8 servings *LC, LCh, D. V, v, Ml, K, k*

Combine in glass bowl or jar, whisking until well blended:

2 tablespoons **lemon juice**
2 tablespoons **orange juice concentrate**
2 tablespoons **oil**
2 tablespoons **stock** or water (*K:* use water)
½ teaspoon dry mustard
¼ teaspoon lemon pepper
¼ teaspoon cumin
Salt to taste

Add and marinate overnight:

1 14-ounce can artichoke hearts, drained

When ready to serve, drain artichoke hearts, reserving marinade. Arrange on platter or in shallow bowl:

1 head iceberg and 1 head romaine lettuce, washed, dried, torn, and tossed with ½ cup of marinade

2 avocados, peeled and sliced (*LC:* use 1 avocado and 2 green peppers, sliced)

(*Recipe continued on next page*)

16 cherry tomatoes or 2 medium tomatoes, cut in wedges
Garnish with artichoke hearts and:
1 small red onion, thinly sliced and separated into rings
Sprinkle salad with remainder of marinade and serve immediately.

(223)

Vegetables a la Russe

4 to 6 servings *D, v, k, B**

Combine in large bowl:
1 cup diced cooked carrots, chilled
1 cup diced cooked beets, chilled (*D:* omit)
1 cup diced cooked potatoes, chilled
1 cup cooked green peas, chilled
or use 4 cups of any permitted vegetables, cooked and chilled.
Combine in small bowl:
½ cup sour cream
⅓ cup low-fat **buttermilk**
2 tablespoons finely chopped fresh dill or 1 teaspoon dried
Salt to taste
Add sour cream mixture to vegetables. Toss to coat vegetables with dressing. Chill well. Garnish as desired with:
Paprika
Fresh parsley sprigs

* Except those on low-residue diets.

(224)

Vegetable Slaw

4 to 6 servings *LCh, V, v, Ml, K, k*

Combine in glass or earthenware salad bowl:
1 medium cabbage, shredded
2 cucumbers, thinly sliced
1 green pepper, diced
3 carrots, coarsely shredded
1 large red onion, sliced and separated into rings

In another bowl, combine and blend well:

2 tablespoons **sugar** or **fructose** or to taste
1 cup vinegar
⅓ cup water
⅓ cup **apple juice concentrate**
½ cup **oil**
1 to 2 tablespoons **salt** to taste
Pepper to taste
3 cloves garlic, crushed

Pour dressing over salad and toss well. Cover. Let marinate in refrigerator for 3 days or more. Remove garlic cloves before serving.

(225)

Watercress-Apple Salad

3 to 4 servings *LC, LCh, D, LS, V, v, P, Ml, k*

Prepare 1 recipe:

BUTTERMILK DRESSING (**250**) (except *LS*, *V*, or *Ml*) *or*
LIGHT ORANGE VINAIGRETTE (**261**) *or*
SWEET-AND-SOUR DRESSING (**272**) (except *D*)

When ready to serve, combine in salad bowl:

1 bunch watercress, washed and trimmed (*LS:* use romaine lettuce)
1 apple, scrubbed, evenly sliced, and sprinkled with **lemon juice**
1 red pepper, thinly sliced
½ small red onion, thinly sliced and separated into rings

Pour dressing over and toss well.

(226)

Watercress, Mushroom, and Tomato Salad

4 to 6 servings *LC, LCh, V, v, P, Ml, k*

Prepare 1 recipe:
LIGHT VINAIGRETTE DRESSING **(258)**
Add to dressing, whisking together well:
½ cup dry white **wine**
2 tablespoons **apple juice concentrate**
Salt to taste (*P* and *LS:* omit)
Pepper to taste (*P:* use white)
Toss in dressing and marinate for 1 hour:
3 cups sliced mushrooms
When ready to serve, fill bottom of small salad bowl with:
1 bunch watercress, washed, dried, and trimmed
Mound the marinated mushrooms in the center of the watercress. Arrange around the edges of the greens:
12 cherry tomatoes

(227)

Watercress, Orange, and Fennel Salad

4 servings *LC, LCh, D*, LS, V, v, P, Ml, K, k*

Wash, dry, and chill:
2 bunches watercress (arugula, romaine, or Boston lettuce may be substituted; *LS:* use substitute)
Combine and chill for 1 hour:
2 to 4 tablespoons slivered fennel (from stalks and bulb)
2 tablespoons **lemon juice**
2 tablespoons **orange juice concentrate**
2 scallions, thinly sliced
6 small black olives, thinly sliced (*LS* and *P:* use 2 tablespoons minced pimiento)

¼ teaspoon ground coriander
¼ teaspoon dry mustard

Beat in:

1 tablespoon **oil** (*P:* omit; use 1 tablespoon **stock**)

Arrange in salad bowl, the greens and:

2 navel oranges, peeled, and sectioned or sliced
½ cup alfalfa sprouts (Opt.)

Just before serving, toss salad with dressing.

* Except those on diets restricted in simple carbohydrates, such as fruit.

(228)

Salad Bar for Mix and Match Salads

In separate bowls or dishes, serve a variety of salad ingredients geared to meet the needs of your special guests. Create your own salads from the list of ingredients that follows. Combine flavors, textures, colors—make each salad a work of art, mixing and matching according to dietary needs, the season, the rest of your menu, or your own personal whim.

Add cumin and fresh chilies to a salad accompanying a Mexican dinner, caraway and paprika when the meal has a German accent. Add salt and pepper as desired, then toss and taste. Adjust seasonings and add a sprinkle of wine or tarragon vinegar, perhaps some juice, if appropriate, and 1 or 2 tablespoons of oil. Toss and taste again. For guests avoiding oils, let them add their own oil and vinegar at the table, as desired.

The following are suitable for all diets except bland and those specified in parentheses with an "X." Those suitable for bland dieters avoiding fiber are so labeled.

SALAD INGREDIENTS

Greens

Boston
Bibb
Cabbage

(*Recipe continued on next page*)

Chinese cabbage
Chinese celery
Curly endive (chickory)
Escarole
Iceberg
Red cabbage
Romaine
Savoy cabbage
Spinach (X *LS*)
Watercress (X *LS*)

Raw Vegetables
Beets (X *LS*)
Broccoli
Carrots (X *LS*)
Cauliflower
Cucumbers
Celery (X *LS*)
Fennel
Green Beans
Jicama
Onions
Peppers, red and green
Radishes
Snow peas
Sunchoke
Tomato
Turnip (X *LS*)
Zucchini

Cooked Vegetables
Artichoke hearts
Asparagus
Beets (X *LS*)
Belgian Endive
Broccoli
Carrots (X *LS*)
Cauliflower
Celery Root (X *LS*)
Chick peas (*LS:* unsalted)
Green beans
Kidney beans (*LS:* unsalted)
Mushrooms

Potatoes
Snow peas

Fruits
Apples
Avocados
Bananas
Grapes
Mangoes
Melons
Oranges
Papaya
Peaches
Pears
Raisins

Toppings
Caraway seeds
Cheese, shredded or grated
Corn kernels
Croutons (See **bread**)
Nuts (almonds, peanuts, pecans, pine nuts, walnuts, etc.) (X *P; LC:* limited)
Pumpkin seeds (X *P; LC:* limited)
Sesame seeds (X *P; LC:* limited)
Soy bits (X *LS* and *P*)
Sunflower seeds (X *P; LC:* limited)
Water chestnuts

Flavorings
Apple juice (*B*)
Chives
Dill (*B*)
Fennel
Garlic
Herbs of all kinds (*B*)
Horseradish
Lemon juice (*B*)
Lime juice
Mint
Mustard (*LS:* unsalted or dry)
Onion

(*Recipe continued on next page*)

Parsley (*B*)
Pepper (black, white, pink, red; X *B; P:* avoid black)
Pickles (X *LS* and *P*)
Pimiento
Salt (*B*)
Salt substitute
Scallions or green onions
Spices
Tomato juice (*B*)
Vinegars
Wine

Rice, Macaroni, and Potato Salads

(229)

Bulgur-Tofu Salad

4 to 6 servings *LCh, D, V, v, Ml, k*

Combine in serving dish:
2 cups cooked bulgur
8 to 12 ounces tofu, cut in ½-inch cubes
1 cup chick peas
1 cup chopped plum tomatoes
1 cup shredded zucchini
2 medium scallions, thinly sliced

Combine in separate bowl, blending well:
1 to 2 tablespoons **mayonnaise** (*D:* use unsweetened mayonnaise; *V:* use SOYO-NAISE (**264**))
½ teaspoon **soy sauce**
¼ to ½ teaspoon Dijon-style mustard
½ teaspoon oregano

To serve, toss bulgur mixture in dressing.

(230)

Macaroni a la Russe

8 to 10 servings *D, v, k, B*

Prepare:
1 recipe VEGETABLES A LA RUSSE (**223**) doubling the sour cream mixture
Cook according to package directions:
½ pound macaroni shells
Drain shells and rinse in warm, then cold water. Combine shells with vegetables. Season as desired with:
Salt
Pepper (*B:* omit)
Finely chopped parsley *or*
Finely chopped dill
Chill. Garnish with:
Paprika
Parsley sprigs

(231)

Curried Potato-Apple Salad

4 to 6 servings *LC, LCh, LS, V, v, P, Ml, k*

Boil until tender:
2 pounds small potatoes, scrubbed but not peeled
Drain. Cool enough to handle, peel if desired, and dice.
Combine in small bowl:
½ cup dry white **wine**
¼ cup **wine** vinegar
3 tablespoons **apple juice concentrate**
1 teaspoon **soy sauce** (*LS:* omit)
Pour this mixture over the potatoes, tossing carefully to coat. Chill.
Meanwhile, prepare and toss in a bowl:
4 MacIntosh or Granny Smith apples, scrubbed, cored, and diced
1 cup finely diced celery (*LS:* use diced green or red pepper)
4 tablespoons **lemon juice**

1 tablespoon chopped parsley
¼ cup chopped scallions or shallots

Combine cooled potatoes with apples and celery. Add and toss:

½ teaspoon curry powder
2 teaspoons toasted sesame seeds

Chill salad, taste for seasoning and correct. Serve garnished with:

Chopped parsley

(232)

Mustard-Dill Potato Salad

4 to 6 servings *LCh, D, LS, v, P, k*

Cook until just tender:

6 medium potatoes, scrubbed

Peel, if desired, and slice. While still warm, pour over potatoes a mixture of:

2 tablespoons white **wine** (*D:* use **stock**)
2 tablespoons white **wine** vinegar or tarragon vinegar (*D:* use tarragon vinegar)
⅛ teaspoon paprika
⅛ teaspoon white **pepper**
¼ teaspoon **salt** (*P* and *LS:* omit)
4 teaspoons Dijon-style mustard (*LS:* use low-salt variety or dry mustard to taste)

Toss gently and let marinade soak in. When potatoes are cooled, add to them:

¼ cup finely sliced celery (*LS:* omit if prohibited)
¼ cup finely diced red and green pepper
¼ cup julienned zucchini
2 large scallions, finely sliced
1 tablespoon minced parsley
1 tablespoon dried dill or ¼ cup fresh, finely minced

Add and toss well but gently:

¼ cup low-fat **yogurt**

Garnish with:

Fresh dill

(233)

Potato-Vegetable Salad

10 to 12 servings *LC, LCh, D, LS, P*

Boil until tender:

2 pounds small potatoes, scrubbed but not peeled

Drain. When cool enough to handle, dice potatoes. Combine in small bowl:

½ cup dry white **wine** (*D:* use **stock**)
¼ cup **wine** vinegar (*D:* use tarragon vinegar)
2 tablespoons **apple juice concentrate**

Pour this mixture over the potatoes, tossing carefully to cover. Cool. Meanwhile, prepare and combine in small bowl:

¼ cup finely sliced scallions
1 cup finely diced celery (*LS:* omit)
1 cup minced green and/or red pepper (*LS:* increase to 1½ cups)
2 tablespoons chopped pimiento
1 cup peeled, seeded, and finely diced cucumber
½ cup finely sliced carrots
½ cup finely chopped parsley
1 cup diced zucchini

Blanch in boiling water for 3 minutes or cook briefly in microwave oven:

2 cups small fresh cauliflower florets

Cool immediately under cold running water; drain. Combine carefully potatoes, cauliflower, and other vegetables in large bowl. Toss with:

1 cup SOYO-NAISE **(264),** (for non-dieters, use **mayonnaise,** or combination of **mayonnaise** and sour cream)
¼ teaspoon paprika
Salt to taste (*LS* and *P:* omit)
Pepper to taste

Serve chilled, garnished with:

Cherry tomatoes
Chopped parsley

(234)

Gourmet Rice Salad

10 to 12 servings *LCh, D, V, v, Ml, k*

Combine in bowl and toss lightly:

6 cups cooked rice, cooled
2 6½ ounce jars marinated artichoke hearts, sliced and drained (reserve liquid)
6 ounces pitted black olives, sliced (drained weight)
¾ cup minced celery
1 8-ounce jar or can pimientos, drained and minced
½ cup minced shallots or scallions
½ cup finely chopped parsley
¼ cup reserved liquid from artichoke hearts
2 tablespoons tarragon vinegar
1 to 2 tablespoons dried tarragon to taste
2 teaspoons Dijon-style mustard

Chill well to let flavors blend before serving.

(235)

Green Rice Salad

4 to 5 servings *LC, LCh, D, LS, V, v, P, Ml, k*

Combine in bowl:

2 cups cold cooked rice
6 black olives, sliced (*P* and *LS:* omit)
1 to 2 tablespoons sliced scallions, including tops
2 tablespoons **wine** vinegar (*D:* use tarragon vinegar)
1 teaspoon **apple juice concentrate**
1 teaspoon Worcestershire sauce (*V* and *v:* use steak sauce)
½ cup chopped green pepper
½ cup diced zucchini
¼ cup finely chopped parsley
2 tablespoons finely chopped dill (Opt.)
Salt to taste (*LS* and *P:* omit)
Pepper to taste (*P:* use white)

Toss well, serve chilled.

(236)

Rice, Snow Pea, and Water Chestnut Salad

8 servings *LC, LCh, D, V, v, P, Ml, k*

Combine in serving bowl:
3 cups cooked rice, cooled
3 scallions, finely sliced
1 cup finely diced celery
24 snow peas, washed and plunged into boiling water for 1 minute, cooled in cold water, and trimmed
8 water chestnuts, thinly sliced

In separate bowl, combine, and stir to blend:
2 tablespoons **soy sauce**
2 tablespoons white **wine** (*D:* use 1 tablespoon vinegar plus 1 tablespoon **stock**)
2 tablespoons **pineapple juice concentrate**
1 teaspoon **oil** (Opt.; *P:* omit)
½ teaspoon dry mustard
¼ teaspoon ground ginger
¼ teaspoon garlic powder
2 tablespoons **wine** or rice vinegar (*D:* use rice vinegar)

Pour dressing over rice and vegetable mixture; toss carefully, but thoroughly. Serve chilled.

Main Dish Salads

(237)

Avocado-Halibut Salad

4 servings *LC, LCh, D, LS, k, B**

Combine:

2 cups cold poached lean fish (haddock, halibut, etc.)
2 small avocados, peeled, pitted, and cubed

Toss with:

½ cup ORANGE YOGURT DRESSING **(263)** (*D:* use LIGHT ORANGE VINAIGRETTE **(261)**)

Serve on:

Finely shredded lettuce leaves

VARIATION: Add to salad one of the following† (except: *B*):

1½ cups cubed papaya
1½ cups cubed mango
1½ cups cubed melon

Or dress with:

LIGHT ORANGE VINAIGRETTE **(261)** (except *B*)

* Except those on low-residue diets.
† Except those on diets restricted in simple carbohydrates, such as fruit.

(238)

Halibut-Stuffed Avocado

4 servings *LC, LCh, D*, LS, k*

Combine and toss well:
- 2 cups cold poached lean fish (haddock, halibut, etc.)
- 1½ cups cubed melon or papaya or mango
- ½ cup ORANGE YOGURT DRESSING (**263**)

Halve and pit:
- 2 avocados

Brush open face with:
- **Lemon juice**

Fill each shell with ¼ of the fish-melon salad.

* Except those on diets limited in simple carbohydrates, such as fruit.

(239)

Artichoke-Halibut Salad

4 servings *LC, LCh, D, P, k, B*

Combine:
- 2 cups cold poached lean fish (haddock, halibut, etc.)
- 2 cups sliced canned artichoke hearts, drained

Toss with:
- ½ cup ORANGE YOGURT DRESSING (**263**) *or*
- LIGHT ORANGE VINAIGRETTE (**261**) (except *B*)

(240)

Halibut and Melon Salad

6 to 8 servings *LC, LCh D*, LS, Ml, k*

Halve, and scoop out seeds of:

1 medium-sized cantaloupe

Dice or cut into balls with a melon scoop and put into a bowl. Cut into bite-sized chunks:

2 pounds poached halibut

Combine melon and fish in a colander lined with paper towels. Allow to drain for 20 minutes.

Meanwhile, in a small bowl, combine:

2 tablespoons **lime juice**

1 tablespoon **apple juice concentrate**

1 teaspoon **oil**

In a dry bowl, combine fish and melon with dressing. Toss to coat. Chill salad for 1 hour in refrigerator. Serve in individual glass bowls set over ice and lined with:

Dark green lettuce leaves

Garnish with:

Lime wedges

* Except those on diets limited in simple carbohydrates, such as fruit.

(241) *HALIBUT AND PEACH SALAD*

6 to 8 servings *LC, LCh, D*, LS, Ml, k, B*

In HALIBUT AND MELON SALAD (**240**), substitute for melon:

4 cups sliced, unsweetened, cooked or canned peaches, well drained

* Except those on diets limited in simple carbohydrates, such as fruit.

(242)

Brown Rice and Bean Salad

4 main course or
8 side dish servings

LCh, D, LS, V, v, P, Ml, k

Tip: Prepare day before

Combine in large bowl and set aside:
- 4 cups cooked brown rice
- 1 16-ounce can dark red kidney beans, drained (*LS:* use dried beans cooked without salt)
- ⅔ cup finely minced onion
- 1 cup finely chopped green pepper
- 1 cup finely chopped red pepper
- ⅓ cup chopped walnuts (*P:* omit)

In 2-cup measuring cup, combine and blend well:
- 2 tablespoons **safflower** or **corn oil** (*P:* omit and substitute 2 tablespoons **stock** or water)
- ¼ cup white **wine** (*D:* use **stock**)
- ¼ cup **wine** vinegar (*D:* use tarragon vinegar)
- ¼ cup **apple juice**
- ¼ teaspoon dry mustard
- **Salt** to taste (*LS* and *P:* omit)
- **Pepper** to taste (*P:* use white)

Toss rice/bean mixture with dressing until thoroughly blended. Chill well before serving.

(243)

Curried Tuna Nestled on Mango Slices

4 servings

LCh, LS, Ml, K, k

Combine in bowl and toss gently to mix:
- 2 6 to 7-ounce cans water-packed tuna, drained (*LS:* use unsalted, if required)
- 2 apples, washed, cored, and diced
- ¼ cup **mayonnaise**

½ cup finely diced celery (*LS:* omit)
¼ cup raisins (Opt.)
½ cup diced red pepper
½ cup diced green pepper
2 tablespoons finely diced onion
1 to 2 teaspoons curry powder, or to taste

Peel, pit, and slice:
2 small mangoes

Arrange slices in rings on 4 dinner plates. Mound curried tuna in the center of the rings. Sprinkle with:
Sliced almonds

(244)

Dilled Salmon on Avocado Half Shell

6 to 8 servings *K, k*

Combine in bowl and toss lightly:
2 1-pound cans salmon, drained and boned
½ cup chopped gherkins
2 tablespoons finely chopped onion
½ cup sour cream
2 tablespoons **mayonnaise**
2 tablespoons **yogurt**
2 tablespoons minced fresh dill or ½ teaspoon dried
2 teaspoons **lemon juice**
½ teaspoon grated lemon peel
½ teaspoon **salt** or to taste

Halve and pit:
3 or 4 small avocados

Place avocado halves, open side up on individual plates lined with:
Dark greens

Rub cut surface with:
Lemon juice

Fill avocados with the salmon mixture. Garnish plates with:
Sliced cucumbers

(245)

German Tuna Salad

4 servings *LC, D, Ml, K, k*

Combine in bowl:

4 tablespoons sour cream (*Ml:* use **mayonnaise**)
2 tablespoons **mayonnaise**
4 teaspoons mustard, hearty-style
4 teaspoons chopped fresh dill (or increase to taste)
2 teaspoons **apple juice concentrate**
2 teaspoons sweet paprika or to taste
1 teaspoon caraway seed or to taste
¼ teaspoon garlic powder

In separate bowl combine and toss well:

2 7-ounce cans solid white tuna in water, flaked
2 cups tiny broccoli flowerets
1½ cups chopped apple
⅓ cup chopped green pepper
⅓ cup chopped red pepper
⅓ cup chopped onion

Toss dressing lightly with tuna-vegetable mixture. Taste and season with:

Salt to taste
Pepper to taste

Chill well. Garnish with:

Paprika
Fresh dill sprigs

(246)

Salad Nicoise

4 servings *LC, LCh, D, P, Ml, K, k*

Prepare triple recipe of:

LIGHT MUSTARD VINAIGRETTE **(260)**

Chill. Meanwhile, boil or steam in jackets:

2 pounds small red salad potatoes (*K:* bake in foil or use canned)

Do not overcook. While still warm, slice and toss gently with:

2 tablespoons dry white **wine** or dry vermouth (*D:* use **stock**)
1 tablespoon **apple juice concentrate**
2 tablespoons **stock**

When potatoes have absorbed all the liquid, add and toss gently again with ½ cup of the VINAIGRETTE. Add to taste:

Salt (*P:* omit)
Pepper (*P:* use white)

Cool the potato salad. Meanwhile, cook until barely tender:

1 pound green beans, trimmed (*K:* use raw beans, or frozen beans defrosted)

Toss with beans ¼ cup of the reserved VINAIGRETTE, and chill. Hard cook and peel:

4 to 6 **eggs** (*LC, LCh, D,* and *P:* use whites only)

Chill the eggs. Combine salad as follows before serving: Fill bottom of large salad bowl with:

1 head Boston or romaine lettuce, washed, dried, and torn

Toss lettuce with ¼ cup of the VINAIGRETTE. Attractively arrange on the greens, the potatoes, the beans, and:

1 6 to 7-ounce can water-packed tuna, drained and flaked
2 medium tomatoes, cut in eighths

Garnish with hard-boiled eggs, quartered, and:

8 black olives (*P:* use pimiento strips)
8 anchovy fillets (Opt.; *LC* and *P:* omit)

Drizzle remaining VINAIGRETTE over salad and serve immediately.

(247)

Tuna Hawaiian

4 servings *D, Ml, K, k*

In bowl, combine and stir:

¼ cup **pineapple juice concentrate**
¼ cup **mayonnaise**
2 teaspoons prepared mustard

Refrigerate until ready to use. When ready to put salad together, combine and toss with dressing:

2 6 to 7-ounce cans white meat tuna, drained and flaked
¾ cup pineapple chunks in **unsweetened** juice, drained for ½ hour on paper towels

(*Recipe continued on next page*)

½ cup chopped red and green peppers
¼ cup finely chopped celery
¼ cup broken walnut pieces
¼ cup chopped red onion

Serve on large paper platter on a bed of:

Bright greens

Garnish with:

8 green pepper rings, halved

(248)

Thai Tuna Salad

4 servings *LC, LCh, D, P, Ml, k*

Combine in small bowl and allow to marinate at least one hour:

4 tablespoons **lime juice**
4 teaspoons **soy sauce** (*P:* reduce to 2 teaspoons)
2 garlic cloves, peeled and slashed
1 tablespoon **oil** (*P:* omit)
2 chopped fresh or canned chili peppers
¼ teaspoon coriander
½ teaspoon ground ginger
4 tablespoons vegetable **stock**
1½ tablespoons **apple juice concentrate**

Blanch in boiling water for one minute:

16 pea pods, trimmed

Drain, cool immediately under cold water. Drain well. Combine in bowl with pea pods and half the marinade:

2 7-ounce cans tuna, water pack, drained
10 average scallions, finely sliced
1 red pepper, diced

Pour remaining marinated dressing over:

4 cups bean sprouts, rinsed and dried

Toss well. On a serving platter arrange:

10 ounces fresh spinach leaves, washed and torn

Mound bean sprouts in center of leaves. Arrange tuna mixture around them. Sprinkle with:

Roasted peanuts (*P* and *LC:* Pass nuts separately)

(249)

Viva La Salad

8 servings *LCh, D, LS, V, v, Ml, K, k*

Combine in bowl:

2 quarts mixed romaine, Boston, and bibb lettuce, torn
10 ounces fresh spinach, washed and trimmed (*LS:* omit; use additional greens)
2 cups sliced mushrooms
1 cup sliced red cabbage
1 cup shredded carrots (*LS:* use shredded sunchoke)
¼ cup chopped nuts (*LS:* use unsalted nuts)
¼ cup seeds (*LS:* use unsalted seeds)
¼ cup raisins (*D:* omit, or pass separately)

Garnish with:

Hardboiled **eggs,** sliced (*LCh:* use whites only; *LS* and *V:* leave out)

Serve with:

BUTTERMILK DRESSING (**250**) (*V* and *Ml:* Use LIGHT ORANGE VINAIGRETTE (**261**); *LS:* use LIGHT ORANGE VINAIGRETTE (**261**) for those permitted only low-sodium milk)

Salad Dressings

(250)

Buttermilk Dressing

About 1½ cups ***LC, LCh, D, LS*, v, P, k***

Combine in blender and puree until smooth:

1 cup low-fat **buttermilk** (*LS:* use unsalted buttermilk)
½ cup low-fat **cottage cheese** or **hoop cheese** (*LS* and *P:* use **hoop cheese** or unsalted **cottage cheese**)
2 tablespoons chopped onions
2 tablespoons minced parsley
1 tablespoon fresh dill, minced
½ teaspoon dry mustard

Add:

1 garlic clove, peeled and slashed

Marinate for 2 hours or more. Remove garlic before serving.

* Except those permitted only low-sodium milk.

(251) *BASIL BUTTERMILK DRESSING*

About 1½ cups *LC, LCh, D, LS*, v, P, k*

To basic BUTTERMILK DRESSING (**250**) add 1 tablespoon finely chopped fresh basil.

* Except those permitted only low-sodium milk.

(252)
Buttermilk-Chive Dressing

1½ cups *LC, LCh, D, LS*, v, P, k*

Combine in blender and puree:

1 cup low-fat **buttermilk** (*LS:* use unsalted **buttermilk**)
1 cup low-fat **cottage cheese** or **hoop cheese** (*P* and *LS:* Use **hoop cheese** or unsalted **cottage cheese**)
2 tablespoons minced chives
Salt to taste (*P* and *LS:* omit)
White **pepper** to taste

Refrigerate to allow flavors to blend for at least 1 hour.

* Except those permitted only low-sodium milk.

(253)
Creamy Citrus Dressing

About 1½ cups *LC, LCh, D, LS*, v, P, k*

Combine in blender and puree:

¾ cup **pot cheese** or **hoop cheese** (*LS* and *P:* use **hoop cheese** or unsalted **pot cheese**)
¼ cup **buttermilk** (*LS* and *P:* use unsalted **buttermilk**)
1 tablespoon **apple juice concentrate**
1½ teaspoons Dijon-style mustard (*LS:* use unsalted prepared mustard, or dry mustard to taste)

(*Recipe continued on next page*)

1 garlic clove, crushed
2 tablespoons fresh **lime juice**
1 tablespoon fresh **lemon juice**
¼ teaspoon **salt** (*LS* and *P:* omit; *P:* use **soy sauce**)
⅛ teaspoon **pepper** (*P:* use white)

Set aside. Combine in small saucepan:

1 tablespoon **lemon juice**
1 tablespoon **apple juice concentrate**
1 tablespoon white **wine** vinegar (*D:* use tarragon vinegar)
½ teaspoon unflavored **gelatin**

Blend and let stand 1 minute. Heat mixture just to boiling, stirring constantly. Blend into cheese mixture. Pour into bowl and refrigerate for several hours, or until set.

* Except those permitted only low-sodium milk.

(254)

Coriander Dressing

⅓ cup *LC, LCh, D, LS, V, v, P, Ml, k*

Combine in small bowl:

2 tablespoons **stock**
1 teaspoon **lime juice**
1 teaspoon **lemon juice**
1 tablespoon **wine** vinegar (*D:* use tarragon vinegar)
¼ teaspoon ground coriander
½ teaspoon cumin
1 garlic clove, slashed

Whisk in:

1 tablespoon **oil** (*P:* omit)

Chill in refrigerator for several hours. Before serving, remove garlic clove. And add, to taste:

Salt (*P:* omit)
Pepper (*P:* use white)

(255)

Garlic Mayonnaise

About 1 cup *D, v, Ml, k*

Combine in blender and process at high speed for 30 seconds:

1 **egg**
1 teaspoon dry mustard
¾ teaspoon **salt**
2 to 3 garlic cloves

Add and blend for another 15 seconds:

1 tablespoon **lemon juice**

Uncover blender jar and continue blending at high speed, gradually adding, drop by drop:

1 cup **oil**

If mixture becomes so thick that blades won't turn, stop machine and stir the mayonnaise down from the sides of the jar to the center. Cover and blend again for a few seconds at high speed. Add as needed to taste:

Salt
Pepper

(256)

Garlic Sesame Dressing

½ cup dressing *LC, LCh, D, LS, V, v, Ml, k*

In skillet, heat:

2 tablespoons **oil**

Sauté in oil until lightly browned:

1 garlic clove, finely chopped
1 tablespoon sesame seeds

Transfer to a bowl and let cool. Add, blending well:

2 tablespoons **wine** vinegar (*D:* use tarragon vinegar)
3 tablespoons **stock**
Coarse **salt** to taste (*LS:* omit)
Pepper to taste

(257)

Italian Dressing

About 1 cup *LC, LCh, D, LS, V, v, P, Ml, K, k*

In a small glass bowl or jar, steep for 1 hour:

½ cup **stock**
⅓ cup **wine** vinegar (*D:* use tarragon vinegar)
2 cloves garlic, mashed
½ teaspoon oregano
¼ teaspoon basil
¼ teaspoon fennel seed, crushed

Strain steeped mixture into:

2 tablespoons **oil** (*P:* omit; increase stock by 2 tablespoons)

Whisk in:

1 teaspoon **lemon juice**
Salt to taste (*LS* and *P:* omit)
Pepper to taste (*P:* use white pepper)

VARIATION: Stir in:

2 flat anchovies, mashed well (Except: *LS, V, v, P*)
or
2 tablespoons grated **cheese** (Except: *V, Ml, K; LS:* use unsalted cheese)

(258)

Light Vinaigrette

About 1 cup *LC, LCh, D, LS, V, v, P, Ml, k*

Measure into bowl:

⅔ cup vegetable **stock**

Gradually whisk in:

1 tablespoon **oil** (*P:* omit)

Add to mixture:

1 clove garlic, peeled and slashed
1 teaspoon fresh tarragon, finely chopped, or ¼ teaspoon dry
1 teaspoon finely chopped fresh basil, or ¼ teaspoon dry
2 teaspoons finely chopped parsley

Marinate mixture for several hours in refrigerator. Remove garlic. Whisk in:

- 2 tablespoons white **wine** vinegar or red **wine** vinegar (*D:* use tarragon vinegar)
- 4 tablespoons **lemon juice**
- **Salt** to taste (*P* and *LS:* omit)
- **Pepper** to taste (*P:* use white)

Store in refrigerator. Whisk before serving.

(259) *LIGHT LEMON VINAIGRETTE*

About 1 cup *LC, LCh, D, LS, V, v, P, Ml, k*

In basic LIGHT VINAIGRETTE (**258**), substitute **lemon juice** for vinegar.

(260) *LIGHT MUSTARD VINAIGRETTE*

About 1 cup *LC, LCh, D, LS, V, v, P, Ml, k*

To basic LIGHT VINAIGRETTE (**258**) add: 1 teaspoon Dijon mustard or ¼ teaspoon dry mustard, or to taste. (*LS:* use unsalted mustard or dry mustard)

(261) *LIGHT ORANGE VINAIGRETTE*

About 1 cup *LC, LCh, D, LS, V, v, P, Ml, k*

In basic Vinaigrette or LIGHT VINAIGRETTE (**258**), substitute 2 tablespoons **orange juice concentrate** for 2 tablespoons of **stock.** Blend in 1 teaspoon dry mustard.

(262)

Spicy Orange Dressing

Enough for 4 to 6 servings *LC, LCh, D*, LS, V, v, P, Ml, k*

Combine in small saucepan:

2 tablespoons cornstarch
½ teaspoon dry mustard
½ teaspoon paprika
¼ teaspoon coriander

Gradually blend in, stirring to dissolve the cornstarch:

1 cup orange juice

Bring mixture to a boil over medium heat and boil for 1 minute, stirring constantly. Remove from heat. Stir in:

2 tablespoons tomato paste (*LS:* use unsalted tomato paste)
¼ teaspoon tabasco

Chill and stir before serving.

* Except those on diets limited in simple carbohydrates, such as fruits.

(263)

Orange Yogurt Dressing

About 1½ cups *LC, LCh, D*, LS†, v, P, k, B*

Combine and blend well:

1 cup low-fat **yogurt**
¼ cup **orange juice concentrate**
¼ cup **lemon juice**
¼ teaspoon paprika

Chill for several hours to blend flavors.

* Except those on diets limited in simple carbohydrates, such as fruit.
† Except those limited to low-sodium **milk**.

(264)

Soyo-Naise

About ¾ cup *LC, LCh, D, LS, V, v, P, Ml, k*

Combine in blender:

1 pound soft tofu (bean curd)
3 tablespoons **lemon juice**
½ teaspoon dry mustard
1 teaspoon **salt** (*LS:* omit; *P:* use ½ teaspoon **soy sauce**)
1 teaspoon **apple juice concentrate**
White **pepper** to taste

Process until smooth. Refrigerate for 1 hour before using. Use as mayonnaise. If mixture thickens too much, beat in 1 teaspoon of water before serving.

(265)

Soyo-Naise with Oil

About ¾ cup *LC, LCh, D, LS, V, v, Ml, k*

Blend gradually into recipe of SOYO-NAISE (**264**), 1 tablespoon of **oil.**

(266)

Soyo-Naise with Egg White

About ¾ cup *LC, LCh, D, v, Ml, k*

For a lighter dressing, gradually blend into SOYO-NAISE (**264**), 1 egg white.

(267)

Garlic Soyo-Naise

About ¾ cup *LC, LCh, D, LS, V, v, P, Ml, k*

Add to one of basic SOYO-NAISE (**264–6**), recipes: 2 small garlic cloves, pureed.

(268)

Green Soyo-Naise

About ¾ cup *LC, LCh, D, V, v, Ml, k*

Add to one of basic SOYO-NAISE (**264–6**), recipes: 2 tablespoons chopped fresh spinach or watercress, 1½ tablespoons chopped fresh chives or basil, 2 tablespoons chopped fresh parsley. Blanch herbs for 1 minute, cool, drain, and pat dry. Puree, removing any excess liquid, and add to SOYO-NAISE.

(269)

Curried Soyo-Naise

About ¾ cup *LC, LCh, D, LS, V, v, P, Ml, k*

Add to one of basic *SOYO-NAISE* (**264–6**), recipes: 1 teaspoon curry powder or to taste.

(270)

Soyo-Remoulade

About 1 cup *LCh, V, v, Ml, k*

Prepare:
1 basic SOYO-NAISE (**264**) recipe
Combine with SOYO-NAISE, blending gently:
2½ teaspoons chopped capers
2 teaspoons chopped sweet gherkins
1½ teaspoons chopped parsley
¾ teaspoon anchovy paste (*V* and *v:* leave out)
Refrigerate for 1 hour or more to allow flavors to blend. Serve cold.

(271)

Sweet-and-Sour Soyo-Naise

About 1¼ cups *LC, LCh, LS, V, v, P, Ml, k*

Blend into basic SOYO-NAISE (**264**) recipe: 3 teaspoons **lemon juice** and 3 teaspoons **apple juice concentrate,** or to taste.

(272)

Sweet and Sour Dressing

Abour ¾ cup *LC, LCh, D*, LS, V, v, P, Ml, k*

Combine in small bowl and let stand 1 hour:
4 teaspoons mustard seeds
4 teaspoons dry mustard
1 teaspoon tarragon
½ cup boiling water
Meanwhile, combine in small saucepan and bring to a boil:
6 tablespoons tarragon or **wine** vinegar (*D:* use tarragon vinegar)
2 tablespoons **apple juice concentrate**

(*Recipe continued on next page*)

¼ cup chopped onion
2 teaspoons minced garlic

Simmer for 5 minutes. Pour mixture into blender or food processor. Add mustard mixture and blend well for 2 minutes. Add and blend again:

2 tablespoons **apple juice concentrate**
6 tablespoons **orange juice concentrate**

* Except those on diets limited in simple carbohydrates, such as fruit.

Relishes

(273)

Chutney

4 cups *LC, LCh, LS, V, v, P, Ml, k*

Combine in heavy, large saucepan and bring to a boil:

3 cups fresh pineapple chunks (½-inch chunks) or other almost ripe fresh fruit (mango, peaches, apricots, plums, apples, etc.), peeled and seeded
1¼ cups white vinegar
½ cup **apple juice**
½ cup **apple juice concentrate**
1 medium onion, finely chopped
2 hot green peppers, finely chopped
2 garlic cloves, minced
1 teaspoon chopped fresh ginger
¾ cup raisins

(*Recipe continued on next page*)

½ cup dates, chopped
½ cup chopped papaya
½ fresh lime, peeled, seeded, and chopped
1 tablespoon brown **sugar** (*P:* omit)
1 teaspoon cinnamon
1 teaspoon garam masala
1 teaspoon grated orange rind
½ cup walnuts or slivered almonds (Opt.; *P* and *LC:* omit)

Simmer for 1 hour, stirring frequently. Remove from heat, stir in:

¼ cup **lemon juice**

Simmer an additional 5 minutes. Chill or cool for several hours before serving.

(274)

Homemade Horseradish

About 3 cups *LC, LCh, D, LS, V, v, P, Ml, K, k*

Combine:

2 cups grated or chopped peeled horseradish root
1 cup vinegar
¼ cup **apple juice concentrate**
1 cup cooked or canned beets, drained and chopped (*LS:* if permitted, use unsalted beets; if prohibited, omit and use additional **apple juice concentrate** to taste)

Chill for several hours.

VARIATION: Add to each 2 tablespoons horseradish:

¼ cup **mayonnaise** or SOYO-NAISE (*LC, LCh, D, LS, V, P:* use SOYO-NAISE)
½ to 1 teaspoon **lemon juice**

Combine prepared horseradish and **mayonnaise** (*K*)

(275)

Jersey Pepper Relish

6 to 8 servings *LC, LCh, LS, V, v, Ml, K, k*

Combine in glass bowl or jar:

3 red peppers, finely chopped
3 green peppers, finely chopped
1 small onion, chopped
½ teaspoon salt (*LS:* omit)
⅓ cup sugar
⅓ cup cider vinegar

Marinate for 3 to 4 hours in refrigerator before serving.

Fish

(276)

Baked Fish Fillets in Mustard Sauce

4 to 6 servings *LC, LCh, Ml, k*

Chop and set aside:
    ¼ cup sweet gherkins
Heat in **non-stick** skillet over medium flame:
    ½ to 1 tablespoon **margarine**
Sauté until lightly browned:
    ⅔ cup finely chopped onion
    ½ teaspoon finely minced garlic
Add and cook briefly:
    2 tablespoons red **wine** vinegar
Add and bring to a boil, stirring:
    ½ cup fresh fish or vegetable **stock**
    1 tablespoon tomato paste

Salt to taste
Pepper to taste
Add and let simmer 5 minutes:
½ teaspoon thyme, dried, or one sprig, fresh
Remove from heat. Stir in gherkins and:
1 tablespoon Dijon-style or other imported mustard
Set aside.
In **non-stick** baking dish, arrange:
2 pounds fish fillets
Sprinkle fillets with:
Cumin
Lemon juice
Pepper
Salt
¾ cup dry white **wine**
Bake at 375° F for 10 to 20 minutes, or until fish is opaque and flakes easily. Do not overcook.
Warm sauce gently and serve over fish

(277) *HERRING IN MUSTARD SAUCE*

8 to 10 appetizer servings ***LCh, Ml, k***

Prepare:
1 recipe MUSTARD SAUCE (**276**) without fish
Serve tossed with:
2 8-ounce jars herring in **wine** sauce, rinsed and drained

(278)
Chilean Fish Stew

6 servings ***LC, LCh, D, LS, P, Ml, k***

In a small saucepan, cook together for 10 minutes, stirring often:
1 cup canned tomatoes, drained, or fresh tomatoes, peeled and seeded (*LS:* use unsalted canned or fresh tomatoes)
1 clove garlic, minced
Add, and continue cooking over low heat for another 15 minutes, stirring frequently:

(*Recipe continued on next page*)

3 medium onions, sliced
3 green peppers, cut in strips
2 teaspoons paprika
¼ teaspoon saffron

In a **non-stick** casserole or Dutch oven, heat:

½ tablespoon **oil** (*P:* omit)

Brown in casserole on both sides:

6 thick slices (about 2 pounds) sea bass, snapper, pike, or other fillet

Add to the casserole the tomato mixture plus:

2 bay leaves
¼ teaspoon dried ground red pepper
1½ cups dry white **wine** (*D:* if prohibited, use **stock**)
1½ cups fish **stock** or water
1 tablespoon **wine** vinegar
Salt to taste (*LS* and *P:* omit and increase wine vinegar if necessary)
White **pepper** to taste

Bring mixture to a boil. Add:

½ cup uncooked rice

Cover and cook over low heat for 25 minutes or until rice is tender.

(279)

Halibut Linguata

4 servings *LC, LCh, D, LS, P, Ml, k*

In a **non-stick** pan, heat:

2 tablespoons **oil** (*P:* omit)

Stir in and **sauté** until golden:

2 large onions, sliced and separated into rings

Stir in and bring to a boil:

½ cup white **wine** vinegar (*D:* if prohibited, use tarragon vinegar)
½ cup dry white **wine** (*D:* if prohibited, use **stock**)
1 tablespoon **lemon juice**

Remove from heat. In a **non-stick,** flameproof pan, arrange:

4 6 to 8-ounce halibut steaks

Sprinkle steaks with:

Salt to taste (*LS* and *P:* omit)
Pepper to taste (*P:* use white)

Baste with onion mixture and bake at 400° F for 4 minutes on each side, basting twice on each side during baking. Fish is ready when it flakes easily with a fork. When ready to serve, place halibut steaks under the broiler for a few minutes until they are lightly browned. Do not overcook. Transfer to a serving dish. Spoon remaining onion mixture over them and garnish with:

Lemon wedges
Parsley

(280)

Herbed Fish Steaks

2 servings *LC, LCh, D, LS, P, Ml, k, B*

Rinse and wipe dry:

2 6-ounce permitted fish steaks (salmon, halibut, snapper, etc.)

In small saucepan, combine:

2 teaspoons fresh rosemary, or ½ teaspoon dried
2 teaspoons fresh tarragon, or ½ teaspoon dried
2 teaspoons fresh thyme, or ½ teaspoon dried
2 teaspoons fresh or frozen chives (*B:* omit)
2 teaspoons chopped fresh fennel or ½ teaspoon dried fennel seed) (*B:* if permitted)
2 to 4 tablespoons **butter** or **margarine** (*LC:* use 1 tablespoon plus 2 tablespoons dry white **wine;** *P:* omit; use 3 tablespoons dry white **wine**)

Heat herbs and shortening or wine over low heat until well blended. Sprinkle steaks with:

2 tablespoons **lemon juice**
Salt to taste (*LS* and *P:* omit)
Pepper to taste (*P:* use white; *B:* omit)

Brush herbed butter on both sides of fish steaks. Broil in **non-stick** pan for 5 to 7 minutes on each side, or until fish flakes easily. Do not overcook.

(281) *ROSEMARY FISH STEAKS*

2 servings *LC, LCh, D, LS, P, Ml, k*

Follow recipe for HERBED FISH STEAKS (**280**) but substitute 2 tablespoons fresh rosemary or 2 teaspoons dried for mixed herbs. Add ½ teaspoon minced garlic.

(282)

Fish Paprikash

4 to 6 servings *LC, LCh, D, LS, P, k*

Heat in **non-stick** skillet over medium heat:
 1 tablespoon **oil** (*P:* omit)
Sauté in skillet for 10 minutes or until golden brown:
 4 medium onions, chopped
Blend in:
 2 teaspoons paprika, preferably Hungarian
Arrange over the onions:
 2 pounds fish fillets (sea bass, lake trout, whitefish, flounder, etc.)
Sprinkle with:
 White **pepper**
 Salt (*P* and *LS:* use **lemon juice**)
Add:
 1 cup fish **stock,** vegetable **stock,** or water
 1 cup crushed tomatoes (*LS:* use unsalted canned, or fresh)
Cook, covered, over low heat for 25 minutes.
With broad spatula, carefully remove fish to serving dish. Keep warm. Taste sauce for seasoning; correct if necessary. Cook sauce for 10 minutes to reduce slightly. Stir into sauce:
 ½ cup low-fat **yogurt** or **buttermilk** (*LS:* omit for those limited to low-sodium **milk;** for others, use unsalted **buttermilk** or **yogurt**)
Gently reheat sauce, but do not boil. Pour sauce over fish, and serve garnished with:
 Lemon wedges
 Chopped parsley

(283)

Kippered Herring with Onions

4 to 6 servings *LCh, D, Ml, k*

Heat large **non-stick** skillet. Add:

1 very large onion, or 2 large onions, sliced

Cover and steam over low heat for 10 minutes, stirring occasionally, until onions are nicely softened. Add to skillet:

2 kippered herrings

Cook herrings for 4 to 5 minutes on each side, or until browned. Stir onions frequently. Drain excess fat. Serve with:

Individual baked potatoes *or*

Sliced boiled potatoes

Garnish with:

Parsley

(284)

Poached Whole Fish

Servings depend upon size of fish *LC, LCh, D, LS, P, Ml, k, B*

Prepare in large pot:

1 recipe COURT BOUILLON (**296**) (Double recipe for fish over three pounds)

Wrap in cheesecloth:

1 large fish (salmon, bass, salmon trout, etc.; about ¾ pound per person) cleaned but with head still on

Set fish in a poacher or a pot large enough to hold it. (Or, if necessary, cut it in half and put it back together to serve later.) Heat COURT BOUILLON to boiling and pour over the fish. Cover poacher or pot and simmer (do not boil!) for about 5 to 8 minutes a pound. Thickness is a factor, too, so thicker fish will take longer. Check by flaking with a fork. Fish is done when it flakes easily. Remove fish from bouillon as soon as it is done. If skin is to be removed, do so while fish is still warm. Cool. Bone if desired. Arrange on a long platter; garnish with:

Cucumber slices

Dill sprigs

(Recipe continued on next page)

Coat with an aspic, if desired. (see GEFILTE FISH EN GELEE **(171)**)
Serve with one or more of the following sauces, depending upon diet.

DILL SAUCE **(421)**
ORANGE DILL SAUCE **(422)**
SAUCE VERTE **(426)**

(285)

Curried Salmon Kedgeree

4 servings *LC, LCh, D, k*

Melt in saucepan:
4 teaspoons **margarine** or **butter**
Blend in gradually, stirring over low heat for 3 minutes:
3 tablespoons **flour**
Gradually blend in, stirring constantly until mixture thickens:
1½ cups skim **milk**
¼ cup evaporated skimmed **milk**
1 to 2 tablespoons curry to taste
Salt and **pepper** to taste
Remove from heat.
Combine ⅔ cup of the sauce with:
3 cups cooked rice
Layer rice mixture in **non-stick** double boiler or mold with:
1 pound canned or fresh cooked (baked, broiled, or poached) salmon or other fish
4 sliced hard-cooked **eggs** (*LCh:* omit yolks)
¼ cup chopped parsley
Top with remaining sauce. Heat thoroughly over hot water. Unmold to serve or serve over:
CREAMED SPINACH **(393)** (Opt.)

(286)

Bland Fish Kedgeree

4 servings *LC, LCh, D, k, B**

Prepare double quantity of sauce as in CURRIED SALMON KEDGEREE **(285)** but omit curry and pepper. Combine half of sauce with:

2 cups chopped spinach, well cooked

Combine rest of sauce with:

1 pound cooked (baked, broiled, or poached) non-fatty fish (sole, halibut, haddock, flounder, etc.)

3 cups cooked white rice

Serve over spinach

* Except those on milk restricted or low-residue diets.

(287)

Salmon Mousse I

8 servings *LC, LCh, D, P, k*

Tip: Prepare 4 to 6 hours or more before serving

In **non-stick** pan, heat over medium flame:

1 tablespoon **oil** (*P:* omit)

Add and **sauté** until just golden:

1½ cups minced scallions or onions

Set aside. Combine ¼ cup water with:

2 tablespoons unflavored **gelatin**

Allow gelatin to soften for 1 minute. Meanwhile, combine in saucepan and bring to a boil:

1¼ cups **stock**

½ cup dry white **wine** (*D:* if prohibited, use **stock** or water)

Stir in gelatin mixture. Cool, but do not chill. Meanwhile, puree in blender or processor:

2 1-pound cans salmon, drained

(*Recipe continued on next page*)

Stir into salmon:
4 tablespoons **lemon juice**
1½ cups low-fat **yogurt**
Add salmon mixture to cooled liquid. Stir in onions and:
½ cup very thinly sliced celery
½ cup finely diced sweet red pepper
⅓ cup slivered almonds (*LC* and *P:* omit)
½ cup chopped fresh dill weed, or 1 tablespoon dried
Taste for seasoning. Add, if needed:
Salt to taste (*P:* omit)
Pepper to taste (*P:* use white)
Lemon juice
Pour into 2-quart **non-stick** mold, and chill for several hours until set.
Unmold on platter garnished with:
Watercress
Cucumber slices
Quartered tomatoes

(288)

Salmon Mousse II

4 to 6 servings *LCh, LS, k, B**

Puree in blender:
1 1-pound can salmon, drained (*LS:* use unsalted if required)
3 tablespoons **lemon juice**
Transfer mixture to a bowl. In blender, process:
1 small avocado, peeled and pitted
3 tablespoons finely chopped dill, stems removed
Add avocado mixture to salmon along with:
2 tablespoons sour cream
In a small saucepan, combine:
1 envelope unflavored **gelatin**
¼ cup water
Let stand for 1 minute until gelatin is softened. Bring to a boil over medium heat, stirring constantly. Remove from heat and stir into salmon. Add to taste:
Salt (*LS:* omit)
Pour mixture into 4-cup **non-stick** mold and chill until set. Unmold to serve and garnish with:
Avocado slices

VARIATION: Stir into salmon mixture: 1 cup drained canned petits pois or 1 4-ounce can of mushrooms, drained (*LS:* omit).

* Except those on low-residue diet.

(289)

Stuffed Fillets in Cheese Sauce

4 servings *LCh, D, k, B**

Rinse and wipe dry:
 1½ pounds fish fillets
If frozen fish is used thaw according to package directions. Then soak thawed fillets in refrigerator for 1 hour in:
 1 cup skim **milk**
Turn once during soaking.
In **non-stick** skillet, melt over medium flame:
 1 tablespoon **margarine**
Sauté in margarine until just tender (*B:* soft):
 3 cups sliced fresh mushrooms
 ½ teaspoon thyme
 ½ teaspoon **salt**
Add to skillet and blend well:
 ¾ cup **bread** crumbs
 ½ tablespoon **margarine**
Drain milk from fillets. Spoon ¼ of mushroom mixture in center of each fillet. Roll up fillets and place seam side down in greased baking dish. Drizzle over fish:
 ½ teaspoon **lemon juice**
Sprinkle with:
 ½ teaspoon paprika
Refrigerate until 20 minutes prior to serving. Then, bake in preheated oven at 350° F for 5 minutes. Pour over fish:
 1 recipe CHEESE SAUCE **(419)**
Continue baking for 5 to 10 minutes or until fish flakes easily with fork. Serve immediately, garnished with:
 Paprika
 Lemon wedges
 Parsley sprigs

* Except those on diets limited in milk products.

(290)

Stuffed Fish in Phyllo

4 servings *LC, LCh, D, LS, Ml, k*

Bring to room temperature according to package directions:
Package of phyllo leaves
Prepare COURT BOUILLON (**296**).
Prepare one of the following stuffings:
I. *LCh, D, LS, Ml, k*
Combine in a bowl:
½ cup chopped parsley
¼ cup chopped walnuts
1 tablespoon crushed fresh rosemary, or 1 teaspoon dried
1 tablespoon crushed fresh thyme, or 1 teaspoon dried
1½ teaspoons **lemon juice**
II. *LC, LCh, D, LS, Ml, k*
Heat in **non-stick** pan:
1 tablespoon **lemon juice**
Add and **sauté** lightly:
1 cup sliced mushrooms
Stir in and remove from heat:
½ cup chopped parsley
1 tablespoon crushed fresh rosemary or 1 teaspoon dried
1 tablespoon crushed fresh thyme or 1 teaspoon dried
III. *LC, LCh, D, Ml, k*
Combine in small bowl:
½ cup chopped parsley
2 tablespoons capers, chopped
1 tablespoon **lemon juice**
Salt and **pepper** to taste
Poach in the COURT BOUILLON until it flakes easily with a fork:
4 8 to 10-ounce trout or baby salmon, boned and cleaned, heads and tails removed
Or
1 2 to 3-pound sea bass, sea trout, or salmon, boned and cleaned, heads and tails removed
Estimated cooking times: 7 to 10 minutes for the smaller fish; 10 to 15 minutes for the larger. Don't overcook.
Remove fish from poaching liquid. Drain on paper towel. Spread prepared stuffing in each fish.

Melt:

1 tablespoon **margarine** or **butter**

Count out 8 phyllo leaves. Return remainder to refrigerator. Spread 1 leaf on damp towel. Brush leaf with melted margarine. Place a second leaf over the first. Then wrap a small fish in the leaves, making a neat package. Do the same with the other leaves and the additional fish, tucking in the ends.

If you are using large fish, arrange overlapping leaves, spread with the melted margarine, and roll them neatly around the fish. Tuck in the ends.

In a **non-stick** skillet, heat:

1 tablespoon **oil**
1 tablespoon **margarine** or **butter**

Sauté the phyllo-wrapped fish in the pan for about 1 or 2 minutes on each side or until golden.

Serve hot.

(291)

Tandoori Fish

6 to 8 servings *LC, LCh, D, LS, P, k*

Tip: Begin the day before.

Combine in saucepan:

1 large or 2 to 3 small beets (*LS:* if prohibited, omit this step)
1 cup water

Cover and boil until beets are tender, about 15 to 20 minutes. Drain well, reserving the liquid as beet-root color extract. Set aside. Combine and seep for about 5 minutes:

2 tablespoons boiling water
1 teaspoon saffron threads

Brush this mixture generously over:

8 boned trout or baby salmon or bluefish or other small fish

Let stand at room temperature for 20 minutes.

Puree in processor or blender:

2 ounces garlic cloves (about 8 large)
2 ounces fresh ginger root, peeled and cut into small pieces

Transfer to a bowl and add beet-root extract made earlier and:

2 tablespoons fresh **lemon juice**
1 heaping tablespoon ground coriander

(*Recipe continued on next page*)

1 teaspoon paprika
1 teaspoon **salt** (*P* and *LS:* omit)
½ teaspoon ground red pepper
½ teaspoon ground cumin
1 cup low-fat **yogurt**

Stir to blend well. Brush this mixture generously on fish. Marinate, covered, in refrigerator for 12 hours. Baste every few hours. Shortly before serving, preheat oven to 500° F. In a lightly buttered (*P:* omit) **non-stick** roasting pan, arrange the fish. Sprinkle with:

2 tablespoons melted **butter** or **margarine** (*P:* omit)

Bake for 10 minutes. Reduce oven temperature to 350° F and continue baking until fish flakes easily, about another 5 to 10 minutes. Do not overcook.

Serve garnished with:

Radish roses
Lemon and lime wedges
Green chilies (*LS:* use unsalted or fresh)

Pour remaining marinade into saucepan and heat gently. Do not boil. Serve on the side.

(292)

Baked Trout with Filberts

4 servings *LCh, D, LS, Ml, k*

Wipe with a damp cloth:

4 6 to 8-ounce trout, cleaned and boned

Sprinkle inside and out with:

Salt to taste (*LS:* omit)
Pepper to taste

Sprinkle inner cavities of fish with (in total):

2 tablespoons **lemon juice**
2 tablespoons finely chopped parsley

Insert in cavities (in total):

2 lemons, sliced thinly

Dip fish in:

1 **egg** white, lightly beaten

Then dip in a mixture of:

1 cup ground, lightly toasted filberts or almonds
¼ cup wheat germ

Each fish should be lightly coated with nuts. In baking dish just large enough to hold the fish, heat in 450° F oven for 3 minutes:

1 tablespoon **butter** or **margarine**

Add the fish and bake for 15 to 20 minutes or until fish flakes easily. In a **non-stick** skillet, **sauté**:

½ cup thinly slivered filberts or almonds

Transfer fish to serving platter. Sprinkle with sliced nuts. Garnish with:

Chopped parsley

(293)

Trout Sauté with Almonds, Pine Nuts, and Raisins

4 servings *LCh, D, LS, Ml, k*

Place in shallow dish:

4 6 to 10-ounce whole trout, or sole (*LS:* use fresh fish)

Sprinkle with:

Juice of 1 lemon
Salt to taste (*LS:* omit)
Pepper to taste

Let fish stand one hour, then dust with:

Flour

Heat in large **non-stick** skillet over medium flame:

1 tablespoon **oil**
1 tablespoon **butter** or **margarine**

Sauté fish in shortening for 5 to 6 minutes on each side, or until they flake easily with a fork. Transfer to serving platter and keep warm. Add to skillet and **sauté** until golden:

¼ cup sliced almonds
¼ cup pine nuts

Remove nuts from pan with slotted spoon; set aside. Add to pan and cook until raisins are plumped:

⅓ cup white **wine** (*D:* use 2 tablespoons **apple juice,** 2 tablespoons water)
¼ cup raisins

Spoon sauce over fish. (*D:* pass separately) Sprinkle with toasted nuts.

(294)

Turban of Fish, Spinach Sauce

4 to 6 servings *LCh, D, k, B**

Rinse and pat dry:
  2 pounds non-fatty fish fillets (sole, flounder, haddock, snapper, etc.)
If frozen fish is used, soak fillets, refrigerated, for 1 hour in:
  2 cups skim **milk**
Turn fillets once during soaking.
In small saucepan cook over low heat, stirring occasionally:
  1 10-ounce package frozen chopped spinach
  ⅔ cup skim **milk**
  ¼ teaspoon **salt**
When spinach is cooked (*B:* very soft), allow to cool.
In large **non-stick** skillet melt over low heat:
  ½ to 1 tablespoon **margarine**
Sauté in skillet until just softened (*B:* very soft):
  2 cups fresh mushrooms, stems trimmed, sliced
  ½ teaspoon dried dill or 1 tablespoon fresh chopped
  ¼ teaspoon **salt**
Combine mushrooms with:
  3 cups cooked rice (*B:* use white rice)
Beat together to blend, and add to mushroom-rice mixture:
  ⅓ cup evaporated skimmed **milk**
  2 **egg** whites
Stir in:
  1 tablespoon fresh dill or ½ teaspoon dried
  Salt to taste
  Pepper to taste (*B:* omit)
If soaking fillets, drain and pat dry. Line greased ring mold with fish fillets overlapping each other and the outer rim of pan.
Spoon rice mixture into inner ring formed by fish. Fold overlapping ends of fillets over rice to cover. Place sheet of buttered wax paper on top of mold. Perforate in center to allow steam to escape. Place mold in oven in pan filled with hot water halfway up the sides of ring mold. Bake in preheated oven at 325° F for 30 to 40 minutes or until fish is springy to touch. While turban bakes, combine cooled spinach mixture in blender with:

2 ounces **cream cheese** or **hoop cheese** (*LCh:* use **hoop cheese**)
⅓ cup low-fat **cottage cheese**
Fresh dill or paprika to taste
Salt to taste

Puree in blender until smooth. Heat over low heat in saucepan. When turban of fish is done, let settle 10 minutes out of oven. Turn over on wire rack to drain excess water. Unmold and pat dry with paper towel. Brush with:

Melted **margarine**

Top with Spinach Sauce and serve immediately.

* Except those on milk restricted or low-residue diets; if milk is permitted, but spinach is not, substitute chopped broccoli for spinach.

(295)

Yucatecan Fish

4 servings *LC, LCh, D, LS, P, Ml, k*

In a small bowl, combine to make marinade:

4 garlic cloves, mashed
1 teaspoon achiote seed (a Latin spice available in Spanish markets)
½ teaspoon oregano
½ teaspoon cumin
Salt to taste (*LS* and *P:* omit)
Pepper to taste (P: use white)

Stir in:

6 tablespoons orange juice
2 tablespoons **lemon** or **lime juice**

Arrange in a ceramic or glass dish:

4 7 to 10-ounce fish fillets (sea bass, snapper, or sole)

Coat fillets with marinade and let stand for 30 minutes. Place the fish and marinade in a **non-stick,** flameproof pan just large enough to hold the fish. Add in layers:

1 large onion, thinly sliced
2 medium tomatoes, peeled, seeded, and thinly sliced
2 green peppers, thinly sliced
2 pimientos, thinly sliced

(*Recipe continued on next page*)

1 canned serrano pepper, seeded and chopped, or 1 fresh chili pepper, chopped (*LS:* use fresh)

Combine in a small bowl:

¼ cup tomato juice (*LS:* use unsalted)
½ teaspoon achiote
¼ teaspoon cumin
¼ teaspoon oregano
2 tablespoons **orange juice concentrate**
1 tablespoon **lemon juice**

Pour this mixture over the fish and vegetables. Cover the dish with foil and simmer for 15 minutes, or until the fish flakes easily. Garnish with:

Chopped parsley
Orange slices

(296)

Court Bouillon for Poaching

About 8 cups *LC, LCh, D, LS, P, Ml, k, B*

In **non-stick** pan, heat over medium flame:

1 tablespoon **oil** (*P:* omit)

Sauté in pan:

2 garlic cloves, minced (*B:* omit)
1 cup sliced onions (*B:* omit)
1 cup sliced celery (*LS:* use ½ cup)
1 cup sliced carrots (*LS:* use sliced parsnips)

Transfer mixture to a poacher or large pot. Add and simmer for 10 minutes:

8 cups water
1 cup dry white **wine** (*D* and *B:* if prohibited, use ¼ cup vinegar plus ¾ cup water)
1 bay leaf
5 sprigs parsley
4 peppercorns (*B:* omit)

Strain liquid and return to poaching pot.

Poultry

(297)

Cold Glazed Chicken Breasts, Nut and Duxelles Stuffing

6 servings *LCh, D, LS, Ml*

Tip: Prepare a day ahead

Have a butcher prepare:
3 whole chicken breasts left unsevered
Spread each breast on a sheet of wax paper. Cover with another sheet and, with the broad side of a cleave, flatten slightly. In a kettle large enough to hold chicken, combine:
6 cups chicken **stock**
6 peppercorns
2 dried red hot peppers
1 garlic clove, split

(*Recipe continued on next page*)

Bring the mixture to a boil and add the breasts. Simmer, covered, for 5 to 10 minutes, or until breasts are just tender. Let chicken cool in stock.

When cool, carefully bone and skin chicken breasts, keeping each breast in 1 piece. Return skin and bones to stock pot. Bring to a boil over high heat and cook until stock is reduced by half. Strain through a sieve lined with cheesecloth into a bowl. Let cool and skim off fat.

In blender, chop:

¼ pound blanched almonds
1 clove garlic

Transfer almonds to a bowl and add 3 to 4 tablespoons of the reduced stock to make a thick paste. If necessary, add a bit more stock. Add to taste:

Salt (*LS:* omit)

In blender, chop:

¼ pound shelled, unsalted, pistachio nuts, husks removed
1 clove garlic

Transfer mixture to a bowl and add 3 to 4 tablespoons of the reduced stock to make a thick paste. Add to taste:

Salt (*LS:* omit)

Chill remaining stock.

Finely chop:

½ pound mushrooms

Squeeze the moisture out of mushrooms in a towel. In a **non-stick** skillet, heat:

1 to 2 tablespoons **oil** or **margarine**

Add mushrooms and:

2 shallots, finely minced

Cook over low heat until all moisture has evaporated. Season with:

Salt to taste (*LS:* omit)
Pepper to taste

Transfer chicken breasts to a flat surface. Slice in half flatways. With a spatula spread a ⅓-inch thick layer of the almond mixture on the bottom of each breast. Over that, spread a ⅓-inch thick layer of pistachio mixture. Add a layer of the mushroom duxelles next. Continue layering the stuffings until all the stuffing has been used. Replace tops of chicken breasts to form 3 whole breasts. Arrange them on a large serving platter. Chill overnight, covered tightly with plastic wrap.

Next day, heat stock *just* until it liquifies. Let it cool to the consistency of syrup. Spoon 3 or 4 coatings of stock over chicken to glaze, chilling chicken after each coating until glaze is set. Garnish with:

Finely chopped parsley or watercress (*LS:* use parsley)
Cherry tomatoes

And remaining jellied stock, chopped.

(298)

Cold Glazed Chicken Breasts, Duxelles Stuffing

6 servings *LC. LCh, D, LS, P*

Prepare chicken as for COLD GLAZED CHICKEN BREASTS, NUT AND DUXELLES STUFFING **(297),** but substitute mushroom duxelles made from 2 pounds of fresh mushrooms, 2 to 3 tablespoons oil (*P:* omit), and 6 shallots *or* 1 cup scallions *or* onions, chopped, for the nut stuffing. **Salt** and **pepper** to taste (*LS* and *P:* omit **salt**; *P:* use white **pepper**).

(299)

Apple-Stuffed Chicken Breasts

8 to 10 servings *LC, LCh, D*, LS, P, Ml*

Split, bone, and skin:

  6 whole chicken breasts

Reserve bones for stock. Place the 12 single breasts between layers of wax paper and pound each with the side of a cleaver or a mallet until very thin. Heat in **non-stick** skillet over medium flame:

  1 tablespoon **oil** or **margarine** (*P:* omit)

Sauté in skillet until golden:

  1 cup chopped onion
  2 garlic cloves, minced

Add to skillet, stirring over low heat until well mixed:

  2 medium apples, peeled, cored, and grated
  1 cup soft **bread** crumbs
  ½ teaspoon **salt** (*P* and *LS:* omit)
  ½ to 1 teaspoon **crushed** rosemary
  ½ teaspoon basil *or* thyme

Fill each breast on the bone side with 2 or 3 tablespoons of the apple mixture. Roll up, tucking in ends. Secure with toothpick or string, if necessary.

(*Recipe continued on next page*)

Roll each breast in:
Flour
Heat in **non-stick** skillet:
1 tablespoon **oil** or **margarine** (*P:* omit)
Brown chicken in skillet on all sides. Add to skillet:
¾ cup **apple juice**
¼ cup chicken **stock**
¼ cup dry white **wine** (*D:* if prohibited, use **stock**)
3 tablespoons apple brandy (*D:* omit; *P:* use dry white **wine**)
1 tablespoon **lemon juice**
Simmer covered for 20 to 25 minutes or just until tender. Remove toothpicks or string. Transfer breasts to a heated platter with a slotted spoon. Blend together:
1 tablespoon cornstarch
1 tablespoon water
Stir cornstarch mixture into pan juices, stirring over low heat until thickened. Spoon juices over chicken rolls. Garnish platter with:
GLAZED APPLE RINGS (**432**)
Watercress sprigs

* Except those on diets limited in simple carbohydrates, such as fruit.

(300)

Burgundy Chicken

4 to 6 servings *LC, LCh, LS, Ml*

Skin and bone:
3 whole chicken breasts, split
Discard skin, reserve bones. Cut boned chicken into bite-size pieces. Dust with mixture of:
3 tablespoons **flour**
2 teaspoons garlic powder
1 teaspoon paprika
½ to 1 teaspoon **salt** (*LS:* omit)
¼ teaspoon **pepper**
Heat in **non-stick** skillet over medium flame:
1 tablespoon **oil** (Opt.)

Sauté chicken pieces in skillet, turning until they lose pink color. Remove from skillet and reserve; refrigerate. In large, heavy, **non-stick** saucepan, heat:

1 tablespoon **oil**

Sauté in oil until slightly softened:

3 cups sliced onions
1 tablespoon minced garlic

Add to saucepan reserved chicken bones and:

2½ cups Burgundy or other dry red **wine**
2 cups chicken **stock**
12 to 16 small boiling onions, peeled, ends trimmed
1 tablespoon tomato paste (*LS:* use unsalted tomato paste) or 3 tablespoons tomato puree (*LS:* use unsalted)
2 teaspoons thyme or sweet marjoram
1 bay leaf
1 large garlic clove, speared with toothpick

Stir over medium-low heat until blended. Bring to a simmer, cover, and cook 1 hour. Remove bones, bay leaf, and garlic. Meanwhile, melt in **non-stick** skillet over medium flame:

1 tablespoon **margarine**

Sauté in margarine until slightly softened:

1 pound mushrooms, washed, stems trimmed, and sliced.

Sprinkle over:

3 tablespoons **flour**

Blend, stirring constantly over very low heat for 2 to 3 minutes. Add 1 cup Burgundy sauce to pan and stir until smooth. Add this mixture to remaining Burgundy sauce and cook over medium-low heat, stirring constantly until mixture is thick. Add reserved chicken pieces, and continue to stir for 5 minutes, or until chicken is heated through. Serve, if desired, over:

Noodles tossed with 1 tablespoon **margarine** and chopped parsley (*LCh:* use yolkless noodles)

(301)

Chicken Breasts with Mushrooms

6 servings *LC, LCh, D, LS, P, Ml, B*

Halve, skin, and bone:
3 whole chicken breasts
Flatten them between sheets of wax paper with a mallet or the side of a cleaver.
Sprinkle breasts with:
Salt (*LS* and *P:* omit)
Pepper (*P:* use white; *B:* omit)
Lemon juice
Dip them in:
3 **egg** whites, lightly beaten (*LS:* use 1 white plus 2 tablespoons water)
Coat with:
1 cup **bread** crumbs
In a **non-stick** skillet, heat over medium flame:
½ tablespoon **oil** (*P:* use 2 tablespoons dry white **wine**)
½ tablespoon **margarine** (*P:* omit)
Sauté the breasts on both sides in the skillet until nicely browned. Transfer them to a heated platter and keep warm. Add to the skillet:
3 cups sliced fresh mushrooms
Sauté mushrooms for 3 or 4 minutes or until lightly browned. (For *B:* cook until very soft) Spoon mushrooms over chicken breasts and serve.

(302)

Stuffed Chicken Breasts in Phyllo

4 to 6 servings *LC, LCh, D, LS, P, Ml*

Bring to room temperature according to package directions:
1 package phyllo leaves
Skin and bone, reserving bones for making stock:
6 single chicken breasts
In a large **non-stick** skillet, melt over medium flame:
½ tablespoon **margarine** (*P:* omit)

Sauté in skillet until golden:
½ tablespoon minced garlic
Add to skillet and continue to sauté over medium-low heat:
1 pound fresh mushrooms, sliced
1 tablespoon tarragon
¼ teaspoon **salt** (*LS* and *P:* sprinkle with **lemon juice**)
When mushrooms are soft, sprinkle with:
1 tablespoon **flour**
Blend over medium heat for 2 to 3 minutes. Add:
¼ cup plus 2 tablespoons sherry **wine** (*D:* if prohibited, use ¼ cup **stock** plus 1 tablespoon tarragon vinegar; *P:* use dry white **wine**)
Stir over low heat until thickened. Set aside.
Flatten chicken breasts between sheets of wax paper with a mallet or the side of a cleaver. Dust with:
White **pepper**
Sweet paprika
Divide mushroom mixture among flattened breasts. Roll up tightly and place each on 1 phyllo leaf folded in half. Fold sides of phyllo over chicken, then roll up tightly from bottom. Place rolls on **non-stick** baking sheet. Brush with:
Egg white
Sprinkle with:
Sesame seeds
Bake in a preheated oven at 350° F for 10 minutes.

(303)

Chicken Cacciatore

5 to 6 servings *LC, LCh, D, LS, P, Ml*

Combine:
½ cup **flour**
¼ teaspoon garlic powder
Dredge in this mixture:
2½ pounds chicken breasts, skinned and quartered
Heat in **non-stick** skillet:
1 tablespoon **oil** (*P:* omit)

(*Recipe continued on next page*)

Add to pan and brown:

2 cups chopped onions
2 green peppers, cut in thin strips
2 tablespoons chopped fresh parsley
2 teaspoons minced garlic
2 teaspoons fresh oregano or 1 teaspoon dried
1 teaspoon dried basil
½ teaspoon marjoram
Pepper to taste (*P:* use white)
Salt to taste (*LS* and *P:* use wine vinegar to taste plus dash **apple juice concentrate**)

Add:

2 cups tomatoes, crushed (*LS:* use fresh or unsalted canned)
¼ cup tomato paste (*LS:* use unsalted)
1 cup dry red **wine** (*P:* use dry white **wine;** *D:* if prohibited, use **stock**)

Cook 15 minutes and add:

2 cups sliced fresh mushrooms

Continue cooking until chicken is tender, about 10 minutes more. Serve with pasta.

(304)

Chicken with Chick Peas

4 to 6 servings *LC, LCh, D, P, Ml*

Heat in **non-stick** skillet over medium flame:

1 tablespoon **oil** (*P:* omit)

Sauté in skillet until soft:

2 onions, chopped
2 garlic cloves, minced

Add:

½ teaspoon ground turmeric
½ teaspoon coriander
⅛ teaspoon cumin

Brown in onion mixture on medium heat:

6 single chicken breasts, halved

Remove chicken and onion to casserole.

Deglaze skillet with:

½ cup chicken **stock**

Add to casserole. Combine and add to casserole:

1 cup chicken **stock**
¼ cup **lemon juice**
2 garlic cloves, minced
Salt to taste (*P:* omit)
Pepper to taste (*P:* use white)

Cover and simmer mixture for 30 minutes. Add:

2 cups chick peas (*LC* and *D:* use 1 cup)
1 10-ounce package frozen artichoke hearts, defrosted

Simmer partially covered for 30 minutes, or until chicken is tender.

(305)

Chicken Curry

8 servings *LCh, LS, P, Ml*

Skin and bone:

5 pounds chicken breasts, about 10 single breasts

Discard fat; reserve skin and bones for stock. Combine in bowl large enough to hold the breasts:

½ cup **lemon juice**
½ cup dry white **wine**
½ teaspoon ground ginger
2 teaspoons curry powder
½ teaspoon white **pepper**
4 teaspoons finely chopped onion

Marinate breasts in this mixture for at least an hour in the refrigerator. Meanwhile, prepare a stock from the chicken bones and skin. Combine bones and skin in large stock pot with:

10 cups water
4 stalks celery, sliced (*LS:* use 2 stalks if permitted; if not, omit)
5 carrots, sliced (*LS:* use 2 if permitted plus 1 parsnip; if not, omit)
2 leeks, white parts only, sliced
1 parsnip, sliced
1 onion, an *x* cut in the bottom
8 sprigs of parsley
1 bay leaf
2 garlic cloves
Salt to taste (*LS* and *P:* omit)

(*Recipe continued on next page*)

Bring stock ingredients to a boil and simmer for 2 hours, uncovered. Strain stock, reserving vegetables and chicken from bones for family eating. Discard garlic and bay leaf and skim fat from stock. In saucepan, make a roux from 2 tablespoons of the stock and:

1 tablespoon **margarine** or **oil** (*P:* omit)
¼ cup **flour**

Cook roux, stirring, for a few minutes. Gradually add to roux 2½ cups of the stock, stirring constantly until smooth. Continue cooking over low heat, stirring frequently until sauce is thickened. Add:

2 tablespoons curry powder
½ teaspoon ginger powder
½ teaspoon cumin
¼ cup **apple juice concentrate**
1 fresh chili pepper, finely chopped (Opt.)

Heat in **non-stick** skillet over medium heat:

2 teaspoons **oil** (*P:* omit)

Brown chicken breasts lightly in skillet. Remove breasts and add to skillet:

1¼ cups finely chopped onion
1 bay leaf

Cook, stirring frequently for 2 or 3 minutes. Add:

2 teaspoons finely minced garlic
2 green peppers, cut in very thin strips

Continue cooking, stirring frequently, for another 3 minutes. Stir in curried sauce and simmer for 2 minutes. Return chicken to skillet and simmer for 10 minutes. Add:

2 large apples, peeled, cored, and cut into small cubes
4 bananas, sliced in half lengthwise
½ cup currants or raisins

Taste for seasoning. Add more curry or, if desired:

Cayenne
Salt to taste (*LS* and *P:* omit)

Simmer for 5 minutes more or until chicken is just tender. Serve hot, garnished with:

Coriander (Cilantro)

Pass separately:

Shredded coconut (except *LCh* and *P*)
Sliced almonds or unsalted peanuts (*P:* omit)

(306)

Chicken Breasts Florentine

8 servings *LC, LCh, D, LS, P, Ml*

Heat in **non-stick** skillet over medium flame:

2 teaspoons **oil** (*P:* omit)

Sauté quickly while stirring until brown:

¼ cup minced shallots or scallions

1 teaspoon minced garlic

Stir in and simmer for 3 minutes or until shallots are soft:

¼ cup dry white **wine**

Add to skillet and simmer for 5 minutes:

4 cups chopped fresh spinach *or*

2 10-ounce packages frozen chopped spinach, defrosted and squeezed dry (*LS:* use finely chopped broccoli)

¼ to ½ teaspoon nutmeg to taste

½ teaspoon paprika

¼ teaspoon white **pepper**

Transfer spinach mixture to a large bowl. In skillet, simmer together until mushrooms are slightly softened:

2 cups sliced fresh mushrooms

¼ cup dry white **wine** (*D:* if prohibited use **stock**)

¼ cup **stock**

Add mushrooms to spinach mixture along with:

½ cup whole-wheat **bread** crumbs

Skin and bone, reserving bones for future stock making:

5 pounds chicken breasts, about 10 medium breasts

Flatten breasts by pounding between sheets of plastic wrap or wax paper. Sprinkle each side of each breast with:

Lemon juice

White **pepper**

Fill each breast with spinach mixture. Roll up and secure with toothpick. Dip each roll first into:

1 lightly beaten **egg** white

and then into mixture of:

¾ cup whole-wheat **bread** crumbs

½ teaspoon garlic powder

½ teaspoon Sauté Onion

½ teaspoon onion powder

(*Recipe continued on next page*)

1 teaspoon paprika
½ teaspoon **salt** (*LS* and *P:* omit)

Heat in **non-stick** skillet over medium flame:

2 teaspoons **oil** or **margarine** (*P:* omit)

Brown chicken quickly in skillet on all sides, over medium-high heat. Place rolls side by side in a 9 x 9-inch or 10 x 10-inch **non-stick** baking pan. Pour over rolls a mixture of:

¼ cup dry white **wine** (*D:* if prohibited, use 1 tablespoon **apple juice concentrate** and 1 tablespoon tarragon vinegar)
½ cup chicken **stock**
1 tablespoon **lemon juice**
Salt to taste (*LS* and *P:* omit)

Bake at 325° F for 15 to 20 minutes, or until breasts are tender. Spoon pan juices over and serve hot.

(307)

Garden Italian Chicken

4 servings *LC, LCh, D, LS, P, Ml*

Cut into 1-inch cubes:

4 skinless, boneless chicken breasts

Lightly dust with:

1 tablespoon cornstarch

Place wok or large **non-stick** skillet over high heat for 30 seconds. Add:

1 tablespoon **oil** (*P:* use 2 tablespoons **stock** or dry white **wine**)
2 garlic cloves, minced

Stir fry for 10 seconds. Add chicken and continue to **stir fry** until it loses its pink color. Remove from pan and reserve. Wipe skillet clean. Heat in skillet over medium heat:

½ tablespoon **oil** (*P:* use 1 tablespoon **stock** or dry white **wine**)

Add:

2 cups fresh or frozen Italian-cut green beans
1 cup diced red pepper
½ cup thinly sliced scallions (white part only)
2 tablespoons fresh chopped basil or ½ teaspoon dried
½ teaspoon oregano
½ teaspoon **salt** (*LS* and *P:* omit)

Stir-fry over medium-high heat until beans are crisp-tender. Add:

4 medium fresh tomatoes, coarsely chopped
1 cup fresh, small button mushrooms, washed and stems trimmed
2 tablespoons pimientos, sliced
2 tablespoons capers (*LS:* omit)
1 to 2 tablespoons **lemon juice**

Stir-fry 1 minute to heat through. Add reserved chicken and:

¼ cup **stock** or dry red **wine** (*D,* if prohibited, and *P:* use **stock**).

Cook, stirring constantly until sauce is slightly thickened and chicken is heated through. Do not overcook. Turn onto heated platter and sprinkle with:

1 teaspoon cayenne pepper

(308)

Lemon Chicken with Mushrooms and Hazelnuts

4 to 6 servings *LCh, D, LS, P, Ml*

Remove skin and fat from:

2½ pounds of chicken breasts

Cut breasts into quarters. Rub with:

¼ cup **lemon juice**

Sprinkle with:

Salt (*LS* and *P:* omit)
Pepper (*P:* use white)

Coat lightly with:

Flour

Sauté chicken until golden in **non-stick** pan in:

1 to 2 tablespoons **oil** (*P:* omit)

Sprinkle with:

4 teaspoons grated lemon rind
½ teaspoon thyme

Add to pan:

1 lemon, thinly sliced
1 cup chicken **stock**
3 tablespoons **apple juice concentrate** *or*
3 tablespoons brown **sugar** (*P* and *D:* use 2 tablespoons **apple juice concentrate**)

(*Recipe continued on next page*)

Cover pan and cook chicken over medium heat until just tender, about 15 minutes. Remove chicken from pan to serving platter; keep warm. Bring pan juices to a boil; add and cook until just softened, about 3 minutes:

1 cup sliced fresh mushrooms

Stir in:

1 teaspoon arrowroot, mixed with 1 tablespoon water

Cook sauce until thickened and smooth. In small, **non-stick** skillet, heat over medium heat:

1 teaspoon **oil** (*P:* omit)

Sauté in skillet until lightly browned:

⅔ cup chopped hazelnuts (*P:* use roasted chestnuts)

Add nuts to sauce. Stir and taste for seasoning; correct to taste. Pour sauce over warm chicken and serve.

(309)

Chicken Mayan Style

6 servings *LC, LCh, D, LS, P, Ml*

Tip: Begin marinating chicken 1 day ahead

In mortar mash together:

4 garlic cloves, chopped
2 teaspoons achiote seed (a Latin spice available in Spanish markets)
1 teaspoon **salt** (*LS* and *P:* omit)
½ teaspoon oregano
¼ teaspoon cumin seed
12 whole peppercorns

Transfer mixture to a bowl and add:

¾ cup orange juice
¼ cup **lemon** or **lime juice**

Skin and cut into small pieces:

3½ pounds chicken breasts skinned and quartered (about 7 or 8 individual breasts)

Marinate in the juice mixture in the refrigerator for 24 hours, turning 4 or 5 times.

Cut heavy-duty aluminum foil into 7 or 8 12-inch squares. Place the foil on a damp surface and oil it lightly with **non-stick** spray. (*P:* omit)

Divide the chicken pieces among the squares. Divide over each chicken portion:

2 green peppers, sliced in rings

Spoon marinade over the chicken pieces. Fold the foil over the mixture and crimp edges tightly to seal. Arrange packets in a baking dish and bake, covered, in a preheated oven at 325° F for 25 minutes. Slit packets open and serve chicken with:

Rice

(310)

Chicken-Noodle Bake

4 servings *LCh, D, Ml, B*

Cook according to package directions:

8 ounces medium or broad noodles (*LCh:* use no-yolk noodles)

Meanwhile, heat in **non-stick** skillet over medium flame:

1 to 2 tablespoons **margarine**

Sauté in skillet until very soft:

2 cups fresh sliced mushrooms

Drain noodles, rinsing with cool water. Shake out excess moisture. Toss with sautéed mushrooms and add, tossing well:

2 cups shredded, cooked chicken (*LCh, D,* and *B:* white meat only)
1 **egg** or 2 **egg** whites (*LCh* and *D:* use whites only)
¼ cup finely chopped parsley
Salt to taste
Pepper to taste (*B:* omit)

Spread mixture evenly in **non-stick** 10 x 10 inch baking pan. Combine in small bowl, tossing well:

1 cup **bread** crumbs (*B:* use white only)
1 tablespoon melted **margarine**

Spread crumbs evenly over noodle mixture. Bake at 350° F for 25 to 30 minutes, or until crumbs are golden brown.

(311)

Scarborough Fair Chicken

4 to 5 servings *LC, LCh, D, LS, P, Ml*

Set on individual squares of foil:
 5 single chicken breasts, skin removed
Peel and divide among breasts:
 10 garlic cloves
Wash and slice and divide among breasts:
 2 medium zucchini
In a small bowl, combine:
 1 teaspoon rosemary
 1 teaspoon sage
 1 teaspoon thyme
 ½ cup chopped fresh parsley
 ⅛ teaspoon white **pepper**
Blend herbs together and divide among chicken packets. Drizzle over each packet:
 2 tablespoons **lemon juice**
Sprinkle with:
 White **pepper**
 Salt, if desired (*LS* and *P:* omit)
Close packets, crimping edges to seal. Bake at 325° F for 20 to 25 minutes or until chicken is just tender. Do not overcook.

(312)

Tangerine Chicken

4 servings *LC, LCh, D, P, Ml*

Toss together:
 1½ pounds skinned and boned chicken breasts, cut into 1-inch cubes
 1 teaspoon cornstarch
Heat in large **non-stick** skillet over medium flame:
 ½ tablespoon **oil** (*P:* use dry white **wine**)
Sauté in skillet for 2 minutes over medium-low heat:
 1 tablespoon minced garlic

Add chicken and cook until it loses pink color. Reserve. Combine in bowl:

½ cup diced onion
4 medium scallions, thinly sliced

Combine in separate bowl:

¼ teaspoon Szechuan peppercorns, crushed (Opt.)
2 teaspoons grated fresh ginger

Combine in another bowl:

2 tablespoons **orange juice concentrate**
2 tablespoons **soy sauce** (*P:* reduce to 1 teaspoon)

Prepare:

2 tablespoons tangerine or orange peel, finely julienned
1 tangerine, segments halved and pitted (*D:* omit for those on diets limited in simple carbohydrates)

Heat in **non-stick** skillet until very hot:

½ tablespoon **oil** (*P:* use 1 tablespoon **stock** or water)

Add peppercorns and ginger; stir fry 10 seconds. Add tangerine pieces and onion-scallion mixture; stir fry another 30 seconds. Mix in chicken and juice mixture and stir fry 45 seconds. Serve hot, if desired with:

FLUFFY WHITE RICE (**370**)
or
Brown Rice

(313)

Tunisian Chicken Breasts

4 servings *LC, LCh, D, Ml*

Skin and bone:

2 large chicken breasts, about 1½ pounds each

Slice breast meat in strips about 2½ x ⅜ inches. Sprinkle with:

½ teaspoon **salt**
½ teaspoon **pepper**
½ teaspoon ground cumin

Let stand 20 minutes. Sprinkle with:

4 teaspoons cornstarch
2 teaspoons **oil**

(*Recipe continued on next page*)

Turn to mix and let stand 20 minutes. Fold in:

1 unbeaten **egg** white

Let stand 15 minutes.

Heat in large, heavy, **non-stick** skillet over medium flame:

2 teaspoons **oil**

Add chicken and **sauté** 4 to 5 minutes or just until opaque throughout and golden. Remove and set aside. Add to skillet:

2 teaspoons **oil**

Add and **sauté** until tender:

2½ cups finely chopped onion
1 cup diced green pepper
2 cups finely julienned eggplant
2 garlic cloves, mashed

Stir in:

2 teaspoons paprika
2 teaspoons cumin
¼ teaspoon crushed red pepper
½ cup minced parsley
¼ cup **lemon juice**
1 teaspoon **apple juice concentrate**
3 tablespoons chopped green olives (Opt.)

Heat through. Return chicken to skillet and add:

20 whole green olives, pitted (*LC:* use only 10 olives)

Gently heat. Serve over:

3 to 4 cups cooked rice, brown or white

(314)

Roast Turkey

14 to 16 servings *LC, LCh, D, LS, P, Ml, B*

Preheat oven to 450° F. Place on rack in large roasting pan, washed dried, and stuffed, if desired:

12 to 15-pound turkey

Sprinkle with:

Salt (*LS* and *P:* omit)
Pepper (*P:* use white pepper; *B:* omit)
Garlic powder (*B:* omit)
Paprika

Prepare:

1 recipe basting sauce (see ROAST TURKEY WITH APPLE CHAMPAGNE SAUCE **(315)**, ROAST TURKEY WITH APPLE-PRUNE STUFFING **(317)**, ROAST APRICOT TURKEY **(316)**

Brush some basting sauce under turkey skin (*P:* remove skin). Soak a piece of cheesecloth, large enough to cover turkey, with:

Oil or **stock** (*P:* use **stock**)

Lay cloth loosely over bird. Add to roasting pan:

2 celery stalks, sliced (*LS:* use 1 small zucchini, sliced)
2 carrots, sliced (*LS:* use 1 carrot plus 1 parsnip, sliced)
1 onion, diced
4 sprigs parsley
1 bay leaf
Water to 1-inch depth

Turn turkey on one side on rack and place in oven at 450° F for 15 minutes. Turn turkey to second side. Roast another 15 minutes. Baste with sauce and turn breast down. Reduce heat to 325° F and roast for 2½ hours, basting every half hour. Remove cheesecloth and turn bird breast-side up. Continue roasting until internal temperature reaches 180° F and stuffing, if any, at center is 165° F.

(315)

Roast Turkey with Apple-Champagne Sauce

10 to 12 servings *LC, LCh, D*, LS, P, Ml, B*

Prepare:

1 recipe CHESTNUT-APPLE STUFFING **(320)**

Stuff into a:

14 to 16-pound turkey

Prepare a basting sauce from the following:

1 cup champagne (see **wine;** *D* and *B:* use **stock**)
½ cup brandy (see **wine;** *D, P,* and *B:* use **apple juice**)
⅓ cup **apple juice concentrate**

Proceed as for ROAST TURKEY **(314)**. When turkey is done, remove from roasting rack. Remove vegetables and bay leaf from pan and discard. Skim fat from drippings. In small dish, combine and blend

(*Recipe continued on next page*)

thoroughly with 1 tablespoon of skimmed drippings (*B:* if meat extractives are prohibited, use vegetable **stock** or water):

1 tablespoon **oil** (*P:* use 2 tablespoons drippings)
2 tablespoons **flour**

Slowly blend into mixture ½ cup liquid from roasting pan. (*B:* if meat extractives are prohibited, use vegetable **stock** or water.) Stir into remaining liquid in roasting pan, blending well. Stir in:

1 cup champagne or dry white **wine** (*D* and *B:* if prohibited, use **stock**)
¼ cup apple brandy (*D:* use **stock;** *P* and *B:* use **apple juice**)
1 cup **apple juice**
1 cup **stock**

Scrape up browned bits from sides of roasting pan. Bring mixture to boil and simmer for 3 minutes. Strain sauce. Season to taste with:

Salt (*LS* and *P:* omit)
Pepper (*P:* use white; *B:* omit)

Heat to serve, but do not boil. Serve turkey with sauce on the side.

* Except those on diets limited in simple carbohydrates, such as fruit. Substitute SAVORY STUFFING AND GRAVY (**322**) for CHESTNUT-APPLE STUFFING and pass these separately for low-sugar dieters.

(316)

Roast Apricot Turkey

10 to 12 servings *LC, LCh, D*, LS, P, Ml, B*

Prepare:

1 recipe APRICOT MATZO STUFFING (**319**)

Stuff into a:

14 to 16-pound turkey

Prepare a basting sauce from the following:

1 cup dry white **wine** (*D* and *B:* use **stock**)
½ cup brandy (*P, D,* and *B:* use **apple juice**)
¾ cup **apple juice concentrate**
1 16-ounce can **unsweetened** apricots, drained and pureed

Proceed as for ROAST TURKEY (**314**). When turkey is done, remove from roasting rack. Remove vegetables and bay leaf from pan and discard. Skim fat from drippings.

In **non-stick** skillet, heat over medium flame:
  1 tablespoon **oil** (*P:* omit)
Sauté in oil until golden:
  1 cup finely minced onion
  1 garlic clove, finely minced
Sprinkle over onion-garlic mixture:
  2 tablespoons matzah flour or potato starch
Gradually stir in the skimmed drippings (*B:* if meat extractives are prohibited, use vegetable **stock**) from the roasting pan. Add:
  ¼ cup **apple juice concentrate**
  1 cup dry white **wine** (*B* and *D:* if prohibited, use ½ cup **apple juice** plus ½ cup **stock**)
  1 16-ounce can **unsweetened** apricots, drained and pureed
Continue stirring over low heat until sauce is thickened and smooth.
Season to taste with:
  Salt (*P* and LS: omit)
  White **pepper** (*B:* omit)
Heat to serve, but do not boil. Serve turkey with sauce and stuffing on the side.

* Except those on diets limited in simple carbohydrates, such as fruit. Instead of APRICOT MATZO STUFFING substitute SAVORY STUFFING AND GRAVY (**322**) and pass separately for low-sugar dieters.

(317)

Roast Turkey with Apple-Prune Stuffing

10 to 12 servings *LC, LCh, D*, LS, P, Ml*

Prepare:
  1 recipe APPLE-PRUNE STUFFING (**318**)
Stuff into a:
  14 to 16-pound turkey
Prepare a basting sauce from the following:
  1 cup dry white **wine** (*D:* use **stock**)
  ¼ cup brandy (*P* and *D:* use **apple juice**)
  ⅓ cup **apple juice concentrate**

(*Recipe continued on next page*)

Proceed as for ROAST TURKEY (**314**). When turkey is done, remove from roasting rack. Remove vegetables and bay leaf and discard. Skim fat from drippings.

In **non-stick** skillet, heat over medium flame:

1 tablespoon **oil** (*P:* omit)

Sauté in skillet until softened:

1 cup chopped onions

1 teaspoon minced garlic

Add and continue **sautéing** until softened:

2 cups shredded peeled apple

Puree onion-apple mixture. Return to skillet. Sprinkle with:

2 tablespoons **flour**

Blend in well, stirring over low heat. Stir in:

1 cup dry white **wine** (*D:* if prohibited, use **stock**)

1 cup **apple juice**

1 cup skimmed pan drippings plus **stock,** if needed, to make 1 cup

Continue stirring until smooth thick sauce is formed. Add to taste:

Salt (*LS* and *P:* omit)

White **pepper**

Heat to serve, but do not boil. Serve turkey with sauce and stuffing on the side.

* Except those on diets limited in simple carbohydrates, such as fruit. Substitute SAVORY STUFFING AND GRAVY (**321**) for APPLE-PRUNE STUFFING and pass these separately for low-sugar dieters.

(318)

Apple-Prune Stuffing

About 10 cups stuffing *LC, LCh, D, LS, V, v, P, Ml, k*

In **non-stick** skillet, heat over medium flame:

1 tablespoon **margarine** or **oil** (*P:* omit)

Sauté in skillet until soft:

2 onions, chopped

2 cups sliced celery (*LS:* reduce to 1 cup)

1 teaspoon minced garlic

Add and toss in:

4 tart apples, peeled, cored, and cubed (*D:* omit for those on diets limited in simple carbohydrates)

Turn apple-onion mixture into large bowl. Add:

2 cups cooked rice
2 cups cooked wild rice
1½ cups chopped pitted prunes (*D:* omit)
¾ cup toasted pine nuts (*P:* omit)
½ cup chopped parsley
1½ teaspoons thyme
½ cup **stock**
Salt to taste (*LS* and *P:* omit)
Pepper to taste (*P:* use white)

Toss well; taste and correct seasonings.

VARIATION: (*B*) Toss melted margarine, apples, white rice, pitted prunes, thyme, stock, and salt only. Omit all other ingredients.

(319)

Apricot-Matzo Stuffing

10 to 12 cups *LC, LCh, D*, LS, P, V, v, Ml, k*

Combine in bowl and soak until matzo farfel is softened:

⅔ cup **orange juice concentrate**
1⅓ cups **stock**
4½ cups whole-wheat matzo, processed in blender to farfel size (¼ to ½-inch crumbs)

Sauté in **non-stick** pan until golden:

3 large onions, chopped
5 garlic cloves, minced
6 celery stalks, sliced thinly (*LS:* omit; use 2 cups chopped red or green peppers)

Meanwhile combine in saucepan and simmer until fruit is soft:

6 ounces dried apricots, chopped (*D:* reduce to 4 ounces)
1 cup white raisins (*D:* use ½ cup)
1½ cups orange juice

Combine **sautéed** vegetables, matzo farfel, and fruit in large bowl with:

½ cup white **wine** (*D:* if prohibited, use **apple juice** and water, half and half)
½ cup chopped walnuts (*P:* omit; *D:* increase to ¾ cup)
1 tablespoon sage, or to taste

(*Recipe continued on next page*)

½ cup chopped parsley
Salt to taste (*LS* and *P:* omit)
White **pepper** to taste

Stuff mixture into large turkey.

Bake any remaining stuffing in a shallow, **non-stick** pan until golden brown.

VARIATION: (*B*) Combine and soak till matzo farfel is softened:

⅔ cup orange juice
1⅓ cups **stock**
4½ cups matzo farfel or white matzo processed to farfel size

Add and blend:

2 16-ounce cans **unsweetened** apricots, peeled
2 cups shredded carrots
2 tablespoons very finely chopped parsley
Sage to taste
Thyme to taste
Salt to taste

* Except those on diets limited in simple carbohydrates, such as fruit. Substitute instead SAVORY STUFFING AND GRAVY (**321**) and pass separately for low-sugar dieters.

(320)

Chestnut-Apple Stuffing

Approximately 10 cups *LC, LCh, D, LS, P, V, v, Ml, k*

Heat in large **non-stick** skillet over medium flame:

1 tablespoon **margarine** or **oil** (*P:* use 1 tablespoon dry white **wine**)

Sauté in skillet for 1 minute:

2 teaspoons minced garlic

Add to skillet and sauté until golden brown:

3 cups chopped onions
3 cups finely diced celery (*LS:* omit)

Remove vegetables to a large bowl and add to skillet, **sautéing** until soft:

1 cup chopped green pepper (*LS:* increase to 2 cups)
1 cup chopped red pepper (*LS:* increase to 2 cups)
4 cups peeled, cored, and diced apple

Add the peppers and apples to the onion mixture. Add and toss well:

4 cups whole-wheat **bread** cubes, toasted at 325° F for 10 minutes
1 cup chopped parsley
2 teaspoons thyme or to taste
2 teaspoons sage or to taste
½ cup **apple juice**
½ cup **stock,** or enough juice and stock to moisten but not soak stuffing
1 pound chestnuts, boiled, peeled, skinned, and coarsely chopped
Coarse **salt** to taste (*LS* and *P:* omit; add additional **apple juice** to sweeten if desired)
Pepper to taste (*P:* use white)

Stuff mixture into large turkey—or follow vegetarian alternatives. Any remaining stuffing can be baked separately in shallow, **non-stick** pan.

VARIATION: (*B*) Combine only:

1 tablespoon melted **margarine**
4 cups peeled, cored, and diced apple
2 cups grated carrots
4 cups white **bread** cubes
Thyme to taste
Sage to taste
½ cup **apple juice**
½ cup **stock,** or enough to moisten, but not soak, stuffing
2 tablespoons very finely chopped parsley
Salt to taste

(321)

Savory Stuffing and Gravy

About 10 cups *LC, LCh, D, V, v, P, Ml, k*

Heat in **non-stick** skillet over medium flame:

1 tablespoon **oil** (*P:* use dry white **wine**)

Sauté in skillet for 1 minute:

1 teaspoon minced garlic

(*Recipe continued on next page*)

Add and **sauté** until golden brown:

3 cups finely chopped onion
3 cups finely diced celery

Remove vegetables to a large bowl and add to skillet, **sautéing** until soft:

1 cup chopped green pepper
1 cup chopped red pepper
2 cups sliced fresh mushrooms

Combine peppers and mushrooms with onion mixture. Add and toss well:

4 cups whole-wheat bread cubes, toasted at 325° F for 10 minutes *or* 4 cups whole-wheat matzo, broken into farfel-size bits
1 cup finely chopped parsley
1½ teaspoons thyme or to taste
1½ teaspoons sage or to taste
¾ cups stock or enough to moisten, but not soak, the stuffing
1 pound chestnuts, boiled, peeled, skinned, and coarsely chopped
Coarse **salt** to taste
Pepper to taste (*P:* use white)

Stuff mixture into large turkey or bake separately in shallow **non-stick** pan. Mixture may also be used in MOCK TURKEY (**350**). When turkey is finished, skim drippings in roasting pan. Combine 2 tablespoons of the skimmed liquid with:

2 tablespoons **flour**

Blend until smooth. Stir into remaining drippings and heat, stirring, until thickened.

Meats

(322)

Individual Apple Veal Loaves

4 servings *LC, LCh, D, LS, P, Ml, B*

Prepare:
2 recipes APPLE-VEAL BALLS (**160**)
Divide into 4 portions and form small loaves from each. Place on **non-stick** baking sheet or in 3 individual **non-stick** loaf pans. Bake in preheated oven at 350° F for 20 to 30 minutes, or until firm but not dry. (*B:* Do not allow to become crusty)

(323)

Cassoulet

8 to 10 servings *LCh, D, Ml*

In large pot bring to a boil:

2½ quarts water

Gradually add to pot:

1 pound dry white beans, such as Great Northern or Small White California

Bring rapidly back to a boil and boil for 2 minutes. Remove from heat and let stand for 1 hour. Drain and rinse in cold water. Meanwhile, boil in 1 quart water for 1 minute:

1 pound veal sausage, cut into chunks

Drain. Repeat, but do not drain. Set aside to cool. Return soaked beans to large pot. Add the following bouquet garni tied in a cheesecloth bag:

2 to 3 sprigs parsley
1 bay leaf
1 sprig thyme or ½ teaspoon dry thyme
4 garlic cloves, peeled
1 or 2 whole cloves

Skim any accumulated fat from sausage liquid. Add along with sausage to bean pot along with:

12 to 15 small white onions, peeled
Water to cover

Bring to a simmer and skim off film. Simmer slowly, uncovered, for 1½ hours or until beans are tender. Add boiling water if needed to keep beans covered with liquid. Discard bouquet garni. Add:

Salt to taste
Pepper to taste

In a **non-stick** skillet, heat over medium flame:

1 tablespoon **oil** (Opt.)

Brown in skillet:

1½ pounds veal cut in 2-inch cubes
1 chicken, cut in eighths, skin removed

Transfer veal and chicken to a large casserole. In the same skillet, **sauté** until golden brown:

2½ cups chopped onion
3 garlic cloves, minced

Transfer onion mixture to casserole. Deglaze skillet with:

1 cup dry vermouth (see **wine;** *D:* if prohibited use **stock**)

Add the vermouth to the casserole along with:

3 tablespoons tomato paste

Salt to taste

Pepper to taste

Simmer for 30 minutes.

In a large casserole or crock pot, layer meats, beans, sausage, ending with sausage. Add liquid from first casserole and additional liquid from beans to almost cover. Be sure all beans are covered with liquid.

Combine in a small bowl:

2 cups **bread** crumbs

¼ cup chopped parsley

Spread half of crumbs over top of casserole. Bake in moderate oven at 350° F for 45 minutes. Or cook according to directions in a slow cooker. Press crust of bread crumbs down into dish. Add remaining crumbs to allow new crust to form. Bake another 45 minutes.

(324)

Chili Con Carne

4 servings *LCh, D, LS, P, Ml*

In **non-stick** skillet, **sauté** until it loses pink color:

1 pound ground lean veal or beef (*P* and *LCh:* use veal)

Drain off and discard any fat, reserving meat. Wipe out skillet with paper towel and heat:

1 tablespoon **oil** (*P:* omit)

Sauté in oil until golden:

2 cups chopped onion

1 cup chopped green pepper

2 tablespoons minced garlic

Return meat to skillet and add:

1 tablespoon ground cumin, or to taste

5 tablespoons chili powder, or to taste

1 tablespoon oregano

Continue to sauté, stirring occasionally for 10 minutes. Transfer to large heavy saucepan and add:

(*Recipe continued on next page*)

1 16-ounce can tomatoes in puree, chopped coarsely (*LS:* use 4 cups fresh or unsalted canned)
1 6-ounce can tomato paste
⅓ cup dry red **wine** (*D* and *P:* omit, unless permitted)
1 teaspoon **apple juice concentrate**
Salt to taste (*LS* and *P:* use 1 tablespoon red **wine** vinegar)
Cayenne pepper to taste
Black **pepper** to taste (Opt. *P:* use white)

Bring to a boil over high heat. Reduce heat to low and simmer, stirring occasionally, for 1½ hours, adding tomato puree if chili becomes too thick. Stir in:

1 16-ounce can dark red kidney beans, rinsed and drained (*LS:* use unsalted canned or dried cooked without salt)

Cook 30 minutes longer. Serve with:

Chopped onions
Tortilla chips *or* crusty **bread**
Shredded lettuce
Chopped tomatoes
Chopped green peppers
Chopped jalapeño peppers or chili peppers

(325)

Rice and Ground Meat Bake

4 servings *LCh, Ml, B*

Combine and toss well:

2 cups FLUFFY WHITE RICE **(370)**
1 tablespoon melted **margarine**
Salt to taste

Combine in bowl and blend well:

1 pound finely ground lean beef
1 **egg** or 2 **egg** whites (*LCh:* use whites)
1½ teaspoons **salt,** or to taste
2 carrots, pureed in blender or processor
¼ teaspoon thyme

In a small loaf pan, spread a thin layer of ground beef. Add a layer of rice, then another layer of beef, more rice, and then more beef. Pour over all:

1 cup tomato juice

Bake at 375° F for 30 to 40 minutes.

(326)

Stuffed Cabbage a la Cranberries

6 to 8 servings *LC, LCh, D*, LS, P, Ml*

In boiling water or in freezer in plastic bag for 1 hour, soften:

1 large cabbage

Meanwhile, combine in bowl:

1½ pounds ground lean veal
¼ cup raw rice
3 **egg** whites, lightly beaten (*LS:* use 2 whites plus 2 tablespoons water)
1 carrot, shredded
1 large onion, finely chopped
¼ teaspoon garlic powder
⅛ teaspoon white **pepper**
Salt to taste (*LS* and *P:* omit; add 1 tablespoon **apple juice concentrate** plus 1 tablespoon **wine** vinegar)

Set mixture aside. In large **non-stick** Dutch oven, heat over medium flame:

1 tablespoon **oil** (*P:* omit)

Sauté until golden:

1 large onion, diced

Add to Dutch oven:

1 15-ounce can tomatoes (*LS:* use fresh tomatoes or unsalted canned)
1 cup whole, fresh or frozen **unsweetened** cranberries
1 can whole-berry cranberry sauce (*D* and *P:* omit, use ⅓ cup **apple juice concentrate**)
⅓ cup **unsweetened** cranberry apple juice
2 tablespoons **lemon juice**
⅛ teaspoon ground ginger (Opt.)

Simmer for 5 minutes. Taste, and adjust seasonings. Separate softened cabbage leaves. On each large leaf, place a portion of the reserved meat mixture. Fold up bottom of leaf over filling, and fold in both sides. Fold down top, tucking it in securely. Gently place cabbage rolls in sauce. Simmer 1½ hours, covered.

(*Recipe continued on next page*)

VARIATION: (*B*) Combine veal, grated carrots, white rice, egg whites, and salt in a bowl. Form into balls. Simmer in a sauce of: 1 can jellied cranberry sauce, 1 cup tomato juice, and 2 tablespoons lemon juice. Add salt to taste.

* Sauce should be avoided by those who must limit intake of simple carbohydrates, such as fruit.

(327)

Stuffed Shoulder of Spring Lamb, Cumberland

6 to 8 servings *LC, LCh, D, LS, P, Ml,*

In **non-stick** skillet, heat over medium flame:
- ½ tablespoon **oil** or **margarine** (*P:* omit)

In skillet, **sauté** until lightly brown:
- ¼ cup pine nuts (*P:* omit)

Transfer nuts to a bowl. Add to skillet:
- 1 tablespoon **oil** or **margarine** (*P:* omit)

Sauté in skillet until soft:
- ½ cup finely chopped celery (*LS:* if prohibited, use chopped onion)
- 1 teaspoon minced garlic
- ¼ cup finely chopped shallots or scallions

Remove from heat. Add to skillet, tossing to mix, the pine nuts and:
- 1½ cups cooked brown or white rice

In small saucepan, heat together, simmering for 5 minutes:
- ½ cup currants or raisins (*D:* omit for those on diets limiting simple carbohydrates)
- 2 tablespoons **orange juice concentrate**

Stir in:
- 1 teaspoon grated orange rind
- ½ teaspoon grated lemon rind

Toss this currant mixture with the rice and vegetables. Add:
- **Salt** to taste (*P* and *LS:* omit)
- **Pepper** to taste (*P:* use white)

Stuff this mixture lightly into:
- 3½-pound boned shoulder of lamb, trimmed of visible fat

Sew up or truss up opening. Rub outside of meat with a mixture of:

2 tablespoons **flour**
½ teaspoon paprika
1 teaspoon garlic powder
1 teaspoon **salt** (*LS* and *P:* omit)
¼ teaspoon **pepper** (*P:* use white)

Roast at 400° F for 30 minutes. Reduce heat to 350° F and roast 1 hour more.

Serve with CUMBERLAND SAUCE (**420**).

VARIATION: (*B*) Prepare a stuffing of:

1½ cups cooked white rice
¼ cup chopped stewed prunes, pureed if required
2 tablespoons **orange juice concentrate**
1 teaspoon **lemon juice**
½ cup shredded apple
Salt to taste

Serve with CUMBERLAND SAUCE (**420**)

(328)

Veal Prince Orloff's Smarter Brother

6 to 8 servings *LC, LCh, D, LS, P, Ml, B*

Dry thoroughly with paper towels:

3½-pound boneless veal roast, tied for roasting

In a **non-stick** pan, lightly brown the veal on all sides over moderately high heat.

Meanwhile, in a **non-stick** saucepan heat over medium flame:

1 tablespoon **margarine** (*LC* and *P:* use **stock**)

Sauté in saucepan for 5 minutes:

¾ cup sliced onion (*B:* omit)
¾ cup sliced carrots (*LS:* if prohibited, use parsnips)
¾ cup green peas

Transfer vegetables to a heavy **non-stick** casserole, just large enough to hold the veal. Sprinkle browned veal with:

Salt (*LS* and *P:* omit)

(*Recipe continued on next page*)

Add veal to casserole along with:

2 stalks celery with leaves, cut in halves (*LS:* omit)

1 bay leaf

½ teaspoon thyme

Cover veal with foil, then cover casserole with lid. Set in lower third of oven and roast in preheated oven at 325° F for 1 hour. Remove cover of casserole and insert meat thermometer through foil into center of veal. Bake for another 15 to 20 minutes or until internal temperature of veal reaches 175° F. Meat is done when juices run clear yellow. Let meat rest for 30 minutes on a carving board. Save any juices that accumulate. Set them aside, skimming fat when juices are cooled. Discard celery from casserole. Strain remaining vegetables, collecting any juices and skim these too. Reserve vegetables and juices. While veal is standing, prepare stuffing mixture. Squeeze out the liquid in a paper towel from:

2 cups finely chopped fresh mushrooms (about ½ pound)

Heat in a **non-stick** skillet:

½ to 1 tablespoon **margarine** or **oil** (*P:* use **stock** or dry white **wine**)

Sauté in skillet until soft:

1 cup finely chopped onions or scallions (*B:* omit)

Add to skillet, and continue sautéing until juices are evaporated, the mushrooms and:

1 tablespoon **lemon juice**

Remove from heat and stir in:

Salt to taste (*P* and *LS:* add additional **lemon juice** if needed)

White **pepper** (*B:* omit)

Combine mushroom duxelles with:

1 cup cooked rice (*B:* use white)

Puree the set-aside vegetables in a blender. Combine with reserved skimmed meat juices in large saucepan along with:

Stock to make 3 cups (*B:* if meat juices are not allowed, use all vegetable **stock** with the pureed vegetables)

¼ teaspoon thyme

Make a paste of:

2 tablespoons **flour**

2 tablespoons **stock**

Stir additional liquid from saucepan into this paste, stirring to make a smooth thickener for the sauce. Stir this paste into the sauce over medium-low heat, stirring constantly, until sauce is thickened. Add half of the sauce to the rice mixture, reserving the other half. Carve the veal into serving slices about ¼-inch thick, placing them on a

heat-proof serving dish as you do so. Spread some of mushroom-rice mixture on each slice, then top with reserved sauce.
If veal is not to be served within the hour, refrigerate. About 30 minutes before serving time, heat in preheated 375° F oven for 2 to 3 minutes, or until heated through. Serve garnished with:
Asparagus tips

(329)

Veal Tarragon with Brazil Nuts

6 to 8 servings *LCh, D, Ml*

Cut into 1½-inch cubes:
2 pounds boneless shoulder of veal (or other lean cut)
Dust veal with blend of:
2 tablespoons **flour**
1 teaspoon **salt**
1 teaspoon sweet paprika
1 teaspoon garlic powder
¼ teaspoon pepper
In **non-stick** skillet, heat:
½ tablespoon **oil** (Opt.)
Add half of the veal cubes to skillet. Remove when browned on all sides. Repeat process with remaining veal cubes in:
½ tablespoon **oil** (Opt.)
Wipe skillet clean with paper towel and melt over low heat:
½ tablespoon **margarine**
Sauté in margarine until golden:
1 cup finely chopped onion
1½ teaspoons finely minced garlic
Return veal to skillet and sprinkle with:
1½ tablespoons chopped fresh tarragon or 1½ teaspoons dried
Add:
1⅓ cups white veal or chicken **stock**
¼ cup dry white **wine** (*D:* if prohibited, use **stock**)
Simmer veal covered, over low heat, stirring occasionally. After 1 hour or when veal is tender, transfer to a heated serving dish with slotted spoon and keep warm. Put 2 tablespoons of the hot cooking liquid in a small dish and dissolve in it:

(***Recipe continued on next page***)

1½ tablespoons Dijon or other imported mustard

Stir mustard mixture into skillet liquid. Add:

1 cup coarsely chopped Brazil nuts, toasted

Pour over veal and serve with:

Rice *or* pasta *or* spaetzel

(330)

Veal Roast, Minted Cranberry Glaze

8 to 10 servings *LC, LCh, D*, LS, P, Ml*

Blend together:

1 teaspoon coarse **salt** (*LS* and *P:* omit)
1 teaspoon rosemary, crushed
½ teaspoon garlic powder

Rub this mixture on:

1 4 to 6-pound veal roast

Place veal in roasting pan with:

1 carrot, cut in chunks
2 celery ribs, cut in chunks (*LS:* use ¼ head iceberg lettuce, cut in chunks)
1 onion, sliced

Cover with foil and roast at 350° F for 30 minutes. Meanwhile, heat in a saucepan:

½ cup mint jelly (*LC* and *D* use dietetic, artificially sweetened, apple jelly, plus 1 teaspoon dried mint; or *LC, D,* and *P:* use ¼ cup **apple juice concentrate** plus 1 teaspoon dried mint)
1 can jellied cranberry sauce (*LC* and *D:* use dietetic cranberry sauce, artificially sweetened; or *P, D,* and *LC:* use 1 cup fresh cranberries plus ¼ cup **apple juice concentrate**)
3 tablespoons **lemon juice**

Remove foil from veal and brush with minted cranberry mixture. Continue roasting for 1 to 1½ hours or until internal temperature reaches 170° F. Baste every 10 minutes with minted cranberry glaze. Serve garnished with:

Peach halves each filled with 1 teaspoon mint jelly and 1 teaspoon cranberry sauce, or with fresh cranberries

* If dietetic jelly and cranberry sauce are used in this recipe, it is suitable for low-sugar dieters. If **apple juice concentrate** is used, it is suitable for low-sugar dieters who do not have to limit their intake of simple carbohydrates, such as fruit.

(331)

Veal and Turkey Pie

6 to 8 servings *LCh, D, LS, P, Ml*

Heat in **non-stick** skillet over medium flame:
1 tablespoon **oil** (*P:* omit)
Sauté in skillet until softened:
1 large onion, finely chopped
2 stalks celery, finely chopped (*LS:* omit if prohibited)
2 small carrots, finely chopped (*LS:* reduce to 1 carrot)
1 small parsnip, finely chopped (*LS:* increase to 3 parsnips)
½ teaspoon marjoram or thyme
Cut into bite-sized pieces:
1 pound veal for stew, fat well trimmed
1 pound boned turkey breast
Dredge in a combination of:
¾ cup **flour**
Salt to taste (*LS* and *P:* omit)
Pepper to taste (*P:* use white)
1½ teaspoons paprika
½ teaspoon garlic powder
Add to skillet and brown meat, stirring frequently. Turn meat and vegetables into a 6-cup **non-stick** casserole. Add:
1 to 1½ cups chicken **stock** (to almost cover meat)
1 cup dry red **wine** (*P:* use white; *D:* if prohibited, use **stock**)
Cover dish and bake in preheated oven at 350° F for 30 minutes. Remove from oven and cool slightly. Meanwhile, prepare:
1 recipe QUICHE CRUST **(58)** rolled and kept chilled until ready to use, *or*
4 sheets phyllo dough, brought to room temperature (*P* and *LC*)
Increase oven temperature to 425° F. Cover casserole with pie crust, rolled and trimmed to fit, cutting a star or circle in the center to allow steam to escape. Or, for phyllo dough crust, cover the casserole with four sheets of phyllo dough, brushed with some of the liquids from the casserole, and trimmed to overlap at the edges of the casserole. Cut several slits in phyllo. Brush top layer of phyllo or pie crust with:
1 beaten **egg** white
Sprinkle with:
Sesame seeds
Bake 10 to 15 minutes or until crust is golden brown.

Vegetable Main Courses

(332)

Broccoli Lasagna

4 to 6 servings *LCh, D, v, k*

Cook according to directions, *al dente:*
  8 ounces lasagna noodles, white, whole-wheat, or spinach
In **non-stick** skillet, heat over medium flame:
  1 tablespoon **oil**
Sauté in skillet until browned:
  4 medium onions, sliced
  2 garlic cloves, minced
Add, blending well with onions:
  1 tablespoon **apple juice concentrate**
Continue cooking, stirring to glaze. Add and continue cooking until broccoli begins to soften:
  1 large bunch broccoli, chopped *or*
  2 10-ounce packages frozen chopped broccoli

Combine in a bowl:

3 cups low-fat **pot cheese** or **hoop cheese**
3 tablespoons grated **cheese**
2 tablespoons chopped fresh basil or 1 teaspoon dried

In large, **non-stick** lasagna pan, layer alternately lasagna, cheese, and broccoli, beginning with lasagna. Top final layer of broccoli with:

1 to 2 tablespoons grated **cheese**
3 ounces part-skim mozzarella, sliced thin (Opt. *LCh* and *D:* use low-fat, low-cholesterol **cheese**)

Bake lasagna at 400° F for 15 minutes, or until cheese is melted and browned.

(333)

Cottage Cheese and Noodle Bake

6 to 8 servings *LC, LCh, v, k, B**

Tip: ⅛ of recipe equals 1 *LC* serving

Combine in large bowl:

8 ounces medium-width noodles, cooked according to package directions until soft
2 cups low-fat, small-curd **cottage cheese**
1 egg plus 4 **egg** whites (*LCh:* use 6 egg whites)
½ cup skim **milk**
½ cup sour cream or low-fat **yogurt** or ⅓ cup low-fat **buttermilk** (*LCh* and *D:* use low-fat **yogurt** or **buttermilk**)
2 tablespoons melted **margarine** or **butter**
Salt to taste
White **pepper** to taste (*B:* omit)

Turn into a 9 x 13-inch **non-stick** baking pan or casserole. Sprinkle top with:

1 cup soft **bread** crumbs

Bake at 250° F for 1 hour, or until crumb topping is golden brown.

* Except those on milk-restricted diets.

(334)

Crown of Noodles and Spinach, Creamed Mushroom Sauce

4 to 6 servings *LCh, D, v, k, B**

Grease inside of 4-cup ring mold with:
Margarine
Cook according to package directions until soft, then drain:
1 10-ounce package frozen chopped spinach
Cook according to package directions:
8 ounces medium-width noodles (*LCh:* use yolkless noodles)
Rinse in warm water and drain well. Combine spinach with noodles, toss to blend well, and set aside.
In a **non-stick** saucepan, melt:
1 tablespoon **margarine**
Add and blend well, stirring over low heat for 3 minutes:
2 tablespoons **flour**
Add gradually, stirring as you do:
¾ cup skim **milk**
¼ cup evaporated skimmed **milk**
Continue stirring over medium-low heat until sauce is thickened and smooth. Stir into sauce until melted:
4 ounces **cheese** shredded (*LCh* and *D:* use low-fat, low-cholesterol **cheese;** *B:* use mild American **cheese**)
Combine cheese sauce with spinach-noodle mixture. Toss until well-blended. Stir in to blend well:
1 **egg** or 2 **egg** whites, slightly beaten (*LCh:* use egg whites)
Season to taste with:
Salt
Pepper (*B:* omit)
Nutmeg or paprika (*B:* use paprika)
Pour into prepared ring mold, smoothing the top. Place mold in pan of hot water filled to halfway up sides of ring. Bake in preheated 350° F oven for 30 to 35 minutes or until set. Meanwhile, heat in **non-stick** skillet:
1½ teaspoons **margarine**
Sauté in skillet over low heat until just soft (*B:* very soft):
1 pound fresh mushrooms, washed and stems trimmed, sliced
Dill or tarragon to taste
Salt to taste

Blend into mushrooms until smooth, stirring for 2 to 3 minutes:
  1½ tablespoons **flour**
Add and simmer over medium-low heat, stirring constantly:
  1 cup skim **milk**
Simmer until sauce thickens, stirring constantly. Keep sauce warm. Unmold noodle ring on large platter and spoon mushrooms over.

* Except those on milk-restricted or low-residue diets.

(335)

Macaroni and Peas Au Gratin

4 servings *LCh, D, v, k, B**

Prepare according to package directions:
  12 ounces elbow macaroni
Drain, rinse in warm water, and set aside. In **non-stick** skillet, heat over medium heat:
  2 tablespoons **margarine**
Add and **sauté** until very soft:
  2 cups sliced fresh mushrooms
Blend into mushrooms for 2 to 3 minutes until smooth:
  2 tablespoons white **flour**
Gradually add over low heat, stirring constantly:
  2 cups skim **milk**
Continue stirring for about 5 minutes, until thin, smooth sauce is formed. Stir in:
  1½ cups grated **cheese** (*LCh* and *D:* use low-fat, low-cholesterol **cheese**; *B:* use mild American or mild Swiss **cheese**)
Continue cooking over low heat, stirring constantly until cheese is melted. Combine cheese sauce with macaroni and toss in:
  1 cup frozen peas
Turn into **non-stick** casserole. Sprinkle casserole with mixture of:
  ½ cup **bread** crumbs (*B:* use white **bread**)
  ½ tablespoon melted **margarine**
Bake in preheated 350° F oven for about 30 minutes, or until top of casserole is golden brown.

* Except those on milk-restricted diets.

(336)

Pasta Del Sol

6 to 8 servings *LC, LCh, D, v, k*

Heat to boiling in small saucepan:

3 cups water

½ teaspoon **salt**

Place strainer in saucepan. In strainer, blanch for 2 to 3 minutes each, until vegetables are crisp tender, 1½ cups each of any 5 of the following vegetables:

Green beans, trimmed and cut into 1-inch lengths

Unpeeled zucchini, cut into 1-inch matchsticks

Very small broccoli florets, and peeled and sliced stems

Asparagus spears, cut into 1-inch lengths

Green pepper, cut into 1-inch strips

Cauliflower, broken into small florets

After blanching each kind of vegetable, remove from water in strainer and hold under cold running water to refresh. Drain and put in large bowl. Also blanch for 1 minute:

¾ cup fresh peas (for frozen peas blanch 30 seconds)

Blanch for 2 to 3 minutes:

1 cup red pepper cut into 1-inch strips

When all vegetables have been blanched, refreshed, drained, and put in bowl, set them aside.

Heat in a large skillet over medium heat:

1 tablespoon **oil**

Add to skillet and **sauté** for 3 minutes until soft but not brown:

½ cup chopped scallions

1 teaspoon finely chopped garlic

Add and sauté an additional 1 to 2 minutes:

2 cups sliced mushrooms

½ cup finely chopped Italian parsley

Salt to taste

Pepper to taste

Stir in:

½ cup coarsely chopped fresh basil leaves or 2 teaspoons dried

Add vegetables to skillet if there is room. If not, combine skillet contents and vegetables in a large pot. Stir carefully to heat through, about 2 or 3 minutes. Set aside, keeping warm.

In large heavy pot or skillet, large enough to hold pasta and vegetables, melt:

2 tablespoons **butter** or **margarine**

Stir in and bring to a simmer:

1 cup vegetable **stock**

½ cup dry white **wine** (*D:* if prohibited, use 6 tablespoons **stock** plus 2 tablespoons tarragon vinegar)

Cover and set aside, keeping warm.

Cooking according to package directions, *al dente:*

1 pound pasta (fettucine, spaghetti, vermicelli)

Add pasta and vegetables to sauce in heavy pot. Toss together with:

½ cup freshly grated **cheese** (*LC, LCh,* and *D:* use low-fat, low-cholesterol **cheese**)

½ cup pine nuts, toasted in the oven until golden

If sauce seems dry, add a bit more **stock**.

Serve on heated plates. Pass more:

Grated **cheese**

(337)

Cold Pasta Primavera

4 to 5 servings *LC, LCh, D, V, v, P, Ml, k*

Use any or all of the following fresh vegetables, when available. Steam over boiling water for 3 minutes, or until crisp-tender:

1 cup broccoli florets, cut in 1-inch lengths

Steam for 2 minutes, or until crisp-tender:

2 small zucchini, cut into 1-inch matchsticks

Steam for 5 minutes, or until crisp-tender:

4 asparagus spears, cut into 1-inch lengths

Steam for 7 minutes, or until crisp-tender, a combination of:

½ pound green beans, trimmed, cut into 1-inch lengths

2 tablespoons minced fresh oregano or ¾ teaspoon dried

Steam for 3 minutes, or until just tender, a combination of:

½ pound fresh peas, shelled

2 tablespoons minced fresh thyme or ¾ teaspoon dried

Drain vegetables on paper towels.

(*Recipe continued on next page*)

In a **non-stick** skillet, heat over medium flame:

1 tablespoon **oil** (*P:* use **stock** or dry white **wine**)

Sauté in skillet for 3 minutes:

1 red pepper, sliced in 1-inch strips

1 green pepper, sliced in 1-inch strips

Add and continue to sauté, stirring occasionally, for 2 minutes more:

2 cups sliced fresh mushrooms

1 teaspoon finely chopped fresh hot pepper or ¼ teaspoon crushed dried

¼ cup finely chopped parsley

Combine the skillet mixture and the vegetables in a large bowl.

In the same skillet, heat:

1 tablespoon **oil** (*P* and *LC:* use **stock** or dry white **wine**)

Sauté for 1 minute:

2 teaspoons finely minced garlic

Stir in:

¼ cup chopped fresh basil or 1 teaspoon dried basil crumbled with 2 tablespoons chopped parsley

Stir vegetable mixture into skillet, sautéing lightly, stirring gently, for about 2 minutes or until heated through. Transfer to a large serving bowl.

Combine in a small bowl:

¾ cup LIGHT VINAIGRETTE **(258)**

1 tablespoon **oil** (*P:* omit)

Salt to taste (*P:* omit)

Pepper to taste (*P:* use white)

Toss vinaigrette with vegetables and marinate at room temperature for 10 minutes. Meanwhile, prepare according to package directions, *al dente:*

½ pound pasta, preferably fresh (*P:* use whole grain)

Drain, cool under cold running water, and drain again. Combine pasta and vegetables in the serving bowl and toss well. Add and toss again:

⅓ cup freshly grated cheese (*P:* use **hoop cheese** or low-fat **cottage cheese** pureed; *V* and *Ml:* omit)

¼ cup toasted pine nuts (*P:* omit)

Salt to taste (*P:* omit)

Pepper to taste (*P:* use white)

Garnish with:

Chopped parsley *or* chopped basil

Serve chilled or at room temperature.

(338)

Cold Pasta Primavera with Buttermilk Dressing

4 to 5 servings *LC, LCh, D, v, P, k*

Prepare COLD PASTA PRIMAVERA (**337**) recipe. Instead of LIGHT VINAIGRETTE dressing, use:

1½ cups BUTTERMILK CHIVE DRESSING (**252**)

Pass separately:

Appropriate grated **cheese**

(339)

Pasta with Peas, Mushrooms, and Pine Nuts

4 servings *LCh, D, LS, V, v, k*

In **non-stick** skillet, heat over medium flame:

1 to 2 tablespoons **oil**

Sauté in **oil** over low heat for 1 minute:

½ teaspoon minced garlic

Add and continue to sauté for about 5 minutes:

2 cups sliced fresh mushrooms
¼ cup pine nuts
¼ cup finely chopped parsley
½ teaspoon oregano
½ teaspoon basil
Salt to taste (*LS:* omit)

When mushrooms are just softened, sprinkle skillet mixture with:

1 tablespoon **flour**

Stir to blend well and add to skillet:

½ cup vegetable **stock**
1½ cup fresh peas, blanched in boiling water for 1 minute *or* frozen peas, defrosted (*LS:* use fresh peas)
2 tablespoons dry white **wine** (*D:* if prohibited, use 1 tablespoon **stock** plus 1 tablespoon tarragon vinegar)

(*Recipe continued on next page*)

Continue to cook over medium-low heat, stirring constantly, until sauce thickens. Toss sauce into:

1 pound spaghetti, cooked according to package directions

Pass separately:

Salt

Pepper

Grated Parmesan **cheese** (*LCh* and *D:* use low-fat and low-cholesterol **cheese;** *LS:* use low-sodium **cheese;** *V:* leave out)

(340)

Spinach-Mushroom Sformato

6 servings *LC, LCh, D, v, k*

Steam until tender:

20 ounces fresh spinach *or*

2 10-ounce packages frozen chopped spinach

½ teaspoon **salt** or to taste

Squeeze out any excess moisture and chop the spinach if using fresh. Set aside. In **non-stick** pan, heat over medium flame:

½ to 2 tablespoons **oil**

Sauté in the oil until soft:

1 large onion, thinly sliced

1 whole garlic clove

Discard garlic when it is golden brown. Add to the onions:

½ cup finely chopped parsley

½ pound fresh mushrooms, sliced

Sauté over medium low heat until mushrooms just begin to soften, about 5 minutes. Remove from heat and cool for a few minutes. Combine with spinach. Beat together, lightly:

5 **egg** whites

1 **egg** yolk

¼ teaspoon **salt**

Fresh ground **pepper**

½ cup grated **cheese** (*LC, LCh,* and *D:* use low-fat, low-cholesterol **cheese**)

Pour egg mixture over spinach and mushrooms, and mix well. Coat inside of round 2-quart casserole with:

1 tablespoon **oil**

And sprinkle surface with:

½ to ¾ cup unseasoned **bread** crumbs

Shake crumbs until they cling evenly to bottom and sides of casserole. Add the egg-spinach and mushroom mixture. Sprinkle top with:

½ cup unseasoned **bread** crumbs

Bake in preheated oven at 375° F for 20 to 25 minutes, or until the eggs are set and the crumbs well toasted. Unmold to serve by passing a knife around inner edge of casserole. Serve hot, or at room temperature.

(341)

Individual Roulades

4 servings *LC, LCh, D, LS, V, v, P, Ml, k*

Bring to room temperature according to package directions:

1 package of phyllo leaves

Heat in a **non-stick** skillet over medium flame:

1 tablespoon **oil** (*P:* omit)

Sauté in skillet until onions are starting to brown:

1 cup sliced onions
½ teaspoon minced garlic

Add to skillet and continue sautéing, stirring frequently:

½ cup thinly sliced celery (*LS:* omit)
1 cup shredded zucchini
1 cup sliced mushrooms
1 cup shredded cabbage
½ cup grated **cheese** (*LC, LCh, D:* use low-fat, low-cholesterol **cheese** or omit; *LS:* use low-sodium **cheese,** or omit; *V, P,* and *Ml:* omit)
¼ cup dry white **wine** (*D:* if prohibited, use **stock**)
½ teaspoon dry mustard
½ teaspoon dried tarragon
Salt to taste (*P* and *LS:* omit)
White **pepper** to taste

When vegetables are crisp-tender, stir in:

¼ cup pine nuts (*P:* omit)

Remove from heat.

(*Recipe continued on next page*)

Combine in small bowl:
½ cup whole-wheat matzo or **bread** crumbs
2 tablespoons melted **margarine** (*P* and *LC:* omit)
Count out:
8 phyllo leaves
Return remainder to refrigerator.
Spread 1 phyllo leaf on a damp towel. Fold it in half. Spread it with a few crumbs and, if desired, melted margarine. Top with second folded leaf and repeat crumbs and margarine. Spoon ¼ of filling into center and fold one long side over filling. Turn in two shorter sides; and finally, tuck in second long side. Place in **non-stick** baking pan. Repeat with remaining leaves and filling, making 4 roulades in all. Brush tops of roulades with remaining melted margarine, if desired. Otherwise, brush with:
1 **egg** white, lightly beaten (*LS* and *V:* use 2 teaspoons melted **margarine**)

VARIATION: Prepare a MUSHROOM DUXELLES (**298**) and spread it between the top and bottom phyllo leaves of the roulade. Complete roulade as directed.
Serve, if desired, with:
MUSHROOM SAUCE (**424**)
CHEESE SAUCE (**419**) (Except *LCh, LS, V,* and *Ml*)

(342)

Apple-Prune Stuffed Phyllo Log

8 to 10 servings — *LCh, LS, V, v, Ml, k*

Bring to room temperature according to package directions:
1 package of phyllo leaves
Prepare:
1 recipe APPLE-PRUNE STUFFING (**318**)
In a small saucepan, melt:
2 tablespoons **margarine**
Blend with:
2 tablespoons vegetable **stock**
On large **non-stick** baking sheet arrange overlapping layers of phyllo leaves the length of the baking sheet, and wider than the sheet. Brush leaves with the margarine-stock mixture. Add another layer of overlapping phyllo leaves and again brush them with the margarine-stock

mixture. Add 1 more layer. Now arrange down center of the leaves the stuffing mixture. Shape with hands into a long log the length of the baking sheet. Wrap phyllo leaves around the log, tucking excess lengths under. The final product should resemble a Yule log. Brush with a mixture of:

1 **egg** white (*LS* and *V:* Use 2 teaspoons melted **margarine**)
¼ teaspoon steak sauce (*LS:* use ½ teaspoon **apple juice concentrate**)

Sprinkle with:

Sesame seeds

Bake at 400° F for 45 to 50 minutes or until nicely browned.

(343)

Apricot-Matzo Gâteau

10 to 12 servings *LC, LCh, LS, P, V, v, Ml, k*

Combine in bowl and soak until farfel is softened:

⅔ cup **orange juice concentrate**
1⅓ cups **stock**
4 ½ cups coarse whole wheat matzo crumbs, processed in the blender to farfel size (¼ to ½-inch crumbs)

Heat in **non-stick** pan:

1 tablespoon **oil** (*P:* omit)

Sauté in pan until golden:

3 large onions, chopped
5 garlic cloves, minced
6 stalks celery, thinly sliced (*LS:* omit if prohibited; use 2 cups chopped red or green peppers)

Meanwhile, combine in saucepan and simmer until fruit is soft:

6 ounces dried apricots, chopped (*D:* omit)
1 cup white raisins (*D:* use ¼ cup)
1½ cups orange juice

Combine sautéed vegetables, soaked matzo farfel, and fruit in large bowl with:

½ cup white **wine** (*D:* if prohibited, use ¼ cup **apple juice** plus ¼ cup **stock**)
1 cup chopped walnuts (*LC* and *P:* omit)
1 tablespoon sage or to taste

(*Recipe continued on next page*)

½ cup chopped parsley
Salt to taste (*LS* and *P:* omit)
White **pepper** to taste

In large, **non-stick** baking dish, arrange:
2 whole-wheat matzos

Spread over matzos, ⅓ of stuffing. Arrange on top of stuffing:
2 whole-wheat matzos

Add half of the remaining stuffing and top with:
2 whole-wheat matzos

Add a final layer of stuffing and top with:
2 whole-wheat matzos

Combine in small bowl:
4 **egg** whites or 2 whole **eggs** (*LC, LCh, P:* use **egg** whites; *LS:* use 2 whites plus 3 tablespoons water or **stock**; *V:* use ½ cup **stock**)
1 cup **stock**
Salt to taste (*LS* and *P:* omit)
White **pepper** to taste

Pour mixture over gâteau and bake at 350° F for 30 minutes or until nicely browned.

(344)

Bean Curd and Chinese Mushrooms

4 servings *LC, LCh, D, V, v, Ml, k*

Combine in heavy skillet and simmer covered for 10 minutes:
1 pound firm-style bean curd (tofu), drained and cut into 1-inch cubes
1 8-ounce can straw mushrooms, drained
½ cup vegetable **stock**
1 tablespoon **soy sauce**

Turn or baste during soaking. Remove tofu and mushrooms with slotted spoon. Reserve cooking liquid in separate bowl. In skillet, heat over medium heat:
1 tablespoon **oil**

Sauté in oil 1 minute:
2 teaspoons minced garlic

Add and continue to sauté for 3 minutes:
2 small scallions, thinly sliced

¼ cup finely chopped red pepper
1 slice fresh ginger, ¼-inch thick, crushed, or ¼ teaspoon dry
3 grinds fresh white **pepper**
Reserved cooking liquid

Add to skillet and simmer 1 minute, stirring:

2 tablespoons **apple juice concentrate**
1 tablespoon rice vinegar
¼ cup vegetable **stock**

Prepare a paste of:

1 tablespoon cornstarch
2 tablespoons vegetable **stock** or water

Add cornstarch mixture to skillet and stir until sauce begins to thicken. Add tofu and mushrooms. Toss with sauce until coated, and sauce is thickened.

(345)

Stuffed Eggplant

16 baby eggplant halves or 4 main course servings — *LC, LCh, D, LS, V, v, P, Ml, k*

Wash, trim tops from, and cut in half lengthwise:

8 baby eggplants *or* 2 medium eggplants

With a melon scoop or grapefruit knife, remove pulp from eggplants, leaving a ¼ inch shell. Reserve pulp.

Brush eggplant halves with:

Lemon juice

Place, cut side down, on **non-stick** baking sheet and bake in preheated oven at 350° F for 5 minutes (the baby eggplants) or 10 minutes (the larger eggplants). Cool.

Meanwhile, heat in **non-stick** skillet over medium flame:

1 tablespoon **margarine** (*P:* omit)

Stir fry in margarine 1 minute:

½ teaspoon minced garlic

Add to skillet and continue to **sauté** for 5 minutes:

1 cup finely chopped onion
½ cup chopped green pepper
½ cup chopped apple
½ teaspoon coriander

(*Recipe continued on next page*)

½ teaspoon cumin
½ teaspoon turmeric
½ teaspoon paprika
½ teaspoon coarse **salt** (*LS:* omit; *P:* use ½ teaspoon soy sauce)

Stir in reserved eggplant. Add, and continue sautéing until softened:

1½ cups sliced mushrooms

Add, blending well over low heat:

1 cup cooked brown rice (*LS* and *P:* use CHIVE RICE **(368)** cooked without salt)
¼ cup **bread** crumbs
¼ cup pine nuts (*P:* omit)
½ tablespoon melted **margarine** (*P:* omit)

Taste and season if desired with:

Salt (*LS* and *P:* omit, using **lemon juice** to taste)
Pepper (*P:* use white pepper)

Fill reserved eggplant shells with this mixture. Place in **non-stick** baking dish which will hold eggplants snugly. Pour boiling water into bottom of pan to ⅛-inch depth. Bake in preheated oven at 350° F. for 10 minutes (baby eggplants) or 20 to 30 minutes (larger eggplants), or until eggplants are tender and filling is heated through. Serve warm or at room temperature.

(346)

Chilean Vegetable Stew

6 servings *LC, LCh, D, LS, V, v, P, Ml, k*

In a small saucepan, cook together for 10 minutes, stirring often:

2 cups canned tomatoes, drained, or fresh tomatoes, peeled and seeded
4 cloves garlic, minced

Add, and continue cooking over low heat for another 15 minutes, stirring frequently:

5 medium onions, sliced
5 green peppers, cut in strips
3 to 4 teaspoons paprika to taste
¼ teaspoon saffron

In a **non-stick** casserole or Dutch oven, heat over medium flame:

½ tablespoon **oil** (*P:* omit)

Brown in casserole on both sides:

12 slices tofu (1 pound)

Add to casserole the tomato mixture plus:

2 bay leaves

¼ teaspoon dried ground red pepper

1½ cups dry white **wine** (*D:* if prohibited, use **stock** and increase vinegar if necessary)

1½ cups vegetable **stock** or water

1 tablespoon **wine** vinegar (*D:* if prohibited, use tarragon vinegar)

Salt to taste (*P* and *LS:* omit; increase **wine** vinegar, if necessary)

White **pepper** to taste

Bring mixture to a boil. Add:

1 cup uncooked rice

Cook, covered, over low heat for 25 minutes or until rice is tender.

(347)

Falafel Pie

1 pie (8 wedges) *LCh, D, V, v, P, Ml, k*

In small bowl, soak, covered with cold water for 15 minutes:

½ cup bulgur wheat

1½ cups coarse crumbs made from whole-wheat pita **bread**

Drain thoroughly, squeezing out excess water. Then process in electric blender or food processor until smooth:

1 can chick peas (garbanzos) drained

¼ cup **lemon juice**

2 teaspoons minced garlic

1 teaspoon coriander

1 teaspoon cumin

1 teaspoon crushed red pepper

1 teaspoon **salt** (*P:* omit)

¼ teaspoon **pepper** (*P:* use white)

Combine mixture with bulgur wheat and pita crumbs, mixing well. Press into a **non-stick** 9-inch pie pan. Bake at 350° F for 30 minutes. Cut into wedges and sprinkle top with:

1 large tomato, coarsely chopped

2 scallions, chopped

Serve plain or with:

TAHINA DIP (**123**)

(348)

Flageolets au Gratin

8 servings *LCh, V, v, Ml, k*

In large pot, combine and bring to boil, boiling for 2 minutes:
2 cups dried flageolets or small white beans
6 cups water
Let stand for 1 hour. Meanwhile, fill a cheesecloth bag with:
6 sprigs parsley
1 clove garlic, unpeeled
1 bay leaf
2 sprigs thyme or ½ teaspoon dried
Drain beans and place in a heavy casserole with cheesecloth bag and:
1 onion stuck with 2 cloves
2 to 3 teaspoons **salt**
Water to cover by 1 inch
Bring to a boil. Skim off froth, lower heat, and simmer beans for 1½ hours or until they are tender. Drain, discard the cheesecloth bag and onion. In a **non-stick** skillet, heat over medium flame:
1 tablespoon **oil**
Sauté in skillet:
2 medium onions, finely chopped
Add:
2 tomatoes, peeled, seeded, and cut into strips
2 garlic cloves, crushed or minced
½ teaspoon cumin
½ teaspoon coriander
Simmer mixture for 5 minutes. Add:
1½ cups **stock**
Bring mixture to a simmer and gently stir in the beans. Add:
Salt and **pepper** to taste
Transfer mixture to a **non-stick** shallow au gratin dish. Sprinkle with:
¾ cup whole-wheat **bread** crumbs
Dot with:
1 to 2 tablespoons softened **margarine**
Bake in 375° F oven for 30 minutes, or until crumbs are nicely browned. Sprinkle with:
Chopped parsley

VARIATION: Combine **bread** crumbs with ¾ cup grated **cheese** (*LCh, V, Ml:* omit)

(349)

Mock Fish in Phyllo

3 to 4 servings *LCh, D, V, v, Ml, k*

Bring to room temperature according to package directions:
1 8-ounce package phyllo leaves
Meanwhile, combine in a bowl:
½ cup chopped nuts
½ cup chopped parsley
½ cup **feta cheese** or **pot cheese** (*V* and *Ml:* omit; *LCh:* use **hoop cheese** or low-fat **pot cheese**)
2 cups cooked brown rice
1 tablespoon minced fresh rosemary or ½ teaspoon dried
1 tablespoon minced fresh thyme or ½ teaspoon dried
Toss until well mixed. Add:
Salt to taste
Pepper to taste
Melt:
2 tablespoons **margarine**
Arrange an overlapping layer of phyllo leaves on a large **non-stick** baking sheet. Brush with melted margarine. Arrange another layer of phyllo leaves and brush with the melted margarine. Repeat one more time. Spread filling down the center of the phyllo leaves. Wrap leaves around the stuffing, forming the shape of a fish with head and tail. Brush crust with margarine. Make a hole with your finger for the eye. Bake at 400° F for 25 to 30 minutes or until crust is golden. Garnish with a black olive for the eye.

(350)

Mock Turkey in Phyllo

8 to 10 serviings *LCh, V, v, Ml, k*

Bring to room temperature according to package directions:
1 package of phyllo leaves
Heat in **non-stick** skillet over medium flame:
1 to 2 tablespoons **oil**

(*Recipe continued on next page*)

Sauté in skillet:

2 large onions, chopped
4 garlic cloves, minced

When onions turn opaque, add and continue sautéing until soft:

4 cups thinly sliced celery

Transfer vegetables to a very large bowl and add:

3 large tart apples, peeled and finely sliced or cubed
10 slices whole-wheat **bread,** lightly toasted and cubed
1½ cups chopped pitted prunes
1 pound chestnuts, scored, boiled, peeled, and chopped
1 bag frozen fried onion rings, heated in oven until crisp, and chopped (*V* and *Ml:* pareve-milkless and meatless)
1 package onion soup mix (*v:* pareve-milkless and meatless)
1 cup **apple juice** or more to moisten
1 cup water or vegetable **stock** or more to moisten
½ cup wheat germ
½ cup sunflower seeds
Salt to taste
Pepper to taste

Add additional juice or water to mixture so that it holds together. Do not make it too wet. In skillet, brown:

12 ounces soy protein sausage, chopped, or textured vegetable protein (*V* and *Ml:* pareve-milkless and meatless)

Add to mixture. Adjust seasoning to taste. Count out:

12 phyllo leaves

Brush each lightly with:

Oil or melted **margarine**

Arrange 5 of the leaves in an overlapping pattern on the bottom of a large **non-stick** baking pan or sheet. On the center of the leaves, form stuffing into a large mound in the shape of a roast turkey. Wrap leaves around stuffing; cover with additional leaves, tucking excess under turkey. Tuck lollipop sticks or wooden skewers into "turkey" sides for drumstick bones. Prepare a basting sauce of:

2 tablespoons melted **margarine**
2 tablespoons **apple juice concentrate**
¼ cup dry white **wine** or champagne

Brush basting sauce on "turkey." Bake at 400° F until "skin" is golden brown and crisp, and inner temperature of stuffing is 165° F. Baste several times during baking. Serve with, if desired:

CHAMPAGNE SAUCE (**418**)

(351)

Nut Loaf

6 to 8 servings *LCh, D, V, v, Ml, k*

Combine and mix thoroughly:

1¼ cups peanuts, walnuts, or cashews, or combination, chopped
2 carrots, grated (about 1 cup)
2 cups finely sliced celery
1 cup chopped onion
1 cup chopped mushrooms
¼ cup wheat germ
1¼ cup whole-wheat **bread** crumbs
1 cup chopped eggplant or cauliflower or chopped green beans
1 package onion soup mix (*V* and *Ml:* pareve-meatless and milkless)
½ to ¾ cup water, or enough to make mixture hold together, without making it wet
Salt to taste

Bake mixture in greased **non-stick** loaf pan at 400° F for 1 hour, or until well-browned. Cool. Run knife around edge of loaf and invert on cookie sheet. Return to oven at 425° F for 5 to 10 more minutes, or until nicely browned. Serve, if desired with:

CHEESE SAUCE (**419**) (*V* and *Ml:* omit)
or
MUSHROOM SAUCE (**424**)

(352)

Minted Cranberry Nut Loaf

6 to 8 servings *LCh, D, V, v, Ml, k*

To basic NUT LOAF (**351**) recipe, add:

1 cup raw cranberries, chopped
½ to ¾ teaspoon dried mint
½ to ¾ teaspoon rosemary, crumbled

(353)

Rice-Stuffed Phyllo Cumberland

4 servings *LCh, D, LS, V, v, P, Ml, k*

In a **non-stick** skillet, heat over medium flame:
½ tablespoon **oil** or **margarine** (*P:* omit)
In skillet, **sauté** until lightly brown:
½ cup pine nuts (*P:* use chopped chick peas)
With slotted spoon, transfer nuts to a bowl. Add to skillet:
½ to 1 tablespoon **margarine** or **oil** (*P:* omit)
Sauté in skillet until soft:
½ cup finely chopped celery (*LS:* use chopped red and/or green peppers)
1 teaspoon minced garlic
¼ cup finely chopped shallots or scallions
In small saucepan, heat together, simmering for 5 minutes:
½ cup currants or raisins (*D:* omit for those limiting simple carbohydrates)
2 tablespoons **orange juice concentrate**
Remove from heat, and stir in:
1 teaspoon grated orange rind
½ teaspoon grated lemon rind
Toss this mixture with pine nuts and:
1½ cups cooked brown rice
Salt to taste (*LS* and *P:* omit)
Pepper to taste (*P:* use white)
Wrap this mixture in:
Phyllo leaves (see MOCK TURKEY (**350**)) *or*
Brioche dough
Serve with CUMBERLAND SAUCE (**420**)

(354)

Stuffed Vegetarian Cabbage a la Cranberries

6 to 8 servings *LC, LCh, D*, LS, V, v, P, Ml, k*

In boiling water for a few minutes, or in freezer for 1 hour, soften:
- 1 large head cabbage

Meanwhile, combine in a bowl:
- 1 cup raw brown rice
- 2 carrots, shredded (*LS:* use 1 large apple, peeled, cored, and chopped)
- 1 large onion, finely chopped
- ½ cup ground nuts (*P:* use ground chick peas)
- 3 medium **egg** whites, lightly beaten (*LS:* use 2 whites plus 2 tablespoons water; *V:* use ⅓ cup water)
- ½ teaspoon garlic powder
- 2 teaspoons **apple juice concentrate**
- ⅓ teaspoon white **pepper**
- **Salt** to taste (*LS* and *P:* use 2 additional tablespoons **apple juice concentrate**)

Set aside. In large **non-stick** Dutch oven, heat:
- 1 tablespoon **oil** (*P:* omit)

In Dutch oven, **sauté** until golden:
- 1 large onion, diced

Stir in:
- 1 15-ounce can tomatoes (*LS:* use fresh or unsalted canned)
- 1 cup whole fresh or frozen **unsweetened** cranberries
- 1 can whole-berry cranberry sauce (*D:* use artificially sweetened diet cranberry sauce, or ⅓ cup **apple juice concentrate** plus ⅔ cup **unsweetened** apple-cranberry juice; *P:* use juice mixtures)
- 1 cup **apple juice** (*D:* use ½ cup apple juice plus ½ cup water)
- 2 tablespoons **lemon juice**
- Dash ground ginger (Opt.)

Simmer for 5 minutes. Adjust seasonings, adding, if needed, more:
- **Apple juice concentrate**
- **Lemon juice**

Separate cabbage leaves, cutting from core with a sharp knife. On each leaf, place a portion of the reserved rice mixture. Fold up bot-

(*Recipe continued on next page*)

tom of leaf, then fold sides over. Finally, tuck in top of leaf. Gently place stuffed cabbage rolls in sauce. Simmer 1½ hours, covered. Add additional water during cooking, if necessary.

* Unless sauce is made with diet cranberry sauce, it should be avoided by those who must limit intake of simple carbohydrates, such as fruit.

(355)

Baked Tofu

4 servings *LCh, D, V, v, Ml, k*

Combine in small dish:
⅓ cup **bread** crumbs
⅓ cup chopped walnuts
White **pepper**
Slice into ⅜-inch slices:
1 pound tofu
Combine in small bowl one of the following three groups of ingredients: I
1 tablespoon **soy sauce**
1 teaspoon **oil**
1 teaspoon garlic powder
or II (*D:* omit)
1 tablespoon honey
2 tablespoons **apple juice concentrate**
or III
3 tablespoons SOYO-NAISE (**264**)
1 teaspoon **oil**
Dip tofu first into one of the above mixtures, then into crumbs. Bake on a **non-stick** or greased cookie sheet at 400° F for 10 minutes on each side.

VARIATION: Serve Version I with TERIYAKI DIPPING SAUCE (**124**) if desired.

(356)

Tofu Paprikash

4 to 6 servings *LC, LCh, D, LS, P, V, v, Ml, k*

Heat in **non-stick** skillet over medium flame:
 1 tablespoon **oil** (*P:* omit)
Sauté in skillet for 10 minutes, or until browned:
 4 medium onions, chopped
 2 green peppers, seeded and chopped
 2 red peppers, seeded and chopped
Blend in:
 2 teaspoons Hungarian paprika, or to taste
Arrange over vegetables:
 1 pound tofu, sliced
Sprinkle with:
 White **pepper**
 Salt (*P* and *LS:* use **lemon juice**)
Add:
 1 cup **stock** or dry white **wine** (*D:* use **stock**)
 1 cup crushed tomatoes (*LS:* use unsalted canned, or fresh)
Cook, covered, over low heat for 25 minutes.
With broad spatula, carefully remove tofu to serving dish. Keep warm. Taste sauce for seasoning; correct if necessary. Cook sauce for 10 minutes to reduce slightly. Stir into sauce, if desired.
 ½ cup low-fat **yogurt** or **buttermilk** (*LS:* omit for those limited to low-sodium **milk;** for others, use unsalted **buttermilk** or **yogurt;** *V* and *Ml:* omit)
Gently reheat sauce, but do not boil. Pour sauce over tofu, and serve garnished with:
 Tomato wedges
 Chopped parsley

(357)

Vegetarian Chili

4 to 6 servings *LCh, D, V, v, P, Ml, k*

Tip: Freeze tofu 1 week before preparing this dish

Heat in **non-stick** skillet:
  1 to 2 tablespoons **oil** (*P:* omit)
Sauté over low heat in skillet until onion is softened, about 5 minutes:
  1½ cups onion
  2 garlic cloves, minced
  1 chopped green pepper
Stir in:
  1 pound tofu, frozen for at least 1 week, and defrosted and crumbled
Increase heat to medium and continue cooking until tofu and onions are browned. Stir frequently. Add:
  1 28-ounce can tomatoes in puree
  4 tablespoons chili powder, or to taste
  2 teaspoons brown **sugar** or **apple juice concentrate** (*D* and *P:* use juice)
  2 teaspoons ground cumin, or to taste
  1 teaspoon **salt,** or to taste (*P:* omit)
  ¼ to ½ teaspoon cayenne or to taste
  ⅛ teaspoon **pepper** (*P:* use white)
  1 tablespoon oregano
  1 6-ounce can tomato paste
Bring to a boil over high heat and simmer for 1 hour, adding water or tomato puree if chili becomes too thick. During last 30 minutes of cooking, stir in:
  1 20-ounce can dark red kidney beans, drained
  1 10½-ounce can pinto beans, drained
  1 cup fresh corn kernels (Opt.)
Serve with any of the following, passed separately:
  Shredded lettuce
  Chopped onions
  Chopped tomatoes
  Chopped green peppers
  Shredded **cheese** (Monterey Jack or Cheddar) (*V, P,* and *Ml:* omit)
  Chopped jalapeño peppers or chili peppers
  Sour cream (*LCh, D, V, P,* and *Ml:* omit)

Side Dishes

Pastas

(358)

Angel Hair Pasta with Match-stick Zucchini

4 side-dish servings *LC, LCh, D, LS, V, v, P, Ml, k, B*

Prepare according to package directions:
 4 ounces very fine pasta (*P* and *LS:* use **lemon juice** instead of salt in water)
Drain. Meanwhile, steam:
 2 small zucchini, cut into 1-inch matchsticks
Toss zucchini with pasta. Serve with, according to diet:
 TOMATO SAUCE **(425)** *or*
 Grated **cheese** *or*
 CHICKEN CACCIATORE **(303)** *or* other main dish

(359)

Whole-Wheat Noodles and Cauliflower

4 servings *LC, LCh, D, LS, V, v, P, Ml, k*

Cook according to package directions:
 8 ounces whole-wheat noodles (*LCh:* use yolkless noodles; *V:* eggless; *LS* or *P:* do not salt water; add **lemon juice** instead)
Steam:
 1 small head cauliflower, separated into florets
Meanwhile, heat in **non-stick** skillet over medium flame:
 1 tablespoon **oil** or **margarine** (*P:* omit)
Sauté in skillet until golden brown:
 1 cup chopped onion
 1 garlic clove, minced
Stir into skillet:
 ½ cup **stock**
Then add the drained noodles, the steamed cauliflower, and:
 Salt to taste (*LS* and *P:* omit)
 Pepper to taste
Serve immediately.

Potatoes

(360)

Apple-Stuffed Yams

4 to 8 servings *LCh, D*, LS, V, v, P, Ml, k*

Bake in microwave or conventional oven until soft:
 4 large yams or sweet potatoes
 2 large apples, peeled, cored, and sliced
Halve yams and remove centers, leaving ⅜-inch shells. Mash, process, or blend together apples, yam pulp and:

1 teaspoon orange rind
1 tablespoon **apple juice concentrate**
1 tablespoon **orange juice concentrate**

Refill shells with mixture. Bake at 375° F for 20 minutes.

* Except those who must limit intake of simple carbohydrates, such as fruit.

(361)

Dutchess Potato Nests

6 servings *LC, LCh, D, LS, v, P, Ml, k, B*

Cook until tender in salted boiling water:

2 pounds potatoes, peeled

Drain and return to heat for a few minutes to evaporate any excess moisture. Transfer to blender or food processor and puree until smooth with:

2 tablespoons **margarine** (*LC* and *P:* use 1 to 2 tablespoons skim milk to obtain desired texture)
1 **egg** or 2 **egg** whites (*LC, LCh,* or *P:* use whites; *LS:* use 1 white)
Salt to taste (*LS* and *P:* omit)
Pepper to taste (*P:* use white **pepper;** *B:* omit)
Dash nutmeg (*B:* omit)

Transfer to pastry bag with large decorating tip. Pipe 4-inch circles on a **non-stick** cookie sheet; flatten circles with a spoon. Add a decorative ring around edge of each circle about 1-inch high. Brush with slightly beaten mixture of:

1 **egg** white
1 tablespoon cream (*LC, LCh,* and *P:* use evaporated skimmed **milk;** *Ml:* omit)

Place under broiler for 1 to 2 minutes or until lightly browned. Fill nests with:

Asparagus tips *or*
CREAMED SPINACH **(393)** (*LS*: use CREAMED BROCCOLI **(394)**)
or
Creamed mushrooms
Baby June peas

VARIATION: Use DUTCHESS POTATOES **(361)** around hot dishes as garnish.

(362)

Parsleyed Yogurt Potatoes

6 servings *LC, LCh, D, LS, v, P, k, B*

Steam or microwave cook:

18 small red potatoes (peeled, if desired)

Slice while still warm and toss with:

¼ cup low-fat **yogurt**

Salt to taste (*LS* and *P:* omit)

Pepper to taste (*P:* use white; *B:* omit)

½ cup finely chopped parsley

Serve warm or at room temperature, garnished with:

Parsley

Rice

(363)

Brown Rice and Triticale Pilaf

4 to 5 servings *LCh, D, LS, V, v, P, Ml, k*

In **non-stick** saucepan, heat over medium flame:

½ tablespoon **oil** (*P:* omit)

In saucepan, **sauté** until lightly browned:

½ cup finely chopped onions

Add and continue sautéing, lightly browning the grains:

¾ cup brown rice

⅓ cup triticale (a hybrid grain available in health-food stores)

Add:

2½ cups boiling **stock**

Salt to taste (*LS* and *P:* omit)

Bring mixture back to boil; cover and cook over low heat for 25 minutes, or until all liquid is absorbed.

(364)

Rice and Celery Pilaf

6 to 8 servings *LC, LCh, D, V, v, P, Ml, k*

In **non-stick** saucepan, heat over medium flame:
  1 tablespoon **oil** (*P:* omit)
Sauté in saucepan until golden:
  1 onion, finely minced
  1 teaspoon finely minced garlic
  2 cups finely sliced celery
Add:
  1 cup brown rice
Stir rice in vegetable mixture for several minutes, allowing it to brown slightly. Add:
  2½ cups boiling **stock**
  Salt to taste (*P:* use ½ teaspoon **soy sauce**)
Cook for 25 minutes on low heat, covered, or until all liquid is absorbed and rice is tender.

(365)

Chutney Rice

4 to 6 servings *LC, LCh, LS, V, v, P, Ml, k*

Toss until combined:
  3 cups cooked brown rice (*LS* and *P:* cooked without salt)
  1 cup CHUTNEY **(273)**

(366)

Moroccan Rice

4 to 5 servings *LCh, LS, V, v, k*

Cook according to package directions:
 1 cup white or brown rice (*LS:* prepare without **salt**)
Add to hot rice, tossing well:
 1 tablespoon **margarine** or **butter**
 ⅓ cup white raisins, plumped in brandy or sherry or **wine**
Transfer rice to serving dish and sprinkle with:
 ½ cup toasted sliced almonds
 ¾ cup very crisply fried onions

(367)

Rice with Peas

4 to 5 servings *LCh, V, v, Ml, k, B*

Cook according to package directions:
 1 cup white rice
Toss with:
 1 tablespoon **margarine** or **butter**
 2 cups heated canned petits pois or well-cooked fresh or frozen peas
 1 teaspoon very finely chopped parsley
 ½ teaspoon crushed dried tarragon (Opt.)

(368)

Chive Rice

4 to 5 servings *LC, LCh, D, LS, V, v, P, Ml, k*

Combine and cook according to package directions (*LS:* omit **salt**):
 1 cup rice
 2 tablespoons finely chopped chives
 Water or **stock**

(369)

Five-Grain Pilaf

8 to 10 servings *LC, LCh, D, LS, V, v, P, Ml, k*

In **non-stick** saucepan, heat over medium flame:
 ½ to 1 tablespoon **oil** (*P:* omit)
In saucepan, **sauté** until lightly browned:
 1 cup onions, finely chopped
Add and continue sautéing, lightly browning the grains:
 ⅔ cups brown rice
 ⅓ cup triticale (a hybrid grain availabe in health-food stores)
 ⅓ cup millet (available in health-food stores)
 ⅓ cup converted white rice
 ⅓ cup wild rice
Add:
 5 cups boiling **stock**
 Salt to taste (*LS* and *P:* omit)
Bring mixture to a boil and simmer, covered, for 25 minutes or until all the liquid is absorbed.

(370)

Fluffy-White Rice

LC, LCh, LS, V, v, Ml, k, B

Cook white rice according to package directions.* When it is finished, place a folded towel or folded paper towel over rice. Cover. Excess moisture will be absorbed, leaving rice light and fluffy.

* *LS:* Cook without salt in rich stock.

(371)

Saffron Rice

6 to 8 servings *LCh, D, LS, V, v, Ml, k*

Melt in medium saucepan over medium high heat:
    1 to 2 tablespoons **butter** or **margarine**
Add and **sauté** briefly:
    1 cinnamon stick, crushed
    3 bay leaves, crushed
    ¼ teaspoon cumin
Add and continue sautéing until onion is golden and coated with spices:
    ½ cup chopped onion
    4 wholes cloves (Opt.)
    ¼ teaspoon tumeric
Add and **sauté** until grains are coated:
    2 cups long-grain converted rice
Add:
    4 cups boiling water
    1 teaspoon **salt** (*LS:* omit)
    ¼ teaspoon saffron threads
Bring mixture to a boil and stir several times. Reduce heat to lowest setting and cook until water is absorbed and rice is tender, about 25 minutes. Garnish with:
    Slivered or sliced almonds

(372)

Zucchini Rice

4 to 6 servings *LC, LCh, D, LS, V, v, P, Ml, k*

Heat **non-stick** skillet. Add and **sauté** at medium heat until soft:
    1 medium onion, chopped
    2 tablespoons dry white **wine** (*D:* if prohibited, use **stock**)
Add to skillet:
    2 tablespoons dry white **wine** (*D:* if prohibited, use **stock**)
    2 cups julienned zucchini

Sauté for 2 minutes. Add and toss to heat:
1½ cups cooked rice
Season to taste with:
Salt (*LS* and *P:* omit)
Pepper (*P:* use white)

Vegetables

(373)

Alu Gobi (Cauliflower and Potatoes)

8 to 10 servings — *LC, LCh, LS, V, v, Ml, k*

Melt in **non-stick** skillet over medium flame:
1 tablespoon **margarine**
Sauté in the margarine until lightly browned, stirring frequently:
1 pound potatoes, peeled and cut into 1-inch cubes
Remove potatoes from heat. In heavy saucepan, heat:
1 tablespoon **oil**
Add to saucepan when oil is hot but not smoking:
1 teaspoon black or white mustard seeds
Cover pan and shake constantly until seeds pop. Add and brown lightly:
1 cup chopped onion
Reduce heat and add, blending thoroughly:
1 teaspoon **lemon juice**
¾ teaspoon ground coriander
¾ to 1 teaspoon ground cumin
¾ teaspoon tumeric
½ teaspoon ground red pepper
½ teaspoon paprika
Add:
2 fresh tomatoes, cut into 1½-inch cubes
2 tablespoons chopped fresh coriander or cilantro (Chinese parsley) (Opt.)
2 teaspoons slivered fresh ginger root
1 to 2 fresh jalapeño peppers, seeded and chopped (Opt.)
½ to 1 teaspoon **salt** (*LS:* omit)

(*Recipe continued on next page*)

Stir in:

½ cup **stock**

Add to mixture the potatoes and:

3 pounds cauliflower, broken into florets, and some tender green leaves from base

Reduce heat to low, cover tightly, and cook 15 to 25 minutes, until vegetables are cooked but still firm. Serve garnished with:

Chopped onion
Cilantro leaves

(374)

Broccoli with Capers

4 to 6 servings *LC, LCh, D, V, v, Ml, k*

Steam:

1 bunch fresh broccoli, trimmed and sectioned

Meanwhile, combine in saucepan:

1 tablespoon **margarine**
¼ cup **stock**
2 tablespoons capers, drained and chopped

Heat until margarine is melted. Transfer to blender and puree. Pour sauce over cooked broccoli and serve.

(375)

Lemon Broccoli with Pistachios

4 to 5 servings *LCh, D, V, v, Ml, k*

Toast in oven by spreading flat in pan and baking at 300° F for 10 to 15 minutes:

½ cup shelled pistachios

Chop and set aside. Steam until tender:

1 bunch fresh broccoli, cut into spears, or 2 10-ounce packages frozen broccoli spears

Melt in **non-stick** saucepan:

1 to 2 tablespoons **margarine**

Sauté in margarine for 3 minutes:

2 garlic cloves, minced fine

Add and stir:

1 tablespoon **lemon juice**
¼ cup **stock**

Toss broccoli with lemon-garlic mixture until well-covered. Sprinkle with toasted pistachios.

(376)

Brussels Sprouts with Chestnuts

8 servings *LC, LCh, D, LS, V, v, Ml, k*

Steam or cook for 10 minutes:

2 pounds Brussels sprouts, washed and trimmed

Drain and refresh sprouts under cold water. Dry. Arrange them in a **non-stick,** flameproof baking dish just large enough to hold them all in one layer. Sprinkle lightly with:

Salt (*LS:* omit)
Pepper
Lemon juice

Add:

¼ cup **stock**

Bring to a simmer over high heat. Cover with greased sheet of wax paper and a sheet of foil. Braise in preheated oven at 350° F for 20 minutes, or until tender. In a large **non-stick** skillet, melt:

1 to 2 tablespoons **margarine**

Add:

1 pound chestnuts, shelled and husked

Shake over low heat until they are well coated with margarine. Add to cover by 1 inch:

Stock

Dissolve in 1 tablespoon of **stock:**

1 tablespoon tomato paste (*LS:* use unsalted tomato paste)

Add mixture to skillet, blending in thoroughly. Add:

1 stalk celery (*LS:* omit if prohibited)
4 sprigs parsley
1 bay leaf

Bring to a boil and simmer chestnuts until tender but not mushy, about 40 to 45 minutes. Remove chestnuts with slotted spoon and transfer to bowl. Remove vegetables and bay leaf. Cook remaining

(*Recipe continued on next page*)

liquid over high heat until reduced by half. Return chestnuts to skillet. Add Brussels sprouts and their juices to skillet and gently shake pan over medium heat until sprouts are hot. Taste juices for seasoning. Add:

Salt to taste (*LS:* omit)
Pepper to taste
1 to 3 tablespoons **margarine,** cut into small pieces

Stir to glaze the sprouts and chestnuts. Serve in heated dish.

(377)

Cabbage au Pecans

6 servings *LCh, D, LS, V, v, Ml, k*

Shred:

1 medium head cabbage (about 4 to 5 cups shredded cabbage)

Melt in large **non-stick** skillet:

1 tablespoon **margarine**

Stir in the cabbage and:

1 cup thinly sliced onion

Cook, over medium-low heat, stirring frequently, until vegetables are well coated with margarine, about 1 to 2 minutes. Add:

¼ cup dry vermouth (see **wine;** *D:* omit if prohibited; use ¼ cup **stock**)
2 tablespoons fresh minced or 1 teaspoon dried dill weed
½ teaspoon **salt** (*LS:* omit)
⅛ teaspoon white **pepper**

Continue to cook, stirring, for 3 minutes more. Add:

½ cup oven-toasted pecan halves

Stir until heated through, about 1 minute. Taste and adjust seasonings.

(378)

Baby Belgian Carrots

8 servings *LC, LCh, LS*, V, v, Ml, k, B*

In large saucepan, combine:
- 2 pounds fresh or frozen baby carrots, preferably Belgian
- ½ cup **pineapple-orange juice concentrate** *or*
- ¼ cup **pineapple juice concentrate** plus ¼ cup **orange juice concentrate**

Cover and cook over medium heat until juices are melted and begin to simmer. Reduce heat and cook until carrots are tender (*B:* cook until soft). If desired, serve sprinkled with:
- Cinnamon

* Except dieters who are prohibited such high-sodium vegetables as carrots.

(379)

Gingered Carrots

4 to 5 servings *LC, LCh, LS*, V, v, P, Ml, k*

Combine in heavy saucepan:
- 1 10-ounce bag of baby carrots (preferably Belgian)
- ¼ cup **pineapple juice concentrate**
- 2 tablespoons water
- 1 tablespoon **orange juice concentrate**
- ¼ to ½ teaspoon ground ginger
- 1 tablespoon grated orange peel

Mix well and cook, covered, over low to medium heat until carrots are just tender, about 20 to 30 minutes.

* Except dieters who are prohibited such high-sodium vegetables as carrots.

(380)

Glazed Carrots, Turnips, and Peas

8 servings *LC, LCh, D, LS*, V, v, P, Ml, k, B*

Steam separately until just tender (*B:* until *very* tender):

4 cups peeled and julienned carrots
4 cups peeled and julienned turnips (*B:* omit)
2 cups peas

Before ready to serve, heat in **non-stick** skillet over medium flame:

½ to 1 tablespoon **margarine** (*P:* omit)
1 tablespoon **apple juice concentrate** (*D:* **use pineapple-orange juice concentrate**)
2 teaspoons **orange juice concentrate** and/or **pineapple juice concentrate** (*D:* use **stock**)

Add carrots and heat in glaze, shaking pan frequently until liquid is reduced and they are coated with glaze. Set aside; add to skillet:

½ to 1 tablespoon **margarine** (*P:* omit)
1 tablespoon **apple juice concentrate** (*D:* use **pineapple-orange juice concentrate**)
2 teaspoons **orange juice concentrate** and/or **pineapple juice concentrate** (*D:* use **stock**)

Add turnips and heat in glaze, shaking pan frequently, until liquid is reduced and turnips are coated with glaze. Set aside; add to skillet:

½ to 1 tablespoon **margarine** (*P:* omit)
1 tablespoon **apple juice concentrate** (*D:* use **pineapple-orange juice concentrate**)
2 teaspoons **orange juice concentrate** and/or **pineapple juice concentrate** (*D:* use **stock**)

Add peas to skillet, and heat in glaze, shaking pan frequently, until peas are coated with glaze. Toss all three vegetables together, and serve warm.

* Except those who are prohibited such high-sodium vegetables as carrots and turnips.

(381) *GLAZED ZUCCHINI, PARSNIPS, AND PEAS*

8 servings *LC, LCh, D, LS, V, v, P, Ml, k, B*

In GLAZED CARROTS, TURNIPS, AND PEAS **(380)**, substitute zucchini and parsnips, julienned, for carrots and turnips.

(382)

Chinese Vegetables

4 servings *LC, LCh, D, V, v, Ml, k*

Heat wok or **non-stick** skillet. Add:

1 tablespoon **oil** (Opt.)
½ cup **stock**
2 tablespoons sherry **wine** (*D:* use 1 tablespoon vinegar)
1 tablespoon **soy sauce**
1 tablespoon **apple juice concentrate** or brown **sugar** (*D:* use **apple juice concentrate**)
¼ to ½ tablespoon shredded fresh ginger to taste
1 teaspoon minced garlic

Stir fry in this mixture, one at a time each until just crisp-tender:

1 cup sliced celery
1 cup broccoli florets and stems, sliced
1 cup asparagus stems and tips, cut into 2-inch lengths *or*
1 green pepper, thinly sliced
1 cup celery cabbage or bok choy

Also toss briefly in this mixture, but do not cook:

½ cup straw mushrooms, canned
½ cup dried black mushrooms, reconstituted

As each is cooked, transfer to a large bowl. Add to remaining liquid in the wok or skillet:

½ cup **stock**
2 tablespoons **soy sauce**
2 tablespoons sherry **wine** (*D:* omit)
¼ cup **apple juice concentrate** or brown **sugar** (*D:* use 1 tablespoon **apple juice concentrate**)
1 to 2 teaspoons shredded fresh ginger or ¼ to ½ teaspoon ground ginger or to taste
2 tablespoons rice vinegar or other mild vinegar
1 teaspoon dry mustard

Combine in small bowl:

2 tablespoons water
1 tablespoon cornstarch

Add cornstarch mixture to liquid in wok or skillet and blend over medium heat, stirring until thickened and smooth. Return vegetables to wok and toss, adding:

(*Recipe continued on next page*)

1 15-ounce can baby corns, drained

Quickly heat all by covering and cooking for one minute. If desired, serve with:

FLUFFY WHITE RICE **(370)**

or

Brown rice

(383)

Crudités and Crisp-Tender Vegetables

Crudités are simply raw vegetables. They can be cut in sticks or strips, chips or rounds, or florets, or left whole. Good for serving with dips are:

Asparagus tips
Beets (except *LS*)
Belgian Endive
Broccoli
Carrots (except *LS*)
Cauliflower
Celery (except *LS*)
Cherry tomatoes
Cucumber
Fennel
Green beans
Mushrooms
Radishes
Red and green pepper
Scallions
Sunchoke
Turnips (except *LS*)
Zucchini

If you prefer to serve vegetables that are somewhat more tender, blanch in boiling water for 1 to 3 minutes, then chill. Or steam until crisp tender. Or cook for a minute or 2 in the microwave oven. Vegetables that lend themselves to parcooking include:

Asparagus
Broccoli
Brussels sprouts

Cauliflower
Celery Root
Green beans
Snow Peas
Zucchini

(384)

Green Beans Almondine

4 to 5 servings *LC, LCh, LS, D, V, v, Ml, k*

Wash and trim:
    1 pound fresh green beans
Melt in saucepan (preferably a waterless or other heavy pan):
    1 tablespoon **margarine**
Add the beans and:
    2 tablespoons **stock** or water
Toss beans well with stock and margarine. Cover and cook over low to medium heat until beans are just crisp-tender, shaking pan frequently. Meanwhile, toast in oven at 300° F for 5 to 10 minutes, checking frequently to prevent overtoasting:
    ¼ cup sliced almonds
When ready to serve, sprinkle almonds over green beans.

(385)

Green Beans au Gratin

4 to 5 servings *LC, LCh, LS, V, v, Ml, k, B*

Steam until just tender (*B:* very tender):
    1 pound whole green beans, washed and trimmed
Arrange beans in a small casserole. In a small bowl toss together:
    1 tablespoon melted **margarine** or **butter**
    ½ cup **bread** crumbs
Spread crumbs on beans. Bake at 350° F for 10 to 15 minutes, or until crumbs are golden brown.

VARIATION: Toss beans with 1 tablespoon **butter** or **margarine** before arranging them in casserole.

(386)

Minted Green Beans

4 to 5 servings *LC, LCh, D, LS, V, v, Ml, k*

Melt in wok or **non-stick** pan:
2 teaspoons **margarine**
Add and blend:
1 tablespoon water
10 mint leaves, crushed, or ½ teaspoon dried mint
Stir fry in mixture, stirring constantly until vegetable is tender:
1 pound whole green beans, washed and trimmed
Serve warm.

(387)

Curried Lentils

6 to 8 servings *LCh, D, LS, V, v, P, Ml, k*

Bring to a boil in a large saucepan:
1 quart water
Add and stir:
2 cups dried lentils
1½ teaspoons curry powder
½ teaspoon **salt** (*LS* and *P:* use 1 teaspoon **lemon juice**)
Let simmer, covered, until lentils are tender and have absorbed most of the liquid, about 20 to 30 minutes. Meanwhile, melt in a **non-stick** skillet over medium heat:
½ to 1 tablespoon **butter** or **margarine** or **oil** (*P:* omit)
Sauté in skillet until golden:
1 cup chopped onion
Add:
½ teaspoon coarse **salt** (*LS* and *P:* omit)
2 teaspoons cumin
1 teaspoon ground red chili
1 teaspoon turmeric
Raise heat to high and cook, stirring constantly, for 30 seconds. Reduce heat and stir in:

¾ cup coarsely chopped peanuts (*P:* omit)

Add lentils and toss lightly. Adjust seasonings to taste, and serve garnished with:

1 tablespoon chopped fresh coriander
Chopped tomato

(388)

Mushrooms and Zucchini

4 to 6 servings *LC, LCh, D, LS, V, v, P, Ml, k*

Heat in **non-stick** skillet:

2 teaspoons **oil** (*P:* use **stock**)

Sauté in skillet for 3 minutes:

2 medium cloves garlic, minced

Add and toss until well combined:

1 pound fresh mushrooms, cleaned and sliced
2 tablespoons fresh **lemon juice**

Add and toss well again:

4 cups sliced zucchini (about 1 pound), unpeeled
¼ cup chopped fresh parsley
1 to 2 tablespoons fresh basil, chopped, or 1 teaspoon dry
1 teaspoon **salt** (*LS* and *P:* omit; use 1 teaspoon **apple juice concentrate**)
Pepper to taste

Cover and cook over medium-high heat until vegetables are crisp tender, about 3 to 5 minutes, shaking pan frequently.

(389)

Okra and Tomatoes

6 to 8 servings *LC, LCh, V, v, Ml, k*

Steam until fork-tender:

1½ pounds okra, ends trimmed

Spread to cool in a single layer. Heat in a **non-stick** saucepan:

1 tablespoon **oil**

Sauté in saucepan for 5 minutes:

¼ cup chopped shallots or scallions

Add and stir in:

1 cup crushed tomatoes in juice
1 garlic clove, crushed
¼ cup red **wine** vinegar
Salt to taste
Pepper to taste

Simmer 15 minutes, then stir in:

2 tablespoons chopped sweet gherkins
¼ cup small capers or chopped large capers

Cool sauce. Spoon over okra. Serve at room temperature.

(390)

Sweet and Sour Onions

8 servings *LC, LCh, D*, LS, V, v, P, Ml, k*

Combine in saucepan:

1 pound pearl onions, peeled
½ cup **wine** vinegar (*D:* use white vinegar)
½ cup sherry **wine** (*D:* use ½ cup **apple juice;** *P:* use ¼ cup dry white **wine** plus ¼ cup **apple juice**)
2 tablespoons **apple juice concentrate**

Cover and simmer over low heat for 25 to 30 minutes or until onions are tender. Sprinkle with:

2 tablespoons brown **sugar** (*P* and *D:* use additional **apple juice concentrate**)
1 tablespoon **apple juice concentrate**

Continue cooking onions, uncovered, for several minutes, or until onions are nicely glazed and liquid is reduced. Serve warm, cold, or at room temperature.

* Except those on diets limited in simple carbohydrates, such as fruit.

(391)

Peas a la Française

8 servings *LC, LCh, D, LS, V, v, P, Ml, k*

Melt in heavy **non-stick** skillet:

1 tablespoon **butter** or **margarine** (*P:* omit)

Stir in:

4 cups shelled new peas or frozen new peas (*LS:* use fresh peas)
1 head iceberg lettuce, quartered
24 small white onions, peeled and blanched in salted (*LS:* use vinegar to taste) water for 5 minutes, or small frozen onions, defrosted
4 sprigs parsley
1 bay leaf
1 teaspoon fresh or ¼ teaspoon dried thyme
1 teaspoon **sugar** or **apple juice concentrate** (*D* and *P:* use **apple juice concentrate**)
1 teaspoon **salt** or to taste (*LS* and *P:* omit)
½ cup water or **stock**

Simmer, tightly covered, for 15 to 20 minutes, or until tender. Remove bay leaf. With slotted vegetable spoon, transfer peas and onions onto serving platter. Cut the lettuce into strips and add to peas. Heat remaining juices in skillet until reduced and thickened slightly. Stir into sauce:

1 tablespoon **butter** or **margarine,** cut into pieces (*P:* omit)
Salt to taste (*LS* and *P:* omit)
Pepper to taste

Pour sauce over vegetables and serve warm.

(392)

Ratatouille

8 servings *LC, LCh, D, LS, V, v, P, Ml, k*

Heat in large **non-stick** skillet:
1 to 2 tablespoons **oil** (*P:* omit)
Sauté in skillet until lightly browned:
3 cups diced eggplant, peeled
3 cups unpeeled ½-inch slices of zucchini
Remove from pan with slotted spoon. Add to skillet and **sauté** until soft:
3 cups thinly sliced onions
1½ cups julienned green peppers
1 tablespoon minced garlic
Add to skillet:
2 cups peeled, seeded, and diced fresh tomatoes
Cover skillet and cook over medium low heat for 5 minutes. Uncover and cook at higher heat for 3 to 4 minutes or until juices have almost entirely evaporated. Add eggplant and zucchini and toss well. Add:
4 tablespoons tomato paste (*LS:* use unsalted tomato paste)
1 tablespoon **apple juice concentrate**
Salt to taste (*P* and *LS:* use **wine** vinegar to taste)
Pepper to taste (*P:* use white **pepper**)
Simmer over low heat for 10 minutes covered. Then uncover and continue to cook for an additional 10 minutes, or until most of liquid is evaporated. Serve hot or cold.

(393)

Creamed Spinach

4 servings *LC, LCh, D, v, k, B*

In **non-stick** skillet, heat:
1 tablespoon **margarine**
Sauté in margarine until golden:
¾ cup finely chopped shallots or scallions

Sprinkle with:

1 tablespoon **flour**

Blend well, stirring constantly for 2 to 3 minutes. Add gradually, continuing to stir:

¾ cup evaporated skimmed **milk** (*LC:* use skim **milk;** *LS* and *B:* if **milk** is limited, use ¼ cup evaporated skimmed **milk** plus ½ cup **stock**)

Continue to cook over medium heat, stirring constantly until thickened and smooth. Add and stir to blend well:

1 10-ounce package frozen chopped spinach, cooked and drained

Season as desired with:

1 teaspoon **apple juice concentrate** or **sugar** (*D:* use concentrate)
Salt (*LS:* omit)
Pepper (*B:* omit)
Paprika or nutmeg (*B*: use paprika)

Continue cooking over low heat, stirring occasionally, for 10 minutes.

(394) *CREAMED BROCCOLI*

4 servings *LC, LCh, D, LS*, v, k, B†*

In CREAMED SPINACH **(393)** recipe, substitute finely chopped broccoli for spinach.

* Except those limited to low-sodium milk.
† Except low-residue diets.

(395)
Tsimmes

12 servings *LC, LCh, D*, LS, V, v, P, Ml, k, B*

In a large **non-stick** pot, heat (*B:* omit this step)

1 tablespoon **oil** (*P:* omit)

Sauté in pot until nicely browned (*B:* omit this step)

2 medium onions, sliced

Add, stirring to mix ingredients:

4 cups sliced carrots (*LS:* reduce to 2 cups, or, if prohibited, omit)

(*Recipe continued on next page*)

2 medium yams or sweet potatoes, cut into 1-inch cubes (*LS:* increase to 3 or 4)
2 medium potatoes, cut into 1-inch cubes (*LS:* increase to 3 or 4)
1½ cups **apple juice**
¼ cup **apple juice concentrate,** or to taste
16 prunes, pitted and quartered (*D:* omit)

Bring mixture to a simmer and cook over low heat for 1 hour or more or until all ingredients are soft and well blended. Stir occasionally, and add more **apple juice** if mixture seems dry.

(396)

Carrot Tsimmes

12 servings *LC, LCh, D,* V, v, P, Ml, k, B*

Tip: This recipe is lower in calories than TSIMMES with potatoes.

In recipe for TSIMMES **(395),** substitute for potatoes and sweet potatoes:

4 additional cups carrots

* For those who must limit their intake of simple carbohydrates, such as fruit, omit the **apple juice concentrate** and add additional water as needed. The resulting dish will be less sweet, but still tasty.

(397)

Steamed Vegetables

All diets, depending on vegetables used

Vegetables are steamed over—not in—boiling water. An adjustable steamer basket works well and fits into pots of almost any size. Because steaming can discolor green vegetables and intensify the tastes of strong flavored ones, it's best to keep cooking time at the minimum. Cutting vegetables into small pieces (cubes or julienne) will help keep cooking time down. To steam, fill saucepan with 1 to 2 inches of water. Put steamer in place. Add vegetables. Cover and bring to boil over medium heat, steaming until just tender. (*B:* cook until very tender) Vegetables are done when they can be pierced with a sharp knife.

VARIATION: Season with any of the following before beginning steaming:

Salt, white or black **pepper**
Lemon juice, salt, white **pepper**
Lemon juice, white **pepper**
Sliced onions
Garlic powder
Fresh or dried herbs (dill, parsley, tarragon, basil, thyme, etc.)
Ginger
Nutmeg

(398)

Stir-Fried or Pan-Fried Vegetables

All diets, depending on vegetables used

First prepare vegetables. They should be cut in small pieces of the same size to allow for faster and more even cooking. Long-cooking vegetables such as carrots or turnips are best parcooked by steaming or blanching or in the microwave oven. Vegetables requiring similar cooking times can be stir fried together.

Next, heat in a **non-stick** skillet (which allows you to use a minimum of oil or none at all):

½ to 1 tablespoon **oil,** or enough to thinly coat bottom of pan

For Pritikin or other low-fat diets, you can substitute:

Stock and/or white **wine**

Add vegetables and cook rapidly over moderate heat, stirring or shaking pan constantly.

Vegetables may be seasoned with any of the following permitted on the diet you are cooking for:

Salt and/or **pepper**
Unpeeled, mashed garlic clove browned in **oil** before vegetables are added
Chopped onions, scallions, or shallots
Mashed garlic and chopped parsley
Lemon juice
Herbs or spices
Toasted nuts
Soy sauce

(399) *STIR-FRIED KALE AND JULIENNED CARROTS*

LC, LCh, D, V, v, P, Ml, k

Stir fry kale and carrots separately, then toss together

(400) *STIR-FRIED BROCCOLI*

LC, LCh, D, LS, V, v, P, Ml, k

Stir fry broccoli broken into small florets and diced stems separately.

Barbecues

(401)

Lean Beef Patties with Sautéed Mushrooms

2 to 4 servings *Ml, B*

Combine in bowl and blend well:
- 1 pound ground lean beef
- ½ cup soft **bread** crumbs
- **Salt** to taste
- 1 **egg**

Form mixture into 4 patties. Broil or grill but do not allow to become crusty. Meanwhile, heat in **non-stick** skillet:
- 1 tablespoon **margarine**

Sauté in skillet until very soft:
- 2 cups sliced fresh mushrooms

Season with:
- **Salt** to taste

Serve patties with sliced mushrooms and:
- White burger buns (see **bread**)

(402)

Chicken Breasts in Foil with Nectarines

2 to 4 servings *LC, LCh, D*, P, Ml*

Remove skin from:
4 single chicken breasts
Combine in a small bowl:
½ cup **apple juice concentrate**
¼ cup dry white **wine** (*D:* if prohibited, use 1 tablespoon **lemon juice**)
1 teaspoon finely minced garlic
1 tablespoon **orange juice concentrate**
1 teaspoon **soy sauce**
Dash white **pepper**
½ teaspoon dried sage
Peel, pit and halve:
4 ripe nectarines
Marinate chicken for 1 hour or more with nectarines in above mixture. Then, arrange breasts, each on a 12 x 15-inch sheet of heavy aluminum foil. Brush each breast with the marinade. Top each with 2 nectarines. Brush additional marinade on nectarines, using up all the marinade. Wrap breasts, sealing by crimping edges of foil. Bake in hot coals for 10 minutes, or until tender. Do not overcook.

* Except those who are on diets limited in simple carbohydrates, such as fruit.

(403)

Grilled Garlic Chicken

4 servings *LC, LCh, D, LS, P, Ml*

Remove the skin from:
 5 large single chicken breasts
Place breasts between layers of wax paper and flatten with side of cleaver.
Brush with:
 Lemon juice
Rub with cut side of half of:
 Garlic clove
Combine and blend well:
 ½ cup **flour**
 ½ teaspoon garlic powder
 ½ teaspoon paprika
 ½ teaspoon **salt** (*LS* and *P:* omit)
 ¼ teaspoon **pepper** (*P:* use white)
Brush breasts with:
 1 tablespoon **oil** (*P:* omit)
Dip into:
 1 slightly beaten **egg** white (*LS:* omit)
Then coat well with flour mixture. Place on a greased grill 6 to 12 inches above the hot coals and grill for about 10 minutes on each side, or broil in broiler.

(404)

Chicken Sate

4 servings *LCh, D, Ml*

Combine in blender and process until smooth:
 1 cup finely chopped onion
 3 garlic cloves, chopped
 ¼ cup **soy sauce**
 5 tablespoons **lemon juice**
 2 tablespoons natural unsalted peanut butter

(*Recipe continued on next page*)

¼ teaspoon chili powder or hot pepper sauce
¼ teaspoon turmeric
3 tablespoons **apple juice concentrate** or brown **sugar** (*D:* use **apple juice**)
1 tablespoon **oil** (Opt.)
2 teaspoons grated fresh ginger or ¼ teaspoon ground dried
Peel of 1 lemon, thinly sliced
2 tablespoons water

Marinate in this mixture at room temperature for 1 to 2 hours, basting and turning occasionally:

2 pounds chicken breasts, skinned, boned, and cubed

String chicken on skewers. Grill over hot coals until brown but not dry, about 3 to 4 minutes. Do not overcook.

VARIATION: Alternate chicken with fresh pineapple cubes, marinated in same sate sauce.

(405)

Hawaiian Chicken Kabobs

4 to 6 main course or 12 appetizer servings — *LC, LCh, D*, LS, P, Ml*

Combine in large glass bowl:

3 whole skinless and boneless large chicken breasts, cut into bite-sized pieces
1 20-ounce can **unsweetened** pineapple chunks, with juice, or 2 cups fresh pineapple chunks plus ½ cup **unsweetened** pineapple juice.
2 large nectarines, unpeeled and cut into wedges (or 2 tangerines, peeled, seeded, and segmented)
1 large green pepper, cut into large chunks
1 large red pepper, cut into large chunks
4 scallions, thinly sliced
1 large onion, chopped
¼ cup chopped shallots
¼ cup **pineapple juice concentrate**
¼ cup **orange juice concentrate**
¼ cup **apple juice concentrate**
¼ cup sherry **wine** (*D* and *P:* omit)
2 tablespoons grated fresh ginger root

2 tablespoons red **wine** vinegar
1 tablespoon garlic powder
1 to 2 tablespoons **oil** (Opt.; *P:* omit)
1 tablespoon **lemon juice** (*LS* and *P:* increase if desired)
1 teaspoon white **pepper**
Salt to taste (*LS* and *P:* omit)

Marinate, refrigerated, for 6 to 12 hours, turning and basting occasionally. Arrange chicken, pineapple, nectarines, and peppers on skewers. Preheat broiler or grill. Grill kabobs for 3 to 5 minutes. Turn and grill 3 to 5 minutes more, basting with the marinade. When done (meat has turned white inside), serve immediately. Do not overcook.

* Except those who must limit their intake of simple carbohydrates, such as fruit.

(406)

Grilled Fish Steaks

4 servings *LC, LCh, D, LS, Ml, k, B*

Wash and pat dry:
4 ¾-inch thick salmon steaks or other fish steaks

Place steaks in a glass baking dish just large enough to hold them. Sprinkle with:
2 tablespoons **lemon juice**
2 tablespoons finely minced dill
2 tablespoons finely minced garlic (*B:* omit)

Turn once or twice during marinating.

When ready to grill the fish, melt:
2 tablespoons **butter** or **margarine**

Blend with:
2 tablespoons **lemon juice**

Spread lemon-butter mixture on salmon steaks. Cook on a well-greased or **non-stick** grill over moderately hot coals for 4 minutes on each side. Sprinkle, if desired, with:
Salt (*LS:* omit)
Pepper (*B:* omit)

Or brush with:
ANCHOVY BUTTER (**427**) (*LS* and *B:* omit)

(407)

Herbed Fish Flambé

4 servings *LC, LCh, D, LS, P, Ml, k*

Wash and pat dry:
4 whole, firm-fleshed permitted fish
If keeping head and tail on, cover with foil. Make 3 slashes on each side of each fish. Brush fish with:
Oil (*P:* omit)
Sprinkle with:
Salt (*LS* and *P*: use **lemon juice**)
Pepper (*P:* use white)
Lay a few sprigs of any of below herbs across each side of fish:
Fennel
Basil
Tarragon
Thyme
Dill
Or sprinkle with dried herb. Fasten in a greased wire-hinged rack and grill for 4 minutes on each side, sprinkling once again on each side during grilling with:
Oil (*P:* omit)
Arrange cooked fish on flameproof platter. Sprinkle with:
¼ cup brandy (see **wine**; *D* and *P:* omit)
Flame. Serve with, passing separately:
Lemon wedges
SOYO REMOULADE **(270)** *or*
Tartar Sauce *or*
GARLIC SOYO-NAISE **(267)**

(408)

Grilled Fish Teriyaki

4 servings *LC, LCh, Ml, K, k*

In 9 x 12 x 2-inch glass baking dish, combine:
- ½ cup **soy sauce**
- ⅓ cup **pineapple juice concentrate**
- 2 tablespoons **oil**
- 3 garlic cloves, mashed
- 1 tablespoon shredded ginger root (or ¼ teaspoon ground ginger)
- 1 tablespoon brown **sugar**
- ¼ cup sherry or medium dry white **wine**

Marinate in this mixture for 1 hour or longer in refrigerator:
- 4 halibut, salmon, or swordfish steaks

Have barbecue fire ready about 10 minutes before serving fish. Or preheated broiler. Grill fish on non-stick sprayed grill for 4 to 6 minutes on each side, time depending on thickness of steaks. Do not overcook. Brush with marinade frequently during grilling.

(409)

Grilled Stuffed Trout or Baby Salmon

4 servings *LCh, LS, Ml, k*

Wash and pat dry:
- 4 8 to 10-ounce whole baby salmon or trout

Heat in **non-stick** skillet:
- 1 tablespoon **oil** *or* **butter** *or* **margarine**

In skillet, **sauté** until golden:
- ½ cup finely chopped shallots, scallions, or onions
- ½ teaspoon finely minced garlic

Add and **sauté** just until softened:
- 1 cup sliced fresh mushrooms

Stir in to blend:
- ½ cup cooked rice (*LS:* cooked without salt)
- ⅛ teaspoon thyme

(***Recipe continued on next page***)

½ cup chopped spinach, well drained (*LS:* if prohibited, use chopped broccoli)
Pinch sage
2 tablespoons pine nuts
1 tablespoon fresh grated lemon peel
Salt to taste (*LS:* omit)
Pepper to taste

Fill fish with stuffing mixture. Brush skin with:

Oil
Lemon juice
Salt and **pepper** (*LS:* omit salt)

Grill on well-greased wire-hinged rack over hot coals about 5 minutes on each side, until skin is browned and fish flakes easily.

(410)

Grilled Tofu Teriyaki

4 servings *LC, LCh, V, v, Ml, k*

Combine in bowl:

¼ cup **soy sauce**
3 tablespoons **pineapple juice concentrate**
1 tablespoon **oil**
1 garlic clove, mashed
1 teaspoon shredded ginger root (or ¼ teaspoon dried, ground ginger)
1 teaspoon brown **sugar**
2 tablespoons sherry or medium dry white **wine**

Cut into ½-inch slices:

1 pound firm tofu

Marinate slices in teriyaki marinade for 1 hour or longer. Grill over hot coals or in broiler until browned on each side, basting with marinade during grilling. To serve, drizzle with additional marinade, and sprinkle with:

Sesame seeds

(411)

Grilled Herbed Eggplant

8 to 10 servings ***LC, LCh, D, V, v, Ml, k***

Salt and place in a colander to drain for 30 minutes:

2 pounds (about 3 medium) eggplants, cut into ¼-inch slices

Rinse and pat dry. Meanwhile combine:

2 tablespoons **oil**
2 tablespoons **stock**
2 tablespoons fresh oregano or 2 teaspoons dry
2 tablespoons coarsely chopped fresh mint or basil, or 2 teaspoons dry
¼ teaspoon **pepper**

Brush one side of each eggplant slice with herbed mixture. Grill herbed side down over hot coals (or broil herbed side up). While grilling, baste with mixture. When first side is browned, turn and brown second. Keep warm while preparing additional slices. If desired, pass separately:

Grated **cheese** (*V* and *Ml:* omit)

(412)

Grilled Curried Eggplant

8 to 10 servings ***LC, LCh, D, LS, V, v, Ml, k***

Follow directions for salting and draining of eggplant in GRILLED HERBED EGGPLANT (**411**). Brush eggplant with mixture of:

2 tablespoons **oil**
1 tablespoon **wine** vinegar
1 teaspoon curry powder, or to taste
1 tablespoon **apple juice concentrate**
¼ teaspoon onion powder
⅛ teaspoon ground ginger
⅛ teaspoon white **pepper**
¼ teaspoon **salt** (*LS:* omit)

Let marinate for ½ hour or more. Brown over hot coals on both sides, basting as you do. Or, if desired, broil. Serve with:

Chutney (except *D*)

(413)

Veggieburgers

5 to 6 servings *LC, LCh, D, LS, v, P, Ml, k*

Combine and blend well:

1 cup chopped cooked or canned chick peas (*LS:* use unsalted chick peas)
1 cup chopped, parcooked green beans
½ cup finely chopped onion
2 cups **bread** crumbs
½ cup chopped nuts (*P:* use chopped boiled chestnuts, or additional chick peas)
½ cup wheat germ (*P:* use **oats** or **bran**)
3 large **egg** whites (*LS:* use 2 whites and 2 tablespoons **stock** or water)
½ teaspoon thyme
½ teaspoon rosemary, minced
½ teaspoon garlic powder
Salt to taste (*LS:* use 1 teaspoon **lemon juice; *P:*** use ½ teaspoon **soy sauce**)
Pepper to taste (*P:* use white)

Chill mixture for 1 hour or more. When ready to cook, form mixture into patties. Coat patties with:

Flour

Grill on barbecue, broil in oven, or pan fry in **non-stick** pan. Serve as burgers.

(414)

Vegetable Sate

LC, LCh, D, V, v, Ml, k

Prepare:

Marinade for CHICKEN SATE (**404**)

Marinate any or all of the following vegetables in the mixture for 1 to 2 hours:

Mushrooms, whole
Eggplant cubes, presalted, drained, and dried

Zucchini cubes
Apples chunks
Green peppers squares
Red peppers squares
Artichoke hearts, canned or frozen and defrosted
Cherry tomatoes
Cucumber chunks

Skewer combinations of vegetables and grill over coals for 3 to 5 minutes, basting with some of marinade while cooking. Serve, if desired, with additional marinade as dip.

(415)

Coal-Roasted and Foil-Grilled Vegetables

All diets, depending on vegetables used

To roast vegetables—or even fruits—in the coals, first wrap tightly in a double layer of heavy-duty foil. Place them in or around the white coals, turning 2 to 3 times during cooking. Test for doneness by piercing foil with a long fork. Vegetables may also be cooked in foil packets on the grill, following the same directions, but placing on grill above the coals. If blackened hard crust on potatoes is desired, cook in coals, unwrapped. Good candidates for coal roasting include:

Whole potatoes
Whole onions
Whole eggplant
Husked corn
Whole zucchini

For top-of-grill cooking, try:

Sliced zucchini
Sliced potatoes
Sliced onions
Sliced carrots
Sliced green peppers
Whole mushrooms

Season before wrapping with any of the following permitted:

Margarine or **butter** *or* **oil** *or* **stock**
Lemon juice
Salt
Pepper

Sauces and Garnishes

(416)

Avocado Sauce

About 1½ cups *LC, D, v, k, B**

Puree in blender or food processor:

1 medium avocado, peeled and pitted
½ cup sour cream
½ cup low-fat **cottage cheese**
½ teaspoon **lemon juice**
½ teaspoon **salt,** or to taste
Water to desired consistency

* Except fat-restricted, milk-restricted, or low-residue diets.

(417)

Broccoli Sauce

About 3 cups *LC, LCh, D, LS*, v, P, k*

In **non-stick** skillet, **sauté** until soft:

½ teaspoon minced garlic
¼ cup chopped onion
¼ cup chopped parsley, loosely packed

Cook over low heat 10 minutes:

1 10-ounce package frozen chopped broccoli
½ cup skim **milk**
¼ teaspoon dried dill or tarragon (Opt.)

Puree broccoli and onion mixture in blender or food processor with:

8 ounces potato, boiled and peeled
½ cup evaporated skimmed **milk**

Season, as desired, with:

Salt to taste (*LS* and *P:* omit)
Pepper to taste (*P:* use white)

* Except for those restricted to low-sodium milk.

(418)

Champagne Sauce

About 4 cups *LC, LCh, LS, V, v, Ml, k*

In **non-stick** skillet, melt:

2 tablespoon **margarine**

Blend into margarine to make a roux:

4 tablespoons **flour**

Stir over low heat for 3 minutes. Slowly add, stirring constantly:

2 cups **stock**
1 cup **apple juice**
1 cup champagne or dry white **wine**

Stirring steadily, simmer over low heat until thick and smooth.

(419)

Cheese Sauce

About 1½ cups *LCh, D, v, k, B**

In small saucepan, melt over low heat:

1 tablespoon unsalted **margarine**

Add and blend well to make smooth paste, stirring over low heat for 2 to 3 minutes:

1 tablespoon **flour**

Add gradually, stirring constantly:

1 cup skimmed **milk**

½ cup evaporated skimmed **milk**

Continue to cook over low heat, stirring constantly, until sauce is thickened and smooth. Add and stir until melted:

1 cup grated **cheese** (*LCh* and *D:* use low-fat, low-cholesterol melting **cheese;** *B:* use mild American)

Season as desired with:

Salt to taste

Nutmeg or paprika (*B:* use paprika)

White **pepper** (*B:* omit)

* Except low-residue diets or diets limited in milk products.

(420)

Cumberland Sauce

About 2 cups *LC, LCh, D, LS, V, v, P, Ml, k*

Combine in small saucepan:

1 tablespoon brown **sugar** or **apple juice concentrate** (*D* and *P:* use **juice concentrate**)

1 teaspoon dry mustard

¼ teaspoon ground ginger

Dash cayenne

1 cup Port or other medium sweet red **wine** (*P* and *D:* use **orange juice**)

Simmer, covered, for 10 minutes.
Combine and stir until smooth:
- 2 teaspoons cornstarch
- 2 tablespoons cold water

Stir cornstarch mixture into sauce and simmer for 2 minutes more, stirring constantly. Stir in:
- ¼ cup red currant jelly (*D:* use dietetic, artificially sweetened apple jelly; *P:* use ¼ cup **apple juice concentrate**)
- 2 teaspoons fresh grated orange rind
- 1 teaspoon fresh grated lemon rind
- ⅔ cup **orange juice**
- 2 tablespoons **lemon juice**
- ¼ cup currants (*D:* omit)

Serve over lamb or other meats or poultry or over vegetarian alternative.

VARIATION: Combine in saucepan and simmer for 5 minutes:
- 1 tablespoon brown **sugar**
- 1 cup **orange juice**

Combine and stir until smooth:
- 2 teaspoons cornstarch
- 2 tablespoons cold water

Stir cornstarch mixture into sauce, stirring over low heat until thickened. Stir in:
- ¼ cup red currant jelly
- ⅔ cup **orange juice**
- 2 tablespoons **lemon juice**

Serve as for CUMBERLAND SAUCE (**420**)

(421)

Dill Sauce

About 1 cup *LC, D, LS*, v, k*

Puree in blender or food processor:
- 2 tablespoons sour cream
- 6 tablespoons low-fat **cottage cheese**

Add, continue to process:
- ½ cup sliced scallions
- 1 cup fresh dill, loosely packed, or 2 teaspoons dried

(*Recipe continued on next page*)

2 teaspoons Dijon-style mustard (*LS:* use unsalted prepared or dry to taste)
Coarse **salt** to taste (*LS:* omit, use **lemon juice** to taste)

Chill before serving.

* Except for those restricted to low-sodium milk.

(422)

Orange Dill Sauce

About 1¾ cups *LC, LCh, D*, LS, v, P, k*

Puree in blender or food processor:

1 cup low-fat **yogurt**
¼ cup **orange juice concentrate**
¼ cup fresh dill, loosely packed, or 1 teaspoon dried
4 tablespoons sliced scallions
2 tablespoons low-fat **cottage cheese** (*LS:* use **hoop** or unsalted **cottage cheese**)
2 teaspoons **apple juice concentrate**
1 teaspoon fresh grated orange rind
1 teaspoon dry mustard

Chill well.

* For those on diets limited in simple carbohydrates, use DILL SAUCE (**421**) instead.

(423)

Easy Hollandaise

⅔ cup *v, Ml, k, B*

In mixing bowl whip with a fork until thoroughly blended and pale yellow:

2 **eggs**
2 tablespoons water
3 teaspoons **lemon juice**

Melt over low heat in heavy **non-stick** skillet:

4 tablespoons unsalted **margarine**

Add egg mixture slowly, stirring constantly until sauce is thickened. Do not overcook. Before serving, season with:

Salt to taste
Cayenne to taste (Opt.; *B:* omit)

(424)

Mushroom Sauce

About 2 cups *LC, LCh, D, LS, V, v, Ml, k, B*

In **non-stick** skillet, melt over medium heat:

1 tablespoon **margarine**

Add and **sauté** over reduced heat:

2 cups sliced mushrooms

When mushrooms are just softened (*B:* very soft) sprinkle with:

2 tablespoons **flour**

Blend flour in well over low heat, stirring constantly for 2 minutes. Gradually add, blending in well:

1 cup vegetable **stock**

Continue to cook over medium high heat, stirring constantly, until sauce is thickened. Season to taste with:

Salt (*LS:* omit, adding **lemon juice** to taste)
Pepper (*B:* omit)

(425)

Tomato Sauce

About 4 cups *LC, LCh, D, LS, V, v, P, Ml, k*

Combine in large saucepan:

1 16-ounce can crushed tomatoes, plus 1 can water (*LS:* use fresh or unsalted canned)
2 tablespoons tomato paste (*LS:* use unsalted paste)
1 medium onion, sliced thinly, and separated into rings
1 medium green pepper, chopped

(*Recipe continued on next page*)

1⅓ tablespoons **apple juice concentrate**
2 teaspoons oregano
2 teaspoons basil
1 large garlic clove, pierced with a toothpick
1 teaspoon dried parsley or 2 tablespoons fresh

Simmer over low heat for 1 hour, stirring occasionally. Season with:

Salt to taste (*LS* and *P:* omit)
Pepper to taste (*P:* omit)

Remove garlic clove.

(426)

Sauce Verte

About 3 cups | *LC, LCh, D, v, k*

Prepare:

1 recipe CREAMED SPINACH (**393**)

Transfer to blender or food processor and puree with:

1 cup low-fat **cottage cheese**
1 cup parsley leaves, loosely packed
1 cup watercress leaves, loosely packed
2 tablespoons sliced scallions, white part only
2 tablespoons **mayonnaise** (*LCh:* use yolkless **mayonnaise** *or* SOYO-NAISE (**264**))
2 teaspoons Dijon-style mustard
1 teaspoon **lemon juice** or to taste
1 teaspoon capers, rinsed and drained, *or*
1 teaspoon anchovy paste (*v:* use capers)
1 teaspoon chervil

Taste and season if necessary with:

Salt
Pepper

Serve warm, at room temperature, or cold.

(427)

Anchovy Butter

About ⅓ cup *LCh, D, Ml, K, k*

Combine and blend until smooth:

¼ cup softened **butter** or **margarine**
2 teaspoons anchovy paste
1 teaspoon **lemon juice**

Use as a spread on crackers or for grilling fish or chicken.

(428)

Fruited Yogurt

About 1 cup *LC, LCh, LS*, D, v, P, K, k*

Combine and stir well:

¾ cup **yogurt**
¼ teaspoon fresh grated orange rind
½ teaspoon fresh grated lime rind
¼ teaspoon fresh lemon rind
1 tablespoon **orange juice concentrate**
1 tablespoon **pineapple juice concentrate**
1½ teaspoons **apple juice concentrate**
½ teaspoon cinnamon or to taste

* Except for those limited to low-sodium milk.

(429)

Lime Sauce

About 1½ cups *LC, LCh, LS, V, v, P, Ml, k, B*

Combine in small saucepan:

1 cup water
⅓ cup **apple juice concentrate** or to taste
6 tablespoons lime juice
2 teaspoons fresh grated lime rind (*B:* omit)
1 tablespoon cornstarch

Cook and stir over medium heat until sauce comes to a boil and is smooth and thickened.

(430)

Berry Sauce

About 3 cups *LC, LCh, D*, LS, V, v, P, Ml, k*

Combine in a saucepan and bring to a boil:

2 cups berries (blueberries, strawberries, raspberries, etc.)
½ cup **apple juice**
¼ cup **apple juice concentrate**
2 teaspoons **lemon juice**
2 teaspoons fresh grated lemon rind
1 teaspoon vanilla extract

Simmer for 3 minutes or until berries are slightly cooked. In bowl, combine and blend until smooth:

1 tablespoon water
1 tablespoon cornstarch

Add cornstarch mixture to berry sauce, stirring over low heat until thickened. Remove from heat. Serve warm or cold.

* For those limited in simple carbohydrates, use only ¼ cup of sauce over a food that contains little or no simple carbohydrates.

(431)

Berry Filling or Topping

About 2½ cups *LC, LCh, D*, LS, V, v, P, Ml, k*

Combine in saucepan and bring to a boil:
- 2 cups berries (blueberries, strawberries, raspberries, etc.)
- ¼ cup **apple juice concentrate**
- 1½ teaspoons **lemon juice**
- 1 teaspoon fresh grated lemon rind
- ¾ teaspoon vanilla extract

Simmer for 1 minute. In bowl, combine and blend until smooth:
- 1 tablespoon water
- 1 tablespoon cornstarch

Add cornstarch mixture to berries, stirring over low heat until thickened.

* Use as a garnish only for those on diets limited in simple carbohydrates, such as fruit.

(432)

Glazed Apple Rings

10 to 12 rings *LC, LCh, D*, LS, P, V, v, Ml, k, B*

Wash, core, and cut into rings (*B:* peel):
- 2 large cooking apples

Heat in **non-stick** skillet over medium flame:
- 1 tablespoon **margarine** (*P:* omit)

Place rings in skillet and sprinkle with:
- 2 tablespoons brown **sugar** plus
- 2 tablespoons **apple juice concentrate** *or*
- ¼ cup **apple juice concentrate** (*P* and *D:* omit **sugar,** use all juice concentrate)

Cover and simmer apples until tender. Uncover and, stirring frequently, allow apples to glaze.

* Use as a garnish only for those on diets limited in simple carbohydrates, such as fruit.

(433)

Glazed Chestnuts

Servings vary *LC, LCh, D*, LS, P, V, v, Ml, k*

Score and boil until tender:

½ pound chestnuts

When cool enough to handle, peel and remove skin. Heat in **non-stick** skillet over medium flame:

1 tablespoon **margarine** (*P:* omit)

Place chestnuts in skillet and sprinkle with:

2 tablespoons brown **sugar** plus 2 tablespoons **apple juice concentrate**

or

¼ cup **apple juice concentrate** (*D* and *P:* omit **sugar,** use all juice concentrate)

* Use as garnish only for those on diets limited in simple carbohydrates, such as fruit.

Desserts

(434)

Airy Apple Parfait

6 to 8 servings *LC, LCh, D, LS, v, P, Ml, k*

Tip: This dessert has about 1½ (*D*) sweetness allowances per serving and should be omitted for those limited to less.

Combine in small saucepan and simmer for 5 minutes:
- ½ cup **apple juice**
- ½ cup white raisins (*D* and *B:* omit; *B:* use 1 cup shredded apple)

Drain; reserve juice and raisins. In small bowl, combine:
- 2 envelopes unflavored **gelatin**
- ¼ cup **apple juice**

Let stand 1 minute to soften. Meanwhile, heat to boiling reserved juice, plus:
- **Apple juice** to make 1 cup

(*Recipe continued on next page*)

Add gelatin mixture to hot juice and stir until dissolved. Stir in:

2¼ cups **apple juice**

1 tablespoon **lemon juice**

Chill gelatin mixture until it begins to thicken. Do not allow to set. Stir into thickened mixture the raisins, plus:

1 cup shredded apples (*B:* omit)

Whip until stiff:

2 **egg** whites

¼ teaspoon cream of tartar

Fold egg whites into gelatin mixture until all whites are gone. Spoon into individual parfait glasses. Chill. Serve sprinkled with:

Sliced almonds (*P:* use Grape Nuts; *B:* omit)

(435)

Apple-Banana Mold

6 to 8 servings *LC, LCh, D*, LS, V, v, P, Ml, k, B†*

Chill 6-cup mold in the freezer.

Combine in small bowl:

2 envelopes unflavored **gelatin**

½ cup **apple juice concentrate**

Blend to smoothness and let stand 1 minute to soften. In small saucepan, bring to a boil:

1½ cups **apple juice**

Stir gelatin into hot juice. Add, stirring well:

1½ cups **unsweetened** apple sauce

3 tablespoons **lemon** or **lime juice,** or to taste

¼ cup **apple juice**

Turn into chilled mold, rinsed in cold water and dried, and chill until slightly thickened. Stir in:

1 large ripe banana, sliced

Chill until set.

* Except those on diets limited in simple carbohydrates such as fruits. This dessert is equal to about 2 sweetness allowances per serving.

† Except low-residue dieters.

(436)

Apple-Peach Mold

6 to 8 servings *LC, LCh, D, LS, V, v, P, Ml, k, B*

Follow recipe for APPLE-BANANA MOLD (**435**), substituting 1 16-ounce can sliced peaches, in **unsweetened** juice, drained, for banana.

(437)

Apricot-Banana Mold

12 to 14 servings *LC, LCh, D*, LS, V, v, P, ML, k, B†*

Chill in refrigerator or freezer an 8-cup mold.
Combine in bowl, blending until smooth:
 ½ cup **apple juice concentrate**
 1½ envelopes unflavored **gelatin**
Let stand for 1 minute while gelatin softens. Add:
 1 cup boiling water
Stir until gelatin is dissolved and add:
 3 tablespoons **lemon juice**
 ⅓ cup **apple juice concentrate**
 ¼ cup cold water
Chill until thickened but not set. Transfer to mixing bowl and beat together with:
 2 bananas, mashed (*B:* use cooked peaches for low-residue dieters)
Pour into chilled mold that has been dipped in cold water. Chill until set.
Meanwhile, drain, reserving liquid:
 2 16-ounce cans apricots in **unsweetened** juice.
Peel apricots; set aside.
Combine ½ cup of the reserved liquid with:
 2 envelopes unflavored **gelatin**
Let stand 1 minute until gelatin is softened.
Meanwhile, heat to boiling remaining liquid plus:
 Apple juice to make 1 cup

(*Recipe continued on next page*)

Stir hot juice into gelatin mixture until gelatin is dissolved. Add

1½ cups cold **apple juice**

2 tablespoons **lemon juice**

Chill until mixture begins to thicken.

When banana whip is set, arrange in ring half the apricots. Pour ½ the apricot gelatin mixture over apricots. Chill. When set, make another ring of apricots and add remaining gelatin mixture. Chill until firm. Unmold and garnish with additional:

Apricot halves

Banana slices dipped in lemon juice (*B:* use peaches for low-residue dieters)

* Except for those who must limit their intake of simple carbohydrates, such as fruit.

† Except low-residue dieters.

(438)

Apricot Mousse

12 servings *LC, LCh, D, LS, v, P, Ml, k, B*

Tip: Prepare 4 to 6 hours before serving

Chill 2-quart mold in freezer. Drain:

3 cans apricots in **unsweetened** fruit juice (*B:* peel apricots)

Set aside all the juice and the fruit of 1 can. Puree in blender the fruit of 2 cans, until smooth. To ¼ cup of the reserved juice, add and blend until smooth:

2 envelopes unflavored **gelatin**

Combine in small saucepan remaining juices to make 1¼ cups (if more is needed, add **apple juice**). Add:

¼ cup apricot cordial (see **wine;** *P, D,* and *B:* use 3 tablespoons **apple juice concentrate,** plus 1 teaspoon brandy extract)

Heat mixture to boiling. Stir in gelatin mixture, blending well, and then stir in apricot puree. Put mixture in freezer, checking frequently, until it is very lightly jelled or thickened. Do not allow it to become firm. When mixture is thickened remove from freezer. Beat until very stiff:

3 **egg** whites at room temperature

¾ teaspoon cream of tartar

1 tablespoon **sugar** (*P* and *D:* omit)

Then beat in gelatin mixture and fold in:

¼ cup finely sliced almonds (*P* and *B:* omit)

Pour into chilled mold dipped in cold water and dried, and chill for 4 hours, or until set. Unmold and serve garnished with:

Reserved fruit

(439)

Berry Pudding

8 servings *LC, LCh, D, LS, V, v, P, Ml, k*

Combine in large saucepan:

10 ounces fresh or frozen **unsweetened** raspberries or pitted cherries

10 ounces fresh or frozen **unsweetened** strawberries

½ cup **apple juice concentrate**

Cook over low heat, stirring occasionally, for 3 to 5 minutes, or until berries are just thawed if frozen, or just softened if fresh. Puree mixture in blender or food processor and pour through fine strainer to remove seeds, if desired. Return to saucepan. Combine in small bowl to make a smooth paste:

⅓ cup cornstarch or potato starch

¼ cup water

Add cornstarch mixture to pureed berries. Heat, stirring constantly, until mixture thickens and bubbles for 3 minutes. Remove from heat. Stir in:

1 tablespoon **lemon juice**

Pour into heatproof serving bowl. Tap bowl lightly to settle pudding. Cover with plastic wrap and refrigerate for 6 hours or overnight. Garnish if desired with:

Chopped or sliced almonds (*P:* use Grape Nuts)

Serve with:

LIME SAUCE (**429**) (*D:* omit for those who must limit intake of simple carbohydrates)

(440)

Fruit Pudding

8 servings *LC, LCh, D, LS, V, v, P, Ml, k, B*

Substitute for berries in BERRY PUDDING (**439**):

16 ounces fresh or frozen **unsweetened** peaches, peeled and sliced

1 banana, sliced (*B:* use 1 cup apple sauce or 1 cup shredded apple for those on low-residue diets)

Proceed as above. (*B:* omit nuts, Grape Nuts, and LIME SAUCE (**429**))

(441)

Cheesecake

1 10-inch cake *LC, LCh, D, LS*, v, P, k, B†*

Tip: 1/10 of cake is equal to 1 (*D*) sweetness allowance.

Prepare:

1 10-inch recipe for SHREDDIE CRUST (**523**) (*B:* omit, use plain white cookie crumb crust)

Press crust firmly into the bottom and sides of a 10-inch **non-stick** spring-form cake pan. Bake at 350° F for 5 minutes, or until crisp. Meanwhile, combine in blender, letting it stand 1 minute to soften:

½ cup cold **apple juice**

2½ envelopes unflavored **gelatin**

Bring to a boil:

1 cup skim **milk**

Add hot milk to softened gelatin, blending until gelatin is thoroughly dissolved. Add and blend in until smooth:

½ cup **apple juice concentrate**

¼ cup liqueur of choice (see **wine** *P* and *B:* use **apple juice concentrate;** *D:* omit)

2 teaspoons vanilla extract

2 tablespoons **fructose** (*P:* omit; *D:* omit and use **aspartame**)

Gradually add, processing or blending after each addition:

3 cups low-fat **pot cheese** or **hoop cheese** (*LS:* use **hoop** or unsalted **pot cheese**)

Pour mixture into a bowl and chill until slightly set. Do not allow to jell. Meanwhile, bring to room temperature:

2 **egg** whites

When gelatin is ready, beat egg whites until stiff with:

¼ teaspoon cream of tartar

1 tablespoon **fructose** (*P:* omit; *D:* omit and use **aspartame**)

Quickly add gelatin to egg whites, beating in. Do not overbeat. Pour mixture into reserved crust and chill until firm. If desired, top with:

BERRY TOPPING (**430**) (*D* and *B:* omit)

* LS: Except those limited to low-sodium *milk*, and those who must limit intake of milk products.
† B: Except those on limited milk diet.

(442) *FRUITED CHEESECAKE*

1 10-inch cake *LC, LCh, LS, v, P, k*

Add to CHEESECAKE (**441**) recipe before turning into crust:

1½ cups drained fruit, such as crushed canned **unsweetened** pineapple, sliced fresh or **unsweetened** frozen strawberries, whole blueberries

(443) *HAZELNUT CHEESECAKE*

1 10-inch cake *LCh, LS, D, v, k*

Add with pot cheese in CHEESECAKE (**441**) recipe:

½ cup ground hazelnuts

(444)
Farina-Banana Pudding

4 servings *LC, LCh, D*, LS, v, P, k, B*

In small saucepan, bring to a boil:

1 cup cold water

½ cup **apple juice concentrate**

½ cup **apple juice**

(*Recipe continued on next page*)

Stir in and cook until thickened:

½ cup farina

Cool. Stir in:

⅓ cup instant non-fat dry **milk** (*LS* and *B:* omit for milk-restricted dieters)

1 teaspoon vanilla or rum extract

½ teaspoon cinnamon

Set aside. In mixing bowl, beat until stiff:

2 **egg** whites

Beat into the **egg** whites:

2 bananas, mashed and sprinkled with **lemon juice**

Fold farina into egg whites. Mound in individual sherbert glasses and chill. If desired, pass separately:

Cream or evaporated skimmed **milk**

Whipped cream and/or ANGEL CREAM (**543**)

Sliced or chopped nuts (*B:* omit)

* Except for those who must limit intake of simple carbohydrates, such as fruit.

(445)

Filbert Meringues Hélène

8 servings *LCh, v, k*

In a large bowl, soften:

1 quart vanilla ice cream or ice milk (*LCh:* use ice milk)

Blend in:

¼ cup ground filberts (hazelnuts)

¼ cup rum or Amaretto (see **wine**)

Refreeze ice cream. Meanwhile, lightly flour baking sheet and mark 8 3½-inch circles in the flour. In the bowl of an electric mixer combine:

3 **egg** whites

½ teaspoon cream of tartar

Beat until frothy. Gradually, 1 tablespoon at a time, beat in:

¾ cup **sugar**

Continue beating until meringue is very stiff. Add:

½ teaspoon vanilla

½ teaspoon almond extract

Continue beating for 1 minute more. With a small metal spatula, spread a ½-inch thick layer of meringue within the marked circles.

Fill a pastry bag with the remaining meringue and, through a large decorative tip, pipe it around the edges of each circle to form a rim 1 inch high. Measure:

2⅔ tablespoons ground filberts

Sprinkle 1 teaspoon of filberts in center of each circle. Bake meringues in preheated oven at 225° F for 1 hour. Turn off oven and let meringues cool in oven for 3 to 4 hours. In the top of a double boiler, combine:

6 ounces of semisweet chocolate or carob, chopped (*LCh:* use carob)

½ cup heavy cream or evaporated skimmed **milk** (*LCh:* use evaporated skimmed milk)

Stir mixture until chocolate or carob is melted. Add:

1½ tablespoons rum, Amaretto, or brandy (same as used in ice cream)

If mixture is too thick, add additional liqueur. When ready to serve dessert, scoop the ice cream into the meringue shells. Top with sauce. Measure:

½ cup ground, lightly toasted filberts

Sprinkle over each meringue 1 tablespoon of filberts

(446)

Frittatine Zingarella

10 to 12 stuffed crepes *LCh, LS**, v, Ml, k*

Beat together until foamy:

1 **egg** white

1 whole **egg**

Stir in, 1 ingredient at a time:

½ cup **apple juice**

½ cup orange juice

½ cup water

1 tablespoon **sugar**

3 tablespoons cognac or brandy (see **wine**)

1½ cups **flour**

Blend until very smooth. Stir in:

1 to 2 tablespoons melted **margarine**

(*Recipe continued on next page*)

Chill mixture for 2 hours. Meanwhile, cook over low heat until very thick and dry:

4 large pears, peeled, pitted, and cubed
⅓ cup **orange juice concentrate**
3 tablespoons **apple juice concentrate**
3 tablespoons brandy (see **wine**)
1 teaspoon **sugar**

Cool. When batter is chilled, heat in a **non-stick** crepe pan or skillet, coating bottom of pan:

½ tablespoon **margarine**
½ tablespoon **oil**

Pour in just enough batter to coat bottom of pan. Cook until golden brown on both sides. Repeat with remaining batter, stacking crepes gently as you go. To fill, place a heaping tablespoon of pear mixture on each crepe and roll up tightly. Arrange in a **non-stick** baking dish. Beat until soft peaks form:

2 **egg** whites

Very gradually beat in until very stiff:

2 to 6 tablespoons **sugar** to taste

Mound meringue on rolled crepes. Bake in preheated oven at 450° F for 5 minutes, or until delicately browned.

* Omit meringue for those who are limited in the number of egg whites they can have.

(447)

Marzipan-Stuffed Pears

4 to 8 servings *LC*, LCh, D†, LS, v, Ml, k*

Tip: Begin preparation the day before.

Peel, keeping stems intact:

4 Bosc pears

Brush with:

Lemon juice

Set aside.

Combine in saucepan large enough to hold pears:

½ cup **apple juice concentrate**
1 cup **apple juice**
1 cup orange juice
1 lemon, sliced
½ teaspoon vanilla

Add pears and bring to a boil, simmering for 45 minutes or until pears are just tender (test with toothpick). Remove pears and set aside to cool. Bring liquid to a boil again and reduce by half. This takes about 10 minutes.

Meanwhile, combine in a cup and blend until smooth:

1 tablespoon cornstarch
1 tablespoon water

Add cornstarch mixture to reduced liquid and stir constantly over medium-low heat until sauce is thickened.

Prepare:

½ recipe MOCK MARZIPAN (**448**) or use commercial marzipan (except *LC* and *D*)

Halve and core pears. Fill both halves with marzipan and press halves back together again. Chill. To serve, top pears with sauce. If desired, pass separately:

Whipped cream *and/or*
ANGEL CREAM (**543**) *and/or*
Almond-flavored liqueur
Sliced almonds

* Serve ½ pear for weight-conscious dieters.
† Except those who must limit their intake of simple carbohydrates, such as fruit.

(448)

Mock Marzipan

About 1½ cups *LCh, D*, LS, v, Ml, k*

Combine in small bowl and blend until smooth:

¾ cup ground blanched almonds
⅓ cup **apple juice concentrate**
1 tablespoon **orange juice concentrate**
½ cup peeled, cooked, and ground chestnuts
1 teaspoon almond extract
1 tablespoon **fructose** or **sugar** (*D:* use **aspartame**)
2 teaspoons softened **margarine,** unsalted

Whip until stiff:

2 **egg** whites

Fold egg whites into almond mixture thoroughly.

* Except those who must limit their intake of simple carbohydrates, such as fruit.

(449)

Orange Almond Semolina

35 to 40 squares *LC, LCh, LS, V, v, Ml, k, B*

Combine in a saucepan and boil for 15 minutes:
3 cups water
¼ cup **apple juice concentrate**
¼ cup **orange juice concentrate**
¼ cup **sugar**
In another saucepan, melt:
2 tablespoons **margarine**
Stir into this margarine until it is all absorbed:
1 cup semolina or Cream of Wheat
Stir in:
1 teaspoon fresh grated orange rind (*B:* omit)
Add juice-sugar syrup to semolina and stir in:
1 teaspoon almond extract
Turn mixture into **non-stick** baking dish 9 x 13 inches. Bake at 350° F for 10 minutes until all liquid is absorbed. Stir in:
¼ cup sliced almonds (*B:* omit)
Cool. Cut into squares.

(450)

Orange Slices with Hoop Cheese

4 to 6 servings *LC, LCh, LS*, v, P, k*

Peel and thinly slice:
4 large eating oranges
In a **non-stick** skillet heat:
2 tablespoons **apple juice concentrate**
2 tablespoons **orange juice concentrate**
Add orange slices and cook over low heat, turning frequently, until nicely glazed. Set aside to cool.
In blender, combine:
1½ cups **hoop cheese**
2 tablespoons **apple juice concentrate**

2 tablespoons **orange juice concentrate**
¾ teaspoon vanilla

Blend until smooth.
Combine in small saucepan and simmer for 5 minutes:

2 tablespoons **orange juice concentrate**
2 tablespoons **apple juice concentrate**
⅓ cup raisins

Stir in:

1 tablespoon fresh grated orange rind

Stir raisins and their liquid into the cheese mixture and blend well. Add and blend in:

¼ cup Grape Nuts (*LS:* use nuts)

In individual dessert dishes arrange alternate layers of oranges and cheese, beginning with the oranges and ending with the cheese. Chill for at least 2 hours in the refrigerator. Sprinkle with:

2 tablespoons Grape Nuts (*LS:* use nuts)

* Except those who must limit their intake of milk products.

(451)

Orange Slices with Ricotta

4 to 6 servings *LCh, LS, v, k*

Peel and thinly slice:

4 large eating oranges

In a **non-stick** skillet, heat over low-medium flame:

2 tablespoons orange liqueur
2 tablespoons **orange juice concentrate**

Add orange slices and cook over low heat, turning frequently, until nicely glazed. Set aside to cool. In blender, combine:

1 pound part-skim ricotta or **hoop cheese** (*LS:* use **hoop cheese**)
2 tablespoons **fructose** or 3 tablespoons **sugar**
2 tablespoons **orange juice concentrate**
1 tablespoon **apple juice concentrate**

Blend until smooth. Combine in small saucepan:

2 tablespoons orange liqueur
2 tablespoons **orange juice concentrate**
½ cup golden raisins
1 tablespoon fresh grated orange rind

(*Recipe continued on next page*)

Cook mixture until raisins puff, about 3 minutes. Cool. Toast in oven until golden:

½ cup sliced or chopped almonds

Add raisins and their liquid and all but 2 tablespoons of the nuts to the cheese mixture and stir until well mixed. In individual dessert dishes, arrange alternate layers of oranges and cheese, beginning with oranges and ending with cheese. Chill for at least 2 hours. Sprinkle with nuts and:

½ cup orange liqueur (½ tablespoon per serving)

(452)

Peach Cobbler

1 9 x 9-inch cake *LCh, D, LS, V, v, Ml, k, B*

Tip: One 2 x 2-inch piece of peach cobbler is approximately 1 (*D*) sweetness allowance.

Combine in large saucepan and cook over low heat until fruit is tender:

3 cups sliced peaches, fresh or frozen **unsweetened**
⅔ cup **apple juice concentrate**
3 tablespoons **orange juice concentrate**
½ teaspoon cinnamon or more to taste
¼ teaspoon fresh grated orange rind (*B:* omit)

Sprinkle over peaches:

2 tablespoons **flour**

Stir to blend. Set filling aside. Sift together in mixing bowl:

⅔ cup **flour**
1½ teaspoons **baking powder** (*LS:* use 2¼ teaspoons low-sodium **baking powder**)
½ teaspoon fresh grated orange rind (*B:* omit)

Blend in:

⅓ cup wheat germ (*B:* use **flour**)

Cut in with pastry blender or with 2 knives, until it resembles meal:

3 tablespoons **margarine** or **butter**

Stir in to make a soft, smooth dough:

½ cup skim **milk** (*LS, V,* and *Ml:* use **orange juice**)

Turn peach filling into a 9 x 9-inch **non-stick** baking pan. Dot with:

1 tablespoon **margarine** (Opt.)

Drop dough by spoonfuls onto peach mixture. Bake in preheated 425° F oven, for about 20 to 30 minutes, or until crust is lightly golden. Do not overbake. If desired, pass separately:

Evaporated skimmed **milk**

(453)

Pineapple-Banana Mold

6 to 8 servings *LC, LCh, LS, V, v, P, Ml, k, B**

Chill 6-cup mold in the freezer. Drain and set aside liquid and fruit from:

1 20-ounce can crushed pineapple in **unsweetened** juice

Combine in small bowl:

2 envelopes unflavored **gelatin**
½ cup **apple juice concentrate**

Blend to smoothness and let stand 1 minute to soften. In small saucepan, bring to a boil:

1½ cups pineapple juice (liquid reserved from fruit, plus additional to make 1½ cups)

Stir gelatin into hot juice. Add set-aside crushed pineapple and:

⅔ cup **apple juice**
3 tablespoons **lemon** or **lime juice**
¼ cup pineapple juice, heated to a boil
1 ripe banana, sliced

Turn into chilled mold, rinsed in cold water and dried, and chill until set.

* Except low-residue dieters.

(454)

Pineapple-Peach Mold

6 to 8 servings *LC, LCh, LS, V, v, P, Ml, k, B**

Follow recipe for PINEAPPLE-BANANA MOLD (**453**), substituting 1 16-ounce can sliced peaches in **unsweetened** juice, drained, for banana.

* Only if canned, crushed pineapple is permitted. For low-residue dieters, use Pineapple-Peach Mold.

(455)

Fluffy Pineapple Mousse

6 to 8 servings *LC, LCh, D*, v, P, Ml, k, B†*

Tip: This dessert is equal to about 2 (*D*) sweetness allowances per serving.

In a saucepan, combine:

1¾ cups **unsweetened** pineapple juice
¼ cup **pineapple juice concentrate**
¼ cup **apple juice concentrate**

In a separate bowl, combine until smooth:

¼ cup cornstarch
¼ cup **unsweetened** pineapple juice

Stir cornstarch mixture into juice in saucepan. Bring to a boil, and cook for 5 minutes over moderate heat, stirring constantly. When mixture is thick and transparent, remove from heat and cool. Stir in:

1 can crushed pineapple in **unsweetened** juice, drained

In a mixer bowl, beat until stiff:

6 **egg** whites
½ teaspoon cream of tartar

Add ¼ of the whites to the cooled pineapple mixture and fold them together. Add mixture to remaining whites and fold together until no trace of white remains. Chill mousse for at least 3 hours.

* Except those on diets limited in simple carbohydrates, such as fruit.
† Only if canned, crushed pineapple is permitted.

(456)

Fluffy Apple Mousse

6 to 8 servings *LC, LCh, D*, LS, v, P, Ml, k, B*

Tip: This dessert is equal to about 2 (*D*) sweetness allowances per serving.

In a saucepan, combine:
2 cups **unsweetened apple juice**
½ cup **apple juice concentrate**
In a separate bowl, combine until smooth:
¼ cup cornstarch
¼ cup **apple juice**
Stir cornstarch mixture into juice in saucepan. Bring to a boil, and cook for 5 minutes over moderate heat, stirring constantly. When mixture is thick and transparent, remove from heat and cool. Stir in:
1½ cups **unsweetened** apple sauce
In mixer bowl, beat until stiff:
6 **egg** whites
½ teaspoon cream of tartar
2 tablespoons **fructose** (Opt.)
Add ¼ of the whites to the cooled apple mixture and fold them together. Add mixture to remaining whites and fold together until no trace of white remains. Chill mousse for at least 3 hours.

* Except those on diets limited in simple carbohydrates, such as fruit.

Frozen Desserts

(457)

Cassis Sorbet

10 servings *LC, LCh, LS, v, Ml, k*

Tip: Prepare at least 6 hours before serving.

Combine in saucepan:
1 cup **apple juice concentrate**
2 cups water
1 tablespoon **sugar**
Bring to boil over moderate heat and boil for 5 minutes, stirring frequently. Stir in:
2 tablespoons fresh grated lemon rind
Cool. Stir in:
¼ cup **lemon juice**
In blender, puree:
2 large, ripe bananas (about 1 cup)
Stir banana puree into liquid mixture. Pour into trays and place in freezer. Stir every fifteen minutes until mixture is mushy. Remove from freezer and transfer to a mixing bowl. Beat for 1 minute. Add:
1 cup semi-dry white **wine**
⅓ cup crème de cassis (see **wine**)
Freeze mixture again until mushy. Beat until stiff:
2 **egg** whites
Fold egg whites gently into cassis mixture. Freeze again until firm, but not hard, stirring at half-hour intervals. Alternately, don't stir, and sorbet will form two pretty layers that can be served in squares. If sorbet is stirred, serve heaped in sherbert glasses, topped with:
1 teaspoonful of crème de cassis (per serving)

(458)

Easter Egg Ices

Fill egg shaped molds with a variety of colorful sorbets and ices, according to guests' diets. If such molds are unavailable, fill a lamb or other holiday mold with layers of ices. Add each layer as it is almost frozen, spreading evenly. When serving, bring to eating consistency in refrigerator for between 10 minutes and half an hour.

(459)

Ice Cream Rum Ball

4 to 6 servings *LCh, LS*, v, K, k*

Soften:
 1 quart vanilla or coffee ice cream (*LCh:* use ice milk)
Blend in:
 ¼ cup rum
Shape into balls and refreeze. When ready to serve, roll balls in:
 Chopped almonds or walnuts
Serve with:
 Chocolate cookies

* Only if ice cream is permitted.

(460)

Mango Ice

4 servings *LC, LCh, D*, LS, V, v, P, Ml, k*

Process, blend or put through food mill the pulp of:
 3 large or 4 small ripe mangoes (approximately 3 cups pulp)
Add:
 ⅓ cup **lemon juice**
 1 teaspoon fresh grated lemon rind

(*Recipe continued on next page*)

Heat in saucepan, bringing to simmer and simmering for 5 minutes:

1½ cups **apple juice**
2 tablespoons **apple juice concentrate**
2 tablespoons fruit cordial (see **wine**) (*D* and *P:* use **apple juice concentrate**)

Cool and combine liquid with mango puree. Transfer mixture to freezer tray and freeze, stirring every 20 minutes to ensure smoothness, for 3 hours. Serve garnished with:

Mango sections
Fresh mint leaves *or*
White grapes

* Except those on diets limited in simple carbohydrates, such as fruit.

(461)

Cantaloupe Sorbet

4 servings *LC, LCh, D*, LS, V, v, P, Ml, k*

Substitute the meat of 2 small cantaloupes, ripe and sweet, cut in cubes, for mango in MANGO ICE (**460**).

* Except those on diets limited in simple carbohydrates, such as fruit.

(462)

Cantaloupe-Strawberry Sorbet

4 servings *LC, LCh, D*, LS, V, v, P, Ml, k*

Substitute 1½ cups pureed cantaloupe and 1½ cups pureed fresh or frozen **unsweetened** strawberries for mango in MANGO ICE (**460**).

* Except those on diets limited in simple carbohydrates, such as fruit.

(463)

Margarita Ice

6 servings *LC, LCh, LS, v, Ml, k*

Tip: Prepare 4 to 6 hours before serving.

Combine in saucepan:

¾ cup orange juice
¼ cup **orange juice concentrate**
1 tablespoon **sugar** (Opt.)
1 tablespoon tequila
2 tablespoons orange liqueur (see **wine**)

Bring to boil over moderate heat and simmer for 5 minutes, stirring frequently. Stir in:

2 tablespoons fresh grated lime rind
½ cup **lime juice**

In blender puree:

2 ripe bananas (about 1 cup puree)

Stir bananas into liquid mixture. Pour into trays and place in freezer. Stir every 15 minutes until mixture is mushy. Remove from freezer and transfer to mixing bowl. Beat for 1 minute. Add:

3 tablespoons orange liqueur (see **wine**)
2 tablespoons tequila

Freeze again until mushy. Beat until stiff:

2 **egg** whites

Fold whites into mushy tequila mixture. Freeze again until firm but not hard, stirring at ½-hour intervals. Serve heaped in sherbet glasses, topped with:

Grated lime and orange rind

(464)

Orange Sorbet Supreme

6 servings *LC, LCh, LS, V, v, P, Ml, k*

Cut in half, scalloping edges, if desired:
3 large navel oranges
Scoop out pulp and reserve shells. Puree pulp in blender, adding:
Orange juice to make 4 cups
Combine in small saucepan:
2 envelopes unflavored **gelatin**
½ cup **apple juice concentrate**
Let stand 1 minute to soften gelatin. Heat to boiling, stirring until gelatin is dissolved. Remove from heat; add orange mixture and:
¼ cup orange liqueur (*P:* use **apple juice concentrate**)
2 tablespoon **lemon juice**
Fructose to taste (*P:* omit)
Stir mixture well. Freeze in a shallow tray, stirring every 15 minutes to break up ice crystals. When uniformly mushy, divide mixture into 6 orange shells. Freeze until firm.
Meanwhile, prepare and set aside:
1 recipe BERRY SAUCE (**431**)
When sorbet is frozen, and you are ready to serve it, top with sauce. *LS, V,* and *P:* serve as is. For other diets, return to freezer. Whip until stiff:
2 **egg** whites
¼ teaspoon cream of tartar
1½ tablespoons **fructose** or 2 tablespoons **sugar**
Transfer orange shells to large baking sheet. Top each with meringue, spreading to edges of orange shells. Run under broiler for 1 to 3 minutes, or until lightly browned. Serve immediately with additional sauce and:
Sliced or slivered almonds, passed separately

(465)

Peach Sorbet

4 to 6 servings *LC, LCh, D*, LS, V, v, P, Ml, k*

Process, blend, or put through the food mill:

4 to 6 ripe peaches, pitted and peeled (equal to 1¼ cups puree)
1 ripe banana (equal to about ½ cup puree)

Add to this mixture:

3 tablespoons **lemon juice**

Bring to a boil and cook for 5 minutes in small saucepan:

1 cup **apple juice**
3 tablespoons **apple juice concentrate**
2 tablespoons peach brandy (see **wine;** *D* and *P:* use 2 tablespoons **apple juice concentrate**)
1 tablespoon **fructose** (*D* and *P:* omit; *D:* use **aspartame,** if desired)

Cool liquid and combine with peach puree. Stir in, if not using brandy:

1 teaspoon almond extract

Transfer mixture to freezer tray and freeze, stirring every 30 minutes to ensure smoothness, for 3 hours. Serve garnished with:

Slivered almonds (*P:* use Grape Nuts)
Small clusters of seedless grapes

* Except those on diets limited in simple carbohydrates, such as fruit.

(466) *APRICOT SORBET*

4 to 6 servings *LC, LCh, D*, LS, V, v, P, Ml, k*

Substitute apricots for peaches in PEACH SORBET (**465**); use apricot brandy, or almond extract.

* Except those on diets limited in simple carbohydrates, such as fruit.

(467) *NECTARINE SORBET*

4 to 6 servings *LC, LCh, D**, LS, V, v, P, Ml, k*

Substitute nectarines for peaches in PEACH SORBET (**465**); use orange liqueur, or vanilla extract.

(468) *STRAWBERRY OR BLUEBERRY SORBET*

4 to 6 servings *LC, LCh, D**, LS, V, v, P, Ml, k*

Substitute strawberries or blueberries for peaches in PEACH SORBET (**465**); use orange liqueur, or vanilla extract for brandy.

* Except those on diets limited in simple carbohydrates, such as fruit.

(469)
Sabra Sundae

4 to 6 servings *LCh, LS**, v, K, k*

Chill a 5 to 6-cup **non-stick** mold in freezer. Soften:

1 quart vanilla ice cream or ice milk (*LCh:* use ice milk)

Blend into ice cream or ice milk:

¼ cup Sabra liqueur
½ cup ground hazelnuts or almonds
¼ cup small chocolate chips or carob chips (*LCh:* use carob)
1 tablespoon fresh grated orange rind

Press mixture into chilled mold. Refreeze until ready to serve. Unmold by dipping mold quickly into warm water. If desired, garnish with:

Canned mandarin orange slices, thoroughly drained in paper towels
Sliced almonds

* Only if ice cream is permitted.

(470)

Light Tortoni

8 servings *LC, LCh, LS*, v, k*

Tip: Best if prepared 5 or 6 hours before serving

In small bowl, freeze until ice crystals form throughout, about 1 hour:
½ cup evaporated skimmed **milk**
Chill electric mixing bowl and beaters in refrigerator while milk is freezing. Set aside in separate bowl, and allow to come to room temperature:
1 **egg** white
Ready the following ingredients:
3 tablespoons finely ground blanched almonds
1 teaspoon dark rum or rum extract
½ teaspoon almond extract
In chilled bowl at high speed, beat iced evaporated skimmed milk with almonds and rum until milk is stiff and white. Scrape bowl with spatula frequently. Quickly beat egg white in separate bowl until soft peaks form. Gradually add 1 tablespoon of the almonds, plus:
2 tablespoons **fructose** or brown **sugar**
Fold whipped milk into egg whites. Spoon into 8 paper muffin cups or sherbet glasses. Sprinkle with remaining almonds. Freeze. Before serving, top each tortoni with:
A fresh cherry half *or*
Sprinkling of cinnamon *or*
Sprinkling of finely ground blanched almonds

* Except those limited to low-sodium milk.

(471)

Tropical Ice Cream Balls

6 to 8 servings *LS*, v, K, k*

Soften:

1 quart vanilla ice cream or ice milk

Blend into ice cream:

3 to 4 tablespoons rum
¼ cup shredded coconut
¼ cup chopped macadamia nuts

Shape into balls and refreeze, well wrapped in plastic bags. Serve sprinkled with:

Shredded coconut

Garnish with:

Macadamia nuts
Mandarin orange sections, thoroughly drained on paper towels

* Only if ice cream is permitted.

Fruits

(472)

Fruit-Nut Sundae

4 servings *LCh, D*, LS†, v, K, k*

Combine in large bowl and chill:

1 cup pineapple chunks in **unsweetened** juice, drained
1 cup orange slices, halved
1 cup sliced banana
1 cup fresh sliced strawberries
¼ cup shredded **unsweetened** coconut (*LCh:* omit)
¼ cup broken walnut pieces
¼ cup unsalted sunflower seeds

Combine in separate bowl:

1½ cups low-fat **yogurt**
1½ tablespoons **lime juice**
3½ tablespoons unsalted almond butter

(*Recipe continued on next page*)

3 tablespoons **apple juice concentrate**
2 tablespoons plus 1 teaspoon **orange juice concentrate**
¾ teaspoon cinnamon or to taste

Chill. Serve chilled fruit in individual sherbet glasses, and pass topping separately with optional garnish of:

Poppy seeds

* Except those on diets limited in simple carbohydrates, such as fruit.
† Omit yogurt topping for those restricted to low-sodium milk.

(473)

Gingered Fruit

6 servings *LC, LCh, D, LS, V, v, P, Ml, k*

Tip: ½ to ⅔ cup portions of fruit without the juices are equivalent to 1 (*D*) sweetness allowance.

In small saucepan, combine and simmer over low heat for 10 minutes, stirring occasionally:

½ cup **orange juice concentrate**
¼ cup **apple juice concentrate**
¼ cup **pineapple juice concentrate**
Juice from 1 can pineapple chunks in **unsweetened** juice
1 teaspoon ground ginger
½ teaspoon cinnamon

Set aside to cool. Combine 6 to 8 cups of any of the following fruits in a large serving bowl:

Diced papaya
Diced plums
Sliced apples
Sliced peaches
Cubed melons
Diced pears
Seedless whole grapes
Pineapple chunks
Mango cubes
Sliced banana (add just before serving)

Add cooled ginger sauce to fruit. Toss gently to coat, and chill well.

(474)

Fresh Fruit Kabobs

4 to 6 servings *LC, LCh, D, LS, V, v, Ml, P, K, k*

Combine in a bowl as a marinade:

¼ cup **pineapple juice concentrate**
1 tablespoon **orange juice concentrate**
¼ cup appropriate fruit flavored liqueur or Amaretto (see **wine;** *D* and *P:* omit)
1 tablespoon **lemon** or **lime juice**

Cut into bite-sized chunks several (at least 3) varieties of seasonal fruit, up to 3 cups of:

Apples, pears, seedless grapes
Cantaloupe, seedless grapes, strawberries
Banana, papaya, mango
Pineapple, papaya, banana
Peaches, bananas, grapes
Nectarines, bananas, grapes

Combine fruit and marinade and let macerate for at least 1 hour. Skewer fruit on round toothpicks or small wooden skewers, three varieties to a skewer. Try to get a variety of colors and flavors on each skewer.

VARIATION: Marinate fruit in 2 tablespoons honey, to ¼ cup **apple juice concentrate,** 2 tablespoons **orange juice concentrate,** and 1 tablespoon **lemon** or **lime juice** (except *D* and *P*).

(475)

Fresh Fruit Salad

8 to 10 servings *LC, LCh, D, LS, V, v, P, Ml, K, k*

Tip: A ⅔ cup serving without juices is equal to approximately 1 (*D*) sweetness allowance.

Combine in large serving bowl, as available:

1 cup fresh whole strawberries or frozen **unsweetened** strawberries (*D:* increase to 1½ cups)

(*Recipe continued on next page*)

1 cup seedless white grapes (*D:* decrease to ½ cup)
1 cup melon balls (*D:* increase to 1½ cups)
1 cup fresh blueberries or frozen **unsweetened** blueberries
1 15-ounce can pineapple chunks in **unsweetened** juice (*D:* use 1 cup)
1 cup sliced peaches, fresh or **unsweetened** canned
1 cup sliced apples, unpeeled
1 11-ounce can mandarin orange segments, rinsed and drained (*D* and *P:* omit)

Add and toss gently to coat:
¾ cup **apple juice concentrate** (*D:* reduce to ¼ cup)
¾ cup **orange juice concentrate** (*D:* reduce to ¼ cup)
1 cup orange juice
¼ cup **lime juice** or **lemon juice**

Chill well.
Just before serving, slice in:
2 medium-sized ripe bananas

Fruit used may be varied according to season and availability. Serve well chilled. Present in a pretty crystal bowl or in melon shells or melon basket.

(476)

Macedoine of Winter Fruit

8 servings *LC, LCh, D, LS, V, v, P, Ml, K, k*

Tip: A ⅔ cup serving is approximately equal to 1 (*D*) sweetness allowance.

In serving bowl combine:
6 navel oranges, peeled and sliced
8 ounces frozen **unsweetened** strawberries
¼ cup **orange juice concentrate**

Allow to macerate for 1 to 2 hours. Before serving, sprinkle with:
2 tablespoons rolled **oats**

VARIATION: Sprinkle with chopped nuts or chopped coconut (*P:* omit both; use Grape Nuts. *LCh:* omit coconut).

VARIATION: Add 3 tablespoons orange liqueur (see **wine**) to macerating liquid (except *P* and *D*).

(477)

Macedoine of Citrus and Banana Slices

8 servings *LC, LCh, D, LS, V, v, P, Ml, K, k*

Tip: A ⅔ cup serving is approximately equal to 1 (*D*) sweetness allowance.

In pretty bowl, combine:
4 navel oranges, peeled and sliced
2 pink grapefruit, peeled and sliced
2 ripe bananas, sliced
¼ cup **orange juice concentrate**
Allow to macerate for 1 to 2 hours. Before serving, sprinkle with:
2 tablespoons rolled **oats**

VARIATION: Same as for MADEDOINE OF WINTER FRUIT **(476)**

(478)

Wine or Juice-Poached Fruit

6 to 8 servings *LC, LCh, D*, LS, V, v, P, Ml, k, B*

Peel, quarter, and core:
4 small apples
4 small ripe pears
Peel and section:
2 seedless oranges
Place the fruit in a glass, stainless steel, or enamel casserole, poacher, or large pot. Add:
2 cups dry white **wine** (*D, P,* and *B:* use 2 cups juice instead)
¾ cup orange juice
¼ cup **orange juice concentrate**
½ cup **apple juice concentrate**
½ cup raisins (*D:* omit)
2 cinnamon sticks
Bring to a boil and simmer for 15 minutes, covered.

(*Recipe continued on next page*)

Serve warm or chilled, plain or, depending upon dietary requirements, with one or more of the following passed separately:

Cake
Ice cream, ice milk, or frozen yogurt
Fruit SORBET (**457, 460** to **468**)
FRUITED YOGURT (428)
Sliced or chopped nuts and/or Grape Nuts

* Omit juices for those on diets limited in simple carbohydrates, such as fruit.

(479)

Baked Apples

4 servings *LC, LCh, LS, V, v, P, Ml, k*

Wash and core:
  4 large MacIntosh or Courtland apples
Combine in small saucepan and bring to a boil:
  ¼ cup raisins
  2 tablespoons sweet **wine** or cordial or **apple juice concentrate** (*P:* use **apple juice concentrate**)
  2 tablespoons **apple juice concentrate** or **orange juice concentrate**
Simmer for 5 minutes or until raisins are plumped.
Transfer to a small bowl. Add:
  3 tablespoons **oats**
  1 tablespoon **bran**
  1 tablespoon wheat germ (*P:* use **bran** or **oats**)
  2 tablespoons chopped nuts (*P:* use Grape Nuts)
  ½ teaspoon cinnamon
Mix well. Fill apples with this mixture.
Place apples in 8 x 8-inch baking dish. Pour over apples a mixture of:
  ½ cup **apple juice**
  ½ cup **wine** (*P:* use dry white **wine**)
Bake at 375° F for 45 to 50 minutes or until apples are tender.

VARIATION: Fill with chopped figs and walnuts.

VARIATION: Use dates, apricots or other dried fruit instead of raisins.

VARIATION: Just before serving top with meringue and pass under broiler for 2 to 3 minutes to brown (except *LS, V,* and *P*).

(480)

Nut-Filled Baked Apples

4 servings *LCh, D, LS, V, v, Ml, k*

Follow recipe for BAKED APPLES (**479**), but use the following filling, combined in a bowl:

¼ cup rolled **oats**
1 tablespoon **bran**
2 tablespoons wheat germ
¼ cup chopped nuts
¼ teaspoon cinnamon or to taste
¼ cup **apple juice**

(481)

Baked Apple Slices

4 servings *LC, LCh, LS, V, v, Ml, k, B*

Combine in saucepan and melt over low heat:

½ cup **apple juice concentrate**
2 tablespoons brown **sugar**
2 tablespoons **margarine**

Stir in:

1 teaspoon **lemon juice**
1 teaspoon cinnamon

Toss in this mixture:

5 cups peeled, cored, seeded and thinly sliced apples

Transfer to a small **non-stick** baking dish. Top with:

1 cup **bread** crumbs

Bake at 375° F for 30 to 40 minutes or until desired tenderness is reached.

Pass separately, if desired:

Cream or evaporated skimmed **milk**

(482)

Praline-Baked Bananas

4 servings *LCh, LS, V, v, Ml, k*

Melt in small, **non-stick** saucepan:

1 tablespoon **margarine**
2 tablespoons **apple juice concentrate**

Stir in:

1 tablespoon brown **sugar**
½ teaspoon vanilla
½ cup coarsely chopped pecans

Cook over low heat, stirring constantly, until nuts have a golden glaze. Peel:

4 large, ripe bananas

Brush them with a mixture of:

2 tablespoons **orange juice concentrate**
1 tablespoon **lemon juice**
2 tablespoons rum, preferably dark

Arrange them in a **non-stick** baking dish. Pour pecan sauce over, spreading evenly. Sprinkle with:

¼ cup rolled **oats**

Bake at 375° F for about 15 minutes. If desired, pass separately:

Ice cream or ice milk
Whipped cream *or*
Rum-flavored ANGEL CREAM **(543)**

(483)

Fresh Cherries in Kirsch

4 servings *LCh, LS, V, v, Ml, k*

Prepare marinade of:

½ cup kirsch
¼ cup **apple juice concentrate**
¼ cup **orange juice concentrate**
¼ to ½ teaspoon cinnamon

Marinate several hours in refrigerator:
 3 cups fresh cherries, halved and pitted
Turn and baste fruit every hour. Serve alone, or pass separately:
 FRUITED YOGURT (**428**)
 Whipped Cream
 ANGEL CREAM (**543**)

(484)

Seedless Grapes and Orange Slices Sabra

4 servings *LCh, LS, v, K, k*

Combine in small bowl, blending well:
 ½ cup sour cream or **yogurt** (*LCh:* use low-fat **yogurt**)
 2 tablespoons Sabra liqueur
 2 teaspoons **orange juice concentrate**
 ½ teaspoon **apple juice concentrate**
Arrange in individual serving dishes:
 1 large bunch seedless green grapes
 4 seedless oranges, peeled and sliced
Spoon Sabra sauce over fruit.

(485)

Seedless Grapes with Rum and Yogurt

4 servings *LC, LCh, LS, v, k*

Heat in small saucepan to boiling:
 2½ tablespoons dark rum
In a large bowl, combine with rum and let macerate for 15 minutes:
 2 cups sweet seedless grapes, peeled
 1 tablespoon brown **sugar**

(*Recipe continued on next page*)

Meanwhile combine, blending well:

½ cup low-fat **yogurt**
1 tablespoon **apple juice concentrate**
2 teaspoons brown **sugar**

Toss grapes and yogurt mixture and chill for at least 30 minutes. Garnish with, if desired:

Mint leaves *and/or*
Sliced almonds *or*
Grape Nuts

(486)

Marinated Mango

2 to 3 servings *LC, LCh, D*, LS, V, v, P, Ml, K, k*

Peel and slice:

1 large, ripe mango

Combine in small bowl:

2 tablespoons **orange juice concentrate**
¼ cup **lemon** or **lime juice**
2 tablespoons **apple juice concentrate**

Marinate mango in mixture for 1 hour or more. Serve topped with:

2 tablespoons chopped nuts (*P:* use Grape Nuts)

* Except those on diets limited in simple carbohydrates, such as fruit.

(487)

Marinated Pineapple

2 to 3 servings *LC, LCh, D*, LS, V, v, P, Ml, K, k*

Substitute ½ pineapple, sliced, for mango in MARINATED MANGO **(486)**.

* Except those on diets limited in simple carbohydrates, such as fruit.

(488)

Marinated Melon Balls and Blueberries

3 to 4 servings *LC, LCh, D*, LS, V, v, P, Ml, k*

Substitute 2 cups cantaloupe balls and 1 cup blueberries for mango in MARINATED MANGO (**486**).

* Do not serve juice to those on diets limited in simple carbohydrates, such as fruit.

(489)

Melon Cubes with Lime Dip

6 to 8 servings *LC, LCh, D, LS, V, v, P, Ml, K, k*

Arrange on platter and chill:
    6 cups mixed melon cubes (honeydew, cantaloupe, cassaba, etc.)
Prepare dip by combining:
    ¼ cup **lime juice**
    2 tablespoons **orange juice concentrate**
    1 tablespoon **pineapple juice concentrate**
    ½ teaspoon lime rind
    ½ teaspoon corn or potato starch blended in 1 teaspoon water
Heat mixture, stirring constantly, until smooth and thickened. Cool. Serve with melon cubes. Garnish platter with:
    Small clusters of seedless grapes
    Sweet bing cherries

VARIATION: Add 1 tablespoon honey and omit cornstarch; do not heat mixture (except *D* and *P*).

(490)

Tropical Fruit with Lime Dip

LC, LCh, D, LS, V, v, P, Ml, K, k

Prepare lime dip as for MELON CUBES WITH LIME DIP **(489).** Serve with a variety of tropical fruits such as: papaya, mango, banana, pineapple.

(491)

Cheese-Stuffed Nectarines

2 to 4 servings *LC, LCh, LS, v, Ml, k*

Combine in blender and blend until smooth:

¼ cup **farmer cheese** (*LS:* use unsalted **farmer cheese** or **hoop cheese**)

2 tablespoons crème de cassis, or other cordial (see **wine**)

2 tablespoons white raisins

Work in:

1 teaspoon sliced almonds

Wash, halve, and remove pits from:

2 large, ripe nectarines

Rub over exposed surfaces of fruit:

Lemon juice

Fill cavities of fruit with cheese mixture. Press back together to make whole fruit; wrap in plastic wrap (tightly) and chill for 1 hour or more. Garnish with:

Mint leaves

(492)

Poires/Pêches au Gratin

4 servings *LCh, LS, v, Ml, k*

Cut into slices ⅜-inch thick:
 4 firm, ripe pears or 4 large firm, ripe peaches, peeled and cored
Arrange in an 8 x 8 x 2-inch **non-stick** baking pan. Sprinkle with:
 Lemon juice
Combine and blend well:
 ⅓ cup apricot jam, low-sugar variety, forced through a sieve
 ¼ cup dry white vermouth (see **wine**)
Pour this mixture over pears or peaches.
Crumble and sprinkle over fruit:
 3 stale macaroons
Dot the fruit with:
 1 to 2 tablespoons **butter** or **margarine,** cut into tiny pieces
Bake on middle shelf of preheated oven at 300° F for 20 to 25 minutes or until crumbs have browned slightly.
If desired, pass separately:
 Whipped cream *and/or*
 ANGEL CREAM (**543**)
 Ice cream *or* ice milk *or* frozen yogurt

(493)

Pears Baked in Red Wine

4 to 8 servings *LC, LCh, LS, V, v, P, Ml, k*

Combine in flameproof casserole and bring to a simmer:
 1 cup dry red **wine** (*P:* use white **wine**)
 1 cup orange juice
 1 cinnamon stick
Add:
 4 pears, peeled, halved, and cored, and rubbed with **lemon juice**
 2 tablespoons **lemon juice**
Bake at 400° F for 50 to 60 minutes. Serve hot or cold.
Garnish if desired with:
 Chopped nuts (*P:* use Grape Nuts)

(494)

Pears or Peaches Caramel Flambé

4 servings *LCh, LS, V, v, Ml, k*

Blanch in boiling water for 2 minutes:
4 large, ripe peaches
Peel and remove pits. In a skillet, melt:
1 tablespoon **margarine**
Add:
2 tablespoons brown **sugar**
2 tablespoons **apple juice concentrate**
Cook mixture, shaking pan frequently, over moderate heat until it begins to caramelize. Add the peach halves and spoon the caramel over them. Add, when ready to serve:
⅓ cup warmed kirsch (see: **wine**)
Ignite mixture, and shake pan until flames go out.

(495)

Pears or Peaches Flambé

4 servings *LC, LCh, LS, V, v, Ml, k*

Peel and cut into eighths:
4 medium, ripe pears or peaches
Melt over low heat in **non-stick** skillet:
1 tablespoon unsalted **margarine** or **butter**
3 tablespoons **apple juice concentrate**
2 tablespoons **orange juice concentrate**
Place fruit slices in skillet and **sauté** over low heat for 2 minutes, turning after 1 minute. Pour off pan juices, and reserve. Make a smooth paste of:
1 teaspoon cornstarch
1 teaspoon water
Stir into reserved juices, and set aside. Pour over fruit in skillet:
¼ cup Triple Sec or orange liqueur (see **wine**)
¼ cup dark rum

Warm 30 seconds over low heat. Turn off heat. Cover pan for 10 seconds. Ignite sauce, and when flames die down, add reserved juice and cornstarch mixture. Stir over medium heat until sauce bubbles and thickens. Serve immediately.

(496)

Cheese-Stuffed Pears

2 to 4 servings *D, v, k*

Combine in blender and process until smooth:
- ½ cup shredded Cheddar, crumbled Roquefort, or blue **cheese** (*D:* use low-fat **cheese**)
- 2 tablespoons **butter** or **margarine**
- 2 tablespoons **farmer cheese**

Stir in:
- 2 tablespoons coarsely chopped walnuts

Wash and halve:
- 2 large ripe pears

Remove core and brush exposed surfaces with:
- **Lemon juice**

Fill cavity of pear halves with cheese mixture. Sprinkle with:
- About 1 tablespoon finely chopped walnuts

Chill for 1 hour or more. Serve garnished with:
- Mint leaves

VARIATION: Cut off top of pear. Core from above. Fill with cheese, and return cap.

VARIATION: For *LC* use 2 tablespoons low-fat Cheddar plus ¼ cup **farmer cheese.** Add ¼ teaspoon Worcestershire sauce (*v:* leave out).

(497)

Plums in Port

4 servings *LC, LCh, LS, V, v, Ml, k*

In boiling water, blanch for 1 minute:
    4 large, sweet plums
In a small saucepan, bring to a boil:
    ½ cup Port **wine**
Remove from heat and stir in:
    1 tablespoon **orange juice concentrate**
Place plums in shallow dish just large enough to hold them. Pour Port mixture over plums. Sprinkle with:
    1 tablespoon fresh grated orange and/or lemon rind
Let marinate for 1 hour at room temperature or longer in refrigerator.

(498)

Spiced Prunes and Oranges in Port

6 servings *LCh, LS, Ml, k*

Tip: Prunes should marinate for at least 1 week.

Heat to boiling:
    1 cup Port **wine**
    2 cloves, or more, to taste
    1 cinnamon stick
    1 tablespoon fresh grated orange rind
Remove from heat and stir in:
    ¼ cup **orange juice concentrate**
Transfer to glass bowl or jar. Add:
    18 pitted prunes
Cover tightly and marinate in refrigerator for at least 1 week, shaking jar or stirring daily.
One hour before serving, peel and slice:
    3 large naval oranges
Toss oranges with marinated prunes and let stand for 1 hour before serving.

(499)

Strawberries Romanoff

2 to 4 servings *LC, LCh, D*, LS, P, V, v, Ml, K, k*

Wash, hull, and slice:

1 pint fresh strawberries

Toss strawberries with a combination of:

¼ cup Port **wine** (*D* and *P:* use **apple juice concentrate**)

¼ cup **orange juice concentrate**

Marinate several hours and pass separately when serving, one or more of the following:

Sour cream

Whipped cream

ANGEL CREAM (**543**)

Toasted almonds

Grape Nuts

VARIATION: Substitute ¼ cup orange liqueur (see **wine**) for Port **wine** (except *D* and *P*).

* Serve without juice for those on diets limited in simple carbohydrates, such as fruit.

Cakes

(500)

Apple Coffee Cake I

1 12 x 12 x 2-inch cake *LC, LCh, D, LS*, v, P, k*

Tip: One 2 x 3-inch piece of cake is equal to 1 sweetness allowance for those on diets limited in simple carbohydrates.

Combine in saucepan and simmer for 5 minutes:

½ cup raisins
½ cup **apple juice**

Drain raisins, reserve. Reserve juice for use in this recipe. Combine in large mixing bowl:

1 cup **oats**
⅓ cup **bran**
⅔ cup whole wheat **flour**
⅓ cup wheat germ (*P:* use **oats** or **flour**)
½ cup non-fat dry **milk**

Beat in:

½ cup low-fat **yogurt**
⅓ cup **apple juice concentrate**

Raisin liquid reserved plus **apple juice** to make 1 cup
1 ripe banana, mashed
1 teaspoon vanilla
½ teaspoon cinnamon
Fold in raisins and:
⅓ cup walnuts, broken (*P:* use Grape Nuts)
Beat until very stiff:
3 **egg** whites (*LS:* use 2 **egg** whites)
Fold batter into egg whites. Prepare a 12 x 12 x 2-inch **non-stick** baking pan. Cover bottom with:
2 apples, peeled, cored, and sliced
Pour batter over apples and bake at 350° F for 45 minutes to 1 hour or until toothpick comes out clean.

* Except those on diets limited to low-sodium milk.

(501)

Apple Coffee Cake II

1 12 x 12 x 2-inch cake *LC, LCh, D, LS, v, P, Ml, k*

Tip: For *D* one 3 x 4-inch piece of cake is equal to about 1 sweetness allowance for those on diets limited in simple carbohydrates.

Combine in saucepan and simmer for 5 minutes:
¼ cup raisins
¼ cup **apple juice concentrate** (*D:* use **apple juice**)
Drain raisins; reserve liquid and combine with:
½ cup **oats**
1 cup whole wheat **flour**
¼ cup wheat germ (*P:* use **oats** or **flour**)
¼ cup **apple juice concentrate**
¼ cup orange juice
Beat until stiff:
2 **egg** whites
Quickly beat flour mixture into whites, then fold in the reserved raisins and:
½ cup coarsely chopped nuts (*LC* and *P:* use Grape Nuts)
½ teaspoon cinnamon
2 apples, cored, peeled, and cubed
Bake at 350° F for 15 to 20 minutes.

(502)

Carob Party Cake

1 8-inch layer cake *LC, LCh, D, LS*, V, v, P, Ml, k, B*

According to diet, prepare a double of one of the following recipes in 2 **non-stick** 8-inch layer cake pans:

CAROB BROWNIES I **(509)** (*LCh, D, LS, v, k*)
CAROB BROWNIES II **(510)** (*LCh, D, LS, V, v, Ml, k*)
CAROB BROWNIES III **(511)** (*LC, LCh, D, LS, v, P, k*)

Cool cakes on wire cake racks. In blender or processor, puree:

1 pound soft style tofu
¼ cup carob powder or cocoa
⅓ cup **apple juice concentrate**
1 teaspoon vanilla extract

Combine to soften in small saucepan:

1 envelope **unflavored gelatin**
½ cup **apple juice concentrate,** defrosted

Let stand 1 minute to soften. Bring mixture to a boil, stirring. Remove from heat; cool. Stir in tofu mixture. Refrigerate until thickened, but not set. Meanwhile, place bottom layer of cake on serving dish. Cover layer with:

2 ripe bananas, thinly sliced and sprinkled with lemon juice (*D:* omit), *or* sliced, unsweetened strawberries, cherries, apricots, *or* peaches

Spread over fruit about 1 cup of carob mixture. Beat until stiff:

2 **egg** whites
⅛ teaspoon cream of tartar

Beat remaining tofu mixture into egg whites quickly. Frost cake with this mixture. Chill, and decorate appropriately.

* Omit egg whites. Spread frosting until it is thickened.

(503)

Carrot Cake

2 small loaves, or
1 10 x 10-inch square pan

LCh, D, V, v, P, Ml, k

Tip: One 2 x 3-inch piece of cake or ⅛ of small loaf is equal to about 1 (*D*) sweetness allowance.

Cook together in medium saucepan for 10 minutes:
- 1 cup grated carrots
- 1 cup raisins (*D:* reduce to ⅓ cup)
- ½ cup **apple juice concentrate**
- ¼ cup **orange juice concentrate**
- 1¼ cups water
- 1½ teaspoons cinnamon
- 1 teaspoon allspice (Opt.)
- 1½ tablespoons **margarine** (*P:* use 1½ tablespoons water)

Cool this mixture. Meanwhile, mix together:
- 1½ cups whole-wheat **flour**
- 1 teaspoon **baking powder**
- 1 teaspoon **baking soda**
- ¼ cup wheat germ (*P:* use additional **flour**)
- ¼ cup **bran**
- ¼ to ½ cup chopped nuts (*D:* use ½ cup; *P:* omit)

Combine cooled carrot mixture with flour mixture by adding flour mixture slowly to carrot mixture, stirring as you do. When batter is well blended (do not overmix), pour into **non-stick** baking pan. Bake in preheated 325° F oven for 30 to 40 minutes.

(504)

Cranberry-Carrot Cake

2-quart bundt cake *LCh, LS, v, Ml, k*

Sift together:

1½ cups unbleached **flour**
2½ teaspoons **baking powder** (*LS:* use 3¾ teaspoons low-sodium **baking powder**)
½ teaspoon cinnamon

Add:

1 cup whole-wheat **flour**
¼ cup **bran**
¼ cup wheat germ
1 cup grated carrots (*LS:* use grated zucchini if carrots are prohibited)
¾ cup **apple juice**
¼ cup firmly packed brown **sugar**
1 cup whole-berry cranberry sauce
¼ cup granulated **sugar** or **fructose**
¼ cup **oil**
1 **egg** plus 6 whites, lightly beaten (*LS:* use 2 **eggs** plus 2 whites)

Beat mixture until well blended. Meanwhile, cook together, simmering for 5 minutes:

¼ cup chopped dried apricots or raisins
½ cup **apple juice** *or*
¼ cup **apple juice** plus ¼ cup rum (*LS:* increase liquid to total of ⅔ cup)

Stir fruit into cake batter, along with:

½ cup coarsely chopped nuts

Pour batter into well-greased, floured 2-quart bundt pan. Bake in moderate oven (350° F) for 1½ hours, or until top is browned and springs back when lightly touched. Serve plain or topped with:

Fresh or pureed fruit *or*
FRUITED YOGURT (**428**) (except *Ml*) *or*
Melted cranberry sauce

(505)

Carrot-Prune Cake

2-quart bundt cake *v, Ml, k, B*

Stew together:
- ½ cup prunes, quartered (*B:* pureed together with juice if required)
- ¾ cup prune juice

Sift together:
- 3 cups unbleached white or whole-wheat **flour** (*B:* use white only)
- 2 teaspoons **baking powder**
- 1 teaspoon **baking soda**
- ½ teaspoon cinnamon

Add to dry ingredients the stewed prunes and liquid plus:
- 1 cup grated carrots
- ¾ cup **unsweetened** apple sauce
- ¾ cup **apple juice**
- ½ cup **apple juice concentrate**
- ½ cup brown **sugar**
- ¼ cup **oil**
- 2 **eggs** plus 4 **egg** whites

Turn batter into greased and floured 2-quart bundt pan. Bake at 350° F for 1½ hours until brown and top springs back when lightly touched.

(506)

Cinnamon-Raisin Coffee Cake

1 7-inch ring cake, or
1 8 x 8-inch square *LCh, LS, V, v, k*

Combine in saucepan, bring to a boil, and simmer for 3 minutes:
- 1 cup **apple juice**
- 1 cup raisins
- 2 tablespoons **margarine**
- 1 to 1½ teaspoons cinnamon

(*Recipe continued on next page*)

Remove from heat and stir in:
¼ cup **apple juice concentrate**
Cool. Meanwhile, sift together:
2 cups whole-wheat **flour**
2 teaspoons **baking powder** (*LS:* 1 tablespoon low-sodium **baking powder**)
Gradually stir the flour mixture into the juice and raisin mixture. Stir until smooth. Add:
½ cup chopped walnuts
Bake in a greased 7-inch ring pan or an 8 x 8-inch pan at 350° F for 1 hour, or longer, until toothpick comes out clean.

VARIATION: Soak with rum or liqueur before serving.

(507)

Holiday Fruit Cake

1 5-cup ring mold *LC, LCh, LS, V, v, P, Ml, k*

Tip: Prepare several days to 2 weeks ahead of holiday.

Combine in small saucepan and simmer for 5 minutes:
1 cup raisins
½ cup dried apricots, chopped
1 cup dry white **wine** or orange juice
Combine in small bowl with raisin/apricot mixture:
1 cup chopped dried apple slices (or mixture of sun-dried, not candied fruits)
1 cup coarsely chopped sun-dried dates
2 cups whole-wheat **bread** crumbs
¾ cup **oats**
⅓ cup **orange juice concentrate**
⅔ cup **apple juice concentrate**
½ cup chopped nuts or more (*P:* use Grape Nuts)
Rind of one orange, grated
Blend all ingredients well. Press into a **non-stick** ring pan and bake at 350° F for 55 minutes, or until firm. Unmold and cool. Pour over cake ring:
⅓ cup Port, sherry, rum, or liqueur (see **wine**) (*P:* use orange juice only)

Cover with cheese cloth, then wrap tightly in foil. Keep in refrigerator for several days or up to 2 weeks. Add additional liqueur every few days.

VARIATION: For *D* reduce raisins and dates to ¼ cup each; increase nuts to 2 cups. Soak in orange juice. One-eighteenth of a cake is approximately equal to 1 sweetness allowance.

VARIATION: For *B* use CARROT-PRUNE CAKE **(505)**, doused with orange juice before serving.

(508)

Orange-Oat Cake

1 10 x 10-inch cake *LCh, D, LS, V, v, P, Ml, k*

Tip: One 3 x 4-inch piece of cake is equal to approximately 1 (*D*) sweetness allowance.

Combine in saucepan and heat to simmering, cooking for 5 minutes:
- 2 tablespoons currants (*P:* increase to 4 tablespoons)
- ¼ cup orange juice

Drain juice into a large mixing bowl. Reserve currants.
Add to bowl, blending ingredients well:
- ¼ cup wheat germ (*P:* use **oats**)
- ¼ cup **bran**
- ¾ cup **oats**
- ¼ cup **apple juice concentrate**
- 2 tablespoons **orange juice concentrate**
- 1 tablespoon fresh grated orange rind
- ½ teaspoon cinnamon or to taste

Stir in the raisins and:
- 4 dates, chopped
- ¼ cup chopped or sliced unsalted nuts (*P:* omit)
- ¼ cup unsalted sunflower seeds (*P:* use Grape Nuts)

Beat until stiff:
- 2 **egg** whites (*V:* leave out this step; press batter into pan and bake 15 to 20 minutes for bar cookies)

Fold egg whites into batter thoroughly.
Turn batter into a 10 x 10-inch **non-stick** cake pan. Bake at 350° F for 25 to 30 minutes or until toothpick comes out clean.

Cookies

(509)

Carob Brownies I

8 x 8-inch square *LCh, LS, D, v, k*

Tip: Two 2 x 2-inch brownies are approximately equal to 1 (*D*) sweetness allowance. *LS:* two 2 x 2-inch brownies appropriate serving for those on diets limited in eggs.

Combine in medium bowl:
- ⅔ cup whole wheat **flour**
- ½ teaspoon **baking powder** (*LS:* use ¾ teaspoon low-sodium **baking powder**)

Mix together in small bowl:
- 5 tablespoons **unsweetened** carob powder
- 2 tablespoons **oil**
- 2 tablespoons evaporated skimmed **milk**

Beat until soft and fluffy:
- 4 **egg** whites

Add:

¾ cup **apple juice concentrate**
2 tablespoons peanut butter, **unsweetened** and unsalted
1 teaspoon vanilla extract

Blend in carob mixture. Add flour and blend. Fold in:

½ cup broken walnut pieces

Pour into **non-stick** 8 x 8-inch brownie pan. Bake in preheated 350° F oven 15 to 20 minutes, or until toothpick inserted in center comes out clean.

VARIATION: Cook ½ cup raisins for 10 minutes over low heat in ¾ cup apple juice called for in CAROB BROWNIE I recipe. Cool. Add raisin liquid to beaten egg whites with peanut butter and vanilla. Fold in raisins with nuts (except *D*).

(510)

Carob Brownies II

8 x 8-inch square — *LCh, D, LS, V, v, ML, k*

Tip: Two 2 x 2-inch brownies are approximately equal to 1 (*D*) sweetness allowance.

Cook in small saucepan over low heat 10 minutes:

3 tablespoons **margarine**
½ cup **apple juice concentrate**
½ cup **unsweetened** carob powder
½ cup raisins (*D:* reduce to ¼ cup)
1 teaspoon vanilla

Mix together:

¾ cup whole-wheat **flour**
1½ teaspoons low-sodium **baking powder**
½ cup chopped walnuts

Combine with cooled carob mixture. Add:

1 tablespoon **apple juice**

Don't overmix. Pour into **non-stick** 8 x 8-inch brownie tin. Bake at 350° F for 10 minutes. Check with toothpick for doneness. Let cool in pan.

(511)

Carob Brownies III

8 x 8-inch cake pan *LC, LCh, D, LS, v, P, k*

Tip: One 2 x 3-inch brownie is approximately equal to 1 (*D*) sweetness allowance.

Combine and blend together:
- ⅔ cup whole-wheat **flour**
- 2 tablespoons non-fat **milk**
- 1 teaspoon low-sodium **baking powder**

Stir in to form batter:
- ½ cup *unsweetened* carob powder
- ⅓ cup skim **milk**
- ⅔ cup **apple juice concentrate**
- 1½ teaspoons vanilla

Fold in:
- ¼ cup raisins
- 2 egg whites, stiffly beaten

Pour batter into 8 x 8-inch **non-stick** baking pan and bake in preheated oven at 350° F for 20 to 25 minutes. Cut into squares.

(512)

Carob Chip Cookies

18 to 24 cookies *LCh, D, LS, V, v, Ml, k*

Tip: Two or 3 cookies (⅛ of total batch) are approximately equal to 1 (*D*) sweetness allowance.

Combine in mixing bowl:
- ¾ cup pecan meal
- ¼ cup wheat germ
- ¼ cup whole-wheat pastry **flour**
- ½ cup **apple juice concentrate**
- ½ tablespoon vanilla extract
- ½ cup **unsweetened** carob chips (*V* and *Ml:* use raisins)
- 1 tablespoon **margarine**

Mix thoroughly, drop by spoonfuls on **non-stick** baking sheet. Flatten with a fork. Bake at 350° F for 10 to 12 minutes; transfer to platter to cool before serving.

VARIATION: Vary ratio of pecan meal to wheat germ and flour; or add oats.

(513)

Cranberry Crunchies

18 to 25 bars ***LCh, D, LS, V, v, P, Ml, k***

Tip: One to 1½ bars are equal to 1 (*D*) sweetness allowance.

Blend together in a saucepan until smooth:
- ¾ cup orange juice
- 1 tablespoon cornstarch
- ½ teaspoon cinnamon

Add and cook for 5 minutes, stirring occasionally:
- 1½ cups currants or raisins (*D:* reduce to ½ cup chopped)

Stir in:
- ¼ cup **orange juice concentrate**
- 1 tablespoon **apple juice concentrate**
- Rind of one orange, grated
- 1 cup coarsely chopped cranberries (*D:* increase to 1½ cups)

Set aside to cool. Combine in large bowl:
- 2 cups whole-wheat or unbleached **flour**
- 1 cup **oats**

Stir in until mixture resembles coarse crumbs:
- ¼ cup **apple juice concentrate**
- ¼ cup **orange juice concentrate**

Spread half of flour mixture in a **non-stick** pan, pressing down evenly. Spread currant-cranberry filling evenly over it. Add to remaining flour mixture:
- ½ cup chopped nuts (*P:* use ½ cup Grape Nuts)

Pat the mixture over the filling as evenly as possible. Bake at 350° F for 30 to 40 minutes, or until lightly browned.

(514)

Date-Nut Bars

About 32 cookie bars *LCh, D, LS, V, v, P, Ml, k*

Tip: Three 1 x 2-inch bars are approximately equal to 1 (*D*) sweetness allowance.

Process in blender or processor until fine:
 3 whole-wheat matzos (about ¾ cup ground)
Blend meal until crumbly mixture is formed with:
 1 cup finely chopped almonds or walnuts (*P:* use Grape Nuts)
 ⅓ cup **apple juice concentrate**
 1 teaspoon cinnamon
Reserve ¼ cup of this mixture. Firmly pat remainder into bottom of **non-stick** 8 x 8-inch baking pan, making a solid base. Blend in small bowl:
 1 cup pitted dates or raisins, chopped (*D:* reduce to ½ cup; substitute ½ cup nuts, chopped for rest)
 ¼ cup **orange juice concentrate**
 2 teaspoons fresh grated orange peel
Spread this mixture carefully over base. Sprinkle with reserved topping; tap down lightly. Bake at 350° F for 25 to 30 minutes. Cool; cut into squares.

(515)

Date-Nut Crescents

4 to 5 dozen cookies *LCh, LS, V, v, Ml, k*

Combine in saucepan and simmer for 15 minutes, covered:
 ½ cup orange juice
 1 pound pitted dates
Remove from heat and chop in processor or blender. Stir in:
 1 teaspoon fresh grated orange rind
 1 teaspoon cinnamon
 ½ to 1 cup chopped nuts
Set aside.

In large bowl, combine:

- 1 cup unbleached **flour**
- 1 cup whole-wheat **flour**
- 2 tablespoons wheat germ
- 1 cup semolina or Cream of Wheat
- 2½ sticks **margarine**

Cut in margarine until pea-sized. Sprinkle over mixture:

- ¼ cup warm water

Form into ball and turn out onto a floured board. Knead until a smooth dough is formed, adding more water if needed. Chill in freezer for 15 minutes. Divide dough into thirds and then into small balls. Flatten the balls into 2-inch circles. Place 1 teaspoon of filling at the edge of each circle. Roll up into a log and bend into crescent shape. Place on ungreased cookie sheet.
Bake at 350° F for 15 minutes or until lightly browned.

(516)

Nut Crescents

4 to 5 dozen cookies *LCh, D, LS, V, v, Ml, k*

Tip: Four to 5 cookies are equal to 1 (*D*) sweetness allowance.

Prepare dough as for DATE-NUT CRESCENTS (**515**). Use the following filling:
Combine in bowl:

- ¼ cup **orange juice concentrate**
- ¼ cup **apple juice concentrate**
- 1 teaspoon grated orange rind
- 1 teaspoon cinnamon
- 1¼ cups chopped nuts
- ½ cup rolled **oats**

Blend well, making sure that oats are well moistened.

(517)

Fruit Balls

About 24 to 30 balls *LCh, LS, V, v, P, Ml, k*

Combine in bowl:

2 cups mixed sun-dried fruit, chopped (dates, raisins, apples, peaches, pears, papaya, etc.)
½ cup Grape Nuts or chopped nuts (*P:* use Grape Nuts)
¼ cup **apple juice concentrate**

Blend together to form a smooth dough. Roll mixture into small balls, about 1½ inches in diameter. Bake at 350° F for 10 minutes. Cool and serve.

(518)

No Bake Fruit-Nut Balls

About 30 to 36 balls *LCh, LS, V, v, P, Ml, K, k*

Combine in bowl:

2 cups mixed sun-dried fruit, chopped (dates, raisins, apples, peaches, pears, papaya, etc.)
½ cup chopped nuts or Grape Nuts (*P:* use Grape Nuts)
¾ cup rolled **oats**
¼ cup **apple juice concentrate** or enough to moisten mixture

Blend together thoroughly. Form into small balls, pressing very firmly. If balls don't hold together, add more juice concentrate or more oats, as needed. Fruit balls can be chilled or served immediately.

(519)

Fruit Crisps

30 to 36 cookies *LCh, v, P, Ml, k*

Combine in bowl:

2 cups mixed dried fruit, chopped (dates, raisins, apples, peaches, pears, papaya, etc.)

¾ cup Grape Nuts

½ cup **apple juice concentrate**

1 teaspoon cinnamon

Beat until stiff:

2 **egg** whites

½ teaspoon cream of tartar

1 tablespoon **fructose** or **sugar** (*P:* omit)

Fold fruit mixture gently into egg whites. Drop mixture by spoonfuls onto **non-stick** baking sheet. Bake at 350° F for 10 minutes, or until cookies are golden.

(520)

Lace Cookies

About 40 cookies *LCh, LS, V, v, k*

Preheat oven to 325° F. Combine in a small saucepan, blending well and bringing to a boil:

⅔ cup firmly packed brown **sugar**

½ cup plus 2 tablespoons **butter** or **margarine**

½ cup light corn syrup

Remove from heat and immediately stir in, blending well:

¾ cup plus 1 tablespoon chopped walnuts or pecans

1 cup white **flour**

Drop by teaspoonfuls onto heavily greased and floured baking sheet. Bake until set, about 8 to 10 minutes. Quickly remove from baking sheet with metal spatula, handling carefully. Cool on rack.

(521)

Pecan Balls

About 20 cookies *LCh, LS, V, v, k*

In a bowl, cream together until fluffy:

½ cup **butter** or **margarine**
¼ cup **sugar**

Blend in:

¾ cup sifted **flour**
¼ cup wheat germ
1 teaspoon vanilla or rum extract (use almond extract if almonds used)

Work in until dough holds together:

1 cup ground pecans (or ground walnuts, hazelnuts, or almonds)

Form dough into 1-inch balls. Place balls on ungreased cookie sheet and bake at 350° F for 18 minutes.

(522)

Shreddies

About 18 to 24 cookies *LC, LCh, D, LS, V, v, P, Ml, k*

Tip: Suggested serving, 2 to 3 cookies (*LC*); 5 cookies are approximately equal to 1 (*D*) sweetness allowance.

Process in blender or processor until fine:

2 cups spoon-size Shredded Wheat biscuits

Blend in, until a smooth ball of dough can be formed:

½ cup **apple juice concentrate** (*D:* use ⅓ cup **apple juice concentrate** plus water to make ½ cup)

Place ball of dough on the non-shiny side of a piece of foil the size of your cookie sheet. Pat down a bit, then cover with wax paper. Roll out with rolling pin until about ⅛-inch thick. Cut cookies into squares or diamond shapes. Move foil to baking sheet and bake cookies at 350° F for about 5 or 6 minutes, or until lightly browned around the edges. Do not overbake or cookies will be hard.

VARIATIONS: Add to basic dough according to diets, any of the following:

½ teaspoon cinnamon

1 to 1½ teaspoons vanilla, almond, rum, maple walnut, or other extract

¼ cup chopped walnuts and 1 teaspoon maple flavoring (except *LC* and *P*)

¼ cup chopped almonds and 1 teaspoon almond flavoring (except *LC* and *P*)

¼ cup pecan meal and 1 teaspoon vanilla (except *LC* and *P*)

2 tablespoons chopped walnuts and 2 tablespoons chopped raisins and ½ teaspoon cinnamon (except *P*)

(523)

Shreddie Pie Crust

1 10-inch pie crust *LC, LCh, D, LS, V, v, P, Ml, k*

Tip: ⅛ of pie crust is approximately equal to ½ (*D*) sweetness allowance.

Combine ingredients as for SHREDDIES **(522).** Place ball of dough in 10-inch **non-stick** pie pan. Pat down and cover with a sheet of wax paper. Using your fingers, press dough to fit pan evenly.

Use baked, or bake at 350° F for 8 to 10 minutes, or until lightly browned.

VARIATIONS: Use any variation given for SHREDDIES **(522).**

For 9-inch pie crust, use 1¾ cups shredded wheat and 3½ tablespoons **apple juice concentrate.**

(524)

*Cookie Thins**

70 to 80 cookies *LC, LCh, LS, V, v, Ml, k, B*

Cream together until light and fluffy:
6 tablespoons **butter** or **margarine**
2 tablespoons **sugar**
Add:
2 tablespoons **apple juice concentrate**
2 tablespoons vanilla extract
Beat well. Gradually stir in:
2 cups **flour**
Form a ball of dough. If dough does not adhere, add a teaspoon or two of water or juice. Divide the dough into two cubes. Wrap and chill for 1 to 2 hours in the refrigerator. Preheat oven to 350° F. Measure out a piece of aluminum foil that will fit your cookie sheet. Turn it shiny side down and place one of the cubes of dough on it. Soften the dough by rapping a few times with the rolling pin. Then cover with a piece of waxed paper the same size as the foil. Use straight pins to fasten foil and waxed paper together. With the rolling pin, roll the dough between the two sheets as thin as you can. Press down heavily on the rolling pin to achieve this. Dough should reach edges of cookie sheet when rolled out. Lift the foil with the dough on it and transfer to cookie sheet. Remove straight pins and carefully lift off waxed paper. Cut dough diagonally into diamond shapes, being sure to cut all the way through. Bake for about 10 minutes or until cookies are lightly browned. Repeat with second cube of dough.

* Adapted from a recipe in *The Woman's Day Low-Calorie Dessert Cookbook* by Carol Cutler, a book which offers a wide variety of interesting dietetic desserts.

(525) *ALMOND COOKIE THINS*

70 to 80 cookies *LC, LCh, LS, V, v, Ml, k, B*

Substitute 2 tablespoons almond extract for vanilla extract in basic recipe (**524**).

(526) *ALMOND NUT COOKIE THINS*

70 to 80 cookies *LC, LCh, LS, V, v, Ml, k*

Substitute 2 tablespoons almond extract for vanilla extract and add ¼ cup sliced or finely chopped almonds in COOKIE THINS (**524**).

(527) *ANISE COOKIE THINS*

70 to 80 cookies *LC, LCh, LS, V, v, Ml, k*

Add 1½ teaspoons anise to basic COOKIE THINS (**524**) recipe, or substitute anisette liqueur for vanilla extract.

(528) *BLAND COOKIE THINS*

70 to 80 cookies *LC, LCh, LS, V, v, Ml, k, B*

Use only white **flour** in basic COOKIE THINS (**524**).

(529) *CAROB COOKIE THINS*

70 to 80 cookies *LC, LCh, LS, V, v, Ml, k, B*

Increase **apple juice concentrate** to ¼ cup and add 3 tablespoons carob powder, and reduce vanilla to 2 teaspoons in COOKIE THINS (**524**).

(530) *LEMON COOKIE THINS*

70 to 80 cookies *LC, LCh, LS, V, v, Ml, k*

Use fresh grated rind of one lemon plus 2 tablespoons lemon juice instead of vanilla in basic COOKIE THIN (**524**) recipe.

(531) *ORANGE COOKIE THINS*

70 to 80 cookies *LC, LCh, LS, V, v, Ml, k*

Use fresh grated rind of 1 orange plus 2 tablespoons **orange juice concentrate** instead of vanilla in basic COOKIE THINS (**524**).

(532)

Cookie Treats

24 to 30 cookies *LC, LCh, D, LS, V, v, P, Ml, k*

Tip: Suggested (*LC*) serving is 2 per person; 2 to 3 cookies are approximately equal to 1 (*D*) sweetness allowance.

Combine in bowl:

2 cups of **flour** or a combination of any of the following: wholegrain or white **flour,** ground nuts (*P:* omit) wheat germ (*P:* omit), **bran, oats**

¾ cup **apple juice concentrate**

1 tablespoon vanilla or other flavoring

Blend mixture together to form dough. Divide dough into 1-inch balls. Place on a **non-stick** cookie sheet. If desired, press balls flat with fork. Bake at 350° F for 8 to 12 minutes or until lightly browned.

(533)

Orange Cookie Treats

24 to 30 cookies *LC, LCh, D, LS, V, v, P, Ml, k*

Add to basic COOKIE TREATS (**532**) dough:

1 teaspoon fresh grated orange rind

Substitute for ¼ cup of **apple juice concentrate:**

¼ cup **orange juice concentrate**

Omit vanilla.

Pies and Pastries

(534)

Pie Crust

1 9-inch double crust *LCh, D, LS, V, v, Ml, k, B**

Combine in mixing bowl and blend well:

1 cup unbleached all-purpose **flour**

1 cup wheat germ (*B:* use additional cup of unbleached flour)

Cut in with pastry blender or 2 butter knives:

½ cup unsalted **margarine,** chilled

When particles of shortening are the size of large peas, add:

4 tablespoons ice water

Mix only enough to moisten ingredients. Avoid overhandling. Turn dough out onto floured board or wax paper. Divide into two pieces, one slightly larger than the other. Take the larger piece and pat quicky into a ball. Dust it with flour and roll it into a circle about ⅛-inch thick. Line bottom of 9-inch pie pan with dough. Trim edges. Fill pie. Roll rest of dough for top crust. Place it carefully over filling

(*Recipe continued on next page*)

and press both crusts together to seal at edges. Trim excess dough. Flute rim of crust. Bake according to directions in filling recipe.

* Except fat restricted.

(535)

Apple Pie

8 to 10 servings *LCh, D, LS, V, v, Ml, k, B*

Tip: 1/10 of pie is equal to 1 (*D*) sweetness allowance.

Pare, core, quarter, and cut into slices ¼-inch thick:
7 medium baking apples (McIntosh, Rome Beauty, or Greening are good choices)
In large mixing bowl, toss apples with:
¼ to ½ cup brown **sugar** to taste (*D:* use ¼ cup **apple juice concentrate**)
¼ to ½ teaspoon **lemon juice**
1 teaspoon cinnamon, or to taste
Stir apples until syrup is formed, and apples are well coated. Set aside while preparing:
1 recipe PIE CRUST (**534**)
Line 9-inch pie pan with dough for bottom crust. Mound apples high into shell (they will shrink by about ⅓ during baking), drizzling syrup from bowl over them. Dot with:
1 tablespoon unsalted **margarine** or **butter,** cut into pieces
Place top crust over apples. Seal, trim dough, and flute edges. Make design in crust with sharp knife, or prick with fork to allow steam to escape during baking. Bake in a preheated 450° F oven for 10 minutes. Reduce heat to 350° F, and bake 35 to 45 minutes longer, or until golden brown. Let cool 30 minutes before serving. If during baking process, pie begins to brown too quickly, cover it with foil.

VARIATION: Proceed as in above recipe. Add to apples:
⅓ cup broken walnut pieces (*B:* omit)
⅓ cup raisins (*D* and *B:* omit)

(536)

Date-Nut Pie

1 9-inch pie *LCh, LS, V, v, P, Ml, k*

Prepare:
1 9-inch SHREDDIE CRUST (**523**), unbaked
Puree in processor or blender:
½ cup pitted dates
1 pound tofu
¼ cup plus 2 tablespoons **apple juice concentrate**
In small saucepan, combine:
¼ cup **apple juice**
1 envelope unflavored **gelatin**
Let stand one minute to allow gelatin to soften. Heat to boiling. Remove from heat and stir into tofu mixture, along with:
¼ cup chopped, pitted dates
4 dates, pitted and sliced
½ cup chopped walnuts (*P:* use ½ cup Grape Nuts)
Mix thoroughly, pour into prepared pie crust. Chill until set.

(537)

Patriots' Pie

1 9-inch pie *LC, LCh, D, LS, V, v, P, Ml, k*

Tip: ⅛ pie is approximately equal to 1 (*D*) sweetness allowance.

Prepare:
1 9-inch SHREDDIE CRUST (**523**), baked 5 minutes
Cool. In blender or processor, combine and puree until smooth:
1 pound tofu, soft style
¼ cup **apple juice concentrate**
1 teaspoon vanilla
Spread tofu mixture evenly over crust and chill for 1 hour. Decorate pie with rings of red, white, and blue fruit—such as:
Halved cherries
Halved strawberries

(*Recipe continued on next page*)

Raspberries
Whole blueberries
Sliced bananas dipped in lemon juice (add just before serving)

VARIATION: Prepare PATRIOTS' PIE according to directions, but omit SHREDDIE CRUST. Top with cooked and/or pureed fruit of choice, instead of fresh fruit.

(538)

Pineapple Chiffon Pie

1 9-inch pie *LC, LCh, D, LS, v, P, Ml, k*

Prepare:
1 9-inch SHREDDIE CRUST (**523**), baked 5 minutes
Cool crust. Combine in saucepan:
1 tablespoon **lemon juice**
2 tablespoons **lime juice**
2 tablespoons **apple juice concentrate**
Add to juice mixture:
1 envelope unflavored **gelatin**
Let stand 1 minute to soften. Heat to boiling. Drain, reserving juice:
1 20-ounce can **unsweetened** crushed pineapple in juice
Combine juice with gelatin mixture and heat to boiling. Cool on ice or in freezer until just thickened. Do not allow to become jelled. Whip until stiff:
2 **egg** whites
Beat in thickened syrup and:
2 tablespoons **pineapple juice concentrate,** heated to a boil and cooled
1 tablespoon **apple juice concentrate**
Fold in pineapple and pour into crust. Chill 1 to 4 hours before serving, or freeze for up to 24 hours.

VARIATION: (If crushed pineapple permitted), prepare PINEAPPLE CHIFFON PIE according to recipe, but omit SHREDDIE CRUST. Pour filling directly into **non-stick** pie pan.

(539)

Pumpkin Chiffon Pie

1 9-inch pie *LC, LCh, D, LS, v, P, Ml, k, B*

Prepare:
1 9-inch SHREDDIE CRUST (**523**), baked 5 minutes
Combine in small saucepan:
¼ cup **apple juice concentrate,** defrosted
2 envelopes unflavored **gelatin**
Let stand 1 minute to soften gelatin. Heat mixture to boiling, and remove from heat. Stir in:
1 16-ounce can pumpkin puree, **unsweetened,** unseasoned
½ cup orange juice
1 teaspoon cinnamon
½ teaspoon nutmeg (Opt.)
1 teaspoon vanilla
1 tablespoon **apple juice concentrate**
Chill mixture just until it begins to thicken. Do not let it set.
Whip until stiff:
2 large **egg** whites
¼ teaspoon cream of tartar
Beat in:
2 tablespoons **apple juice concentrate**
1 tablespoon **orange juice concentrate**
Then beat in thickened pumpkin mixture until smooth. Do not overbeat. Pour mixture into crust and chill until set, about 2 hours.

VARIATION: Prepare PUMPKIN CHIFFON PIE according to recipe, but omit SHREDDIE CRUST and nutmeg. Turn pie filling directly into **non-stick** pie pan or glass bowl.

(540)

Strawberry-Yogurt Pie

1 9-inch pie *LC, LCh, D, v, P, k*

Prepare:
1 9-inch SHREDDIE CRUST (**523**) (unbaked)

(*Recipe continued on next page*)

In blender, puree:

1 cup fresh strawberries (should equal ¾ cup pureed)

In medium saucepan, combine:

2 envelopes unflavored **gelatin**

½ cup **apple juice concentrate**

Let soften for 1 minute. Then stir in:

½ cup skim **milk**

Stir over low heat until **gelatin** is completely dissolved, about 5 minutes. Beat in, with wire whip or hand beater, the strawberry mixture and:

1 cup low-fat **yogurt**

1 teaspoon **lemon juice**

Chill, stirring occasionally, until mixture is thickened but not set.
Beat until frothy:

2 **egg** whites

¼ teaspoon cream of tartar

Gradually beat in:

2 tablespoons **fructose, sugar** or **aspartame** (*D:* use **aspartame**; *P:* omit)

Continue beating until stiff. Beat strawberry mixture into whites. Turn into pie crust and chill until firm. Garnish with:

10 fresh strawberries, halved

VARIATION: Use blueberries, canned **unsweetened** apricots, unsweetened canned pineapple, or other fruit instead of strawberries.

(541)

Light Baklava

3 to 4 dozen pieces *LC, LCh, LS, V, v, Ml, k*

In small saucepan, melt and mix well:

¼ cup **margarine** or **butter**

¼ cup **apple juice concentrate**

Set aside.

Combine in small bowl and set aside:

1½ cups shelled finely ground unsalted pistachio nuts (lower in calories) or walnuts (*LC:* use ¾ cups **bread** crumbs and ¾ cups nuts)

(*Recipe continued on next page*)

1 teaspoon cinnamon
1 tablespoon brown **sugar**

Bring to room temperature according to package directions:
1 pound phyllo leaves

Keep leaves you are not working with covered with a damp towel. In a **non-stick** 9 x 13-inch baking pan, layer half of the phyllo leaves, brushing every other one with the margarine mixture. Then spread the nut mixture evenly over the top sheet. Layer remaining leaves, again brushing every other sheet with margarine mixture, stirring the mixture frequently. Work quickly. With a sharp knife, cut baklava diagonally at 1½-inch intervals, being sure to cut all the way through. Cut opposite diagonals to form diamond shapes. Bake at 350° F for 45 minutes to 1 hour or until pastry is a golden brown. Cool in oven. Meanwhile, heat to boiling and cook for 5 minutes:
1 cup **apple juice**
½ cup **apple juice concentrate**
2 tablespoons **orange juice concentrate**
2 tablespoons **fructose**
3 tablespoons honey
½ teaspoon lemon and ½ teaspoon fresh grated orange rind
or
1 cinnamon stick and 1 to 6 whole cloves

Remove from heat and add:
1 teaspoon **lemon juice**
1 teaspoon rosewater, rum extract, or almond extract

Drizzle this hot syrup over the cooled pastry.

(542)

Nature-Sweetened Apple Strudel

4 strips *LC, LCh, D, LS, V, v, P, Ml, k, B*

Tip: ¼ of 1 strudel strip is approximately equal to 1 (*D*) sweetness allowance.

Bring to room temperature according to package directions:
1 package of phyllo leaves (you will need 12, but do not separate until ready to use)

Combine and set aside:
1 cup whole-wheat **bread** crumbs (*B:* use white)

(*Recipe continued on next page*)

3 tablespoons finely chopped walnuts (*P:* use Grape Nuts; *B:* omit)
1 teaspoon cinnamon or to taste

Combine and set aside:

½ cup **apple juice concentrate**
2 tablespoons melted **margarine** or **butter** (*P:* omit)

In a small saucepan, combine and heat to boiling, simmering for 5 minutes:

⅓ cup raisins (*D:* omit, or use cranberries; *B:* omit)
¼ cup **apple juice concentrate**

Drain raisins, reserving liquid. Add to liquid:

Apple juice concentrate to make ⅓ cup

Combine this liquid and the raisins in a bowl, and add:

4 large sweet apples, peeled, cored, and very thinly sliced (about 6 cups)
1 tablespoon brown **sugar** (*P* and *D:* omit)
2 teaspoons cinnamon, or to taste

Taste mixture for sweetness. Add, if desired:

More **apple juice concentrate** or brown **sugar** (*D:* omit; *P:* use juice)
1 tablespoon **lemon juice** (omit if cranberries are used)
¼ to ½ cup coarsely chopped nuts or sliced almonds (*LC:* use ¼ cup or omit; *P:* use Grape Nuts; *B:* omit)

Stir in:

¼ cup whole-wheat **bread** crumbs (*B:* use white crumbs)

Count out:

12 phyllo leaves

Return rest of leaves to refrigerator. Keep 12 leaves covered with a damp cloth as you work. Take first sheet, and spread on another damp towel. Brush lightly with the apple juice concentrate-margarine mixture, stirring the mixture to be sure it is well blended. Then sprinkle sheet with the set aside crumb-nut mixture. Add second sheet and repeat. Add a third sheet. Spread apple mixture along one end and roll up tightly. Repeat to make 4 strudel strips. For mini-strudel pieces, use 2 sheets of phyllo per roll, and add a very thin strip of apple mixture to each. Roll up into a strip about 1½-inches wide. Arrange strudel strips on a large **non-stick** baking sheet. Brush each with remaining apple juice concentrate-margarine mixture.

Bake at 400° F for 20 minutes. Reduce heat to 250° F and bake another 10 minutes or until golden brown.

Toppings and Spreads

(543)

Angel Cream

2 quarts or more *LC, LCh, D, LS*, v, P, Ml, k, B*

Separate any time during the day:
 4 **eggs**
Discard yolks, reserve whites; cover tightly and refrigerate.
Just before serving add:
 2 tablespoons **apple juice concentrate**
 ½ teaspoon cream of tartar
Whip to fluffy stage. Add, while still beating:
 1 to 2 tablespoons **fructose** (*D:* use **aspartame** or omit; *P:* omit)
Beat until stiff. With beater still at high speed, add:
 ½ cup **unsweetened** apple sauce
Beat for another 30 seconds.
Serve as you would whipped cream. If you cannot serve immediately, place in freezer, where cream will stay usable for a few hours.

(544) *BRANDIED ANGEL CREAM*

2 quarts or more *LC, LCh, LS*, v, Ml, k, B*

In ANGEL CREAM (**543**) recipe, add to unbeaten egg whites instead of apple juice concentrate:

1½ tablespoons brandy, rum, or liqueur (see **wine**)

Proceed as for ANGEL CREAM

* Pass separately; those on low-salt diets may be limited in the number of egg whites they can consume.

(545)

Honey-Peanut Butter Spread

LCh, LS, V, v, Ml, k

Combine and blend until smooth:

1 part peanut butter, **unsweetened** and unsalted

1 part honey, or to taste

Use as a spread on breads and muffins

(546)

Peanut-Apple Butter

About ¾ cup *LCh, D*, LS, V, v, Ml, k*

Combine and blend until smooth:

¼ cup peanut butter, **unsweetened** and unsalted

½ cup apple butter, **unsweetened**

Use as a spread on breads and muffins.

* To be used in small amounts (1 or 2 tablespoons) by those on diets limited in simple carbohydrates, such as fruit.

(547)

Honey-Tofu Spread

About ¾ cup *LCh, LS, V, v, Ml, k, B*

Combine in blender or food processor:
½ pound soft tofu
¼ cup honey, or to taste
Use as spread on breads and muffins.

(548)

Apple Butter-Tofu Spread

About ¾ cup *LC, LCh, D*, LS, V, v, P, Ml, k, B*

Combine in blender or food processor:
½ pound soft tofu
¼ cup apple butter, **unsweetened**
Use as spread on breads and muffins.

* To be used in small amounts (1 to 2 tablespoons) by those on diets limited in simple carbohydrates, such as fruit.

(549)

Maple-Whipped Cream Cheese

LC, LCh, v, K, k, B

Blend together in processor or blender (*K:* blend with fork):
½ pound whipped cream **cheese** or **hoop cheese** (*LC* and *LCh:* use **hoop**)
2 tablespoons maple syrup or to taste

(550)

Maple-Whipped Butter or Margarine

About ⅓ cup *LCh, LS, V, v, Ml, k, B*

Blend together in processor or blender:

¼ cup **butter** or **margarine**
1½ tablespoons maple syrup or to taste

(551)

Orange-Maple Syrup

Almost 1 cup *LCh, LS, V, v, Ml, k, B*

Combine and stir:

⅔ cup maple syrup
4 tablespoons **orange juice concentrate**
1 teaspoon fresh grated orange rind (*B:* omit)

Beverages

(552)

Hot Juice-ades

LC, LCh, D, LS, V, v, P, Ml, k, B†*

Combine in a pitcher or in a cup, boiling water and one or more of the following, to taste:

Orange juice concentrate
Apple juice concentrate
Pineapple juice concentrate
Grapefruit juice concentrate

Serve with:

Lemon or lime wedges *and/or*
Cinnamon swizzle stick

* Except those on diets limited in simple carbohydrates, such as fruit.
† Using permitted juice concentrates.

(553)

Orange/Apple Tea

LC, LCh, D, LS, V, v, P, Ml, k, B†*

Steep for 5 minutes in boiling water:
Decaffeinated orange or apple tea *(P:* use acceptable tea)
Stir in, to taste:
Orange juice concentrate *or* **apple juice concentrate,** warmed
Garnish with:
Lemon or lime wedge

* Except those on diets limited in simple carbohydrates, such as fruit.
† If tea and juices are permitted.

(554)

Hot Mulled Cider

LCh, D, LS, V, v, P, Ml, k, B*

Heat over low heat, but do not boil:
2 quarts apple cider
1 cinnamon stick
2 or 3 cloves (Opt.; *B:* omit)
Before serving, add:
2 red apples, cored and thinly sliced: (*B:* use cooked apples)

* Except those on diets limited in simple carbohydrates, such as fruit.

(555)

Hot Mulled Wine

LCh, LS, V, v, Ml, k

Tip: To reduce alcohol content: bring wine to a boil and simmer for five minutes.

Combine in a saucepan and bring to a boil, simmering for 5 minutes:

1 cup **apple juice**
½ cup **orange juice concentrate**
¼ cup **apple juice concentrate**
Cloves to taste (a few to 2 dozen) in cheesecloth bag
2 to 3 cinnamon sticks
3 lemons, sliced thinly
2 large oranges, sliced thinly

Add and simmer for 1 or 2 minutes more or until heated:

1 cup **lemon juice**

Heat separately until hot, but do not boil:

2 bottles red **wine**

Combine wine, fruit and juices in large punch bowl or pitcher. Remove bag of cloves and cinnamon sticks.

(556)

Hot Spiced Tea

4 servings *LC, LCh, D*, LS, V, v, P, Ml, k, B†*

Steep together for 3 to 5 minutes:

4 teaspoons decaffeinated tea leaves (*P:* use acceptable tea)
3 cups water

Meanwhile, bring to a boil:

¼ cup **orange juice**
¼ cup **orange juice concentrate**
2 tablespoons **apple juice concentrate**
¼ cup **lemon juice**
3 cloves (Opt.; *B:* omit)
1 cinnamon stick

(*Recipe continued on next page*)

Strain tea after 5 minutes. Combine with juice mixture and serve at once. Garnish, if desired with:

Lemon wedges

* Except those on diets limited in simple carbohydrates, such as fruit.
† If tea and juices are permitted.

(557)

Hot/Cold Spiced Tomato Juice

4 8-ounce servings *LC, LCh, D, LS, V, v, Ml, k*

Combine in saucepan and bring to boil:

4 cups tomato juice (*LS:* use unsalted juice)
½ teaspoon celery seed
½ teaspoon Worcestershire sauce (*LS, V* and *v:* use steak sauce)
4 grinds black or white **pepper**
2 small, or one medium garlic clove, crushed

Simmer over low heat 20 minutes; strain to remove garlic. Serve hot or cold, with:

Lemon or lime wedge
Celery swizzle stick

(558)

Wassail Bowl with Baked Apples

25 servings *LC, LCh, D*, LS†, v, P, Ml, k, B*

Bake for 45 minutes at 350° F:

12 small apples, cored and sprinkled with cinnamon, and set in pan of apple juice

Meanwhile, stir together in a saucepan:

2 cups **apple juice**
½ tablespoon ginger or to taste (*B:* omit)
½ tablespoon nutmeg or to taste (*B:* omit)
6 whole cloves or to taste (*B:* omit)
Allspice to taste
2 cinnamon sticks

Cover and bring to a boil, simmering for 10 minutes.
Combine in large saucepan:

½ gallon apple cider (or sherry or Madeira **wine**)
1 cup **apple juice concentrate**
¼ cup brown **sugar** (Opt.; *D* and *P:* omit)

Bring to a boil and add the spice mix. Simmer cider and spices together for 10 minutes, stirring frequently. Strain mixture. Keep warm.
When ready to serve, whip until rounded peaks form:

8 **egg** whites (*LS:* use 6 egg whites)

Slip whites into a punch bowl. Pour hot mixture very slowly over egg whites, folding gently in. Fold in:

½ cup brandy (see **wine;** Opt.) (*D, P,* and *B:* omit)

Float baked apples in the wassail mixture.

* Except those on diets limited in simple carbohydrates, such as fruit.
† Except those who are very limited in the number of eggs they can eat.

(559)

Mock Sangria

10 to 12 servings *LCh, D**, LS, V, v, P, Ml, k*

Combine in large pitcher:

6 cups **unsweetened** grape juice
1½ cups **apple juice concentrate**
2 tablespoons **lime juice**
2 tablespoons **lemon juice**

Stir to blend, and add:

1 medium lemon, unpeeled, and seeded, cut into half-moon slices
1 medium orange, unpeeled, and seeded, cut into half-moon slices
2 small McIntosh apples, unpeeled, cored, cut into eighths.

Stir well, and chill. Add just before serving:

1½ cups seltzer (unsalted club soda)

Serve in wine glasses over ice.

* Except those on diets limited in simple carbohydrates, such as fruit.

(560)

Mock Strawberry Dacquiri

4 servings *LC, LCh, D*, LS, V, v, P, Ml, K, k*

Puree in blender:

2 cups fresh strawberries
1 cup ice cubes
1 tablespoon **lime juice**
1 teaspoon rum extract or to taste
¼ cup **apple juice concentrate**

* Except those on diets limited in simple carbohydrates, such as fruit.

(561)

Mock Banana Dacquiri

4 servings *LC, LCh, D*, LS, V, v, P, Ml, K, k, B†*

Puree in blender:

2 very ripe bananas, cut into small pieces
1 cup ice
1 tablespoon **lime juice**
1 teaspoon rum extract or to taste
¼ cup **apple juice concentrate**

* Except those on diets limited in simple carbohydrates, such as fruit.
† For those unable to tolerate icy cold drinks, prepare with ¾ cup water instead of ice.
If **lime juice** is unacceptable, use **lemon juice.**

(562)

Blended Fruit Juice, Lime Wedge

6 servings *LC, LCh, D*, LS, V, v, P, Ml, K, k, B*

Combine in pitcher and stir together until frozen concentrates are melted:

4 cups **orange juice**
½ cup **apple juice concentrate**
¼ cup **pineapple juice concentrate**
6 tablespoons **lime juice**

Chill. Stir before serving. Garnish with:

Lime wedges

* Except those on diets in simple carbohydrates, such as fruit.

(563)

Banana Juice Swirl

4 servings *LCh, LS, V, v, P, Ml, k, B*

Combine in blender:

2 ripe bananas, cut in chunks (*B:* for low-residue dieters, use 1 cup sliced **unsweetened** cooked peaches)
3 cups **orange juice** *or* **pineapple juice** *or* **apple juice** *or* a combination of juices (*B:* use acceptable juice)
1 tablespoon **apple juice concentrate**
2 tablespoons **lemon** or **lime juice** (Opt.)

Serve immediately.

(564)

Party Punch

Approximately 24 servings *LC, LCh, D, LS, P, V, v, Ml, K, k, B*

Day before, chill ring mold. Fill with:
- 2 tablespoons **pineapple juice concentrate**
- 2 tablespoons **orange juice concentrate**
- 2 tablespoons **lemon juice**
- 1 tablespoon **lime juice** (*B:* if permitted only)
- 1 small lemon, halved and sliced
- 1 small lime, halved and sliced

Add to fill ring mold:
- Cold water

Freeze solid.
Combine in punch bowl, stirring to blend flavors:
- 1 6-ounce can **pineapple juice concentrate**
- 1 6-ounce can **orange juice concentrate**
- ¼ cup **apple juice concentrate**
- 2 tablespoons brandy or rum extract
- ¼ cup **lemon juice**

When ready to serve, add to bowl:
- 3 28-ounce bottles seltzer or club soda (*LS:* use seltzer)
- 2 cups sliced **unsweetened** frozen strawberries
- *or*
- 2 cups sliced, **unsweetened** cooked peaches (*B:* use peaches)

Place ice block in center of punch bowl and serve.

(565)

Grape Party Punch

Approximately 24 servings *LCh, D, LS, P, V, v, Ml, K, k, B*

In PARTY PUNCH (**564**), substitute for orange juice concentrate:
- 1 6-ounce can **unsweetened** grape juice concentrate or 1 22-ounce bottle grape juice (if bottled juice is used, omit half bottle seltzer)

Index

For convenience, recipes, and pages on which they appear, are italicized; the reference number of each recipe appears in parentheses. For main courses, the page numbers of menus in which they star are included, in order to make menu planning easier. Special diet references are listed according to diet, under "wheat allergy," "gout," "Mormon dietary code," and so on. The first page numbers following an entry are usually the most important.